Passion and Power

Passion and Power

By Fr Shay Cullen

First published October 2006 by Killynon House Books Ltd.
Second reprint November 2006

ISBN: 1-905706-05-7
ISBN: 978-1-905706-05-1

A CIP catalogue record for this book is available from the British Library

Cover design and text layout by Agnieszka O'Toole

Printed and bound in Denmark by Nørhaven Paperback

KILLYNON HOUSE BOOKS
Killynon House, Turin, Mullingar, Co. Westmeath, Ireland
Website: www.killynonhousebooks.com
Email: khbooks@iol.ie

Dedication

For my Father and Mother who gave me life.

For Merly and Alex Ramirez Hermoso without whom it couldn't have been lived like this.

Acknowledgements

This is a true story not only about my life but about the lives of brave and determined Filipino children and youth who endured abuse and suffering with fortitude and overcame it. I thank them for trusting me to tell their story. My heartfelt thanks for the loyalty and friendship of the PREDA staff that made it possible for me to live this life and write about it. For Alex Hermoso for being an intimate part of it. Special thanks to Jason O'Toole, my editor and publisher, who helped me finish the book by his encouragement and determination that the story be told. My thanks to his wife Agnieszka who made the striking cover and layout. I would like to thank my good friend Martin Sheen for promoting this book. Thanks also to Bernard Brady. Finally, warm thanks to the many supporters who are still making it possible for this story to continue.

Introduction

The overriding priority of human rights is to protect those who are vulnerable or at risk. The need to protect the human rights of women and children, of human rights workers and of journalists and people impoverished and oppressed has never been as urgent as in today's troubled world. Human rights defenders come in all shapes, sizes, and walks of life. They may be teachers, journalists, lawyers, religious workers, students, unemployed, elderly, skilled or unskilled. During my term as UN High Commissioner for Human Rights, it gave me particular pleasure to meet those who also spoke with Irish accents and had the humour and practical commonsense which is invaluable in grassroots work. Such a human rights defender is Father Shay Cullen – both ordinary and extraordinary at the same time.

His book, *Passion and Power*, telling of his experiences as an Irish missionary of the Columban Fathers in the Philippines, provides a remarkable story of thirty-seven years defending these rights and working to provide positive life giving alternatives to victims and people marginalized and abandoned.

Our paths crossed but twice. The first was in Kilkenny when I gave a keynote speech as President at the opening of an international conference on Fair Trade. Fr. Shay made a lasting impression on all of us there as he represented the life experience of Filipino artisans and fruit farmers. This book tells a remarkable story of the development of Fair Trade in the Philippines as a life giving solution to thousands of crafts people and farmers.

We met again in Geneva during my UN days, when I

encountered the dedicated and diverse range of adults and young people involved in the Global March to end child labour. The pages of this book are filled with the struggles and hardships involved in defending human rights and with the hard won victories and achievements too. Here we read of the many campaigns undertaken by Fr. Cullen and his courageous Filipino human rights workers taking stands against the death penalty, and extra-judicial executions and their successful campaign to persuade the Congress of the Philippines to bring in new laws to protect women and children.

Passion and Power is an apt way of describing the author's conviction and commitment, shared by his team, in defending human rights which come across with inspirational force. The heart-warming stories of the children rescued from sex slavery and terrible prison conditions give us all encouragement to work on for the realisation of universal respect for human rights and non-violence as the most influential way to bring peace to our divided and anxious world. I strongly encourage everyone to read this inspiring book.

Mary Robinson
New York
September 2006

Preface

The Philippines, a tropical paradise of a seven thousand Island Archipelago in the South China Sea has been my home for thirty-seven years. Since 1974 I have lived in a community composed of social workers, human rights defenders and college students at the PREDA educational centre on a hillside overlooking the expanse of Subic Bay. I speak Filipino and, while still learning, I have experienced the unique character and the best of the Filipino culture. In its unblemished state it's a life-style of quality and value but that is under increasing attack and erosion from within and without. That is what this book is about, what I and dedicated Filipinos have done and are still doing to stem the haemorrhage and bring back spiritual and cultural strength, vitality and dignity to the people from whom so much has been stolen. Filipino culture, the living heart of a nation, the quality of life-style, the sum of its inherent values, the gifted genius of its people has been seriously corroded and corrupted by shameful exploitation, an unredeemable political process, and manmade poverty. Like an invading virus these influences have been allowed to spread aided and abetted by the ruling elite, supposedly the guardians of cultural values and public morality. They have imported a hedonistic lifestyle profoundly lacking in compassion and culture. While there are notable exceptions, most of the patriarchs of power are driven by greed and avarice to exploit the poor and perpetuate their feudalistic fiefdoms with unprecedented violence and cruelty. This is alien and contradictory of true

Filipino culture and traditional values. The dynastic families that make up oligarchy are not true Filipinos. Many have foreign passports, offshore bank accounts, homes abroad and their loyalty is given to other nations and corporations. Their wealth, passion for power and political influence facilitates the shameless exploitation of the natural resources and the people by multinationals.

The heart of real Filipino culture is its deep spiritual belief in the goodness and dignity of the person. In its natural state it is a culture that values highly the efforts of people to be at peace with everybody else. It strives to maintain close family bonds and take responsibility for parents, brothers and sisters, cousins, nephews and nieces, no matter the cost. It respects the elders, the parents, the providers. Its wisdom is to value learning and art, to teach, to know and to understand, to respect and be respected, to love and be loved, to do good to others, to be tolerant and forgiving, to help the needy and ease the pain of poverty. Its generosity is to share food, shelter and clothes, to chat, make music, sing and tell stories and send and receive text messages endlessly.

The courage within the culture is the desire and ability of the people to avoid conflict and confrontation, to negotiate, to pursue justice, to endure all until it is unendurable, to resist oppression and exploitation, to fight only when all else has failed. This is the strength and the beauty of these emotional and excitable people emerging from an ancestral mix of Malayan, Chinese, and a sprinkling of Spanish, Arabic and American people and culture. In this there lies a weakness, a vulnerability that has blighted its blossoms and beauty. It's a weakness marked by excessive openness, and uninhibited desire for friendship, a childlike exuberance to please others, a thoughtless rush to admire and imitate and follow the crowd. A strong desire to be acknowledged and appreciated, accepted and admired, to know and be known, innocent traits in themselves but dangerous before a manipulative exploiter.

They are the psychological traits of the many that make up the nation of have-nots. So many have been treated so badly for so long by leaders and rulers as undeserving, devoid of rights, inferior, uncultured, ignorant, poor and worthless, they have come to believe it themselves. And desperate for redemption from this inculcated inferiority complex they want to be told it is not so.

This book tells how the wily and the wicked, the pimp and paedophiles, the exploiter and abuser, the patriarch, the patron, and the powerful have been able to manipulate and mangle the good and trusting nature of these impoverished people. It tells of the brave and courageous who have resisted and taken a stand to oppose it. Although the story takes place primarily in one location, in the Philippines, it is illustrative of many.

Shay Cullen
Preda Centre,
Olongapo City
Philippines
August 2006

Chapter One

It was fear of what lay before me that troubled me most. My life's journey had reached a crossroads, the final day of commitment had come and there was no turning back.

It was a spring day, Easter Sunday, April 1969, a day that began crisp, clear and pure. The seminary fields stretched away from the monastic-like building where I spent the last six years preparing for the missionary priesthood with twenty-two classmates. It was a beautiful day for the ordination ceremony. Nature was at its best; the lawns were covered with white veils of spider webs quivering with dewdrops, glistening in the morning sun. Rain puddles mirrored the fluffy clouds, billowing like schooner sails, scudding across the blue sky on a journey of certainty. The flowerbeds were alive with budding roses and bright yellow daffodils tossing their heads in the morning breeze.

The ordination ceremony was three hours away. I stepped into the frosty air for a solidarity walk. Many a candidate had pulled back at the last minute, I was fairly sure that I wanted to go ahead but, like marriage, no one can be sure what the future holds. It can all be so different after the ceremony. I walked briskly away from the monastery, head bent, my hands stuffed in the warm pockets of the long black clerical soutane, its skirts blowing about and the short cape flopping in the wind. That's how we were garbed in those days of the clerical cloth. The path led me to that end of all journeys –

the cemetery gates. Beyond, rows of crosses marked the final resting place of Columban Missionaries who had done their bit trying to make this a better world.

Their mission had been certain and clear, mine was muddled by anxieties as to what mine might be. A sharp frosty breeze whipped up a pile of leaves and sprinkled them over the silent graves like a benediction. *Was I visiting my final resting place before my journey had even begun?* I thought. It's now or never I decided and quickly returned to the college where the rites and rituals that would seal my fate awaited.

We walked in a slow solemn procession through the seminary corridors, twenty-three candidates for the priesthood vested in long white albs and holding lighted candles. The church doors swung open, the organ thundered triumphantly and the choir burst into a stirring hymn that lifted our spirits as we moved up the aisle into the sanctuary.

As the ceremonies began, the sanctuary became quiet and solemn. The organ held a long trembling note and then died away. The sharp scent of burning incense drifted across the sanctuary, curling around the candles, making a smoky spiral rising upwards. It was all designed to invoke the sacred, the solemnity, the seriousness of the vows we were taking, in other words there was no backing out. In those days anyone who did quit the priesthood faced repudiation and criticism as a failed priest as if there was something to be ashamed of. It was a tactic to instil fear and shame and prevent priests taking another course in life. Thank God that has faded away. But back then it was a powerful and unfair pressure.

Outside, the clouds parted and with a grand gesture ushered the sunbeams through the high windows. Shafts of blinding light, like great spotlights, poured down onto the carpeted floor where we were now lying face down on the carpeted floor, arms outstretched before the altar and the crucifix, the smell of the carpet and fibers in my nose distracted me from what should have been a moment of deepest prayer. Things don't work out like they should even at the most solemn of times.

The Litany of the Saints was rising and falling, sweeping over the bowed heads of the bishops and priests and our prostrated bodies. The deacon sang the invocation, "All the Holy Martyrs" and the congregation replied, "Ora Pro Nobis" (pray for us). They begged the saints to make us worthy to imitate Christ, to serve the poor and the hungry, to protect us against all dangers, to strengthen us for the hardships to come. I prayed that it would be so. Then silence.

The blue-white smoke of incense from the brass thurible drifted upward on the shafts of sunlight into the church dome. The beams of sunlight inched their way across the sanctuary as if marking each of us for a purpose. We stood and were called one by one before the bishop to have our hands anointed with consecrated olive oil like the Old Testament prophets. We were reminded that our mission was to live the gospel and preside at the celebration of the Lord's Supper.

Soon the moment of ordination arrived, we approached the Bishop again one by one, knelt and he silently laid his hands on our heads. That simple gesture, by which the apostles ordained others, was the moment when we were consecrated to God. We donned new vestments, turned towards our family and friends and saw rows of smiling, happy and proud faces. Applause filled the church. Then, the organ thundered once again and Handel's Hallelujah chorus burst from the choir as we made our way in procession out of the church to a day of celebration

The next day was my first Eucharist celebration with a community in my own home parish of Glasthule, a small village on the Dublin to Sandycove and Dalkey Road, and close to the famous round tower where James Joyce lived and wrote for a while, overlooking Dun Laoghaire and Dublin

Bay. This was where I grew up, playing by the sea and at other times on the wooded hills of Dalkey and Killiney.

My first community mass was a deeply moving experience for my family and neighbours and friends. A group of former classmates from Presentation College was there and we stood around reminiscing about the days when with my best friends Neil McHugh and Pat McDevitt sold newspapers and magazines as student members of the Legion Of Mary on that very pavement. Many a freezing winter morning we went out to sell *The Universe* and *Irish Catholic* and the Columban magazine, *The Far East.* Now I was a member of that famous missionary society and later a writer of *The Universe* and *The Far East* magazine. From there too we marched off to our military duty with the FCA, the part-time soldiering that trained us to be disciplined, shoot straight, be good leaders and serious about life.

I attended elementary at the Parochial Harold School just around the corner from our house. They were tough years when corporal punishment and verbal abuse was the common practice. We endured them without much complaint but the lack of affirmation and encouragement to learn had a detrimental effect on me. I soured on study – I was no scholar – but passed the minimum. In later years, the lessons of the harsh and cruel experience of schoolroom abuse was not forgotten. The following September I was to leave for Manila and the Philippines. My mission had begun.

Chapter Two

The plane taxied to a stop, the stairs were rolled up to the door, and I stepped into a furnace of fire and heat. The blazing sun stabbed me in the back as I walked across the airport tarmac. I took a taxi to the Columban Fathers House on Singalong Street. As the taxi sped along Roxas Boulevard lined with coconut trees I saw Manila Bay off to the left, hotels and restaurants to the right. People were everywhere, in their thousands, in their millions, the runaway population was growing non-stop and so was the hunger, anger and political tension. Campaign streamers hung from buildings, were draped on buses, flags fluttered from lampposts as if a swarm of butterflies had settled. Posters everywhere had one message: vote, re-elect Marcos.

The taxi swung into the Columban Fathers House at speed and skidded to a stop, the driver beaming. I felt blessed to arrive alive. The Columban Fathers Central House is a large three-story building with a wide foyer and a warm and hospitable welcome for everyone. After a few days rest in Manila I received mission orders to proceed to Olongapo City, about three hours drive North West, 139 kilometres from Manila, and report to St. Joseph's Parish for a few weeks before starting language studies in Manila. Well that was what I was told by the good father who had my life planned out. The reality was something altogether different.

Fr Tom was going back to Olongapo and I hitched a ride in his aging spluttering Volkswagen. It was loaded with cartons of Mass wine and we set off in that hot little box without air-conditioning or even a fan through the blistering concrete jungle of Manila. We wore long white *cassocks.* I had been outfitted with one and a spare in the Columban House. It was made overnight by the local tailor. I felt uncomfortable, but it was the strict custom, one I was soon to part ways with, as I did with many more in the months and years to come and upset some of the good fathers.

Dressed in the long skirts, Fr Tom and I began our trip in that spluttering little Volks and passed through Bulacan and Pampanga provinces. Great scenery, first time I'd seen rice fields, green shoots of rice plants were growing out of a sea of water. The Spanish conquered this country in 1521 and these were the first lands they grabbed; I could see why they were so fertile. Further along, other fields were being harvested by hand-sickles and the stalks were passed through little trashing machines driven by a wheezing old tractor. Further down the road we stopped to look at the old-fashioned way of doing it. A band of four ponies harnessed together abreast were running around in a circle trashing the grain with their hooves. A young man held a long rein and urged them on. The scene, the smells, the summer heat awakened my childhood memories of the trashing in my mother's home farm in Emo village in County Laois. I could see my grandmother dressed in black, her grey hair all over the place coming into the field, blowing a whistle and calling for me to come down and get the baskets of brown bread and flasks of sweet tea. Those were the happy days.

Soon we were driving through sugarcane haciendas. Fr Tom began to fill me in on the social realities that I was seeing for the first time. The vast lands I saw are owned by one powerful family and planted with sugarcane. The canes grow twelve feet high and stretched to the horizon on both sides of the road. I saw the cutters, called saccades, slashing at the base of the tall stalks of cane with machetes and others gathering the cut stalks and carrying them on their shoulders up ramps into the waiting trucks. There were little kids there too in that snake and insect infested cane field. Many died from snakebites, Fr Tom said. The Spanish feudal system was still in place and most of the land was owned by the ruling elite. They had it all. A palatial house stood off in the distance. That took the shine off an otherwise pleasant journey in the tropical countryside.

It was a beautiful landscape. The groves of coconut trees and bamboo were swaying in the breeze beside small streams and fishponds. Mountains marked the horizon. The simple bamboo and grass roofed houses of the peasants looked cool in the blazing heat and low and sturdy to withstand the powerful typhoons.

These quaint bamboo cottages were the homes of the cane cutters, the lowest paid humans on earth and they didn't own them. I learned later that they paid rent that was deducted from their earnings, which were so little that slavery would have been a better alternative. At least they would be fed and given medical treatment being a valuable piece of property. The sacadas I saw were throwaway people. Hills appeared as we turned a corner and drove into Dinapupain. A tall white tower sat on a hill. Fr Tom told me it was the communications tower of the US Naval Base at Subic Bay. A United States Naval base slap in the middle of this tropical paradise – that was going to be a sight! Olongapo was the town that squatted at its gates. The narrow bumpy road wound its way through hills covered with tall cogon grass and swaying their white plumes like the sugar cane. *Gorgeous*, I thought looking on them for the first time in my life. All the firsts I was having these days had me in a daze. The old Volks was holding up pretty well on the three-and-half-hour drive that had me sticky with perspiration. As we began the descent towards Olongapo along the then narrow potholed zigzag road, Fr Tom waved towards the grassy treeless hills covered in the tall grass with the dancing plumes. I thought they were gorgeous until he explained that, less than ten years previously, the same hills were covered in rainforest. The canopy was so thick, he said, it shaded the road. Now it was all gone, cut down by loggers with the connivance of local politicians.

We passed the Olongapo City Hall on our way down the main street. People were everywhere, it was baby boom town and I was soon to learn why. We reached a roundabout with a large statue of a warrior's head. *Ulo Ng Apo,* it was called, the chieftain's head, from which the word "Olongapo" was derived. The old Volks coughed and croaked its way through the school gates of St. Joseph's.

We crossed the schoolyard and stopped in the shade of the church and the rectory door. The large school, a two-story wooden building ran the length of the compound. The massive timber columns were once part of the disappearing rain forest, in part because of the corrupt families that ruled the nation and the invention of the chainsaw. Both the church and rectory were modern concrete buildings and I was happy to know I wouldn't be sleeping in the shadows of the dead trees.

I was directed by the Fathers to a room on the second floor that overlooked the school compound. Crowds were streaming into the open sided church. The Mass was in English – thanks to the American colonial period that began in 1899 after the Filipinos had beaten the Spanish and had them surrounded and cowering in Manila. Then the Americans landed to help the insurgents but turned against them and a bloody war that killed as many as 200,000 Filipinos began and ended with occupation until 1945.

So Spanish as the official language died and American-English was introduced. My first few weeks in St. Joseph's was spent getting to know and understand the Filipinos themselves. They are intelligent, smart, uninhibited, and open to friendship. It can be their undoing as they trust too easily and admire too much. Unfortunately, foreigners take advantage and exploit them.

One day I noticed several Caucasians in the congregation at morning Mass. Fr Tom explained they were US Navy men from the nearby Base. They attended mass with their Filipino fiancées. Only a few were Catholic but the Filipino wives-to-be insisted on a Catholic Church wedding and the men had to go along.

Then there was bad news. I was informed by the Columban Superior that I would be staying as long as six months in St. Joseph's and language studies had been postponed. I was greatly disappointed, I had to learn Tagalong. I felt accepted in the community and made good friends, but I needed to be able to understand the language and speak it so that they could share their problems and feelings with me if they needed to. I began to study Tagalong in the rectory with the help of a teacher in the school. It was tough and I didn't make much progress but I learned enough to understand what was being confessed in the confessional and could give advice and encouragement to them to deal with their many family problems. I learned a lot about the problems, feelings and hardships of the people in the confessional. It was the one place they could open up with anonymity and unburden themselves and know they would receive understanding and support. It was a place of spiritual healing.

When the Catholic chaplain was on leave the priests at St. Joseph's were invited to celebrate the Sunday mass. I was assigned sometimes. I met and made friends with many decent upright Americans too, of all religious persuasions and some with none at all. The majority of the navy people were genuinely concerned for the welfare of the Filipinos. Many happily married Filipinos and millions of Filipinos are US citizens.

That October, 1969, I plunged into the busy work of the parish with four other Columbans. The Columban Sisters ran St. Joseph's School with dedication and commitment and gave themselves unstintingly to the development of the students. They knew the future of the youth lay in a good quality education based on Christian values. They had the highest standards of any school in the province. Their students went on to win top slots in college and university scholarship programmes and lead lives of integrity and dignity. They worked hard to help the troubled students and their families and they lost no time in recruiting me to help. I began by giving lessons with the D class. Unlike most Filipino students who are eager to learn and are devoted to their studies, the D class consisted of students out of the "Blackboard Jungle".

They were sceptical and unruly and had little respect for authority. Most of them had serious family problems; some were fathered by US sailors who abandoned them at an early age. Others were left by their Filipino fathers who had a second family or lived with a bar girl. The Olongapo industry of sex and sensuality was taking its toll on the lives of women and children. These teenagers, like hurt youths everywhere, were angry at the world and especially all adults who they felt had failed them. I wasn't surprised they carried resentment and rebel tendencies.

Filipino society has deeply ingrained respect for elders and authority figures. The disturbed and abandoned young people vented their frustration and anger at each other. They formed rival cliques and gangs, took drugs and had gang fights that at times resulted in stab wounds or other serious injuries. Racial slurs – especially when aimed at a student fathered by a black American – were very hurtful.

They were bright, intelligent teenagers, yet their simmering emotional tensions prevented them from showing interest in learning. They needed to solve present problems within their broken families. They had low self-esteem and then low school grades re-enforced that perception.

Despite not being able to speak good Tagalog, I was able to communicate in basic English, yet their poor grasp of it prevented them talking about their deepest problems. I cast aside the long white *cassock* and dressed as they did in jeans and short sleeve shirts. It was the first time they had a priest who did not preach a sermon about their need to reject vice and embrace virtue. I turned the classroom into a discussion group, a kind of therapy, and encouraged them to speak freely about their problems.

I invited a teacher they trusted to translate and they opened up in the group. Attendance increased thirty-five percent the first week. As word spread about the group sharing, there was almost full attendance at all classes so their grades began to improve too. I tried to be a friend and supporter first – and then possibly a teacher. Building trust, rapport and a buddy system with them was the only way to help them discover their self-worth. Hanging out with them after school hours was a great way to break down the traditional barrier between teenagers and authority figures.

We threw around a basketball, went on short trips to the beach, and I visited some in their homes. They came to trust me and I was elated to be making some progress in lowering cultural barriers. After a month I felt that I was getting through to them. There was no physical punishment or insulting verbal reprimands at St Joseph's. The sisters had trained the teachers to maintain discipline through positive means, positive reinforcement, counselling in private and avoid causing loss of face in front of class mates.

That was the worst thing that could happen to a student. It is the most traumatic of all. In my school days, punching, slapping, insults and punishment was the norm. I hated school and buried feelings of anger and thoughts of retaliation against my tormentors. I felt the cruel teachers were picking on me yet most used the cane or leather strap and severely punished us. I went to a public school near home. With some exceptions the teachers were harsh, cynical and at times cruel. It was a school with swishing canes and leather straps the teachers welded with gusto. They knew more about how to punish than how to teach. The school system failed a generation of Irish, as soon as they could they fled abroad, making us a nation of migrants.

Thousands of intelligent and good students dropped out of school as a result of this culture of cruelty in the 1950s and 60s and immediately emigrated to England. When I finished elementary school I continued intermediary education with the Christian Brothers in Monkstown Park. They too had their schoolroom tyrants, brothers and lay teachers. The physical and verbal abuse was so harsh for my brothers and myself that our mother protested and bravely confronted the brother superior about it to no avail. All her complaints fell on deaf ears.

I never forgot that school life. Needless to say I learned little and received low grades. After that I transferred to the Presentation College in Glasthule, closer to our home. That was much better and although I had to repeat one year I managed to pass the final exams.

In the Philippines, graduating from high school and going to college is the dream of every bright young student. Most know it is the only way out of the poverty trap. Finishing school with high grades is the vital and important prize that can open the way to junior college or to a basic job. Without it there is the stigma of being a drop-out or a failure and few will get employment. Most parents sacrifice endlessly to send their children to a good school. Millions of Filipinos have left their children and migrated to work and care for other people's children so their own can have a high school and college education.

One late afternoon before sunset, I left the rectory dressed in casuals and took a short 'jeepeny' ride into the heart of 'Sin City', the centre being right outside the gate of the US Navy Base. The nightclub strip called *Magsaysay Drive* was blazing with neon lights. Loud bands were pounding out rock 'n' roll from bars and clubs on the strip. The Beatles' hit *Get*

Back was vying with The Rolling Stones' *Honky Tonk Woman* and *Judy in Disguise* by the Playboy Band. The street was thronged with American sailors, all bar hopping, leading girls to a cheap hotel or carrying the small little ones in their arms like children. Many of the girls were no more than fifteen or sixteen. The sailors were tall, muscular and macho, dressed in bulging t-shirts and gym shorts, they walked about as if they owned the place, shouting obscenities to each other, waving beer bottles, grabbing the girls that stood in the doorways of the sex bars and clubs. Welcome signs and banners greeted these high paying customers: "Welcome USS Enterprise," said one.

At the doors of the sex clubs, under the flickering neon lights, the older women disguised their hard life of exploitation and abuse behind masks of heavy make-up, artificial eyelashes and mascara highlighted by red burnished cheeks. They lounged in sexually provocative poses.

"Hi Joe, wanna good time? Joe, come on in, I give you special job, Joe!" they called out. If a sailor stopped, his privates were given an instant massage – a sample of more to come. Prudently, I kept to the curb side. The women and young girls were mostly from the far flung provinces where their brothers, sisters and parents lived and died in poverty of disease, malnutrition and neglect.

I walked towards the bridge that separated the city from the base. Throngs of Filipinos were crossing over to work in the naval base and groups of boisterous sailors were coming out. Both groups had their own night shift. At the entrance a barrier was manned by smart uniformed Marines wearing white helmets. They checked everyone's pass or ID card. On the Olongapo side of the bridge a group of hopeful looking streetwalkers beamed practiced smiles and waived to the approaching sailors. It would be a night to remember.

Down a side street on my right, fifty metres from the nightclub scene, was St.Columban's church, high school and college. Students in uniforms of green skirts and white blouses, together with churchgoers, were hurrying with bowed heads and adverted eyes to the church to join evening prayer and meditation. I followed them in and the raucous noise of the street fell away to a distant murmur and quiet reigned. In the corner near the back of the church, a large crucifix showed the impaled figure of the Christ.

A young woman, flashily dressed, stood with her hand on his nailed feet deep in prayer. She appeared to be on her way to work in a bar, and praying for only God knew what. From what I had heard in the confessional I knew that most of the women were doing it to feed a hungry family, pay debts or just to stay alive. Most were trafficked by pimps and sold to club owners.

From the church I went back down Magsaysay Drive and passed the California Jam, Sexton, Body Shaft, American Dream, Blow Heaven and many more sex bars. Their names made it clear they were fronts for prostitution, all operating with permits issued by the city government. They were approved too by the US Navy commander. Suddenly I was bumped off the pavement by a group of shouting, shoving, semi-drunk Marines as they pushed their way along the street. White uniformed sailors with black batons and armbands that said 'shore patrol' patrolled every hundred metres. The bunch of Marines that had bullied their way along the street were now caught up in a fracas at the door of a club. They were kicking, punching and swearing until the shore patrol came running and bundled them into a wire cage on the back of a pick-up and sped away across the bridge into "Little America".

Middle-aged women with young kids were hanging about selling cigarettes, sticks of gum and roasted peanuts. Others barbecued bananas and chicken legs on smoking charcoal braziers along the footpath, filling the air with the acrid smell of kerosene, burnt fat and garlic that stung my eyes and nostrils.

Open fronted shops displayed rows of thick studded leather

belts, sunglasses, vicious looking knives, baseball caps and t-shirts with pornographic images and obscenities, souvenirs prized by the tourists. There was the cynical with the obscene. One t-shirt showed a picture of two US jet fighters climbing into the clouds leaving a nuclear mushroom cloud rising over a city, "Nuke 'em till they glow, then shoot them in the dark," it gloated.

Street children were running about barefooted in dirty shirts and shorts begging and hustling from the sailors. They followed me along the street. "Gimme money, Joe, *pleezze*, gimme money, Joe," they wheedled and pestered until I turned over a few coins and they dashed off to find another willing to give them a handout.

Back at St Joseph's, I sat for a long while in the silent empty church thinking about what I had seen. What should we missionaries be doing about all of this and what impact was it having on the surrounding communities and all the Filipinos? Clark air base, sixty kilometres to the east had a sex industry that equalled Olongapo and the San Miguel communication base in the town of San Antonio, an hour north of Olongapo, had its own smaller version. What impact all this was having on the culture and morality of the Filipinos was never discussed. The level of tolerance and complicity in this industry of exploitation and sexual abuse of women and children was almost total. No one dared criticise the presence of the base or the political family that encouraged and supported it. Most had only good to say of the US military presence.

Chapter Three

Olongapo is a small town on the edge of the South China Sea. You could drive from one end of the built-up area to the gate of the US Navy base in ten minutes when there is light traffic, maybe twenty to thirty minutes at rush hour. There was an estimated minimum of US$32.4 million spent annually by 1966 – most of it by the sailors. This is some small indication the impact of the presence of the US Navy had on the economy of Olongapo. This doesn't include the proceeds of the black economy coming from drugs, people trafficking, prostitution and smuggling. There were about 12,000 regular workers on the base and another 8,000 part-time contract workers employed as domestic helpers, gardeners and construction workers.

This huge income was to be greatly reduced as the Vietnam War drew to a close in 1975. When I arrived in 1969, Olongapo was a built up town with paved roads, basic utilities but a fast growing population of migrants flooding from the impoverished provinces and straining the infrastructure to breaking point.

In 1964 there was a monthly average of ninety-eight US ships docking at Subic Bay. By 1966 the Gordon Family had risen to power and Olongapo had achieved the status of a "chartered city". The status was based on the earnings of the city. That year alone ships visits peaked with one hundred and sixty three ship visits. They docked for repairs, supplies, service and recreational visits. There were as many as nine thousand servicemen and women visiting the area daily for a yearly total of a staggering 3.8 million US personnel. With this number of people spending an estimated ten dollars a day the city was earning a minimum of $32,4000,000 annually.

The spending power of the twenty thousand Filipinos working on the base and the earnings from the sex industry, apartment and room rentals and the purchase of local goods made the city a boom town. There was no other major industry in the city other than "entertainment with sex," as one local official, later a senator, infamously described it. Where all that money went was anyone's guess but the infrastructure was crumbling and little was being done about it. The city frequently called on the US Navy to fix and repair the schools, hospital, water pipes and the electrical system. They willingly obliged, provided that there was a safe and secure environment for the sailors entertainment and satisfaction.

The city and base established a social hygiene clinic to ensure that the girls were clean and free of sexually transmitted diseases to protect the sailors, we were told. No one thought of controlling the men who were carrying the diseases that they picked up in Vietnam and Mombassa. Vietnam Rose was one sexually transmitted disease that was incurable, a form of herpes. Years later when the HIV virus that causes AIDS hit Asia, it was claimed that the sailors were mostly responsible for introducing it to the girls. Then it spread among the sex workers. But as usual, and unjustly, the women were blamed and penalised. A hunt was declared and all sex clubs were penalised if they did not force their girls to have the tests. If they were found to be HIV positive they were fired and even taken to the San Lazarao government hospital in Manila where the US Navy funded a programme.

The Olongapo City hospital is operated by the city administration, although now in a new building, it is still always overcrowded with patients in the corridors and anywhere they can park a trolley. They are understaffed and under-financed, with doctors and nurses struggling to do their best for the poor who cannot afford the basics. There is no free or assisted medical assistance for any person in the Philippines. The patient has to pay as if it were a private hospital. The doctor's fees and some costs can be lowered for charitable reasons. There is a government insurance system called Medicare for those lucky enough to have employment and a good employer who pays their share monthly. Many employers don't and simply bribe their way out of trouble if it comes to a legal dispute with the department of labour. Most employees can't afford to fight in court for their rights.

When the Medicare monthly deductions are paid then the employee can get loans for medical needs. The poor and jobless have to rely on charity or relatives. The sex workers have no medical insurance and no one to turn to when they get sick, apart from the social hygiene clinic.

The women in the bars and brothels were not paid regular wages and had no Medicare contributions or any medical benefits. They received a small payment for every drink they persuaded the customer to buy for him and her. The "ladies drink" was a fake. To take her out of the bar to a hotel for sex the customer paid the bar operator a fixed fee, called a bar fine, and the girl got a small percentage of that.

If the girls got sick or pregnant they had no medical benefits and relied on charity. The hospital will give discounts on ward charges to those who are indigent but the patients still have to buy medicine, needles, gloves, dextrose, and anything used in any procedure. These are available at the pharmacy in the hospital or other private ones outside the gates, some owned by government officials or their relatives. Outsiders can't get the business permit and so competition is eliminated and price fixing rampant. By law generic drugs, as well as branded drugs, have to be named by the doctor when prescribing. Most people don't know about generic drugs being cheaper than the same branded medicine made by a pharmaceutical company and sold at twice the price or even more.

There are many honest, caring doctors who do everything to make it easy and right for the patient. There are the few unscrupulous doctors who have fallen into the temptation to make deals with the pharmaceutical companies to scribble their prescriptions so the generic name is garbled and only the branded medicine stands out. They get a big discount if they buy for their private clinics or gifts for prescribing a monthly quota.

The practice is to over prescribe and even prescribe medicine that is unnecessary. Pharmacies owned by a relative or friend normally don't prescribe the generic named medicine unless specifically asked by the family of the patient who doesn't even know what a generic drug is and never asks for it. Many a good doctor told me about these anomalies in the profession that is subject to greed and avarice like every other. Many years later a people's pharmacy system was begun by honest people and community leaders to make generic low cost medicines available to the poor.

Almost every day the hospital called for a priest to administer the last rites to many dying patients. The hospital building was once used by the Navy and turned over to the city when the boundaries of the naval base were adjusted to put the growing town outside the jurisdiction and control of the base. Hospital infections were rampant as patients admitted with one illness died of another.

Many of the nurses were unpaid volunteers, as is still the practice today, and they leave for abroad to countries like Ireland at the first opportunity. Their experience is extensive, as they have to treat every possible condition under the difficult circumstances. Their endurance, resilience and patience is legendary. The doctors' pay in the hospitals is low and most of them have private practices and use the operating room for their own patients (seen at their private clinic) beside those they get when on duty at the hospital. There are many dedicated and gifted Filipino doctors who are internationally praised for their skills and competence for performing miracles in the operating room everyday and saving countless lives – despite the lack of sterile facilities and monitoring equipment.

Without proper post operating facilities and sufficient medicine many patients didn't survive, especially in 1969. Many young women gave birth to babies fathered by American sailors and were soon abandoned, unmarried and unwanted. These children, called "Amerasians" or Filipino-American (Fil-Am) children faced a hard difficult life, especially those born of Afro-American fathers. Racism is not unknown in the Philippines. I was to meet and help many of them years later. There were thousands of impoverished people who never went to the hospital because they had no money, but instead relied on herbal medicine and village quacks.

Many a woman or teenager died a painful death as the result of a botched abortion or delivering a baby in an unsanitary pool of blood in some tin roofed shanty on a hillside or a back street slum. Here were the results of what went on behind the glare of the neon lights and honky-tonk life of the Olongapo sex industry, which was disgracefully protected and encouraged by the local Mayors and officials that set the scene for exploitation and abuse on a grand scale. I was soon to find them out and the shock and anger I felt at this human neglect and degradation of life set me on a course that was to change my life.

A smell of sickness came forward to greet me the first time I entered the hospital. It followed me through the dirty corridors, growing stronger as I came to the bedsides of the unfortunate and doomed patients. One of the first patients I met was Angi Mendoza, a former sex worker. Angi told me her story. The only help I could give was to listen and see she had the pain killing medicine that I willingly paid for. As a twelve-year-old she had been taken into the palatial house of a big land owner on a sugar plantation near Kabankalan. Her parents and six brothers and sisters lived in a hovel on the edge of the plantation and they all worked day and night planting cane and then harvesting it months later.

It was backbreaking work and to be a domestic servant in the house of the landlord was a great privilege and the envy of her siblings and neighbours. Little did they know that Angi was too terrified to tell how she was repeatedly raped by the owner. The threat to drive her family off the hacienda to starve was enough to seal her lips. These were the lords of lust that used fear and threats to control and dominate their servants and slaves. Slaves because many were in illegal bondage due to debts. Medical debts owed to the patriarch to whom they had to beg for medical help as the child lay dying in the hovel. In return they placed their children as unpaid servants to work it off. They were then the property of the landlord.

At sixteen Angi could no longer endure the abuse and she stole money in the great house and got on a bus and boat to Manila. Arriving at the South Harbor she was picked up by the watchful recruiters who offered food and work. It was just another betrayal and the pimp brought her to Olongapo and sold her to the brothel.

"Sweet sixteen. I was nothing, Father. I had nothing," she said, gripping my hand with a fierce strength as if asking forgiveness. There was nothing to forgive. She felt guilty for running away and leaving her family to starve as she feared they would.

"I sent everything I earned to my family so they could buy food," she told me in a mixture of English and Tagalog. Her voice carried resignation and acceptance of her lot in life. Angi was not alone, the ward was filled with teenagers wasted and dying. It was heartbreaking, I had stinging eyes and a feeling of utter helplessness.

Many women, old long before their years, with sunken cheeks and bony hands, lay on filthy blood stained mattresses. Their large round staring eyes looked up with longing and hope and followed me as I moved from bed to bed but I had little hope to give. I anointed their dry wrinkled skin with the holy oil to give them a mark of respect and dignity, words of comfort and a prayer.

I learned that many patients could not afford the prescribed medicine. They died quickly, their bodies carried to a small morgue at the back of the dilapidated hospital to be buried in a paupers grave – with no one to miss them or mourn. Their soiled bed was soon taken by another. Some who had family or friends could only afford vitamins or dextrose.

There were few fully qualified nurses. The hospital took on volunteer nursing aids, who were promised a future job, promises that were seldom kept as several told me. Unpaid "volunteers" were common in the city work force, especially during the 1980s. It was a "payola" scam. They signed attendance sheets and were processed as employees but someone else collected the wages. I felt despondent, helpless. While millions of pesos were spent daily on frivolous and pernicious entertainment down the road, here the suffering and misery knew no end but death. Mayor Amelia Gordon said that the city had no money to provide medical care for the poor. There were too many.

However, as a personal act of charity, the Mayor did provide simple coffins for the indigent families to bury their dead. The following year St Joseph's began to help the patients at the hospital by donating thousands of pesos worth of medication every month supervised by the staff of the Pope John XXIII Charity Clinic operated at first by Sister Ruth, a Columban sister and later by the Daughters of Charity. They saved hundreds of lives and greatly reduced the suffering. Yet it was never enough and when funds ran out some years later the charity ended. A few years after that an evangelical mission called Helping Hands came in to help sick children.

On another day I was called to pray over a dead child, the first of many. A member of The Legion Of Mary involved in charity work led me to a cluster of clapboard shacks that grew like fungi on the canal banks that passed the city sewerage. There was garbage everywhere. This was a city dump too and the shacks grew out of one another and leaned this way and that to stay upright as they staggered down to the black soup that filled the canal and then hung out over that toxic brew perched dangerously on wobbly bits of wood. Children played in the mire and mud, many hardly more than five and six were furiously scratching at the piles of newly dumped garbage with sticks and metal hooks. Shifting, sorting, gathering and sometimes finding something to eat. I had never seen anything like it.

The shanty was small, tin cans beaten flat and bits of broken plywood formed the walls and rusty iron sheets for the roof. A curtain of old sack served for a door. I bent low to enter and the earthen floor gave off a stench of urine, faeces and vomit, there too the smell of recent sickness and death. There was nothing in the shack other than a sheet of old plywood on bricks serving for a bed and in a corner a cooking pot and jam jars. These apparently were the only possessions of the occupant.

The mother of the dead child sat in a corner. She had the look of total surrender and submission to forces and events beyond her comprehension. Here was a beaten down human being. Here was the pain of loss and a women who blamed nobody but herself. "I did what I could," she told me in Tagalog, translated by the parishioner. "There was no one to help, I had no money."

The little girl was laid out in a box made of scrap plywood taken from the dumpsite by kindly neighbours as poor as herself. Two blobs of cotton wool protruded from her little girl's nose. I was amazed to see a dazzling, white dress, glowing in the flickering light of penny candles. It looked lavish and incongruous on the corpse of the dead child in such impoverished surroundings. As I drew closer, my eyes adjusted to the gloom and then I saw it was a cut out dress made of crepe paper, just laid over her reaching to her ankles, like a first communion dress that she would never wear. Her shroud was a piece of clean paper.

The child's toe nails were freshly painted with cheap red nail varnish given by a neighbour no doubt – the last gesture of a mother's love. The child had died of chronic diarrhoea and dehydration, the last phase of death by malnutrition. If only they had the simple mixture of salt, sugar and clean water, she would have quickly recovered. She simply starved to death in this fat city of incredible excess and vice. I prayed and blessed the dead child and said a few meaningless words of comfort to the mother in the Tagalong that I learned and then I stuffed all the money I had into the little jam jar that held a few donated coins and fled.

Later when I informed my fellow priests at St Joseph's what I had seen, they informed me that I should have asked "Good Mayor Gordon" for a better coffin. They praised her worthy charitable works. The Parish Priest said he would remind the Mayor that many more baby coffins should be made available. He was to celebrate a private mass in her home later that day, it seemed to be a special privilege given to this powerful family. I had my doubts if it was the right thing to do.

Another day, I was called out of the confessional to help a young teenager who told the sacristan that he wanted to make his last confession. In the visitors room I met a troubled, withdrawn, sixteen-years-old boy. I asked him his name. "Francisco," he said not looking at me.

"Why is it your last confession?" I asked.

He was hugging a cardboard shoebox as if it contained his most precious possession.

"Too many problems, Padre, forgive me first please so I do not go to hell when I kill myself," he said slowly in English.

I assured him there was another way to solve his problems, no need to kill himself, just tell me his problem and he would be okay. I persuaded him to open the shoebox and I saw the handgun.

I asked him to give me the gun and I promised to ask his father not to punish him. That seemed to be his greatest fear. He began to cry and released his grip on the box and I slowly took it from him. He then told me his father was a military officer and a strict disciplinarian who beat him. He had run away with his father's gun. Later that day the father showed up and the parish priest took over the case and they left that same afternoon. The boy seemed terrified and helpless. I felt that I had somehow failed him, having promised to intervene. But the parish setting was not the best place for that.

A few weeks later a fifteen-years-old boy, Francisco, was found at the back of the school with slashed wrists. I rushed him to the city hospital for emergency treatment. I had to run out to the nearby pharmacy to buy everything from needles to bandages and all the medicine needed to save his life. Later he told me that his father, an employee at the navy base, had abandoned his mother and two brothers and a sister and went to live with a bar girl. His mother was bringing home sailors to their two room apartment to earn money. It was a common situation, but I had no answer and no solution.

New apostolic ventures for justice and human rights and social ministries were difficult to have approved by the Columban superiors in the early years, especially if they were departed from traditional forms of ministry. What Fr Declan Coyle begun and what I was to venture into for the next thirty-four years was greatly welcomed by many Columban missionaries but looked upon with dismay and trepidation by superiors. They were fearful of political connotations of social involvement or upsetting the ruling family or the like. Some had forgotten the heroic suffering of the early Columbans in China where they ministered to the sick, the hungry, the imprisoned and the oppressed. They served the poor without fear or giving favour to the mighty war lords or the Communists. They were beaten, imprisoned and deported. Somehow when it happened to us, in those days when baptisms and blessings were more important than fighting for justice and freedom, for those of us that were immersed in the human mire of the poors' wretchedness, were misunderstood. If we drew the ire of the ruling powers, we were somehow going beyond the bounds of priestly ministry and wandering too close to the liberation theology so feared by popes and politicians. Solidarity with the poor in the sugar fields and factories, the slums and sweat shops, in the penitentiaries and prisons was not where we were supposed to be in the mind of the saintly sacramentalists.

But we believe too that God was equally present in such sweaty solidarity as in the sacred sanctuary. It was not what we were supposed to be doing. "Well," I asked, "says who?"

They forgot too the declaration of Jesus that the Kingdom is for the poor not the rich, the rich were challenged to go and sell their possessions and share with the poor. Forgotten too were the beatitudes where Jesus declared those who hunger and thirst for justice must have their fill and those who are made suffer and weep will be made glad and happy, and it is for us to make them so. The beatitudes are the challenges every Christian has to meet and to make real. As Jesus said to his Apostles when the five thousand or so people had nothing to eat – feed the hungry! This is what missionaries were now beginning to do everywhere except some of our leaders thought we should be doing what they said. However, the rank and file members of the Columban Missionary Society and the Columban Sisters were themselves involved in many new departures all over the world and in the Philippines too. What Fathers Brian Gore and Niall O'Brien, Mickey Martin and many other were doing in Negros; and Oliver McCrossan, Michael Sinnot, Dan O'Malley, John Keenan, Ray Husband and countless other dedicated Columbans were doing to promote justice and human dignity was what supported and inspired me. They gave their strong support for the work and when the Columban Sisters began in Olongapo and Zambales they started by reaching out to the illiterate, the sick, abused and exploited women and children and began the terrific work for the poor. They were supported by the Columban Fathers in their work. This internal struggle ended when the majority of Columbans gave their approval to the newly defined aim and nature of the Columban Missionary Society that made solidarity with the poor and oppressed the priority value that must guide and inspire out work.

Columban Sisters came to Olongapo in 1953 and dedicated themselves with unstinting sacrifice to building up strong Christian educational schools and colleges. Then by 1969, when Fathers Joe Conneely, Sean Dunne and Tom Vaughen were running St. Joseph's and (that's when I arrived) the missionary work was becoming more socially oriented pushing beyond the purely sacramental. They expanded the ministry reached out through the Pope John XIII centre run by Columban Sisters Pauline McAndrew and Ruth Duckert. It brought hope, dignity and life to the sick and the abandoned. It helped the bar girls and their children and orphans; trained them in new alternative jobs and restored their dignity. In a city where exploitation of women and children filled the money bag of the irresponsible and greedy rich, the selfless work of the Columban Sisters was the salvation of the poor. The education for life and Christian responsibility with a powerful social awareness programme was brought to the young people by Sisters Mary Moylan, Shiela Lucey and Kathleen Coyle through St. Columban's College and the Catechetical Training Centre. Many of these young people educated in St. Columban's College came to join the PREDA staff years later and became agents of change in the whole society that helped us immensely in our struggle against the abuse and exploitation of children. They prepared the minds and hearts of the young to resist the evils of Martial Law and to embrace the people's power movement for justice and peace. It was a school of spirituality that was empowering and inspiring and spreading this great spiritual revolution in the city. Sr Maura Dillan was the power house of energy and inspiration who helped set it up and shaped its course and direction with Sisters Katharine Coyle and Bernadette Dolan between them; all against the surmounting odds of vice and evil that was destroying the fabric of morality and they battled on with truth of light and examples of their faith and personality imbued with the power of God.

They set up the Catechetical Faith and Life Training Centre to empower young people with faith and knowledge and this helped change the tenor of Christian life in the whole province. The catechists it produced had a commitment to defend human rights and the dignity and sacredness of every human being. They brought a new vision of Christianity, moving it away from learning dogmas by rote and practicing little understood rites and rituals. They taught the meaning of love and service to the community and helped transform the Christian youth in parishes throughout the province. The college and this centre is a lasting tribute to all the Columban sisters who went out to meet and confront the daunting tasks facing them in the sick sin city of the orient – Olongapo. They were heroic in their endurance. Eventually, the major part of the work was done and the institutions and spirit had been planted and was blossoming by 1980; it was time to turn it over to the Diocese.

Declan Coyle and the Columban Sisters Kathleen Coyle, Maura Dillon, Mary Moylan and many others gave all important support and encouragement. Some came to the court hearings from time to time to show their solidarity. Years later, in 1983, when I was under pressure from local politicians because of taking an open stand against human rights abuses, the Columban priests rallied around and gave statements of support.

Declan Coyle was a remarkable, charismatic young Columban priest. Tall, good looking and athletic, he was the idol of the young people and he had a great following among the progressive professors and students at St. Columban's College and throughout the province. Declan was ordained a few years after me and was turning the church in Olongapo on its head by challenging all to examine our priorities.

He challenged us to ask ourselves how could we possibly bring God's loving presence into the stink and filth of the sex industry and save the victims and offer conversion and redemption to those caught in its web of evil. He was assistant in the Santa Rita parish and besides having a dynamic apostolate to the poor, he directly challenged the Christian community to awake from their apathy and to question the entire sex industry and the political underpinnings that encouraged and supported it. But that was too much too soon for the traditional Catholics, all of whom made their living working for the Americans or in some part of the Olongapo economy.

He was ahead of his time and realised that to influence the population he needed more than Sunday sermons. He needed radio to broadcast a living message that would bring people to value themselves all the more and restore the value of life. He set up a recording studio in Columban College and gathered teams of people to discuss the social issues from a Christian point of view. It was a vastly popular programme and thousands tuned into it. They never heard anything like this that opened up the hottest issues that were affecting the lives of everyone in the city. Drug abuse, broken families, fake marriages, the exploitation of the women and children and abortion were all tackled. It was phenomenal and it was responsible for a great awaking among the student population that began questioning presence of the US military bases in the Philippines.

This was hitherto a taboo subject. The bases were the source of all that was good and no criticism was permitted. Now, here was a torrent of criticism pouring through the air-waves. The politicians were alarmed and there was political pressure to censor the programme. Eventually they did force it to curtail broadcasts. Abortion was one of the serious issues he tackled to the shock and awe of all. Declan was direct and graphic in bringing home to the public the terrible suffering and pain of the botched abortions that caused the death of many young women, some just teenagers. He used slide shows, pictures, and the testimonies of those victimized by the abortionists. He surely saved the lives of countless unborn children in this campaign for life. Abortion together with the prostitution of children were the great secret sins of the city. Hidden away by a facade of religious ritual and apathy, the killings went on while the church bells tolled, calling the faithful to the Holy Eucharist and the sacraments. Today, many years later, Declan is a much sought after public speaker and human development trainer and is married to Annette Kinne with three beautiful, intelligent children.

Annette is the managing director of Andec Media International that produces broadcast television programmes, educational and training videos and corporate productions based in Dun Laoghaire. She is a well known maker and instructor in documentary film making for television and made an award winning documentary "Taking A Stand" about the work of PREDA, beating more than forty other entrants to win the Radharc Award in 2004, one of Irish television's top awards. The work of Declan and Annette is a continuation of that original commitment to social justice and promotion for human dignity seen so clearly in Olongapo City in the 1970's.

Chapter Four

Poor students, they say, blame their teachers. Well, that was me! After six months in Olongapo, I was finally given permission to undertake language studies at a school in Antipolo, an hour outside Manila. But, unfortunately, the school, which was operated by the Belgium Fathers, was not very professional. We had four teachers and all had different teaching methods and were uncoordinated. It was a frustrating six months. It was to take me a few years to gain any fluency.

When I did start to speak the native tongue with some fluency it was of the greatest importance because I could establish more genuine relationships. It was important that people could open up and share their deepest feelings and thoughts, knowing they would be understood. The foreignness, a feeling of exclusion, was bridged. Eventually, I felt accepted, as if a member of a family. I was reassigned as an assistant to the parish priest, Fr Vinny Lyons in San Marcelino, a rural town about forty-five minutes north of Olongapo. I went there in the latter half of 1970. I objected to this assignment because the language there was Ilocano, very different from Tagalong and, although most people there understand Tagalog, they speak Ilocano. I was not going to learn much there. I thought it was going to be boring in this sleepy unchanging town, which was an hour's drive from the sea. How wrong I was.

The old wooden rectory had a floor of polished mahogany boards and stood beside a solid concrete church with a roof of galvanised iron sheeting. In front of the church was a wide plaza, dotted with a scattering of shady trees. A circular bandstand stood in the centre. To the left of the church there is the Parish School, Saint William's and outside the perimeter wall of the school is the bustling public market. Across the Plaza is the town hall.

The greater part of the municipality of San Marcelino reached many kilometres to the east where the Zambales mountains harboured bandits and Communist rebel groups.

The pace of life in San Marcelino was turtle-like compared to the hectic pace of St. Joseph's Parish in Olongapo. I spent my first few weeks visiting the sick around the town and getting to know the people. I drove the catechists to the distant village schools to give religious instruction. Outside the rectory compound was the market and the day began at four o'clock with the squealing of pigs being brought to market strapped to the sidecar of a motorised tricycle that spluttered angrily and rattled their way under my window making further sleep impossible. We took turns in celebrating the daily Mass at 7am and after that it was a visit to the school or to a distant village to arrange for the catechists to visit and teach Catholic doctrine and moral values. The school was the best place for me to meet people and try to converse with them in Tagalog.

I soon learned that it was a sleepy but dangerous town. The people are known for being hardworking, thrifty and insular. The centre of life for each individual is fulfilling traditional obligations to the extended family members and maintaining good relationships. Outside of that, alliances with other families was of greatest importance. Government people, unless they were relatives, were not well trusted. There was little trust either in the system of justice in resolving disputes. A personal or family affront, a land dispute was frequently settled with the knife or the gun. Family feuds abounded. The sound of gun shots was not unusual. Many people went armed or had a gun at home to protect themselves and their families or settle scores in a shootout.

The first image I had of San Marcelino was that of a sleepy town of rural-tranquillity. That quickly changed when the sudden crack of gunshots woke me in the middle of the night to indicate another funeral.

One day the students came running across the schoolyard to announce that there were dead bodies in front of the Town Hall. I went with them and saw six bloodied corpses riddled with bullet wounds lying on the pavement in front of the police station as a warning to others. The police told me that they were Huks, or Communist rebels, killed in a shoot out with the army.

This undignified display of human corpses from some distant battlefield was appalling. Flies buzzed about the bodies, their blood-splattered faces twisted and broken. The bullet holes were black and putrid; it was my first time to witness human corpses laid out like dead animals after a hunt. No one claimed the bodies and they were not brought to the church. There was to be no funeral, which was the ultimate gesture of contempt for an enemy. I silently prayed over the corpses and gave a blessing to acknowledge their human dignity. I wondered if they had committed any crime at all. An hour later the bodies were thrown into the back of an army truck like sacks of rice and they were driven away to be buried in unmarked graves. I felt nauseated and sick and went back to the rectory to rest and drink water. The tropical sun beat down as I crossed the dusty plaza, the smell of the decaying bodies followed me like a bad dream.

January 1970 began with social unrest and a violent demonstration by two thousand people outside the Palace gates. They were protesting against rising prices and social injustice. In February there were signs of even more growing political unrest in Manila. President Ferdinand Marcos declared that he would not run for a third term having just been re-elected and hinted that the demonstrations were Communist inspired. The tolerance for the Americans and deference shown to them in Olongapo and San Antonio was not shared by my many other Filipinos. On February 18, a crowd of almost three thousand young people demonstrated violently against the Vietnam War and the use of Philippine soil to launch bombing runs against the Vietnamese and Cambodian people.

The Demonstrations against the Vietnam War continued sporadically in Manila through April that year and on April 7 there was a general strike against the increase in oil prices. The street demonstrations against Marcos became more frequent throughout the year. The political situation was getting tense and opposition to Marcos was growing.

On November 27, the priests and Bishop Henry Byrne, along with bus loads of teachers and students, were off to Manila to greet Pope Paul VI. I was scheduled to supervise youth seminars and take care of the parish so I missed the historical occasion.

The speech of Pope Paul was nothing radical and not as hard hitting as that of his successor was to make some years later. Still it gave a lot of encouragement to those in the church to work harder for social justice. The super rich still had it all and they had no intention of letting it go. The Pope called on Marcos to work for a just division of wealth to uplift the poor and to respect human rights.

"We are thinking of an effort to be made through a more equitable distribution of the riches of this country which has been blessed by God, a real and integral development of individuals and communities, a human advancement – especially of the most needy classes – a deeper awareness at all levels, not only of one's rights, but still more and above all of one's duties towards other men, other fellow human beings, and towards the whole community.... By according recognition and respect to the rights of persons, families and groups, and by their care for fairness and for economic and social progress, they do honour to Christianity, from which these virtues derive..." was what he said.

Marcos was already growing rich, powerful and autocratic. The poor were left on the road to economic hell and Marcos and his wife Imelda couldn't care less. He was accumulating gold and she was collecting diamonds – and shoes. She had no sensitivity to the contradiction of being photographed kneeling in prayer holding a dangling rosary made of priceless diamonds, while outside the walls thousands dangled between life and death.

There was no television in Olongapo or the province. The radio was the main source of news or the daily newspaper and it didn't arrive till the afternoon, the road from Manila being notoriously bad. It was only when I turned on the BBC that evening I learned that the Pope had been attacked at the airport by a Bolivian painter disguised as a priest. This incident got the media attention and any impact of the Pope's message calling for social justice and a fair distribution of wealth was lost. But not on many Christians working for social justice who were labelled as Communists for taking an option to serve the poor and organise them to better their communities. This is what my fellow Columban Missionaries were doing in the island of Negros and in parts of Mindanao, although I didn't know it at the time. Later the basic Christian community became a powerful church movement, upholding moral values and social justice. Its spiritual leaders became a threat to the political regime.

There was much talk of revolution and Communist led uprising although that turned out to be Marcos scare tactics. All he had to do was frighten the living daylights out of everybody with the Communist bogeyman and the political opposition would crumble. Church and business leaders ran to shelter under his strongman image. The Huks were nationalist rebels fighting against the landowners of central Luzon and not driven by Communist ideology, although they embraced the same ideals and aspirations of a classless society and socialist state. It spread after WWII and was put down with American help.

The few emaciated bodies of so-called rebels that I had seen in front of the town hall that morning were later said to be tenant farmers driven off their land and had taken to the mountains when evicted. They had surrendered with their antiquated guns but were executed almost immediately. Death squads were nothing new to the Philippines. The armed goons of a greedy landlord had driven them off the land so he could sell it for corporate farming.

Chapter Five

Fr Vincent Lyons was a good-natured, kind and well-liked parish priest but very conservative. We never discussed social issues unless it meant a round of golf and a dinner party. Besides celebrating the Eucharist and administering the sacraments I wanted to do more in development projects in the remote villages. Unfortunately, Fr Vinny didn't see the need for the parish to get involved in anything else. The diocese didn't have a social action centre in those days and whatever went on to uplift the poor and help them to pull themselves out of the manmade misery was left to individuals. It was frowned upon as dabbling in economics or becoming political.

Good old Bishop Byrne was anxious for the Vatican II council reforms to be implemented – slowly. Any innovation, change or modernization was resisted by most of the clergy. I felt it all very frustrating. It was a time when the people needed moral leadership and church-led inspiration to find ways to lessen the poverty and hunger. People were dying for the want of a few dollars worth of basic antibiotics. The church has a role to feed the hungry. I liked to point out that the miracle of the loaves and fishes was really a miracle of sharing. Many had brought food but only when Jesus told the disciples to share their own lunch that others with food had a change of mind and heart and shared with those that had none. That, I pointed out, was our role to begin the sharing no matter how little. If others were to do the same a lot more people will live and poverty can be eliminated.

One day, about an hour before sunset, when Fr Vinny and myself would sit on the small veranda and listen to the BBC and sip a beer, a fusillade of gun shots rang out not far from the rectory. Something big was going on, Fr Vinny took cover in his room and I took cover on the stairs where there were heavy wooden columns to block stray bullets. The cook and the house helpers were under the stairs, which was considered the safest place of all. After a while one of the boys called up to report that there was a shoot-out between the army and a hold-up gang. The grisly scene of the dead farmers in front of the municipal hall returned and I feared another massacre might be taking place.

The town was suddenly silent. The tricycles had stopped, quiet descended on the market. Then we heard furious exchange of shots and shouting across the plaza. The firing then died down so I entered the church by the back door and peeped out the doors that opened onto the plaza. A dozen soldiers in battle gear were behind tree trunks and rubble, aiming at people behind trees across the plaza. He waved at me to go back inside. The shooting started again.

After this went on for half an hour I had an idea. I called to him again to hold fire and said something about letting them surrender to the Church. The officer waited a while, thinking about this, and then shouted something towards the trees and pointed toward the church door. There was a long silence. From the other side of the plaza a white cloth appeared from behind a tree. They were giving up.

The sergeant shouted something in the local language, which I couldn't understand. It was over so quickly. Guns and rifles were thrown out and three men stood up and the soldiers were walking towards them quickly but keeping them covered. I thought they would bring them to the church but instead they were then taken at gunpoint to the municipal hall. I thought they might be shot like the farmers were and it would be my fault so I hurried over to the town hall and the commander told me they were in the jail and would not be harmed. Theyy were bandits. As if by magic people suddenly appeared from all directions. The incident would be the gossip of the market for a week until the next shoot out. I felt very pleased with myself having done what I thought was something really worthwhile.

That exciting incident helped lift me out of a kind of depression. I wondered if I would spend all my life in a place like San Marcelino with a church, school and a rusty Volkswagen to take care of. Many people get into ruts like that and think there is no way out. The Church, business, school or family has unwritten rules by which we are all made to conform and behave in certain ways but we don't know why. I knew I wanted change and it had to be for the better.

In San Marcelino there was no parish plan. What we were doing was already it. I was so bored that I took up my hobby of photography from college days. I set up a darkroom and soon I was out and about with my camera photographing, developing and printing. Shortly after this I also started writing too.

Something changed my life forever one February day in 1976. It happened at a government school in an outlying village of San Marcelino where the parish catechists were scheduled to give religious instruction. Not knowing Ilocano, the local language, brilliantly so I could hardly talk to non-English speaking people. I couldn't even be understood by the children. I felt isolated and cut off without the language.

So I became the bored driver, my life wasting away under the Kiameto tree. I sat like the Holy Buddha for a while and tried to meditate and pray for enlightenment as to what to do with my life. I asked God if life was to be always boring when I craved action. There was no answer, just a gentle stirring of the leaves by a warm gentle breeze. The metal roof of the school shimmered in the blistering sunshine.

I was sweating and decided to take a walk around the schoolyard looking for something to photograph. A tattered flag here, a croaking frog there. Nothing much until I turned a corner and there I stood face to face with a little girl with a huge hole where her nose and mouth ought to have been. One white tooth was sticking out at an angle from this incredibly ugly face. I was visibly startled and stepped back. The poor child looked hideous. It was my first encounter with a child with an untreated cleft palate.

She saw my look of surprise, covered her face in shame and embarrassment, and ran away. I felt awful and, as soon as the classes were over, I asked the catechists why she had never been treated. They explained that it was a childhood deformity and the parents were too poor to get her an operation. I learned also there were many more children with cleft palates in the surrounding villages. I was determined to do something about it.

I talked it over with Fr Lyons and he approved it. His heart was in the right place when it came to immediate needs of the poor. I teamed up with Sr Mary Rose, a religious sister of the Daughters of Charity who lived in the convent at the other side of the school compound. I found the Philippine Band of Mercy, a charity in Manila that was willing to help children in need of surgery, and I scheduled to bring the children there. Sr Rose made a survey of the children that needed surgery and prepared them and their parents to go to Manila. There were some decent people around that willingly donated for the cost of transportation and food in Manila. The Band of Mercy charity arranged with good hearted surgeons to donate their time and skills for an operation. The charity provided the medicine and all other requirements.

The surgery was a great success and the news soon spread around the countryside. Many more parents were bringing their children from the countryside to the parish office to enrol them in the project. Soon many children of all ages were having operations. While the older children were much improved they still had a large scar but soon regained their self-dignity and confidence. Younger children improved immensely. They were no longer teased in the schoolyard but considered something of a celebrity having travelled to Manila, a rarity for village children. I was busy meeting children and parents to put them at ease and make arrangements for their surgery with the great help of a tireless Sr Rose. This was something more practical. The values we preached on Sunday about helping others could be practiced every other day by all of us.

Then I asked how could this deformity be prevented, what caused it I wondered? Then with the catechists and volunteers we began health education classes in the villages for expectant mothers. Firstly to dispel the myth that the birth deformity was some kind of punishment for past misdeeds. This is a repugnant notion, some very stupid people still go about saying that a deformity, sickness, AIDS or a calamity is a punishment from God for some sin. This is heresy or repugnant to say that a loving, compassionate and forgiving God, made present through Jesus Christ, would punish innocent children and mothers with evil of any kind. It might have started as a scare tactic by a witchdoctor, clergy or politician powerful to control the uneducated by fear. People can be paralysed by fear. The fear of hell as a punishment for sin is an old tactic that even got me trembling in church as a small boy as the preacher thundered at us from the pulpit about how we would suffer in the flames of hell for an eternity for our sins. That's what paralysed the poor man that was brought to Jesus and was cured when his sins were forgiven. Maybe that's why the temple leaders got so angry at Jesus. He saw through their terror tactics and took away their weapon of fear by simply forgiving the sins of the man, real or imagined as it might have been.

I set out to dispel that notion by explaining how the deformity happens, how it could be prevented. Hundreds of children were helped and a culture of fear was replaced by an experience of love and care.

The exact causes of cleft palate are not exactly known. Having talked with a few doctors I came up with a plausible explanation. The catechists did the explaining. The developing foetus, they said, was perhaps thumb sucking in the womb and when the mother had a fall or engaged in a lot of rice planting and bending over the washing tub for long periods the child's thumb may pierce the soft tissue of the upper lip. Whether true or not the mothers took greater care during pregnancy. Anyway, the information lifted the fear and shame of guilt associated with the deformity.

The Operation Harelip Project continued for years after I left San Marcelino. Sr Rose developed her own source of funds from the better off families. There were fewer children growing up with disfiguring cleft palates in San Marcelino and later the project spread to other towns.

Young people from neighbouring towns were scared to come to San Marcelino because of the gang warfare. They were seen as intruders and fights in the plaza were common. There was little alternative for the young, the nearest movie house was almost one hour away in Olongapo city; a travelling movie show came twice a year and set up in the plaza, threw up a cloth fence and charged a few cents for a viewing. Starting a youth group was my idea to get them involved in social and church activities. The girls were encouraged to join the catechists going to the out-lying villages on Saturdays and Sundays.

The boys were invited to join a parish group called the *Knights of the Altar* and become active as altar servers and sacristans. It gave me a chance to get them thinking for themselves and making good choices so they could avoid joining a violent gang. It was from this group that one student, Alex

Corpus Hermoso, from a highly respected family whose grandfather had received a papal award, became a highly motivated youth leader. He was later to finish high school, go on to college, graduate with distinction and become a co-founder and a director of the PREDA Foundation, a human rights organisation I set-up a few years later.

The Cursilio was a Catholic apostolate for personal transformation. It was set up and composed entirely of lay Catholics whose mission was to re-evangelise the many nominal Catholics. It came to San Marcelino with the approval of Fr Lyons. I worked with the leaders to recruit some of the most notorious characters, some were known criminals and tough guys. There was little preaching to the choir as it was hard to sell spiritual renewal courses to bring about repentance and a plea to God for forgiveness. The reformed characters became preachers and role models for others. Some of the best lay preachers were the reformed characters themselves. They became role models for the newly inducted members.

The priest had a limited role as one of the several preachers and confessor. It was a great opportunity for me to practice Tagalog as the retreats were held in that language because participants came from many distant places. I became an enthusiastic supporter and chaplain for the retreats. When Fr Vinny took his annual retreat I was left in charge. I had five weeks to try something different in the parish. I called a meeting of the parish leaders and asked them to suggest a more meaningful liturgy. We discussed several options to improve people's participation.

Then we came up with a plan. The following Sunday, the San Marcelino community had a surprise. We celebrated the Eucharist in Ilocano, the language of the people. I had to learn my part well as I have very little ability with it. This was a positive thing as it made the lay parishioners do most of the liturgy. There was modern music and upbeat songs by the youth group. Men and women were assigned as scripture readers. A woman read the gospel and another gave the sermon. All strictly forbidden by church practice then but very necessary so the people could understand the Word of God and feel they belonged to the community. The graduates of the Cursilio retreat were introduced like newly received Christians. Other parishioners read the prayers of the faithful.

Nowadays most of this is commonplace with men and women, Eucharist ministers and deacons, but then it was unheard of. Word spread throughout the parish and the following Sunday there was standing room only and the congregation spilled out into the plaza. The participation of so many made a feeling of togetherness and all were proud to do their share. With three masses a Sunday, many parishioners were involved. As I expected, it only lasted a month and one week. When Fr Vinny returned, the revolution was over and it was back to the old ways again much to the disappointment of all. But they had an unforgettable experience that prepared them for the future change. I suggested to Fr Vinny that if he got more lay people involved he could play a lot more golf. That didn't work either.

It was a night I will never forget. It was a humid tropical night of frog croaking madness accompanied by a concert of a million chirping crickets that filled the night with a sense of alarm and a strange foreboding. I sat on the balcony of the old ramshackle wooden rectory. Fr Vinny had retired to his room.

A gentle breeze drifted down the balcony. The BBC World news and commentary was just ending as I stared out into the clear star speckled sky. It was 8:45. I decided to visit the Sisters' convent at the other side of the school compound and make arrangements with Sr Mary Rose to take some children to Manila for medical treatment that week.

I went down the polished mahogany stairs and out into night. The incessant croaking of the frogs suddenly stopped. I stood for a while, relishing the silence then continued to the convent. The Sisters were all gathered in the community room sewing, reading and writing. One Sister was strumming the guitar.

Half a kilometre away, Mayor Rabanes, his friends and bodyguards sat around a card table on an open patio of a friend's house in a neighbourhood called San Isidro. A narrow sandy road just wide enough for a single vehicle ran outside the bamboo fence that surrounded the small bungalow and dark clad strangers were advancing on the cheerful group playing poker. A teenager was serving beer.

The Mayor's bodyguards had their guns holstered or propped against the wall as they leaned over the back of their chairs watching the fall of the cards. There were sixteen in all. Laughter drifted from the patio into the night as somebody won a game, someone else lost.

In the Sisters' convent I had finished talking with Sr Rose and sat down to strum a few cords on the guitar. At that moment the armed men were surrounding the card players. Down the road a dog suddenly barked viciously, disturbing the silence of the night. The frogs had remained eerily silent.

Just as suddenly the barking stopped with a whelp. I stopped strumming the guitar and sat up and listened in that strange silence that I had come to recognise as a prelude to something ominous. Even the crickets had gone silent. The soft whimpering of a wounded dog was all that could be heard and then it happened.

The night erupted in a roar of automatic gunfire of deafening noise and smoke. A hail of bullets poured across the fence tearing into the Mayor and the group of men sitting around the table. They were caught in a withering crossfire. They spun and fell, crying out in shock and terror, some reaching for their weapons in vain. They were cut down by a dozen bullets.

The sound burst like a huge stone through the convent window. My heart leapt with fright. The vicious gunfire seemed close by and I dropped to the floor, calling to the sisters to "get down, get down"! But there was no need, they were already lying flat on the floor, under tables and chairs. The firing was prolonged and intense. It went on and on. We were frozen with fright, the sisters were praying silently, I was quaking, imagining that the bandits or rebels were attacking the church compound.

Then it stopped as suddenly as it had started. In the silence, we all looked up at each other, still tense, unsure of what had happened but with relief that we were still alive. And then there was another series of short machine gun bursts. They sounded further away. We ducked down again pressing ourselves to the floor as if that alone could save us. The rat-tat-tat filled the room and was coming closer.

Quickly one of the sisters stood up and walked calmly to an open door and closed it. Then lay down on the floor holding the crucifix of her rosary beads close to her lips. My heart was thumping hard, pounding against my chest.

The short rapid bursts of gunfire were closer. I could hear the loud bangs as bullets ripped through galvanised iron roofing and thudded into the wooden walls of nearby houses. Somewhere a window splintered. Then the firing was coming from just outside. The gunmen were passing close, perhaps retreating towards the mountains. I suddenly noticed the lights were still on and, in a panic, I jumped up, found the switch and turned them off. We waited for at least thirty minutes before sitting up and then we sat in darkness. Waiting for the danger to pass.

We were safe but others were not so lucky. Later, I heard that the town hall radio operator, Mario Gonzales, was leaving the building and getting into his jeep at 9.20 when the firing started. He panicked and drove away at breakneck speed towards the firing instead of away from it.

A burst of fire raked the jeep and Mario was hit. Wild with

fear and panic and disoriented, he kept going towards the firing, then swerved on the narrow lane and crashed through a bamboo fence and ran for his life. He escaped. From an upper window in a nearby house an old woman reached to close the shutter. She was met with a burst of fire and cried out in pain, her hand shattered.

When the firing started, hands reached for machetes, knives or any weapon close at hand. Others moved to their secret places and readied their hidden arms. Children wet themselves in fear.

The firing became distant. The card game had come to an abrupt and bloody end. On the patio in San Isidro sixteen people were dead. It was silent, now the firing heard was a long way off. But we were still tense and I began to pray with the sisters for those who had surely died. Then we stopped and listened; there was a great silence over the town broken by a baby crying somewhere across the street. We had imagined the worse, an armed raid by the rebels or bandits. They could have killed a hundred and burnt the whole town. But we were spared all that.

We began to sing a hymn, softly at first, but the sound of our own voices gave us courage and we sang louder, feeling a happiness that comes after a great danger has passed. Then we heard other voices across the street singing too and then some more. It relieved the tension and spread down the street and we sat listening and thanking God to be alive.

A rooster began crowing, a dog was howling. I was worried about Fr Lyons and decided to go back to the rectory. As I came across the schoolyard the crickets started up. He was sitting on the stairs, saying the rosary.

"That was a bad one," he said.

I told him that the sisters were safe. We sat in the dark in silence. I was drinking water; he had a gin and tonic.

At 10:15 we were still wondering what had happened and if the gang would return to terrorise the town once again. We heard a voice calling from outside the rectory. "Father, come quickly. They shot my uncle." It was one of our students. Fr Vinny got the holy oil and I went out to start the pick-up. As I drove slowly in the direction the boy pointed, he told us briefly what had happened. He directed us to the scene of carnage.

I parked with the headlights directed towards the patio of the bungalow. What we saw was shocking. Blood was everywhere like a gruesome scene from a horror movie, but this was real. The walls and doors were splattered with blood and hundreds of bullet holes scarred the walls. Bloodied, twisted bodies were strewn all over the patio. One man was still clutching playing cards. Others were slumped on overturned chairs. The body of Mayor Rabanes was sprawled on the table, it was covered with blood that dripped onto the floor tiles. Another man lay dead in the doorway where he had tried to reach vainly for a weapon before he was cut down by the withering gunfire. The playing cards were scattered all over the ground and pools of blood had formed on the floor near the bodies.

The corpses were torn and mutilated from the continuous hail of bullets from automatic rifles that had poured into them from point blank range. I felt stunned and didn't know what was expected of us. Why were we here? I wondered. What could we do? There were no survivors to comfort, relatives had not yet arrived, we were among the first on the scene. Even the police, fearing a secondary ambush, had not ventured out. The neighbours had been the first to stir from the fearful silence that had descended on the town. There were only a few bodies that could be anointed – the others were too bloodied.

People were beginning to arrive. It seemed gruesome and pointless to anoint these bloodied corpses in this mutilated condition. But not knowing what else was expected of us we went from one body to another praying, blessing and placing a dab of holy oil on to a forehead here and there.

Our presence seemed to give comfort to the relatives that

were now gathered nearby, weeping. One face was so mutilated that someone had covered it with a handkerchief. It was soaked in blood.

More police and relatives began to move the bodies and lay them in a row. I stood there feeling numb, helpless and grim. We stayed a while in solidarity with the relatives and then went back to the rectory. I couldn't sleep that night, the images of the bloodied bodies would not leave my mind. Who could have done such a savage thing? The next day I learned that miraculously there were two survivors. They were hit in the hand and leg and bled profusely but played dead.

For two weeks, day after day, funeral processions slowly wound their way around the town, past the houses of the dead and into the Church for the funeral rites and blessing. Then they made their way to the cemetery.

The bungalow was abandoned after that and the murderers were never caught. It was believed to have been a gang of murderers hired by a political rival to assassinate the Mayor. The leader of the gang was named Fabunan. About a year later his mother's house was still being watched by undercover agents and one night he was seen fleetingly through the window. When the police moved in to capture him he had mysteriously disappeared. But they found a trapdoor and a tunnel that led out into the rice fields and they gave chase and caught him as he emerged from the tunnel. Fabunan, the notorious bandit leader, was riddled with bullets.

During my stay in San Marcelino I kept in contact with the students and teachers in St. Joseph's School in Olongapo City. It was just an hour from San Marcelino and I visited frequently. One day when I arrived at the school campus the gates were locked and I heard there was a teachers' strike demanding better wages and conditions. I realised that the Fathers must be very upset and I just passed through the gate when a police megaphone blared out orders for the gate to be opened. An open top jeep swept into the compound with Mayor Amelia Gordon standing up surrounded by armed men holding automatic rifles and pistols pointing out on all sides.

The Mayor called an impromptu meeting of all the teachers, ordered them to stand beside her jeep and over the megaphone lectured them on the evils of strikes and how they were the tools of Communism. She warned them that if they went on strike in her city they had better be ready to leave Olongapo – or else. That was city policy for years to come, if you were critical and didn't like the city then leave it. Democratic free speech was not considered a virtue in Olongapo. The city was equated with the political family that ran it and some wags suggested it be renamed Gordon City and all it needed was Batman.

During the Mayor's tirade Fr Tom appeared with another priest. They wore white cassocks and were visibly shocked. They may have made a mistake in asking the iron fisted Mayor to negotiate with the teachers but they never expected their teachers to be threatened at gunpoint. That was the end of the strike and the students protest. I was dumbfounded at this naked show of force and gun rule. In San Marcelino family land disputes were settled sometimes with the gun but for a labour dispute to be settled at gun point was a new low for Philippine democracy. Later all the grievances of the staff and students were rectified by the school authorities.

Chapter Six

I left San Marcelino a few months later when I received news that my father was terminally ill with cancer and I was to return home at once after only two years and three months into my assignment. My mission, whatever it would be, had not even begun.

My Father's death made a deep impression on me. He was a quiet, gentle man, faithful to his work and family. I wasn't *emotionally close* to him but his patience and hard work to give us a good home and education was his way of showing affection and love. We were not a well off family but were not poor either. We had a respectable suburban home and a small used car, which we only used occasionally. We all got the opportunity of a good education, although the school system for us boys was hard and disciplinarian to the point of being counterproductive. The harsh treatment turned many away from a love of learning and it was a major obstacle to our success.

In his later years, my Dad's joy and pleasure was for us to go out together for a drive to the Wicklow Hills and enjoy the blooming heather across the mountain side or a walk in the woods on Dalkey Hill and along the Vico Road overlooking Killiney Bay. Our first home had been in Dalkey. Nearby we would drive up the Burma Road to walk in the woods, exercise the dog and sit looking over the beautiful view of Dun Laoghaire Harbour and Dublin Bay. Most of the family emigrated to England in the late 1950s and it was a sad and lonely parting.

Dad worked as an insurance agent for the Hibernian Insurance Company for all his working life. A few years before Dad was to retire it was discovered that he had a weak heart and early retirement was the only option. After a life's faithful service his pension was cut in half. This injustice hurt my mother a lot and I didn't know of it until years later. My parents never discussed their financial problems with us children.

I resented the penny pinching and uncompassionate ways of big business. After my Father died the miserable pension ended and my Mother had nothing to live on. I sent letters of protest to the company, one of the richest in Ireland. A few years later the company relented and changed its policies from miserly penny pinching to one providing social benefits as they should have done years before. They gave my Mother a widow's pension.

I was given an assignment in Ireland in 1972 to undertake recruitment and mission education work in the parishes of the Diocese of Dublin. Our commitment to a *simple life* does not entitle us in the missionary society to a professional salary. I turned to photography in my spare time to earn an income and help my Mother and improve our home. "Rosetta" was a symbol of all that my parents had dreamed of, worked and struggled for – a comfortable home for their children. When my brothers and sisters emigrated to England and Canada, my parents' dreams of growing old surrounded by a loving family with grandchildren to dote over in Ireland vanished. They silently grieved without complaint for their lost dream.

The *Far East Magazine, Columban Mission and Reality Magazine* of the Redemporists Fathers paid well for a lot of my photographs. With this income I was able to help my

Mother. Later, when she had overcome the loss of my Father somewhat, Mother took employment with a friend in a newsagent shop and she loved it. She was a brilliant conversationalist and loved to meet people, listen to their problems and dispense advice. She was a tower of strength to all of us who turned to her for help and advise.

I spent several months of 1972 doing mission education and vocation work around the schools in Dublin. The talks I gave in the parishes during Sunday mass about missionary work was strong on comparing the comparative wealth of life in the developed world and the poverty of the Third World. I appealed to the congregation to subscribe to *The Far East Magazine.* I produced two brochures for aspiring missionaries. One was based on mission as working for justice and peace and one to inspire young people to consider the missionary life as a spiritual journey. Columban Fr John Keenhan, also assigned to the Philippines, was on this work for a while with me. He was involved with the brochure project too. With graphic photographs we showed the horrors of war, hunger and poverty. We challenged people to respond through the inspiration of the Crucified Christ who undertook his prophetic mission of salvation through building a world based on love, friendship, justice and non-violence. I had seen a lot of poverty and global injustice in the Philippines and was outspoken about the wealth and oppression of the poor countries by the West and how Ireland had to take a lead in the struggle for global justice. Some parish priests and wealthy parishioners may have felt uncomfortable by my frank messages.

Towards the end of that year I received a letter from the Superior General Richard Stienhilber and the central administration cutting short my assignment in Ireland and reassigning me to the Philippines. Fr Richard concluded his letter of March 7: "On behalf of the Society I would like to take this opportunity to thank you for the willing way in which you undertook promotion work while you were here at home. No doubt this experience will make you more than anxious to return to the quiet life of the Philippines." I think they had had enough of my outspoken messages and my immediate return would perhaps give them a more "quiet life".

I was happy to get this green light to return to the Philippines. I had begun putting in the central heating system at "Rosetta" as the bitterly cold winters would soon be taking their toll on my Mother. I did much of the work myself, ripping up the floorboards and laying the pipes under the direction of a good plumber who made the plan, all the final connections and installed the boiler. I picked up discarded radiators and fittings for minimum cost.

The spirit of adventure overtook me that March of 1972 and I decided to take an overland route back to Asia. I wrote to companies such as *Trail Finders* and *Encounter Overland* based in London that advertised in the *Sunday Times* travel section. For the modest sum of £180, "fully inclusive", I could travel for three months by road from London to Kathmandu. For £88 I could fly from Katmandu to Calcutta, join Mother Theresa in her work, go on to Burma to visit the Columbans and then go to China and the Philippines. It was an ambitious plan and I bought my ticket on the old Bedford four-wheeled drive converted army truck with twenty-two other adventurers and that June set off on a journey of a life time.

After a sad farewell to my Mother, I left for London from where the *Overlander's* truck departed for the ferry crossing to Ostend in Belgium. My sister Laurie and her husband Terry Smith and the children came to see me off. Before my departure I saw a great family friend Genevieve McNamara who worked in London. Our mothers were close friends and when Gen retired and returned to Ireland she was a next door neighbour and devoted to my Mother, visiting her every day.

We drove the rumbling truck through Brussels and picked

up another traveller and headed into Germany and made our first camp near Frankfurt. By June 29, we were in Austria heading into Yugoslavia. I began a journal by letter and mailed them home to my Mother who kept them faithfully. Among the twenty-two fellow travellers there were three post-graduate students from Cambridge who talked non-stop about history, each vying with the other to impress everyone with their breadth of book knowledge. It was their first trip abroad.

There was a couple of newly weds from Canada, and another couple from Australia, a Malaysian student based in Singapore and a mixed group of young single adventurers. We had five medium sized tents and one big one that folded out from the side of the truck. We all took turns in setting up camp and cooking and washing up the dishes. There was good cooperation and little conflict, which was amazing. The team leader recounted how previous groups never made it out of Europe before people were fighting and arguing and leaving. None dropped out of our group except the American boy who got so sick in Afghanistan from eating contaminated food that he had to be flown out to a hospital.

It was a long, interesting and exciting trip and if I was to tell you every adventure it would be a book in itself. One morning in North East Greece we were camped near a fishing village on the coast. I woke to hear shouting and screaming and the camp in a panic. I thought we were being attacked and looked for rocks or other cover in case there was gunfire. I was ready for anything at that stage. But instead it was only the attack of the killer mosquitoes. The group was running in every direction as a great black swarm of big insects descended on the camp looking for victims like a flock of hungry vampire bats. I dashed into the tent and zipped myself into my sleeping bag until the angry buzzing bloodsuckers had their bloody fill of somebody else. There were a few campers caught in the open near the shore and suffered the painful bites for days.

Istanbul is amazing. There is so much history, magnificent buildings and towering mosques and old city walls where West meets East that I couldn't write about it here. But it was the first step into Asia and as we drove on to a rusty old ferry to make the crossing, I knew I was following a route of the misguided and bloodthirsty conquerors of the past. Here Alexander had crossed, the crusaders, and many more. The Cambridge students came in handy but turned out to be bores. I struck out by myself to explore the ancient city.

Besides the extraordinary historical sights and structures, the street life made a deep impression on me. I wandered the narrow streets around the bazaar and goggled at the human mules that carried incredible heavy loads on their backs up and down the steepest of hills and flights of steps all over the city. Skinny old men carried incredible loads three times their size and weight by the looks of it. They were bent over even without a load with a permanent spine deformity because of carrying gigantic loads from childhood. Nothing was too much for them. They carried big wooden crates, huge bails of cotton one piled on another.

Children were cargo carriers, too. I felt sorry for the kids being treated like beasts of burden. Child labour was taken for granted. The hot tea sellers were weaving their way in and out of the crowds carrying their pots and glasses of steaming tea through the crowded bazaars and markets without spilling a drop. When they found a customer they served it with a flourish and hurried away to find another. Old 1950 vintage American cars drove through the wider streets. Cadillacs and Chryslers made magnificent taxis. We crossed the Bosporos on the bucking rolling ferry that was buffeted by the wake of passing ships passing from the Black Sea to the Sea of Marmara and gratefully we made it and drove up the shore into Asia.

Then we turned south travelling down the coast to visit the many ruins of Roman towns. Ephesus was so well preserved with its great amphitheatre seating thousands where St. Paul made his impassioned speech to the Ephesians. "Here he spoke out boldly and argued persuasively about the Kingdom of God." It was very moving to stand on the very spot where this great man of God had laid his life on the line for his beliefs. Not far away was the ruins of the Temple of Diana where the Oracle had proclaimed doom and gloom, joy and happiness for countless pilgrims. I saw a pile of granite blocks, pillars and ornately carved statues but my imagination gathered them all together to form an image of a magnificent temple that held the ancient world in awe.

We travelled on down the coast and turned off into the mountains to visit the remains of an ancient Roman town. We had a magnificent view of the sea in the distance. I went up to the ruins of an old Roman town long abandoned. I marvelled at the streets of paved stone with ruts cut in them either by chariot wheels or by hand for drainage. But the massive blocks and pillars scattered around the hillside was a reminder of the greatness of the Roman empire that ruled for thousands of years and yet here was the evidence of the fragility of all civilizations and the shortness of human life. There was the remains of an old pagan altar and there, in the glow of the setting sun, I prayed alone and celebrated the Eucharist.

When I reached the camp below it was dark and I ate a hurried supper that the others had left for me and went to my sleeping bag. Whatever unseen power urged me to zip it wide open before climbing in I will never know, the thought of ants perhaps, the hand of God? I shone my flash light and jumped back in fright with a yelp, a big scorpion crawled the length of the bag, its deadly venom only inches away from my hand waiting to kiss me goodnight forever. I held the shaking beam on the deadly creature as it scurried off the cloth into the scrub. There was no sleep for me that night.

Afraid to lay my head down on that infested ground I sat up on a rock with my sleeping bag zipped around me, knees drawn up waiting for the dawn.

There were many more adventures on the road to Katmandu. We met floods, snakes, robbers and drug traffickers on that long fascinating journey of almost four months. We travelled through Northern Turkey along the banks of Lake Vann into Iran, crossed the wide lonely desert and became lost close to the border with Iraq. In a letter dated July 17 to my Mother and sister Aileen back in Ireland I wrote:

Today we carried on from Lake Vann towards the Iranian border and will cross tonight. The countryside is fantastic! Great, open grassy plains and towering snow-capped mountains, and it is in the middle of summer! I am writing this as we drive along dusty mountain roads, and it's bumpy, - oops!

This morning we got a puncture, but were soon on our way again. I invented a washing machine by buying a large plastic container with a large screw cap and fixing it to the top of the cab roof in the box there for baggage. The bumping along the rugged roads sloshes the clothes and water around and washes them white!

I remembered Dad on the 16th (death anniversary) at Sunday Mass, praying for all as I go along into Asia.

It's getting hot and dusty, we will be going down towards the Persian Gulf and the heat will be almost unbearable ...

And so it was. We were soon surrounded by scorching deserts that were so hot the gasoline evaporated before it hit the pistons and we were stranded in an ocean of hot sand. The only solution was to cool the carburettor with our meagre supply of drinking water dripping from plastic bottles on to a cloth placed on the carburettor. We chugged along with a coughing engine sucking gasoline for all it was worth and getting more hot air for propulsion. We were parched from the thirst and doled out small rations of warm water that left our throats raw and dry longing for more. We were like tired panting dogs with lolling tongues.

One of my great discoveries was the use of the turban. I wrapped my towel around my head and across my dried out face and doused it with water when we had an ample supply. I only had to stick my head out the side of the truck to get a warm wind and the sudden coolness of the evaporation process. It was a pleasant relief and useful when we had the water to soak the towel. But this was not possible as we drove further into the desert.

We halted for the night, lost on the bed of a dried up sea. There were no freezing desert nights here. I lay half naked on the desert floor, a warm breeze rolling over a grateful, perspiring body. It was an anxious night for all of us.

Early the next morning we set off with a cooler engine over endless sand dunes following what looked like a rough gravel road. Then cresting a final dune to my astonishment was a scattering of big pipes sticking out of the sand belching and billowing yellow orange flames into the clear blue sky. We were in an oil field where they were burning off the surplus gas.

The road led away from those fiery pipes. I thought of what vast resources were buried under this empty endless desert that they could afford to waste it like this. These were the very sand dunes that would one day become part of *Desert Storm* and countless bodies would litter the desert as far as the eye could see.

I imagined what this place was like a hundred million years before; a lush verdant rain forest, crawling with monster lizards, dinosaurs and millions of unknown creatures now long extinct, all crushed and decayed to oil, their remains shooting up those long funnels into the sky in a blaze of final glory. I later wrote a verse:

They came from cosmic gas, exploding stars that burn,
On waves of burning gas to the heavens they return.
While conscious thought from the universe evolved
to reflect on its own wonders, the why, can never be resolved

Life within the group was going well despite the heat, no

cool drinking water and a few sporadic clashes of personalities. We were still all together and all had changed for the better because of the common challenge to survive this arduous journey. Everyone was more helpful and cooperative. At this stage we were unhappily lost in the desert. It carried with it lingering tension and worry. The pillars of fire in the sand far behind us had brought us no nearer to civilization.

But our daily life had to go on. Nature's call had to be answered. Adventurous and philosophical as my little expeditions as a budding naturalist were behind the sand dunes, I made sure that there were no sand snakes or scorpions about when I dug a hole to squat and answer the call of nature. These were always moments for reflection too.

It was a hazardous life out there in the desert and hot too. I wondered, too, about the effect of our passage on the creatures and life forms around our various camping sites. We left scraps of food, used water and human faeces. Would there be a fiesta, a riot or a major disruption of their life style as the human carnival came to town and stopped in that exact spot perhaps once in a thousand years? A passing camel train perhaps eons ago had passed that way and stopped and now a Bedford truck, I imagined. Did it leave the creatures in the sand longing for more, in disarray and despair or rejoicing at their good fortune at this one time windfall of luck? *Life forms of the desert need a bit of variety too*, I thought, *even if only once in a thousand years.*

On one such stop, when I gratefully completed my call to nature behind a sand dune early one morning, I walked back to our camping site around the dune and to my astonishment I was staring at an empty campsite. They were gone. My heart leapt in fright, they had gone without me. I imagined the worst. They forgot to make the head count before driving off, I was stranded alone, they hadn't missed me and would never find their way back. We were already lost, there were no landmarks just endless dunes. *What will I do?* My heart was pounding now and I broke out in a sea of sweat.

Then I heard wild shouts and boisterous yahoos of jubilation rising from behind another dune and I dashed straight towards it, scrambling up the slippery slope with the sand sliding down around me, my feet sinking and pulling me back as my heart raced faster with ever increasing panic. They were happily driving away without me, I hadn't been missed, I was abandoned and would never be found, without water and food I wouldn't last a day. My fear and panic grew in seconds.

There alone, feeling abandoned on the sand dune, imagining the worst I was paralysed with fright, my legs turned to jelly, my brain refused to function, the commands no longer being transmitted to my feet and legs, but then after a moment's pause to listen and comprehend that rescue was just on the other side of the dune I lunged forward like a Springbok bounding from the jaws of the leaping lion. My legs shot bolts of pain to the brain as they kept scrambling for a foothold in the slippery sand, I was on all fours racing to crest the top of the dune.

Oh dear God help me! Help me! I prayed almost crying. "Wait! Wait!" I croaked with a dried out throat then stifled the cry before it parted my parched cracked lips. I was deprived of the hope of being heard, what could be worse? My eyes stung as tears gushed in a flood of self pity but they dried before they reached my cheek so hot was the blistering sun on my face. I was crying without tears.

In desperation, I finally scrambled and crawled to the top of the sand dune with every neuron firing, every bodily fibre and muscle straining with exertion, I was sweating every drop of moisture left in my already dehydrated body. I saw the truck below on the desert track slowly moving off, someone was still throwing their kit bag on board and scrambling over the side. Everybody was pointing and shouting in delight, they had seen me, I was elated for a second but no they were pointing and looking in the opposite direction. Panic reasserted itself, I looked too, to the direction where they were looking.

A palm tree was showing its leafy crown in the distance, an oasis had been spied, a discovery greeted with raucous shouts of jubilation from the truck-load of weary travellers. At the sight of the truck a wave of relief and happiness swept through me: I was saved! I could reach the truck in time if I ran quickly; I couldn't shout or call out, my throat was parched and hard, a weak croak was all I could manage. No one was looking back to see me, it was all up to me to reach them in time.

I half-ran, half-tumbled down the other side of the dune, arms flailing, legs pumping, desperate to reach the truck. I hit the hard track and stumbled but my feet found traction and with hitherto unknown prowess sped helter skelter for the back of the truck. My chest was heaving, heart bursting, my sandals were flopping and spilling sand, shirt tail flapping as I sped along. I was gaining, gaining, then a final sprint propelled me the last metre and my foot found the rear bumper, and my hand grabbed the top of the tail-board, with this for leverage I soared up and over into the back of the truck, tumbling joyfully into my companions who shouted curses and complaints.

None of them knew I had just had the fright of my life all in the space of minutes. I didn't care what they were shouting at me, I was so deliriously happy to be safe. I was laughing, floating, ecstatic, I'd never felt anything like it, it was an indescribable experience, like being at the point of death and coming out alive, lost and then being found. It must be the feeling a bungie jumper who gets on the way down into the abyss and the sudden reprieve on the end of rubber cord. The elation brought on by the rush of adrenalin. I never strayed far from the truck in the desert again after that.

We had not seen vegetation for over a week. We slowly chugged towards our nirvana. The truck was limping along, its fuel pump was still sucking and spurting more air than petrol into the carburettor, but we were moving and that is what mattered. The petrol had evaporated before it got halfway out of the tank but we gladly squeezed the last of our drinking water onto the cloths covering the carburettor and the petrol pump.

And there it was! A white wall rising out of the desert with a big round sign in blue and red. It declared to the whole world one word: Pepsi! Our eyes were glued on it, there was complete silence as our imaginations conjured up delightful images of downing a cold fizzy drink, bathing in a pool of cool water, luxuriating on a mattress and feasting on kisch-abab. We were like survivors from a shipwreck. We arrived and tumbled from the truck gasping and laughing at our good fortune and ran into the courtyard of this desert tavern. Soon we were standing up to our knees in pools of cool water under the palm trees laughing as we gulped bottles of cold drinks. For us, those simple comforts were most precious in the hard dry world of the vast desert.

Crossing into Afghanistan was a dangerous business. Bribes had to be paid, drug searches endured. There were anxious moments as our passports and visas were scrutinized by tall, slim bushy bearded men in turbans, baggy pants and sandals, complete with old British 303 rifles slung from their shoulders. The very same model that I had in the Irish Reserve Army and prided myself on being a marksman with that big cumbersome rifle and a badge to prove it. Little good all that would do me now as I was told to wait on the dusty veranda as my Irish passport was taken inside. They seldom saw Irish citizens passing this way apparently.

There was a long wait at the border post that consisted of a few low roofed mud brick buildings, housing with tea shops and a small open market. The bronzed faced tribesmen in turbans took hours examining and stamping our passports one by one while our team leader haggled over the amount of grease money that facilitated every transaction. We bought some food and souvenirs to replenish our stores and keep the locals happy. Amazingly, they gave us little paper packets of grass instead of coins for change out of our purchases.

They were packets of marijuana, some of my companions were happily rolling smokes. When I realised what it was I quietly threw it away. I had seen enough bad effects of marijuana on young people in the Philippines. I began to understand why some of my fellow travellers had come to Asia. They were on the drug trail to Katmandu. Many, I am sure, presumed the same of me.

By this time I had the hippy look, gone was the tight clean cut and smart shirt and pants. Life in the wilderness and on the road had worked its unkind effect. My hair had grown long and covered my ears, I wore scruffy jeans and sandals and a long white Afghan shirt with colourful embroidery on the front that I had just bought at the border trading post. My companions invited me to smoke as I surely fitted the image, but I pleaded a possible allergic reaction that could cause an asthma attack. That mollified them and I avoided the peer pressure to get *high* and a wise decision it was too. The long delay meant that we had to camp there for the night and the bonanza of freely available marijuana had many of my companions getting sleepy around the campfire. One wandered off to sleep under a tree and his loose money was stolen. Luckily our passports and valuables had been locked inside the cab of the truck.

The session around the campfire lasted late into the night and many would have passed into a deep drug-induced sleep. That was the time for the thieves to move in with razor sharp knives and slit open sleeping bags and steal passports, money and cameras. It had happened to many a group of inexperienced travellers. But our team leader was wiser and after midnight we were aroused and quietly drove off without lights five miles down the road and turned off into the desert.

We lit our campfires and eat bread and settled in for a good sleep. Then to our alarm, we saw a convoy of vehicles approaching across the desert, their light blazing. They lined up facing us, spotlighting our makeshift camp. It was the local military ordering us back to the border for another customs check. Our group leader tried to negotiate with the captain and offered money, but they weren't satisfied. They wanted us to sleep at the customs compound, no doubt to allow their gang of thieves to clean us out. We promised to drive back after we had finished supper and packed up. The captain said he would wait for us at the border post.

We loaded up the Bedford and headed towards the road without lights, then suddenly turned east, pushed the accelerator to the floor and made a run for it. The old engine wheezed and gasped with exertion as we rumbled along like a big elephant hoping to put as much distance between us and them before they realised that we were not returning to their trap. We drove in the darkness under the clear star lit sky that reached out before us like a great dazzling scarf leading us on towards the sliver of light on the horizon that was the promise of dawn and safety.

We travelled on for several days through rugged valleys, gorges and over mountains to visit the magnificent and awe inspiring statues of Buddha, three hundred and sixty feet high, carved into the sandstone cliffs north of Kabul. These magnificent remains of a Buddhist culture – once prominent in Afghanistan and later to die out – were shamelessly destroyed by the Taliban.

One morning we awoke and moved about the camp, preparing breakfast of fried eggs and tomatoes, the flat pancake like bread from local bakeries and coffee. As the sun climbed into the morning sky, we were amazed to see we were being watched by two warrior-like men on camels holding long rifles silhouetted against the light. We were deeply worried that they were scouts for a group of bandits. But after ten minutes they turned and trotted away. We hurried our departure and headed off once again watching for danger. But there was none. They were probably nomads as curious about us as we were about them.

We entered Iran in the south and travelled to Shiraz and then to Persepolis to see the impressive ruins of the capital of the ancient Persian empire ruled by Darius and destroyed by Alexander. We travelled the length of the country discovering the wonders of Iranian history and reached Teheran, absorbing the life and culture of the country. At the border we had our first major setback that threatened to end the journey there and then – war. There was fighting along the border and we had to wait days before they would let us cross. We camped under the great shade trees and waited. Eventually, we were given visas and gratefully crossed into India.

We toured Northern India and saw the wonders of that ancient civilisation. In Srinagar, Kashmir before the fighting broke out, we drove through magnificent valleys and over great mountains. We stayed on Victorian houseboats once enjoyed by the officials of the British Empire. Then on to Amritsar and the golden temples. The marble temple, the centre of the Sikh faith, is set in the centre of an artificial moat and surrounded by high walls. Thousands of pilgrims stream across the narrow footbridge daily. I gratefully joined them looking more like an Indian Holy Man with my hair touching my shoulders by now.

The temple was small but very beautiful and contains the sacred sword and the Holy Scriptures of the Sikhs. It was open to all and I felt welcome and respected. I joined the worshipers, sat cross legged before the Holy Book. Nearby the holiest Sikh, with flowing white beard, silver bracelet and immaculate turban wearing a garland of flowers around his neck, sat in deep meditation. I, too, turned to meditation. Here I found an oasis of peace and tranquillity. Sadly some years later it became the scene of a bloody siege when separatists took it over and Indira Gandhi ordered a full scale assault and shelled it. This, it was said, led to her assassination by her Sikh bodyguards.

From there we travelled across Northern India to the Punjab. The skies opened to release a deluge of rain that hammered down for two days non-stop. A howling wind knocked down trees that blocked the narrow road. We tied the trucks towing cable to the trees and pulled them off the road and kept going, fearful that the nearby river's raging waters would wash away a vital bridge and we would be stranded. We arrived at the bridge and found the river had overflowed its banks and the bridge was covered by several feet of water. To go back was more dangerous, we had to go on and cross.

We could still see the side railing of the bridge. Our greatest fear was that a section of the bridge had collapsed and just left the railings. So we formed a human chain linking hands and edged across the bridge. The rushing water pulling at our knees, we probed ahead of us with long poles cut from the fallen trees. In this way the truck made its way across. It was still intact and we made it.

We stayed over in a government guesthouse that night. This had been a large Victorian hunting lodge that belonged to a former Raj. Expensive western furniture, richly woven carpets and the smell of damp fungus were everywhere. It was a reminder of the splendour that unashamedly flourished at the hands of the rich in a sea of poverty and enslavement.

But there were no showers and the toilets were primitive. I took a bath in the courtyard beside a faucet with cold running water but I couldn't wash my long hair properly. I had run out of shampoo. There were drawbacks to long hair, I discovered.

We visited Delhi and the Red Fort, the mosques surrounded by flocks of pigeons and only outnumbered by the groups of beggars, mostly children in rags that chased after every foreign tourist that showed up. I was in simple Indian dress and was left alone. We travelled on to Jaipur where the elephants still carried tourists into the courtyards of the great palaces with their lavishly ornate interiors. Then we pressed onto Agra and marvelled at the wonders of the delicate lace designs carved into the white gleaming marble of the Taj Mahal. There were few people there and I could sit undisturbed and enjoy the magnificent reflection of the monument to love in the long pool.

We stopped one day in a small town to buy provisions in the public market. I wandered off alone to take photographs and see daily life. There was shouting and a commotion, and I saw a tall skinny man, with only a loincloth for clothing, being driven out of the market by well-dressed men brandishing long canes. The old man was skin and bones, wrinkled and sunburnt, he shouted back at them as if throwing curses, which infuriated his tormentors all the more and they ran at him. He was an untouchable. Not because he was sacred, just the opposite, he was an outcast, a member of the Dalits.

His group is of the lowest caste of people of India although this is outlawed and many of their members have since achieved much social and political advancement. In the 1970s it was common for them to be ranked as the most despised in Indian society.

He came towards me, still shouting and pointing back at the angry crowd. He suddenly ran over and grabbed my arm and shouted more invective at the crowd. They came closer, almost surrounding us at a distance, not wanting to approach what they considered to be unclean. I stood there allowing him to hold me.

It seemed to me that he was saying to the crowd that was driving him away: "Here I am touching a white man, he accepts me while you despise me."

I began to walk away and he came with me, still clinging to my arm with a vice-like grip. The crowd stood back and parted and together we walked away. I gave him alms and he gave me a great smile and a bow with hands joined in prayer raised to his forehead which I took as a blessing, one I treasured very much.

Then we arrived in the holiest city of Varanasi, sometimes called Benares, the sacred city of the devout Hindu, a shrine city on the banks of the Ganges. The Bedford inched its way along narrow streets following a procession of ox cart pedicabs sacred cows and crowed of brightly robed people.

It was hard for me to take it all in, this city, according to the guidebook, predates Babylon and Nineveh. It lies on the banks of the Ganges and great stone steps lead down to the sacred waters, the Gnats where the pilgrims in droves wash themselves in the holy water seeking salvation and new life. Along the banks, rows of funeral pyres filled the sky with plumes of smoke. The devout Hindu is cremated and the ashes thrown on the waters of the sacred river to be reborn.

Before dawn I went down to the Gnats and there squatted cross-legged near a scattering of young men in loincloths silently performing the exacting exercises of Hata Yoga. Older men, bearded and wrinkled, sat cross-legged and stiffly upright, their eyes were closed as they were deep in meditation striving for that tranquillity and inner peace that is a foretaste of the eternal goal of Raja Yoga. The sun lightened the sky and rose above the horizon, beams of blazing light blessed us as a multitude of pilgrims began to fill the steps at the waters edge and the daily rituals of purification began.

I left this city of a thousand temples and headed north towards the source of the Ganges, the Himalayas in Nepal. We were heading for its capital Katmandu. It is a fascinating city with communities of Tibetan refugees, temples overrun with monkeys and the towering golden temple ornate with the single eye that seemed to be looking in every direction at once. There was nowhere to hide from the all-seeing presence.

There was a thriving drug culture and several of our companions went to the old town where marijuana and heroine were traded like candies. I heard, too, that there was a special section of the cemetery where many a young Caucasian lay buried-dead from a lethal overdose of pure heroin.

The Trail Finders' trip ended in Katmandu. Incredibly, two members of the company were ready to drive the truck all the way back to London and anybody who had a few weeks to spare and wanted a lift home could get it for a minimum price. A few took the return trip, but I left for Calcutta by plane to visit Mother Theresa.

I was welcomed by the community of the *Missionary Brothers Of Charity*, an order of young brothers started by Fr Andrew, an Australian Jesuit to help the work of Mother Theresa and her Sisters in the Calcutta slums. The community house that was once a posh suburb of the city called Kidderpore was taken over by the street dwellers and the slums. There were about fifty brothers living in the three-story house with a flat roof. Many of them were new applicants doing their novitiate and they needed a chaplain.

We lived on the second and third floors of the building and the ground floor was given over to the poor. It was very simple, ascetic living. All unnecessary and superfluous things were eliminated. There were no air-conditioners, only a few fans despite the stifling and oppressive humidity of tropical climate. Bathing was accomplished at a faucet with buckets and taps; there were no showers and the food was of the simplest fare. It was no deprivation for me, who had been camping out for three months in the deserts and on the mountains, eating whatever was available in the village markets.

We all lived exactly the same. No refrigerator, few chairs and tables, no radio or newspapers, or anything that would bring a bit of comfort or relief from the heat and the humidity, and the isolation from the outer world. There were no private rooms and it was a life of extreme evangelical poverty. Few had any personal belongings. Each of us had a sleeping mat and a thin bed sheet, which was all I had to pull over my head as protection against the mosquitoes. At night, the straw mats were rolled out on the hard floor. Some of the brothers went up on to the flat roof where it was cooler and that was where I slept too.

In the morning at 4:15 the mats were rolled up and the large room became the prayer hall and all of us squatted cross-legged in rows and began with the psalms, morning prayer, scripture reading and then the Eucharistic celebration. This was so simple as we sat cross-legged like yogis in meditation. There was the wail of Hindu music and we chanted Christian prayers to the rhythm accompanied by the soft beat of a pair of tom-toms and a small accordion.

I was expected to give a morning reflection on the scripture reading as it applied to our daily life of service to the poor. Then we prayed; members of the community prayed spontaneously from the heart.

We sat on the floor on little cushions in a circle for the celebration of the Eucharist. Bread, baked by the brothers, and a small cup of wine, were offered on a large wooden plate with flower petals and smoking incense sticks. A basket of flower petals was passed around and each of us scattered a few on the offerings of bread and wine. I passed a small bowl of burning incense over the offerings that were resting on a cushion on the floor. The sweet aroma of the incense filled the prayer hall. Then we did what Jesus Christ asked when he said, "Do this in memory of me." That was how we started our day.

I was soon trudging out into the slums with a small band of brothers, making our way through crowds of poor hungry people, many of whom shuffled along from weakness or deformity. I passed emaciated mothers feeding skinny babies from deflated breasts and naked little children with potbellies playing in the filthy gutters. It was a depressing sight and, while I walked with the brothers through this wilderness of human suffering, I longed to be able to change it all. In a world of vast wealth and riches and mountains of surplus food, why were so many starving and dying in pain and loneliness, rejected and abandoned?

I knew something of their hunger too. Breakfast for us was

dry bread and hot tea with one spoon of condensed milk. No more than the poor received on the first floor. We were literally living with the poor. During the day we had a ladle of hot rice spooned into our bowls and a cup of *curry something* poured over it. I dared not ask the ingredients. I was always hungry, especially after a day's work on the streets or in the house of the dying where people found abandoned in the back streets and gutters were brought for medical treatment and care.

I knew hunger – I felt it all day. Then one day, I learned something about solidarity with the poor. We were sitting on the ground floor at rough tables when the tureen of rice and curry was brought out. A brother said grace and then, to my astonishment, the tureen was carried out to be shared with the poor who had gathered in another room. It was to be a day of prayer and fasting. My eyes hungrily followed the food as it passed me by and out the door. My stomach was craving with hunger but I had to settle for some bananas and tea with more condensed milk.

The next day I joined the brothers on their regular medical mission. We entered a yard where a mobile clinic was parked. We drove off, crossed the big bridge that spanned the Hooghly River, it was chocolate brown from pollution and filth. The mobile clinic stopped in the most dilapidated and awful part of the city. There were rats moving about everywhere, unafraid, pausing to look at us with a glint in their beady eyes, and then rummage on through the piles of garbage that were scattered all over the place. An animal stable stank like a cesspool and nearby was a discarded slaughterhouse. It was to this festering armpit of indescribable destitution that the lepers came, as it was one of the few places where they could come for treatment far away from the rest of society. They appeared from clapboard hovels, sewers and tunnels. They were unafraid of the brothers and unashamed of their own rotting putrid flesh festering day by day.

Dirty rags covered the worst of their wounds. They were the stricken, the wretched of the earth, the real untouchables – but not for the brothers. Their cheerful banter with the lepers whom they knew by name showed me how they were friends to these unwanted castaways of humanity. Each had a medical record in the mobile clinic and a history of their treatment. The project was to contact new sufferers and administer drugs that would prevent the leprosy from progressing. With those badly infected there was no chance of recovery.

At first, I recoiled in revulsion; I couldn't help it as it was the first time I had been so close to people so afflicted. The patients were excited and curious by my presence and soon the Brothers were cracking jokes in Urdu with them. I didn't understand but I could feel I was part of the team. I busied myself in my embarrassment and shame in preparing the medicines that were to be distributed and opening boxes of clean bandages. The patients were lining up to have their old bandages removed, wounds dressed and bandaged again.

After an hour there was a long line and the brothers encouraged me to help with the dressings. They gave me a pair of surgical gloves and I couldn't refuse an old man who stretched out his bandaged hand to me. To refuse would be unthinkable, inexperienced as I was. But I had first aid training when I was in the army reserve and knew what had to be done. I cut away the dirty cloth to reveal the decaying fingers. The old man didn't feel anything because the nerve endings were gone so I didn't have to worry about hurting him. I swabbed away the pus and dirt, applied an antiseptic ointment and began to dress and bandage the fingers. Two had already been half-eaten away. It was my first effort and he was so thankful and pleased. It made me feel good.

Soon I was wrapping clean bandages on the rotting fingers of another old man. Then I was dabbing another with cotton wool and iodine. The brothers even performed simple surgery, cutting away flesh with a sterilised scalpel and dressing and wrapping the wounds. The lepers were a cheerful lot – their joking and smiling encouraged me to do a lot more. After an hour, I was shown how to clean a wound and, when I recalled that the patient had no feeling in his limb, I proceeded with greater confidence urged on by the leper vigorously nodding his head in approval. I must be doing the right thing, I thought, as I lobbed off a bit of finger. They were accustomed to it all as their bodies were falling apart bit by bit, the infection gouging itself deeper into their flesh week by week.

We had treated almost fifty by noon. One of the younger men was in a serious state of deterioration. His foot was infected so badly that the disease had eaten a hole to the bone. He would soon have to have it amputated. But that would not stop the progression of the leprosy. We continued to clean and wash their wounds and wrap them in clean bandages and then headed for home, leaving behind a happier group of the truly wretched of the earth weakly waving their bandaged limbs in gratitude.

On another day I put the canvas bag with the first aid kit over my shoulder and, with the brothers leading the way, walked a kilometre through the alleys of this decaying city. The slums were pitiful, thousands of hovels crammed together, clinging to one another. I recalled how similar they were to the slums of Olongapo and the piles of shanties nailed to one another and leaning dangerously over the slime of the canal between the city and the naval base.

If one was removed I thought they would collapse like a house of cards. They seemed to have no ventilation, sanitation or running water. The women and children queued up in long lines with plastic buckets, earthenware jars and tin cans at a single public faucet. Babies clung to their mothers with wide staring eyes as if they had seen too much of the world already and were frightened by what they witnessed: a hostile world of want. Their scrawny bodies were covered with sores and rashes, their shaven heads stained with ringworm.

We went to help those who had survived the early precarious years and were surviving by their own wits. These were the railway children – children that lived like rats in train stations scavenging everything they could lay hands on. It was a dangerous life, running and hiding from the railway police or jumping and swinging onto the trains as their metal might came puffing and hissing into the great smoky stations, disgorging thousands of passengers from every door and window and rooftop.

The boys aged ten to fifteen years were quick and agile and went through the carriages like a dose of salts cleaning out anything of the slightest value and gobbling up the leftover foods with savage glee as they went before the guards could stop them. I watched them swinging like monkeys from the windows, running along the roof of the train and swinging up into the metal girders like gymnasts on the bars. A guard ran along the platform waving a rattan cane but his angry protests were in vain.

The brothers were greatly respected by the railway boys and, after they picked the train clean, they retreated to a safe place until the danger subsided and the train guards had disappeared. Then they came to the meeting place at the end of the platform that was "neutral ground". They ate the food we brought, hungrily stuffing themselves and drinking water from a faucet with their cupped hands. They were laughing and joking, too, recounting a narrow escape or a lucky find. After the boys finished eating and licking the banana leaves which had wrapped the rice cakes, the brothers handed out brushes and soap. The boys gave themselves a good scrub under the supervision of the brothers right there on the platform. This prevented infection from cuts and scabs.

Rivulets of black soot ran down their legs onto the concrete platform. They were carefree and wild. Here they were safe but if caught they were jailed as vagrants. The majesty of justice and the law did not extend to them. They were beaten up, locked in jails and sometimes sexually abused by older male prisoners.

This scrubbing revealed serious wounds and cuts that were hidden under crusts of filth and dirt, if untreated they quickly became infected. Then we went about treating and dressing the wounds and talking to them. I couldn't say anything but some of the boys were being invited to join the street school the brothers operated. This was operation contact. Many had left the railway station life and were learning skills and literacy.

Then a week later, I was invited to help the sisters and brothers in the "House of Life" where we brought the rejected and dying people from streets from where they had been dumped, abandoned and left to die, covered with cockroaches and rats in the garbage dumps and the gutters. I was assigned to the male ward. This was a part of the converted Hindu temple where Mother Teresa herself worked. It was as big as a barn, with little shafts of light penetrating the high windows but it held not the smell of death but the love of life. It was here that Malcolm Muggerge, a convinced atheist, was to interview Mother Theresa and which led to his conversion. I was to meet her years later in Manila and I was deeply moved by her total dedication to the poor.

Those found hopelessly sick and abandoned to die on the streets were brought to the "Dying House" in order to give them whatever medical help available to ease their pain and loneliness, in an effort to allow them to die feeling wanted and loved. Our goal was to bring relief and comfort, to hold the skinny skeletons of skin and bones, make them feel that someone loved them at last.

It helped that the light was dim and soft. Who in the world would want to witness the monumental misery that the dark corners concealed in the shadows? Spread all over the floor on mats and cots were people the uncaring world considered to be the dregs of the human race, the unproductive, discarded outcasts. Here was a place that witnessed countless moments of love and care and respect for the poorest and most deprived humans imaginable.

One day we picked up an old man in a filth strewn alleyway where starving snarling dogs were waiting to eat him. The brothers threw stones at the snarling animals to keep them back from the old man who was in such a state of dehydration and starvation that there was nothing to lift, he was the weight of a sheet of crumpled paper. We placed his frail and fragile bones in a blanket, slung it on a pole and carried him that way through the narrow alleyways. In the old Hindu temple we gently bathed his wounds, anointed his sores and the bites to ease the pain and fed him sips of soup. But he was almost beyond feeding. There was no muscle left to insert a needle for a dextrose drip.

I had lost a lot of weight in the few weeks since I began working here because community meals were meagre and sparse. I had no question about what my mission was here as I had in St. Joseph's Parish and in San Marcelino. The mission here was basic and straightforward. It was simply to love the unloved emaciated people covered in sores, rat bites and in agony. I was to ease their pain and suffering, give them a sense of dignity and whatever comfort was possible. Here I was to love them because no one else did or could, without seeking reward or asking anything from God or humankind in return. It was a mission to love and minister to those who could not give anything in return. It was just to be there for them, to practise pure and simple self-giving and striving to care as Jesus of Nazareth cared for the downtrodden and rejected. This is the love that hundreds of thousand relief workers and missionaries of all faiths do everyday, unknown, unseen and obscure from a world where extravagant living and ostentatious display of wealth holds centre stage. In that world love is the pursuit of selfish gratification and pleasure.

In this world of the sick and the dying I was being taught to respect life in its most dehumanised form. I was a humbled learner. Even though Joseph, as we named him, died days later, it was without pain and we were around him holding his hands, wiping his brow, sharing a smile of encouragement. He died looking into our eyes, a shining light in his eyes said all he could say.

There were many more like Joseph. The sisters and brothers went silently and swiftly about their work of healing and comforting with professional skill and a serenity that inspired me to try and be like them. I took every patient as a personal mission, praying that they would come back to life. Some recovered but most died quickly and every morning our task was to wrap and carry the bodies out to the morgue and then to go out on the garbage heaps and river banks and look for some more to bring home.

They were presumed to be all Hindu and so there was no Christian rites other than a silent prayer of respect and to consign their spirits to the eternal void. I had no sacramental role other than to show the love of Christ in any way possible. I felt priestly in a very different way than that of leading a congregation in prayer or presiding over the Eucharist. I easily imagined that I was at the foot of the crucified Christ on Calvary. What we were doing was respecting life, believing that the Lord of the Universe in his cosmic presence was part of every living creature, and we were privileged to be in his universal presence in this fragment of expiring humanity. It was sacramental, making his presence alive and real through love and action for the poor and the world. I was humbled just to be there with them, they were the least of the brethren and yet we tried to make them the most important of all.

The sisters were of several nationalities and worked as a devoted team. They were in charge and had no hesitation telling me what needed to be done. Nor did I hesitate to do their bidding. Here there was no priestly rank nor did I want any. We were all one in the presence of the living universal presence of unselfish love. This was a sanctuary to a sacred presence.

There was one teenage boy, gaunt-faced, dying of tuberculosis. He had been rejected and abandoned by his family and left lying in the street until we found him. People threw him scraps of food as they would a dog and that kept him alive that bit longer as the ravages of diarrhoea, hunger and disease closed in to claim him. His heels and elbows and shoulder blades had deep holes gouged from lying on a filthy patch of concrete, avoided by all. He was covered with rat bites and in terrible pain. Yet I felt no revulsion or reluctance to touch or hold these dying unfortunates.

We named him Lazarus because he was like the beggar in the Gospel story where it is told that a rich man, called Dives, left Lazarus dying at his gates while he dressed in fine clothes and feasted everyday but would not give the crumbs that fell from his table to the dying man. The story as told by Jesus described how the dogs licked his sores to heal them, the only creatures who showed compassion and care. The greatest sin in the world, according to the story, is the indifference and apathy of the rich in a poverty-stricken world of the abandoned dying of hunger and HIV.

Like most of the patients, he had no muscles; he was just skin and bone, so we couldn't give him a morphine injection to ease his agony. But the sister managed to get a tube into him and fed him a liquid with painkillers mixed in. His wounds were treated with healing balm and we placed cushions to support him and ease the pressure on the sores where his bones protruded.

The relief that he felt was visible. He smiled a faint smile with closed eyes and squeezed my hand with a tenacious grip that kept me bound to him as I squatted beside him in his last hours. He died after a few days, peacefully, still with a faint smile and a tear on his cheek.

Chapter Seven

I got my visa to Burma when I was in Nepal and I wanted to try and visit my fellow Columbans in the northeastern part of the country. The military regime had strict travel restrictions. I was unable to travel further north than Mandalay and spent time in Rangoon. These old British colonial cities had retained much of the old facades of the empire but they were neglected and there was crumbling infrastructure everywhere. There was also a feeling of subdued tension and a foreigner was eyed with curiosity by local people and suspicion by the authorities.

Columban Missionaries had been in Burma since the end of World War II. The Catholic hierarchy was only established in 1955 and the Columban area of missionary activity, Myitkyina, was established as a diocese in 1955 and a Columban, Bishop How, was concentrated as bishop. It was a remote and tough mission, supplies were hard to come by and the area was in a state of constant revolt from Rangoon.

The Katchins, a large ethnic group of highland tribal people, had embraced Christianity. The hard work of the Columbans had built up many communities of dedicated Christians and their own people were flocking to join the priesthood and take up the work. The military regime had forbidden any foreign missionaries to enter Burma since 1966. The Columbans already there had opted to stay and not to leave even for vacation because they knew they would not be allowed to return. It was a brave commitment and they worked under extreme conditions.

That week in September 1972, Archbishop Cardinal Cook of New York was there to ordain twenty-three candidates. Three of these were from the Columban Mission area and it was a very proud moment for everybody. The Columban Superior General Richard Steinhilber was there. The Church in Burma had yet to adopt the reforms of the Vatican Council. It was a pre-Vatican liturgy but was a vibrant and moving ceremony.

St. Mary's Cathedral in Rangoon is a great Gothic structure copied straight out of the turn of the century European architecture. There was nothing ethnic about it except the Christians that filled it to capacity for the ordinations, they all wore native dress, the long chequered sarong and the women's headdress were beautiful and colourful. I was an oddity, dressed in the only kind of clothes I had since trading my western shirts for those of Afghan style. I wore a long white shirt and pants and my hair had grown to my shoulders. I was perhaps a bit of an embarrassment to the extremely conservative and traditional clergy but to their enduring credit they accepted me with courtesy and respect and a warm welcome.

I received an even warmer welcome from the Burmese seminarians who were intrigued and delighted to learn that priests were not exactly the same everywhere. They were excited to learn that there was room for individualism, freedom of choice, discussion and dialogue and opportunities to forge ahead with new ideas and action. The Church in Burma at that time was under great pressure from the military-led government. They had taken over all Catholic schools and Christians were viewed with suspicion and even hostility. The embattled and oppressed Christians grew all the more committed and united in their faith.

That very week in the Philippines, as I was sitting in the cathedral in Rangoon, Ferdinand Marcos was wiping out

Philippine democracy, abolishing civil rights, freedom of the press and arresting his critics and opponents. Constitutionally barred from standing again, he imposed Martial Law to perpetuate himself in power, forestall the election of his rival Benigio Aquino Jr, cover-up his plundering of the national treasury and to appease his domineering and profligate wife Imelda. Dated September 21, signed on the 22 and announced on the 23, the declaration of Martial Law was his move to seize total power and authority. After weeks of street demonstrations, ambushes of dubious culpability and a heightened sense of crises, Marcos ordered the tanks to roll, the troops to arrest and detain and the fig leaf of democracy was stripped away to reveal the naked power of ambition and greed.

Another repressive military dictatorship was starting as I was witnessing the dismal and ghastly effects of the one in Burma that was to endure for many more years becoming increasingly harsher. Marcos declared he was establishing a "constitutional authoritarianism" and a "new society" where all the evils of the old oligarchy, the violence, and corruption and influence peddling, would be brought to an end. There would be land reform and social equality; in effect he would use his absolute power to create Utopia. The gullible believed and served him without thinking, the business elite, who saw advantage for themselves, applauded and those without the means to resist were compliant.

There were those who welcomed Martial Law because of the stability, law and order it promised. They were unable to comprehend what it would do to the country or the human and civil rights of the people. They were fearful and nervous of the civil unrest that Marcos himself had caused. He created the crises and offered the only cure. The business world was pleased, the church leaders were silent, the poor were aghast.

The middle and merchant class were the most frightened at the extremes of the emotional and verbal violence of the protesters who frequently rallied along their streets. They felt their prosperity was resented by the fervent activists whom they believed were agitating for a mass uprising against them. They were perhaps fearful too that they would be the targets of any revolt since their middle class wealth was frequently made with cheap labour and harsh conditions. The student rallies were sights to behold. Exciting, colourful and filled with that sense of purposeful and bonding comradeship and the sense of belonging to a noble cause for which no sacrifice was too much.

I went to a few of these rallies, some held in front of the imposing turn-of-the-century post office near a monument to Bonifacio and witnessed the excitement, fervour and the faith of these thousands of students who believed that they could bring about by their demonstrations an ideal society based on social justice and equality that was the dream of the early patriots. There was no armed wing or underground revolution movement that they were fronting for. When Martial Law was declared, hundreds of the activists were hunted and many were arrested, thousands fled to the mountains to join the newly-established *New People's Army* headed by Jose Sison.

But in 1972 they were caught up in a nationalistic fervour that was essentially non-violent and marched and sang their way to rally after rally. Their huge numbers and well-organised ranks were impressive. At one cross road after another, a new band of students from one college after another would come marching along with their streamers, banners and flags, chanting and singing and letting out a mighty roar as they came close to the main marching body which opened like the parting of the waters and the new comers marched into the ranks which closed around them swelling the great parade.

The students leaders took to the podium and with powerful oratory stirred up the crowd to an excited pitch of anger at some injustice or scandal which resulted in a deafening howl of protest and thousands of defiant fists raised to the sky. Their criticisms of Marcos and his wife Imelda for their conspicuous consumption, political manipulation and ambition to continue in office raised the ire of Marcos and many young students paid dearly for freedom of expression.

They shouted slogans in unison, demanding a sharing of wealth, just wages, tax reform, land reform, an end to the Marcos corruption. It was enough to send shivers of terror down the spines of landowners and wealthy merchants. They slammed closed the steel shutters of their storefronts and retired to their second floor apartments to sit out the days and nights of effigy and tire burning.

Marcos shrewdly spun this to his advantage and gathered enough support among the sectors that felt threatened by the social upheaval. The build up to Martial Law was heightened by playing up the "red scare". Marcos seldom failed to refer to the dangers of activists, the militant students, the so-called imminent Communist uprising, when in fact there was none at that time. The Muslim uprising in the southern island of Mindanao was far more serious but it was isolated and manageable and a wise and just ruler could have ended it with a dedicated programme of social justice and a measure of political autonomy. Years later, it became clear that this was the only possible solution.

There was no organised Communist underground. But there were strong student movements, trade unions, and organised squatter associations. The unsolved problem then, as it is today, was the disparity between the handful of immensely rich and the vast exploding population of millions of ragged poor in water-clogged ghettos festering in their own garbage and disease ridden slums.

When I visited these heaving hives of humanity filled with misery and a million flies buzzing angrily around rotting piles of fish entrails, I was overwhelmed with the pervading hopelessness. It clung to me like the toxic smoke that drifted in all directions, an eye scalding fog, rising from the piles smouldering rubbish where they had pitched their makeshift shacks.

These poor people, the wretched of the earth, the rejects and bone pickers of humanity, were not only clinging to the last vestiges of humanity but were gaunt skeletal humans seemingly on the edge of nervous breakdowns. Carefully picking my way through the mess, my eyes were weeping from the stinging fumes, my heart was breaking from the devastating spectre of poverty that imagination could not picture, and words can hardly describe, I was struck by the sight of the mud-streaked, pot-bellied naked children playing in the brackish brine of an open sewer. In a garbage sorting area the pickers were arguing and fighting over a piece of worthless junk like cats hissing and spitting at each other over the fish bones.

Others nearby were still scratching like fevered chickens with their small hooks at every piece of filth that might yield a scrap that if added to a hundred others might buy a scrawny meal of cheap rice and days old vegetables. I could feel that revolution was inevitable. Sights such as these persisted through the Marcos regime and in recent years have only marginally improved. Then I was seething with anger and frustration at the inhumanity and the kind of unfeeling society, living alone in stupendous luxury in panelled and exclusive mansions with swimming pools and a retinue of servants. Homes had reduced gentle human beings to the edge of madness and starvation. Too hungry to think, too weak to protest, too frightened to rebel at the injustice of it all.

The extent of the inequality was such that righting it was an impossible task. It was overwhelming, crushing, defeating. Five percent of the population at the time controlled ninety-five percent of the wealth. There was no way they were going to lower their privileges or share their wealth or even think about improving the plights of the pool of what was perhaps the cheapest labour in Asia. Only the poor paid taxes and the Philippines was a nation of landless peasants, not a nation on the brink of armed revolution, but a nation moving inevitably towards revolution. It was also a nation with an ambitious and power-hungry president who had failed to bring any meaningful change except to his own bank account and his wife's department store-size wardrobe. The social unrest, a lot of it the result of his own corrupt looting, was something he planned to use to his advantage.

On September 6, 1971, the Philippine Legislative Committee published a report stating that *"no clear and present danger of Communist insurgency or rebellion exists in Central Luzon"*. The possibility that Marcos would impose Martial Law was no secret. The American Embassy knew of it a week before thanks to their well placed CIA mole in the Marcos cabinet who gave Ambassador Byroade an advance copy of the declaration.

Presidential candidate and Marcos foe, Benigno Aquino Jr, later assassinated by Marcos troops, alerted the embassy a week before that. Ambassador Byroade did little more than advise Marcos to back off for a while. But there is no doubt that Marcos felt no US opposition to his plan of autocratic rule. With that tacit encouragement from the US, he made his move with disastrous consequences for the Filipino people.

By September 1972, the Communist scare was working and all that was needed was an incident, the proverbial last straw as an immediate justification of the military takeover. The staged ambush of Defence Secretary Juan Ponce Enrile's car was the pretext. When in 1986 Enrile sensed that the Marcos regime was sinking and the day of reckoning approaching he turned against Marcos and then followed the People's Power Revolution and he was saved. He admitted that the ambush was a ruse.

As troops and tanks rolled into the streets and the arrests began, the chronically inept and inefficient city governments were galvanised into action as never before. With armoured personnel carriers pointing their guns at city halls, the once ebullient Mayors, who had declared with more bravado than conviction that there would be no Martial Law, unless "over our dead bodies", were subservient and obedient. They quickly began to get the streets clean and orderly.

The stinking piles of garbage on main streets and in the business districts that piled up uncollected for weeks miraculously disappeared. The street kerbs took on a fresh coat of whitewash, the sewers, once notoriously clogged and the cause of floods and rat infestation, were clear within days. Street beggars and pimps peddling women and children vanished into the teeming slums to starve to death a bit more sooner as the descending cloud of uncertainty and fear casts its menacing shadow over them and all who dared oppose the rule of the gun. But the immediate law and order, civic responsibility and the dangerous quiet of the midnight to dawn curfew, brought relief and a wide acceptance of Martial Law. But a price had to be paid.

In the first six months as many as thirty thousand people were arrested and jailed without being charged. Eventually, many were released, but many disappeared and were never to be seen again. As armed rebellion grew in strength even more would meet the most agonising torture and death. There was no independent news. They closed seven television stations, twelve radio stations and fifteen newspapers. The Martial Law propaganda boasted a ninety percent drop in crime and six hundred thousand firearms surrendered or picked up by the military. The lower crime rate was interpreted by many as evidence of success. Marcos quickly consolidated his grip on power and a false sense of security prevailed.

I returned to Manila on October 4, 1972, a week after the tanks took over. I worried if any Columban priest would recognise me, burnt brown after three and half months roaming Asia with shoulder length hair, dressed in Afghan shirt and sandals. Not a very priestly looking figure unless one can imagine that Jesus Christ would have been different in attire too. Fr Denis Mescal met me at the airport, cool as always, he didn't bat an eyelid, but just nodded to my kit bag and asked if that was all the luggage I had. He was one of the kindest men I ever knew and he went to his eternal reward a few years ago. I remember him as a friend. That October day he drove me to the Columban House on Singalong Street.

After a few days I began to take an interest in the political situation. Marcos called a constitutional convention and shamelessly influenced the election of delegates. He had hoped it would change the rules and extend his stay in power. During the deliberations, the *Payola Express* scandal was exposed by Edward Quintero, a delegate from Leyte. Imelda Marcos was caught handing out envelopes stuffed with cash to delegates to persuade them to include provisions favourable to a continuation of Marcos' power. One of the delegates, a Marcos loyalist from Olongapo, was Richard Gordon. He denied that he ever took the money. But despite the payoffs it constantly delayed its proceedings, delegates holding out for more perhaps. Marcos could not wait and the declaration of Martial Law was his answer. The convention was being recalled to continue its work on a Marcos constitution, one that would give him more legitimacy, at least on paper.

There was no reliable news. The *Daily Express,* the first newspaper to appear after the freewheeling Philippine press was closed down, was owned and controlled by Marcos and run by the brother of Imelda Marcos, Benjamin "Kokoy" Romuladez. I was unable to find out the real situation. Besides closing the media down he banned all criticism by means of General Order 19 which stated that *"any person who shall utter, publish, distribute, circulate and spread rumours, false news and information and gossip... may be arrested or detained".* He constantly claimed that he was acting according to the authority given to him by the 1935 constitution. But it was a lie – the constitution gave no such power. He needed a fresh constitutional mandate.

After imposing Martial Law, Marcos put increased pressure on the Constitutional Convention and arrested a number of delegates. Gordon was not one of them. The remainder, loyal to Marcos, approved a draft constitution on November 29, 1972. It contained transitory provisions in Article 17, which gave legitimacy to all the decrees, orders and proclamations of the president. It gave him power to remain in office indefinitely. Yet it had to be ratified by the people. On January 17, 1973 he had it ratified in a dubious manner thus sealing his grip on power.

By November 16, a month after the military takeover, Marcos had arrested more than six thousand of his opponents, critics and anyone suspected of opposing him. The crackdown continued. On November 25, he arrested three Americans suspected of being involved in an assassination plot against Marcos himself, allegedly masterminded by the Osmena clan from Cebu. On December 7, Imelda Marcos was stabbed and wounded in the arm during a public presentation, that was all Marcos needed to crack down harder on all dissent, and he did so with a vengeance.

I knew this was the beginning of a dangerous and menacing era. All dissent was banned, freedom of speech was a crime and any criticism was considered subversive. For a foreign missionary it was even more dangerous, especially for those of us who had social awareness and social development projects. In areas of greatest poverty, such as the Manila slums, the island of Negros and Mindanao, there were many religious nuns, priests and lay workers committed to the social change and were now in danger. The Conservative Right said that social work was the expression of Socialism, a step from Communism. Eventually this was to become such an entrenched mind set that working for social justice with and for the poor was seen as a rebellious subversive activity. The years ahead were to test everyone's commitment and faith.

I returned to St. Joseph's Parish in Olongapo about the middle of October and saw that Martial Law did nothing to stop the drug trafficking or the child prostitution. The social problems were worse if anything and the US Naval Base hummed with a new confidence knowing that their strong man was in the seat of power in Manila. The bases were safe as criticism of the US presence was silenced.

The silence of the US Congress and President Nixon at the erasure of Philippine democratic institutions and their support of Marcos was directly related to their interest in having unhampered use of the Clarke Air Base and Subic Bay Naval Base. These were essential for the continuation of the war in Vietnam – just two hours flight across the South China Sea.

I wondered what I could do under these circumstances and was appalled at the extent of drug trafficking and the number of drug dependents among the local children. I met some of my former students and heard the stories of those who had graduated and the many who had failed because of drugs and gang violence. There was a clear need to provide some kind of counselling and a rehabilitation centre but I had no idea what should be done. After a few weeks working in the parish, I began a refresher course in Tagalog at the Inter-Faith Language School in Quezon City.

Myself and another Columban, Seamus Connally stayed at the La Salette Father's House close to the school since the Columban House on Singalong Street was almost an hour drive in the traffic. The La Salette Fathers had two bungalows separated by a wall but with a connecting gate. One was given over to Fr Bob Garon to run a shelter for drug dependents. I quickly took an active interest in the rehabilitation programme – looking for some ideas that might help me get something started in Olongapo.

During the months attending the school and staying at the La Salette House, I did some volunteer work with the drug rehabilitation programme. *DARE Foundation Inc.* was the name of the organisation set up by Fr Bob Garon. It was modelled on the *Daytop Therapeutic Community* in the US.

During these months, I met a Filipino La Salette Father, Joe

Naku, who was involved in social development programmes around Manila. He was connected to an organised community in Tondo called Zone One, near the garbage dump in the infamous Smoky Mountain, as the gigantic heap of rotting garbage was called. Thousands toiled there, destitute and surviving day by day. Smokey Mountain was synonymous with abject poverty and destitution. Old men, shrunken women and skeletal children were scratching daily through the smoking piles of filth and dirt looking for something to eat or sell.

Zone One represented many of the slum dwellers and was strongly opposed to Martial Law. Joe didn't get on well with Fr Garon who was a TV personality with his own talk show dishing out TV counselling. He wrote a column in the *Daily Express*, a Marcos controlled paper and his views were conservative and supportive of Martial Law.

Fr Joe invited me to various meetings and I began to understand the regime's repressiveness and the growing number of human rights abuses. Fr Joe asked me to help a little with the editing of the newsletter, called *Ang Bayan* (The Nation), which Joe was helping to write and circulate. I didn't realise the risk I was taking because this was an underground newsletter supporting the rebel movement.

Fr Joe would appear at odd hours, unannounced, coming through a back entrance through the garden of another house. Unknown to me he was under suspicion by the security forces. One evening when he was visiting, the house was surrounded by troops. A military intelligence officer came to the gate demanding it be opened. Fr Garon was in a panic and rushed about with drugs and syringes confiscated from drug dependents which were illegal to have. They were searching for Fr Joe who was in the basement.

I slipped away to a small storeroom where I had the latest stuff that was to go into the next edition of *Ang Bayan*. In a panic myself, I quickly realised the implications if they found the draft articles for the next edition of the newsletter. They documented human rights abuses and were highly critical of the Martial Law regime. I began to tear up the documents and burn them in the toilet bowl. I grew more panicky because of the smoke and I tried to fan it out the window and then realised the police and soldiers surrounding the house would see it and raise the alert. I turned off the light, then realised the flickering flames would show, so I turned it back on. Then I flushed the remains but the half-burnt documents paper clogged the toilet bowl leaving it blackened with soot.

I was growing more desperate by the second. My shirt was soaking with sweat, my hands were covered with soot too and had to wait what seemed an eternity for the toilet tank to fill up. I flushed again and more went down but the bowl was still black with the soot, if they saw that they would surely know what I was up to. I tried to rub it clean with a crumbled newspaper but it smeared the bowl worse. I was waiting with trembling hands, a pounding heart, a dry throat for the door to be kicked in. I could hear the jackboots pounding around the house as they searched high and low, pulling out filing cabinets, boxes of books and anything that could be considered evidence of subversion. They were getting closer and closer to the bathroom. I realised I couldn't destroy them all and peeped out to see if the corridor was clear. They were in Joe's office. I slipped out and hid the rest under a pile of junk in an adjoining bedroom that was unoccupied.

Then I stepped into my own bedroom and quickly washed up and changed my shirt. I sat on the bed to calm down and gulped water from the faucet. It seemed like hours since they had burst into the compound but it was only about ten minutes and having found Joe and his office they didn't search further. I walked out to the main living room as coolly and as innocently as I could with a quizzical look as if I was amazed by it all. My long shoulder length hair was a give away. They gave me strange looks and I blamed myself for not having had it cut. Long hair was a mark of protest and the Marcos troops were going around picking up longhaired youths and shaving them in public. The captain was shrewd, he looked long and hard at me, asking who I was.

Fr Joe was sitting in the living room with heavily armed soldiers around him. I pretended to look surprised and asked what was happening. Our eyes met with a look of knowing and they said one thing that needed no words: I've been betrayed. His room was being emptied, filing cabinets were taken and boxes of books were being carried out to an army truck parked in the driveway. That explained why they had not reached my room, they had what they were looking for. I went over and began handing out bottles of soda and it relaxed the atmosphere a bit. Fr Garon came in and out a few times.

After a while Fr Joe said he was being arrested and would be taken to Camp Aguinaldo where the political prisoners were detained. The intelligence officer didn't suspect me and only asked my name and what I was doing there. I told him I was a student at the language school. Apparently satisfied they prepared to escort Fr Joe to the waiting jeep.

Before he went with them, he began to say goodbye and came over to hug me and whispered in my ear, "Take the keys, hide them." He slipped them into my hand when we shook and for a moment I saw the officer looking suspiciously at us. Then they left. I slumped into the couch exhausted and weak-kneed, trying to imagine what would happen next. There was no going to bed that night. I went out into the empty garden and when sure I was alone I buried the keys in a flowerbed.

The next day the La Salette Fathers went to the camp to find out what happened to Joe. I stayed in the house. In the afternoon the intelligence officer drove his jeep into the compound again. He was dressed in military camouflage and had a holstered automatic on his belt. My imagination filled with frightening images of Joe being tortured and forced to talk. I feared they had come back for me.

I was right. The captain approached and knew exactly what he was looking for. "Please give me the keys of Father Naku," he ordered.

I stammered, a bit shocked, and realised at once there was no point in denying what they already knew. Joe had told them. But they weren't surrounding me, so I told him that I had thrown them away, into the garden. He ordered me to get them and obediently I did.

"I didn't know what they were for so I threw them there," I explained lamely. Then to my utter relief, without another word, he turned and went out to the jeep and backed out of the driveway. They had the keys to the safe house where those on the run would hide. If they connected Joe to these hideouts, they would have a lot of evidence against him. I hoped and prayed that he hadn't been harmed and waited for news from the La Salette Provincial Superior who had not returned.

About six months later, Fr Joe got out of the stockade on a pretext to visit the dentist, got his guards drunk and made his escape. He went to the French Embassy to ask for asylum but they refused. He was recaptured but then, a year later, he escaped again and got out of the country through the Muslim-controlled part of Mindanao in the South.

I kept a very low profile after that. I had my long hair cut and hoped that my name was not on a list of suspected *Communist sympathizers* as everyone who helped the poor or the prisoners was called. I decided that there was nothing more I could do to help Zone One and, presuming that I was under a cloud of suspicion by the military, decided to pursue a plan to set up a rehabilitation centre in Olongapo. Coming to the end of language studies, I requested my Columban superior Fr John Curry to allow me to join the DARE Programme as a trainee.

Chapter Eight

In March 1973, I was assigned to Botolan, a small town in Zambales province about one and half hours drive north from Olongapo. *Operation Harelip* was still going strong in San Marcelino. Small donations coming into Sr Rose kept it going. Before I could take up residence in Botolan, Fr Curry called me to Olongapo and he was really annoyed. He showed me a newspaper article by Fr Bob Garon in which he wrote about his request to the Columbans to assign me to his project to help drug dependents. Such was his public profile and influence with the Marcos regime it practically obligated the Columbans to agree. I was annoyed too that he had pressured the Columbans to agree, making it appear that I had put him up to it.

His newspaper column reported his visit to Olongapo and the possibility of opening a new centre; it also described the terrible conditions of the city and the jail. He wrote: "Upon returning to Manila I approached Fr John Curry, a district superior of the Columban Fathers and asked them to assign one of their young priests to work with DARE in the new undertaking. Fr Curry was very kind and understanding of the problem. A few days later, he graciously came to my headquarters with Fr Sullivan and said that "Fr Shea (*sic*) Cullen was being given permission to join DARE."

The Columban Superiors believed that Garon would build, run and finance the new centre in Olongapo and I would be assigned there as director. At the time that's the way I understood it too and, bowing to the inevitable, I shelved the hopes of putting up my own project. This was better than nothing.

I settled into the work at the DARE Foundation and, with my fluency in Tagalog improving, I found it much easier to understand the drug dependents and their problems. The DARE method of treating drug dependents was based on the idea that peer group pressure got the kids onto drugs, then drugs were the problem that caused a personality change that led to undisciplined, negative, hostile and rebellious behaviour. The rehabilitation method was based on behaviour modification change by carrot and stick. But it turned out that more "stick than carrot" was on the menu.

Although today that method has changed somewhat, in the early days drug abuse was spreading at an alarming rate and there was no previous experience like it in the Philippines and consequently no programmes had been developed. There was no attempt to understand the psychological background of the drug dependent. The social and family conditions that aggravated his slide into drug abuse were not investigated or taken into account. There was insufficient therapy to reach the deeper roots of family problems. There was a belief that if the drug abuser acted as a good person, he or she would become that good person.

"Act As If" was the slogan. Challenge and confront was the rule of the day, which may be necessary sometimes, but it has to be balanced by positive counselling. Using peer group pressure to bring the new intakes into the routine was used but it quickly got out of control and a clique of bullyboys began to dominate the centre and the new residents. But, despite the abusive regime and not because of it, many did survive emotionally and I am sure went on to lead decent, productive lives.

I soon had reservations and serious doubts about the treatment given to the teenagers when we brought them to the basement of a government hospital, in Quezon City, which had been given over to DARE by Imelda Marcos – *Imelda of the three thousand pairs of shoes.* After my experience at the Eagle's Nest, I saw they needed friendship more than fear, affirmation and understanding, self-discipline and a sense of self-worth rather than being made feel guilty and ashamed. I was repelled by the harsh verbal treatment, the physical work, and the humiliation thought necessary to instil discipline and obedience. Necessary, we were told, for a drug-free life. But I didn't believe this and restrained my criticism because I knew it was likely to jeopardise my chances of operating the Olongapo Centre. I was guilty too for putting personal goals before speaking out sooner against the abuses in DARE.

The DARE programme then seemed to follow the US Marine Corps credo of breaking the spirit of the young people and then claiming to build them up in a new image, a new person. Like playing God. Garon passed around a pictorial magazine describing the marine training method. A photo of a Marine Sergeant poking his face into that of a recruit and screaming at him stuck in my memory and came flashing back years later when I saw the award winning film *Full Metal Jacket* by Stanley Kubrick. The Marine version of attack therapy was similar to DARE's.

Some of the harsh methods drove a few drug dependents to attempt suicide, as they did in that film. One kid tried by jumping off a balcony, many others tried to slash their wrists. At another time one kid was killed when he was beaten to death with a spade by other senior inmates when he tried to escape from the DARE Trece Martirez Centre in Cavite. The boy was from the Olivares family and well connected to the Marcoses. It was almost the end of DARE.

Despite these reservations, I stayed on, vowing that the treatment at the Olongapo Centre would be different. In fact, I stayed with DARE for about nine months. I was learning a lot about what should not be done and trying a positive sincere, affirmative approach. Showing them respect and, making them feel good about themselves, gave them a sense of self-dignity and hope. It was more effective than verbally attacking their traits of human weakness and escapisms.

I was assigned to run a new centre for alcoholics at a rest house loaned by the Araneta family in Novaliches, north of Manila. With the residents we worked out a name, *Pugad Sa Tugatug (The Eagles Nest)* and set it up as an open centre – there were no walls or guards and the modified affirmative therapeutic programme was soon having positive effects. Alcohol and marijuana users did not mix well with heavy drug abusers and needed a different kind of recovery programme and lifestyle. The house was in a lovely open location overlooking a valley and I began using the twelve steps, group therapy, prayer and physical education and games.

There was no compound here to keep the young people locked in so it was a lifestyle based on persuasion, trust and the hope of recovery. There was no need for attack therapy, shouting, humiliation and harsh dehumanising treatment. They responded to respect, affirmation and emotional support far better. There was no bullying either by the senior intakes, so we had a peaceful, prayerful life together and many began to recover quickly. I was also free from military investigations because they had not found my name in any of Fr Joe's files and nobody gave away my participation in the production of the newsletter.

At the new centre I encouraged the residents to plan and manage most of the daily schedule. They organised the house operations, the kitchen and participated in the daily therapy and prepared the schedules. I learned about their families, their childhood and the circumstances that brought them to substance abuse. Rarely was it the drink or drugs that was the root of the problem, rather that was the symptom of deeper troubles. It was inner turmoil that caused them so much anguish and alcohol became their only crutch. That intrigued me and these were the key to understanding the young substance abuser.

You didn't need a university degree to understand that an abusive childhood left wounds, scars and painful memories that lingered on exerting pressure and stress. No wonder the kids were always looking for a pain reliever. Many had cruel and over-disciplined upbringing, while violence and infidelity in the family was common, verbal reprimands and physical punishment – in a home devoid of parental love, care and affirmation – caused severe emotional problems.

I came to accept that – despite being illegal, wrong and dangerous – these troubled people used chemicals to try and change their feelings of anger, pain, and hopelessness; their actions were not justifiable but they were, nevertheless, understandable. Improvement lay in dealing with the underlying causes. Sensible as this may seem there are still many who despise the alcoholic or drug abuser as a selfish, pleasure seeking drop-out who lies, cheats, steals and even turns to violence to get what he wants. For every effect there is a cause and while destructive behaviour cannot be tolerated, rejection is the worst that could happen to a person so afflicted.

We have to understand and help. They are people who have been hurt, rejected and despised as children and grow up without ever having felt genuine love and affection. I wanted to try to ease or even resolve the inner pain and fill the emptiness with positive affirmation, encouragement and create convictions of self-worth and confidence and restored dignity. In a disciplined, ordered and mutually respectful community with therapy and counselling, recovery was possible. One of the important ways to achieving this was to get their parents into the healing process. They, too, needed help, sometimes a lot more than their drug dependent or alcoholic teenager.

The budget was always tight and I had to make the long bus ride into the DARE House at La Salette every two weeks and wait for hours and even days to get the money for the food. Mrs Vega, a friend of Fr Garon, was the keeper of the purse and keep it she did. We hardly got anything. Garon boasted of the enormous support he had and the fine bank account he had when testifying the following May before the Dangerous Drugs Board. We saw little of it and scraped by but it was the beginning of tensions and I began to see that all was not well in the financial management of DARE in those days.

Yet there was no point complaining. DARE had lots of cash donations but was not transparent or providing proper accountability. Public criticism became so strong that an accounting firm volunteered to put the books in order for free but Mrs Vega was not cooperative.

A typist and bookkeeper working in the office, Merly Ramirez, was the cashier when I went to collect the centre's expenses. She was attending college and taking up business management and she really helped me by taking calls and messages, holding any mail, and informing me about the latest mood swings that were engulfing Mrs Vega and Garon. There were times when I had to wait two days before approval would be given for the centre's food. Vega and Garon would disappear and everything would come to a standstill. What they were doing with the money was anybody's guess. Little did I suspect then what was really going on!

I was always hungry when working for DARE and so were the residents. I lost weight. The food was awful and at times inedible. I took some of the residents and went to Caritas where there was food supply designated for a "food for work" project. We got several sacks of oatmeal and bulgur wheat. We ate better after that.

DARE was having other problems as parents began questioning the harsh treatment of their children and there were many who continued to jump the wall and escape. Some even tried to commit suicide both inside the DARE centres and after they ran away. After two months the centre at Novaliches was running well. It was then that the abrupt order came down that the centre was to be closed and the residents returned and dispersed to the other centre. There was no discussion or consultation about it. One day we were achieving something and the next day it was over. Soon after the residents were dispersed they ran away. It was then I began to worry about the future of the centre in Olongapo. Fr Garon showed little interest and he was talking in grandiose terms about taking over some hotel in Antipolo as a National Drug Rehabilitation Centre.

During these months I went to Olongapo frequently to keep the construction going. There were problems with money for the labour and there was none forthcoming from DARE. The City of Olongapo, then under the administration of Dr Lipumano, had worked out an agreement with the Society of American Military Engineers (S.A.M.E.) to help with the construction of the centre. Architect Bener Cruz, then an employee of the US Base, was assigned by the S.A.M.E as project coordinator and a good job he did too.

One day, we climbed a hill with a military engineer, Pat Sherback, who was providing technical help and locating surplus building materials. The site was three kilometres from the city, overlooking the expanse of Subic Bay. It was a beautiful location on public land, ideal for the centre and since it bordered the cemetery we would be having quiet neighbours. I applied to the Department of Environment and Natural Resources for a permit to use the area for what was later to become the PREDA Centre.

During that time, I was still at DARE and following the original agreement to set up the DARE Centre and run it as director. In that capacity, I applied for the land usage permit and signed it as the applicant. Bener Cruz was like a miracle worker. When no one gave the funds, Bener used his own money to pay the workers, and Lieutenant Pat Sherback, of the naval base's Public Works Department, found the materials around the base. Bener was very frustrated that he was getting no financial support, but I promised him I would repay it one day and I did.

The military engineers were able to borrow bulldozers to prepare the site and make an approach road. It was January 1974 when actual construction began. Sherbak was among the most enthusiastic and between himself, Bener Cruz and Captain Clayman Myers, Captain Charles Gibowicz and Mayor Geronimo Lipumano, the building began to take shape. I was commuting there to keep it going and trying to get money for the workers.

Back in Manila, the Novaliches Centre was closed and I was assigned to form a rescue and recover unit to look for the escaped drug dependents before they died from an overdose. Another reason was to reduce the alarming rising numbers of failures at DARE and to stop the flood of complaints from the escapees to the Dangerous Drug Board. They were complaining of mistreatment and requesting a discharge. I was based in an old house on loan to DARE on Gilmore Avenue in New Manila just across the road from the Carmelite Church. There were Irish priests there and I had several hearty meals and good companionship, and remember them all with heartfelt thanks for their kindness and good cheer.

I began training three residents of the centre in basic techniques of locating missing persons. We researched their files, phoned their friends and relatives, asked for them over the phone. Sometimes we visited their old haunts and picked up leads to their whereabouts. Sometimes I would send one of the team to visit their houses under a pretext to see if the escapee was there.

To help us get around we set up a big wall map of the city and planned our early morning visits. The escapee having been committed to DARE by court order could have been arrested by warrant but we were able to persuade them to come voluntarily.

There was a growing paranoia as criticism of the DARE programme grew. The government control body, the Dangerous Drugs Board, were constantly asking for records, accountability, transparency, reform, and a more professional approach. Fr Garon instead criticised the Board in his newspaper column. Many escaped drug users and their parents were appealing to the Board to be released from the court order that incarcerated them in the DARE Centre. A crony Judge would issue arrest warrants against the teenagers for their return. The Judge, who was later to preside over Garon's marriage to one of his staff, routinely signed the commitment orders on Garon's request.

The work with the recovery team was interesting but depressing. At least I felt that we were better to find them before some police squad shot them as was common practice under the Marcos regime. Most of the dependents at DARE were from rich or middleclass families and when I visited their homes I saw the sadness of their wealth.

When I went in search of a very poor resident, I saw the squalor of slum life that was indescribable. One early morning, we went looking for a young teenager who had escaped and our search led me to a squatter settlement on stilts over a fetid marsh where the black liquid bubbled continuously with the rising methane from the raw sewerage beneath the surface. How humans could live in the stinking mess was beyond me. We walked across narrow planks tied to bamboo posts driven into the mud and climbed the stairs leading to the elevated hut above. In the poor light my hand slithered on the faeces that had dropped from the window. We brought the teenager to the hospital building with growing doubts it would do any good It was a work filled with contradictions. In the world around me I was witnessing the growing repression of Martial Law and knew that I had to get back somehow to helping the poor in a more effective way.

We called our recovery team the *Phantom Squad* for fun, because we did a lot of our house calls before dawn and brought the escaped dependents to the basement of the GSIS Hospital in East Avenue, which was now a heavily secured place. The use of this had been procured by Garon's intercession with Imelda Marcos. It was airless and stuffy. Life inside was becoming more like a prison programme than a treatment and recovery service. The facilities were terrible and with the parents I arranged for new showers and toilets to be installed.

Having promised the escapees that they would be well treated, I was bitterly disappointed at the tough treatment they actually received. There were more and more kids running away. I was still going to Olongapo frequently to help move the project along. Architect Bener Cruz was still working wonders using his own money and the Columbans gave some money as well. The building was well advanced by November 1973. As yet DARE had put no money into it. I shared some of my misgivings with Fr Curry about the weakening resolve of DARE to continue with the project. The rumours that Garon was emotionally involved with a young female employee was troubling, his behaviour was becoming erratic.

By March 1974 things were not good and I was close to the end of my year and the future was no clearer. I finally made my opinion known to Fr Garon about the bad treatment of the residents. The lack of good sanitation, showers, healthy food and medical care was the cause of the large number of runaways and the emotional pressure and attack therapy all took their toll. He was really annoyed and angry with this criticism which he called treachery and made remarks to his inner circle that I would never operate the Olongapo centre. He talked a lot about getting the Antipolo Hotel and bringing all the DARE centres under one roof. He had lost interest in the Olongapo project. I considered all the work that I had put into it and I was determined that I would go on with it on my own.

Shortly after our heated meeting I formally wrote to Garon to ask if he would support the Olongapo project and, if he did, would he stick to the agreement to have me run it? He did not answer. I then phoned and asked him point blank and he responded with a torrent of abuse about treachery, double-crossing him and the like. So I hung up and decided to leave. On March 8, I wrote a letter to the Dangerous Drugs Board expressing my intent to operate the Olongapo centre.

A few days later I told Garon that I was resigning and had filed my letter of intent with the Board. He was furious and fired me the next day. On March 14, he passed out a letter making allegations that I was subverting and disrupting the programme and recruiting staff and residents to break from DARE and operate the Olongapo project independently. I had a few things in my favour – the building permit was in my name and I had applied in my name for a public site to set up a rehabilitation centre.

Garon then rushed his own letter of intent to the DDB and hurried to Olongapo and had a meeting with government officials and later in St Columban Parish Rectory met with Bishop Henry Byrne, Fr Curry and other Columbans assigned in Olongapo. I was in a room nearby and soon heard that all had agreed that Garon would get their support in writing.

The Dangerous Drugs Board now had two competing applications to operate the same centre so they began a series of special hearings to reach a decision as to who should get the license to operate. The failure of DARE to finance any part of the centre was a weakness in their claim so at the last hour they rushed to Olongapo and gave five thousand pesos to Bener Cruz to make it appear that they had a stake. It was a trifling sum.

During the first government hearing held by the Dangerous Drugs Board, Fr Garon and George Loiselle were the first to be invited. Garon stated: "DARE has never shown any disinterest in connection with the rehabilitation centre in Olongapo." However Fr Curry stated during another hearing that Garon had only gone to Olongapo twice in two years. "But the thing is that Fr Shay did work on the centre and it was he who brought it about. Fr Bob visited there in 1972 in February and the next time he visited was one month ago."

During the visit of Garon to Olongapo in early March, he

met Bishop Henry Byrne and Fr Curry and his council and separately with Architect Cruz. The Bishop, Fr Curry and his council held a closed door meeting at St Columban's rectory, I was invited but when it became apparent that they were set on backing Garon I left. It was getting a bit too painful.

They decided to support Garon saying that they had a commitment to him. Bishop Henry Byrne wrote to Garon to tell him so and met with him in Manila on March 20, 1974. In a hand written letter Bishop Byrne wrote:

Through Fr Cullen and also through Fr Curry it was made clear to Father Bob that the prelature of Iba, represented by the bishop, would give every support it could to DARE in regard to a foundation in Olongapo. I personally told the same thing to Father Bob when I saw him in Manila on March 20, 1974. Because of that commitment to supporting or backing Father Bob with a DARE Foundation in Olongapo, I could not consider lending support to any alternate or substitute rehabilitation centre without the blessing and goodwill of Father Bob. I consider myself bound in honour to aid him insofar as I can towards the realization and the operation of a centre of the DARE Foundation in Olongapo.

But Garon was far from convinced he would get the approval of the Board where he had made many enemies and was reluctant to invest more money in his claim. According to Fr Curry, Garon told Architect Cruz, "You pay the men there. Don't come to me anymore, I have nothing to do with it. I am not giving anymore money to this project since I don't know where I am, where I stand."

Voluminous documents were submitted to the board by Garon to support his claim that he had planned and constructed the centre. He admitted that he had only given five thousand pesos. But he played up the support of Bishop Byrne. He told the board, "We had a talk with his bishop and his bishop is not supporting him, either his provincial. His provincial has told him point blank in his presence they want DARE to run the centre and so with his boss, Father John Curry."

Perhaps because he was planning to leave the priesthood himself, he made disparaging comments about priests: "Because I have implicit trust in my people and especially priests. But I learned that you shouldn't trust priests too much." Forgetting that he was still one at the time, the board presumably took his advice. To distance himself from the arrest of Fr Joe Naku, Garon told the board: "Our house was raided by the constabulary and a priest friend of mine is now in the stockade and has been there for a year and a half and I suspect that he's gonna be there for quite some time because he has left (his) leaning and there's no question about it and I know it."

Not long after that he left the priesthood and married outside the church, creating a monumental scandal.

Garon offered the board a "donation", others called it a bribe. "Our dream is to become self-sufficient and hopefully someday if the Dangerous Drugs Board would like to have a donation, we would like to be able to write out a cheque for your favourite charity to help maybe some other centres."

He pointed out that his big government connections had given him the free use of buildings to operate his programmes. The chairman of the Dangerous Drugs Board himself had given the use of his house in Baguio to DARE. General Fidel Ramos (later President Ramos), gave Garon the use of a military camp in Cavite where young people were incarcerated for "rehabilitation".

Mrs Ponce Enrile, the wife of the defence minister, gave him another place in Camp Bonifacio and General Rancudo yet another. The First Lady herself, Imelda Marcos, gave him the use of a wing of the GSIS Hospital on East Avenue, he told the board. They had seven centres in all and seemed to be doing the work of the regime. I was ashamed to have been associated with it all but at the time, after nearly being arrested with Fr Naku, I knew that any part I would play to bring about a more just social order in the Philippines would have to be left to the future and I was lucky to slip away into a lower profile work of helping those caught in the web of drug abuse and hopelessness. I felt I could still be effective helping with the victims rather than trying to topple their tormentors. The outcast youth was as good place to start as any other.

Then towards the end of the dialogue with Garon, the board expressed its displeasure at the non-compliance of DARE with the board's regulations. That was a ray of hope for me. I knew I was up against a wily and well-connected opponent who had thrown in his lot with the cruel regime, currying their favour but he had overdone it and became a bit too smug and arrogant. His behind the scenes appeal to his powerful connections seemed not to work. They left it to the board to decide.

Nevertheless, failing to get the message clearly, Garon pressured the board for a quick decision because the inauguration was, according to him, on June 1. The Bishop will be ready to bless it, he said. "Now, I would like to ask the Board if they could kindly as soon as possible give us a decision, you know, so I don't have to be nervous. I didn't eat too well this noon. I mean I am glad you gave me a sandwich and I will take it with me because I really was quite nervous about this. Actually, we have been having a great emotional involvement."

Fr Loiselle was in constant contact with Fr Curry and told the board that Fr Curry had made it clear about Fr Shay: "If he is going to work in Zambales Fr Curry does not intend to name him to this rehabilitation centre. If Fr Shay does not like it, he can go back to Ireland."

The Chairman then said: "Okay, do you want to bring your sandwich? Fr Garon, I will bring my sandwich if the board will allow me. I was just saying that someday I hope we can afford a very beautiful conference room that you have and not only that but afford to give sandwiches to the visitors."

On May 23, I was invited to the meeting of the board. The minutes of that meeting run to thirty-three pages and they asked the history of my involvement with drug dependents in Olongapo and the idea to open the centre. The main thing that the board members wanted to know was the real attitude of my superiors. If I ever did get the license, for example, would my superiors allow me to run the centre?

The previous day, I had anticipated this and had a meeting with Fr Curry. I told him that I had a good chance of getting the license and if the board decided in my favour to operate the centre what would his position be? That put John on the spot, how could he refuse a recommendation of the board that the Columbans run it? Fr John was aghast at the thought that he would have to go against such an authority as the board. He told me if that happened, however unlikely, it would be a "different ball game altogether".

The board asked a lot of questions about my proposed innovative drug rehabilitation programme which I had proposed in my application for the license. They asked about the allegations of Garon against me, which they heard and dismissed, I was glad to note. They seemed satisfied and said they would invite my superiors the next week. It was a time of tension and worry but I felt that if it wasn't from God, then, it wouldn't work out, if it was, it would. With that simple act of faith, I felt more at ease and relaxed.

During the next hearing on May 28, to which Fr Curry, the provincial superior and myself were invited, Dr. Clemente Gaitmaitan, the secretary of justice asked Fr Curry to repeat the questions he had put to the chairman during a private meeting a few days before. That was the first I had heard of it and I realised that there had been behind the scenes lobbying going on.

Fr Curry said he had asked why DARE was not given the license and why would they "entertain an individual applying for a license". Undersecretary Catalino Macaraig of the justice department replied that's what they were trying to decide and if they want to give it to an individual, why not?

Fr Curry then proposed a compromise. He suggested that

the board to give the centre to Garon and for Garon to appoint me as director. *The original agreement that had fallen apart.* The board balked at this and Fr Curry suggested the board itself take over the operation of the centre. This was rejected also and finally the meeting was over and we left. I was asked to wait outside and then invited back in later.

I waited outside in an empty reception room and knew that they were coming to a decision. I resigned myself to the worst. I was deeply hurt after the rejections and lack of support of the past weeks and months and, after all this, a final humiliation. I would have to think seriously about where I would be going after this.

I was called back inside and the chairman, Dr. Gatmaitan, told me that they had reached a decision. I was to be given the license. I was flabbergasted, overjoyed, elated, a huge weight was lifting, pulled upward by a great balloon and I was rising with it. Outwardly I remained calm, thanked them and was shocked when they asked if I could incorporate and register a foundation and be appointed as director, in four days.

The Secretary of Social Welfare Aldaba-Lim said that I would make a good director considering the rehabilitation plans, programmes and methods I had submitted to the board but the catch was I had to incorporate it by the following Monday so the license could be given to a registered organisation. That was four working days away.

"Yes, Mr. Chairman, I suppose I can," I said and I left the building walking on air. I had won! It was unbelievable.

Before me stretched a bureaucratic jungle teeming with unknown pitfalls and obstructions designed to loosen the wallets of foreigners setting up that most desired but unattainable goal of a tax-exempt foundation. In those days only the wealthy and well-connected cronies of Marcos could get official approval. I worried that they would require a military security clearance and my involvement with Fr Naku would be an obstacle. There was no background check required.

The Articles of Incorporation and the by-laws had to be written, typed and duplicated and signed by nine incorporators. I planned to ask friends and supporters who had stood by me in the past year to be on the board. It had then to be submitted to the Security and Exchange Commission and pass a dozen bureaucratic hurdles before it was approved.

There was much to be done as I hurried from the office and across packed streets of Manila and got a jeepney back to the Columban House on Singalong Street. I sat down with an old typewriter and began writing frantically the articles of incorporation and by-laws of what was to become the PREDA Foundation, Inc. The name that I first gave the project was Zambales Rehabilitation Centre (ZARACEN), but by September 1994 I had amended it to the *Prevent and Rehabilitate Drug Abusers Foundation Inc.*

Working most of the night, I had them ready. With no chance to consult a lawyer I just copied the outline of another foundation's articles and by-laws and changed the text to incorporate the goals and aims of the drug rehabilitation that I had envisaged. Then the next day, I went around to all my friends who were on the board and got their signatures. The day after, I took them to the Securities and Exchange Commission and, praying, got the preliminary signatures that attested that the contents were legal and correct. I left them for the approval of the commissioners and said I would be back on Monday. When I got there I was handed a certificate of registration. The final articles of incorporation would be ready in a few days, I was told. On the following Tuesday, I presented the certificate and a copy of the Articles of Incorporation to the Board. They were satisfied and told me that I would hear from them.

Nine days later I received a letter from the Board Chairman, Dr. Gatmaitan, dated June 7, 1974. *This is to inform you,* it read, *that the Dangerous Drugs Board in its meeting of June 4, 1974, resolved to approve your notice of Intent To Establish and Operate a Private Treatment and*

Rehabilitation Centre for Drug Dependents in Olongapo City ... you may now proceed with the establishment and operation of the centre...

With the license at hand I set about starting the centre; I contacted several of the former DARE staffers who had resigned. The most recent who had left was Merly Ramirez, who worked in the accounts department, and had just graduated from college with a degree in management. DARE was becoming increasingly paranoid, the management felt threatened and developed a bit of a siege mentality. The spirit of solidarity and teamwork that had bound us to the work of helping the drug dependent kids was gone.

There was such an air of secrecy, it was like a secret society or a cult. The unanswered allegations of misappropriation of funds hung like a threatening cloud. All wrongdoing was denied and there was no official investigation by the authorities. There were loyalty tests and even the most innocent and ordinary behaviour was questioned and interpreted as signs of disloyalty and betrayal. During this time, Merly Ramirez, under a lot of pressure became a target of suspicion by Bob Garon and Mrs Vega. Others had similar experiences and gave up their jobs and when they heard I was starting the PREDA Centre offered to join the project.

By the end of June 1974, I went to Olongapo with three former DARE staff – Merly Ramerez, Alma Santos and Ofelia Baja. It was the first time that the three former DARE staffers had been to Olongapo. The staff house overlooked Perimeter Street from where they could view the bridge leading to the gate and witness the comic romantic scenes of parting lovers. Hundreds of young Filipinos dressed in mini-skirts and shorts were walking about hand-in-hand with Americans twice their height. It being Martial Law there was a curfew imposed when the National Peoples Army was active in the area. When the siren wailed, the girls ran after the departing sailors for last minute kisses and embraces.

I stayed alone in a bared walled room in the unfinished building on the hillside overlooking Subic Bay. There was no electricity or water. The dark gloom was lit by a few candles at night but I preferred to sit out overlooking the bay, gazing at the heavens and the array of glittering stars and marvel at the wonder of the universe wondering if I could make anything useful out of the project and where life would lead me.

Scaffolding, cement bags, building litter were all over the place but I was glad to be there and set about getting the place organised. Architect Bener Cruz, who passed to his reward peacefully in June 1998, had faithfully stuck with the project throughout the controversy and had done a terrific job. I had promised to find the money I owed him for the labour. Eventually, I did and gladly paid him.

There were still a few workmen who came in to clean and finish the building so that it was habitable. An old military water tank was parked outside and I drew water in a bucket every morning and evening for bathing and cooking. Within a few months, I had the electricity connected. Mayor Geronimo Lipumano was cooperative and helpful. It took another few months until the place was ready for occupation and the driveway was cut out of the hillside, graded, rolled and covered with asphalt.

The majority of US Navy rank and file and officers too were decent, generous people only too willing to try and make life better for the unfortunates of Olongapo but the Navy itself had no objection to the sex industry or the conspiracy of greed that preyed on the helpless and the hapless illiterate women who were duped into believing that there was a paradise behind the glittering lights of the gaudy bars. "You can marry a rich American in no time," they were told. They believed it and turned their bodies and souls over to the *mama san* and bar owners who kept them in endless debt, a slavery they couldn't comprehend, living off empty dreams of making it rich and saving their families. It seldom happened – their life was an unending nightmare.

Many of the Navy's families were unhappy, compassionate and frustrated being buffeted by the swirling squalls of contradictions that pervaded their comfortable world and those that say that they were a big part of the problem were frustrated and angry. Silent detachment was the attitude of many more, knowing they were caught by irreconcilable contradictions. Many wanted no part of Sin City and were not among the pleasure seekers romping about the bars and club and short time hotels. Many were helping individual families, they were generous and kind to their Filipino employees and helped me silently over the years.

Just as we were getting organised an official from the Olongapo arrived with a writ of preliminary injunction against us operating the centre. Fr Garon had lodged a civil action laying claim to the centre and had got the injunction against us. I remember standing there in the half empty building, looking around at the unfinished walls and ceiling and realising that the struggle was far from over. I had a sinking feeling that all that had been won could be easily snatched away. What a test this was going to be.

The DARE included the Dangerous Drugs Board as a defendant as well as myself. I was now in the ironic situation of finding myself in court with the Marcos cabinet members as co-defendants. Garon got a team of lawyers from a well connected and prestigious law firm of which the defence minister of Marcos, Juan Ponce Enrile, was the former leading partner. It was Enrile who later tried unsuccessfully to mount a coup against the dictator Marcos. The plot was discovered before a shot was fired and when cornered in a military camp in Manila was saved by a popular non-violent uprising that brought the downfall of Marcos and ushered Corazon Aquino into power. But all that was in the future and I was now faced with a glittering array of legal luminaries with only a small-town lawyer to counter their threats and legal onslaught.

The big city lawyers wore black legal gowns which was very unusual for provincial courts. The Judge was impressed and from the beginning it wasn't hard to see who he favoured. I saw that I had little chance unless there was a miracle. They made no mention of the Dangerous Drugs Board but targeted me, arguing that I was unable, financially and experience-wise, to operate the centre and a writ of permanent injunction should be granted.

I got the help of a local lawyer, Attorney Val Peralta. He was a good honest man and a great lawyer. In the end after weeks of hearings it all came down to in who's name had the government released the land where the building stood. I had been trying to get this from the land office because I had applied for it in my name but stating that I intended it for a DARE Drug Treatment Programme. So my claim was weaken by this. How was I to know that Garon would change his mind and abandon the centre in favour of a grandiose centralised complex? It was only when he saw what had been built and the magnificent location and that I was determined to operate it that he sprang into action.

After months of paper chasing and countless visits to land offices where I learned that the DARE lawyers had just been, I felt beaten at every step. Without contacts in high places it seemed nothing could be achieved. I was learning about the influence peddling and crony system at every turn. I felt a sense of powerlessness and what it meant to be poor and without influence. I was resigned to the inevitable outcome. But I kept trying and arguing my case with the land officials in Manila asking for the Special Use Permit that would give me the right to use the site.

Then on the day before the closing arguments the case would be set for decision by the Judge, I made one last desperate trip to the land office in Manila, a day when all seemed lost. And there it was, the permit, in my name, signed and waiting. I couldn't believe my good fortune. The next morning, I rushed back to Olongapo and arrived while the court hearings were still going on. Breathlessly, I ran up the rickety wooden planks of the stairway outside the building and sat beside Attorney Peralta. I handed him the permit. Peralta's face lit up with a smile and rose to his feet and interrupted the ranting of the Manila lawyers and asked the Judge to approach the bench. There he showed the Judge the decision of the Bureau of Land Management granting me the lease on the public land. It was over, at that point I knew we had won. The Judge called for a private conference so that the case could be settled. DARE conceded. They signed an agreement to relinquish all claims on the centre.

It had been a hard and difficult time. I felt let down by a few of my fellow priests and the Bishop who had backed Garon's claim. But there were the Columban Sisters who were good friends and we shared a common stand on the Olongapo vice industry. In managing St. Columban's College, they sowed seeds of social awareness and commitment among the staff and students. In later years those seeds were to grow to a rich harvest. Good supporters too were Fathers Colt McKeating, Bill Sullivan, and Declan Coyle who stood by us and gave a lot of much needed encouragement and support. They came to the court hearings from time to time to show their solidarity. Years later, in 1983 when I was under pressure from local politicians for a stand on human rights, the Columban priests rallied around and gave statements of support.

In the Philippines, there was division in the Church between those who made accommodation with Martial Law believing it was the salvation of the Philippines. They turned a blind eye to the human rights violations. But the majority of the bishops and religious were resisting.

Chapter Nine

With church persecution growing, priests and lay leaders were being tagged as subversives and Communists. Some were framed and falsely charged, arrested and tortured and even murdered. But the institutional church as a whole was resisting. There were eighty-three bishops speaking through the Catholic Bishops Conference of the Philippines (CBCP) and 2,500 priests and religious sisters organised through the Association of Major Religious Superiors of the Philippines (AMRSP).

There were approximately 1,200 foreign missionaries all over the country. There were so many reports of human rights violations that the AMRSP organised the Task Force Detainees in January 1974, the same year as PREDA began. Their goal was to monitor such violations and assist the victims. Early that year senior religious leaders of the Protestant National Council of Churches of the Philippines were arrested and tortured.

The office of the AMRSP itself was raided by Marcos troops that December and they were charged with sedition for speaking out through the AMRSP newsletter "Signs of the times".

In Negros Island, about three hundred miles south of Manila, there were many Columban missionaries since 1950.

Impoverished settlers had moved on to denuded forest land and began to carve out small farms. The wealthy land owners were expanding the sugar plantations and laid claim to the property where the settlers had cultivated and developed but had not legally claimed. The farmers were forcing them off the land. There was wholesale pillage and destruction of animals and crops, burning houses, rapes and murder by goons who were frequently moonlighting soldiers in the pay of the rich. Some left and went further up the hills to start again because of the threats and the killings.

The Federation of Free Farmers had worked for years to organise the settlers and help them get legal title to the land they tilled. All who resisted the rich were conveniently labelled "subversives" and they could be hunted "legally" by the military as Communists. Such tactics actually drew in rebel groups and the sons of the poor farmers who were fingered to be executed by the military fled to join them.

The Church in Negros was actively supporting the oppressed farmers since the middle 1950s, they preached, persuaded, campaigned for justice in the Philippines and abroad. In 1969 Bishop Fortich issued a pastoral letter calling for a renewed effort to help the oppressed. A social action centre was set up in Bacolod and the director began to work for stronger solidarity and cooperation between the Farmers Association and the National Federation of Sugar Workers to work for social justice.

There was tension between those committed to social justice and the military. Forty-four sisters and thirty-two priests signed a letter, dated June 18, 1974, addressed to Juan Ponce Enrile, the defence minister, demanding justice for the sugar workers and an end to military violence. The island was the heart of the sugar industry and dominated by the great landowners most of them close allies of Marcos. The letter to Enrile denounced the tagging of officers of the National Federation of Sugar Workers (NFSW) and foreign missionaries as subversives.

In Davao, Mindanao on November 1976, there were two Catholic radio stations closed and about seventy church workers arrested. Two church publications in Manila were closed down for criticising the regime. Two priests, one of them a friend, Fr Eduardo Gerlock and Fr Albert Booms were deported. They had been working in the Manila slums organising Christian communities and were considered dangerous and subversive. In January 1976 Marcos postponed all elections until 1980 citing an opinion poll. The trial of Benigno Aquino began but Aquino boycotted the trial saying it couldn't be fair. The following October, Marcos held a referendum, rigged of course, and got a vote calling for the continuation of Martial Law. There was violence in the streets but it was quickly put down and the protesters hauled off to prison without trial.

By February 1977, the number of arrests of priests and religious had greatly increased. The Catholic Bishops Conference of the Philippines came out with a pastoral letter read in all churches, in part it said: *This evangelising work... has been misunderstood (by the government) and led to the arrests of priests, religious and lay workers, and even the deportation of foreign missionaries.* In the same article the minister of defence denied all the allegations. Nevertheless the mounting political pressure was having some effect and Marcos eased some of the harsher aspects of Martial Law. But he still ruled by decree. Marcos announced that Martial Law would end in January 1981 and that there would be free elections the following June. To appease his critics, he said he would transfer legislative power to an Interim National Assembly. He reinstated the right of habeas corpus with some restrictions, but it didn't apply to the rebel Muslims in the south.

The rebellion by the Muslims under the banner of the Moro National Liberation Front brought the Philippine Army to a standstill and with support pouring in from Middle Eastern Arab countries, the only way to stop the fighting was to grant a measure of autonomy. Marcos did this. Fifty thousand civilians were reported killed during the previous five years.

The following year 1978 Marcos held nation-wide elections for the legislature and his new society party won outright. No one believed the results were anything but fraudulent. However it helped boost his image with Ronald Reagan. In May, Walter Mondale visited Asia and encouraged Marcos to work for freedom and democracy.

Marcos inaugurated the new legislature in June and he was sworn in as the first Philippine premiere. Nothing was changing. The economy was in free fall and poverty was getting worse. Cardinal Jamie Sin spoke out against the continuation of Martial Law.

A critical and active Church was the one thing that he could not control. It infuriated him and Marcos hoped to persuade Pope John Paul II to visit the Philippines, it would be an endorsement of his regime. The Pope rebuffed him and said he would not visit a dictatorship. Marcos then tried to polish his international image and announced a "return to normalcy". With these grand announcements and presenting a false image of democracy to the world, Pope John Paul II was again invited and he agreed. Being the only Christian nation in Asia, the Pope, who had vowed to visit as many Catholic countries as possible, had to visit sometime. But it was fraught with danger that Marcos would use it to cover his bloody reputation as a violator of human rights.

I had kept up my journalism and photography over the years and was having articles and photographs published from time to time and offered to cover the visit for a church news agency and the Columban Fathers magazines.

In the mid 1970's the opposition to Martial Law was growing and it was being suppressed with a growing brutality. There was a culture of fear and silence. To speak critically was an invitation to be arrested, detained and questioned and held indefinitely. Many suspects, critics of the regime, disappeared and joined the ranks of the ten thousand or so human rights victims of the Marcos regime.

The Christian churches were beginning to respond to the growing list of violation of human rights. In 1974 – two years after the start of Martial Law – the Catholic Bishops Conference of the Philippines (CBCP) issued a strong appeal to Marcos to end it and return to democratic rule and Cardinal Sin also made an appeal on September 1. Marcos ignored them and cracked down all the harder against priests and church workers who were being labelled subversives and Communists and therefore subject to arrest and summary execution. On September 17, the Supreme Court, to its shame, now fully behind Marcos, issued a decision establishing the legality of Martial Law.

There was rebellion among the Muslims in the Southern Island of Mindanao and a representative of the Organisation of Islamic Conference (OIC) put forward a peace plan that proposed setting up an autonomous Islamic state. But no action was taken at that time. The growth of the Basic Christian Communities was a positive response to empower people who were otherwise divided, isolated, weak and afraid. The Christian communities, far flung in remote areas, were composed of small groups of believers united together in faith and committed to protecting and helping each other and tasking responsibility for all the social and liturgical activities of the community.

The traditional Eucharistic worship in the parishes was a source of unity and strength among the mostly Catholic population. It became more focused on the primary mission of the church to imitate the stand of Jesus Christ in affirming and standing for the rights and dignity of every human person. Sermons and parish programmes increasingly stressed the need for respect for human dignity and social justice.

Although not all the Bishops were as enthusiastic in their rejection of Martial Law and interpreted social action as

Communist infiltration of the church, it was insufficient to meet the urgent need for group solidarity protection that Christians under persecution needed, especially if they were scattered over mountainous areas where they could not come together for a common celebration. Faith had to be a personal commitment to each other. Many priests had raised their voice in opposition and in protest to the violation of human rights. Some were arrested, jailed and tortured. Some were killed and others forced to flee for their lives and escaped abroad or joined the growing community of rebels in the jungles and mountain strongholds.

The Basic Christian Communities also called Church Communities were growing stronger in the Island of Negros where my fellow Columban missionaries, Niall O'Brien from Dublin and Brian Gore from Australia, and my classmate Donald Hogan and others were already gathering together the scattered flocks to help them protect themselves from the marauding bands of "lost commands", these were groups of soldiers turned loose with a license to kill and terrorise the rural people so that they would be afraid to shelter the Communist rebels. The military high command called them "Lost Commands" and refused to take responsibility for what they did. They were supposed to be disbanded and arrested but, in fact, it was obvious they had lots of emunitions and access to weapons and supplies. They were terror troops turned loose to subdue the population. They were for hire too when rich business and plantation owners wanted areas cleared of tenants or poor communities or to put down a strike at a sugar mill. The church was then the only refuge and the priests were risking their lives by helping the poor in this way. They too were branded as Communist sympathisers, but it was the only way.

The Church in Negros led by Bishop Antonio Fortich took a stand to support the Basic Christian Communities and to provide legal aid through the Diocesan Social Action Centre. Every day bodies were found dumped like carrion beside the road. It was a reign of institutionalised terror that stifled all protest, fettered the judiciary, controlled the press and allowed the cronies of Marcos to grab more land and enrich themselves without protest and legal challenges. Lawyers, who worked for the poor in those days, were at incredible risk. Many were brutally murdered. The military labelled the Christian communities as subversive and a front organisation for the Communist rebels who were growing in numbers and gaining support among the poor.

In Olongapo it was dangerous to speak out even though the local government under Mayor Geronimo Lipumano was no avid supporter of Martial Law. He came to power when the Gordon family fell out of favour with Marcos due perhaps to their unwillingness to support him when he ran for re-election.

The military counter-intelligence was everywhere and when we were guarded in our public statements, I still did not know if they had a file on me because of my connections with Fr Joe Naku. Alex and I were invited to give workshops and seminars against the scourge of drug abuse. We did what we could to counter the feelings of hopelessness that pervaded the people by speaking about the need and right for emotional release therapy – on a personal level, of course, but fell short of suggesting openly that the theory and therapy was just as valid for the release of pent up feelings of social and political repression.

It was a dangerous ploy and could have been taken up as promoting revolution by an astute military undercover agent. We noticed the tension and anxiety in the audience when we pointed out the need to openly protest the repressed pain of injustice and violence. While we never advocated violence we did talk of the need for the internal and even external non-violent facing off with reality, the right to speak and express openly our feelings about the roots of injustice and pain and the emotional release that was necessary to relieve that pain and pressure.

Of course we couched it in the context of the psychological condition of the drug dependent. Friends who heard these presentations saw clearly the political implications and warned us to be careful. Others perhaps were just showing perplexity with our recommendations for therapeutic confrontation with the abusive authority figures of one's childhood and youth. Asian culture strives for consensus, conformity and harmony and eschews conflict and confrontation unless it is to redress a grave affront, a loss of face or personal dignity or is necessary to redress acts of shame brought on the family or clan honour. Confrontation and violence, even emotional and especially military conflict, was the solution of last resort.

Perhaps this is why Marxism seldom penetrated and was not totally absorbed by the Asian spirit. *It had to be imposed.* It is an alien ideology of the West developed in the shadowy corners of the British Museum, a Western imposition on an Asian culture. But traditional Asian values had been greatly distorted and abused. The admirable goals of achieving peace and harmony by giving fidelity to a wise and benign ruler had been manipulated to serve the imperial ambitions of a dictator and was reduced to inculcated submission, docility and a unquestioned obedience to the supreme authority of the emperor as in the case of China or Japan, dictator like Suharto in Indonesia or the tyrant Marcos and his wife Imelda in the Philippines. Also, when it did take hold the same human imperfections arose and the people did not get to the promised land of plenty but the party did. The leader, all too often, cultivated a personality cult and thus one tyrant from the right was replaced by another from the left.

Revolutionaries are not interested to reform the old, considered beyond salvation, but embrace an ideology that would sweep it away making way for the new. They too believed that a new patch on an old jacket does not work and that new wine needs new wine skins. This was the wind of desire for change that was sweeping through the underground movement in the Philippines. Marxism offered a way to replace the ruling and control system of Spanish and American colonial legacy and undo the injustice of historical oppression and excess. The greed, avarice and power hungry dictators could not see that they were digging the pit of their own eventual demise and burial. Yet would this ever happen in the Philippines? Both Christianity and Marxism offered an alternative to the tyrannical rule of the ruthless and brutal dictator. Christianity in its more open and liberal model based on the Gospel vision of the kingdom of justice and peace and peoples participation advocated a non-violent spiritual and social revolution that supported democracy. The traditional institutionalised model of Church did not practice democracy itself being a hierarchical system of government. Marxism offered a Godless ideology that promised an entirely new system for the Philippines based on it avowed programme of communal ownership of wealth, justice and socialism.

Marcos had to protect the bases and American personnel from guerrilla attacks to maintain US aid. That was the main prop for his cruel undemocratic one-man rule. The sailors were very vulnerable to armed attack when visiting the bars, clubs and cheap hotels, but were rarely attacked. The bases were a source of arms and equipment for the rebels who had small detachments deep in the rain forest on the south side in Bataan province. They did not mount attacks on the Americans so as not to invite a crackdown and cut off the supply of goods and ammunition they could pilfer from the base with the help of their members and sympathisers.

In 1976, inspired by what was developing in Negros, we began to organise small Christian groups in the slums and villages around Olongapo to help them empower themselves though prayer and spiritual reflection on their dignity. With self-confidence and organisation they could improve their living conditions through self-help livelihood projects. We got the help of community organisers from a group named ACES brought together by Alice and Denis Murphy, a married couple who were unswervingly dedicated to the poor. Denis was a former Jesuit priest who discovered he was more effective in serving the church of the poor as a married layperson than as ordained priest shackled by the chains of a traditional authoritarian and church system increasingly isolated from the poor.

The small communities we wanted to help were in the garbage dump area called *Pag-asa*, which means hope but there was hardly any. As one wry old scavenger who lived there all his life told me, "The only hope is that of finding something among the garbage that we can eat or sell." We helped the communities on the bank of the Santa Rita River organise themselves and at the Lighthouse area called in Spanish *Parola*. Here the poorest of the poor were living on the edge of starvation. In the Lighthouse, on the edge of Subic Bay area just below the hillside cemetery, we began Bible reflection groups to help the people feel that they were not outcasts but that God was with them and calling them to work together and change their lives. Together they formed a community organisation and drew-up a plan to have a fishing boat that could be shared on a rotation basis. The poor did not have their own fishing boats or nets but they rented them at a very high cost from the wealthy boat owners further up the river.

Ten families could have a decent livelihood with one large boat. With the help of Fr Michael Duffy, who was the Columban social action director of the diocese and very supportive and committed to the formation of the communities, we got a small grant and bought a boat and nets. I remember an excited boisterous group of village folk set off early one morning for Manila to buy the nets and other gear. I was driving them there in the pickup. In Binondo, the old Chinese quarter of Manila, the women did the bargaining, going from one supplier to another until they got the best deal. They bought nets, lamps, floats and hooks and rolls of fishing nylon. It was a four-hour drive back over potted roads and driving rains storms. It was one of the hardest trips I ever made. But the villagers were elated that at last they had the means to work for themselves.

Working together on the boat project helped foster cohesion among the families that had been previously racked by petty jealousies and feuds over trivialities. The spats of community anger that sometimes flared into fights was aggravated by low self-esteem caused by poverty and the unconcern of government. In the eyes of the elite and the military, the poor were pests, they were sub-human who had nothing to contribute to economic growth and had nothing that could be exploited. They too had come to see themselves as of little value. This attitude of resignation was called *Bahala Na* ("Let God Decide"), it seemed to say, "There is nothing we can do to change our lot in life." Now they had something to work for and protect that was theirs to share. They worked out a sharing system so that different families could use the boat on different days and nights. They arranged to share the catch as well. It was a lovely day when the project was initiated. We all gathered on the beach and celebrated mass surrounded by the families and we all prayed for big catches.

At that time Fr Colm McKeating, a Columban colleague, had begun a mission in Cabalan on the southern outskirts of Olongapo. He lived in a small bamboo hut in solidarity with the people and brought them together into three communities, helping them to organise themselves through prayer reflection and action. Traditionally a Catholic's religious duties were fulfilled by attending the Sunday Mass with minimum participation in the sacraments; Baptism and First Communion for the children, then Baptism and the Last Rites for adults. This new model of the Church as a living community where neighbours organised themselves, met, planned and worked together to help and protect each other was a new energizing experience for the people. They felt that they really were "Church" or God's people coming together to implement the gospel values and bring about the kingdom in the here and now. The authority was shared and passing to the community and there was less responsibility for the priest to control and direct everything. As a result there were self-initiated community projects helping youths, unmarried mothers and other needy people.

As missionaries we felt we were doing something long-lasting, useful and meaningful. Unfortunately, Fr Colm's superior did not support the Basic Christian Community model of Church – thinking it was closer to Communism than to Christ. Colm was pulled out and reassigned. The lack of affirmation and support for this pioneering work was a great disappointment to him and left an emotional scar that seemed never to heal. Several of his community leaders were later arrested and imprisoned. Any kind of organising had become increasingly risky. I visited them in the prison at the nearby military camp Cabal to be sure they were safe from the death squad and well treated. There was no replacement for Colm so I decided to continue to visit the growing communities, join their meetings and celebrate the mass in two main centres every Sunday for the following two years. It was an important beginning…

The project for migrant handicraft workers was still thriving and providing a small but steady income to help support the young people at PREDA Bukang Liwayway Centre. We were living a very simple life and were basically self-supporting. We brought in more skilled craftsmen to teach the young people furniture-weaving as a livelihood and had many fine pieces of wicker furniture and baskets for sale. Many were unemployed since the ending of the Vietnam

War in 1974 and the lessening of activity at the Subic Naval Base. Our small training and manufacturing project employed about twenty at this time. Our friends and supporters at the Naval Base were happy to recommend to their friends and neighbours to buy the products. These skilled workers came from the surrounding provinces. They were superb in making rattan-buri chairs, tables and the ornate high fan-backed chair known as a "peacock" chair. The bookshelves with a rounded tops was an elegant and very useful item. We also had a customer in London who imported and sold the furniture for shop window display. Years later, when I passed through Heathrow airport, I was amazed and delighted to see them there showcasing a display of quality soaps and bathroom products. A few years later, many of these workers were to find their way back to the provinces and with help from PREDA set up their own weaving and manufacturing projects in their homes to supplement their rice and vegetable farming. From 1975 we were already participating in the Fair Trade movement that was setting the criteria for good sustainable trading practices.

This project also helped a few of the impoverished families living in makeshift shacks scattered on the barren hillsides surrounding Olongapo. The hills had long since been logged out when the area was released from the control of the US Navy and turned over to local government. The powerful political families then set about exploiting and denuding the rain forest and feuding among themselves over the choice concessions.

Medical care was poor and most women could not afford to go to hospital to give birth but delivered in the shack or shanty where they lived with the help of the village mid-wife. One night in July 1976 a young man dressed in shorts and a t-shirt came hurrying over the hill to ask help. His wife was giving birth on the isolated hillside and was bleeding profusely. She would die shortly from a loss of blood. Immediately, Rolly and some of the residents went to see if they could carry her down the mountain trail in a blanket. There was great excitement the previous week when we had a phone installed, but it had no dial. An operator was supposed to answer when one lifted the receiver but rarely did.

Desperate, I decided to try it. I prayed fervently before lifting the receiver and I was amazed when a voice answered at once – it worked! I could hardly believe it when I was instantly put through to the fire department. More amazingly they said they would send an ambulance. Twenty minutes later, a rescue crew arrived at PREDA and we led the paramedics to the hillside where they met the party of residents carrying the bleeding woman over the difficult terrain and brought her to the hospital. Both she and the baby survived, and I went to Saint Joseph's weeks later and together we baptised him, he was named Francis.

During this time, June 1978, the Basic Christian communities were continuing to spread and leaders were being arrested and detained as subversive organisers. Thirty members of the nearby Half-Moon Beach community wrote to the Mayor informing him of the regular Bible and community meetings and asked him for protection from the local district leader who was accusing them of being Communist rebel supporters. In fact, he was resentful that the community had organised themselves outside of his civil authority and control. Everywhere there was opposition to any community organising activity, especially when it was directed towards helping the poor. I was increasingly worried that the military would soon pay us a visit.

Fr Dermot McCarthy and an Irish RTE documentary team arrived in 1976 to make a report on the situation. They stayed at the centre and followed me about visiting the basic communities, helping the residents in the therapy room and the operation of the craft making. It was broadcast in Ireland and the response from viewers was remarkable. I realised that international support would be increasingly important in the future and the mass media was the way to raise public awareness and action abroad in opposition to the Marcos regime. That video, "Pain is the Price", became a valuable educational tool for us. So I decided to write more on the Philippine situation and began travelling about the Philippines visiting other Columban missions, taking photographs and writing stories. When visiting the development projects of Columbans in Dimataling, Mindanao Southern Philippines, I experienced a mixed community of Muslims and Christian and saw firsthand the overpowering difficulties faced by missionaries. I stayed with Australian Warren Ford who had a fantastic rapport with the Muslim community leaders and my hair stood on end as he recounted in an offhand way the dangers that lurked in the surrounding hills and forests. Marauding bands of Muslim fighters opposing the government attacked Christian settlers believing that they were from the "government side" and that the Christians were encroaching on their ancestral lands. As if to confirm his account that night the silence was punctured with the distant crack of gunfire. In some areas big land grabbers were taking over large areas of Muslim lands and were logging out these areas considered sacred by the Muslims. The environmental destruction was continuing with the connivance of Marcos and his cronies.

As a result in 1979 there was continuous violence between the Philippine military and the Muslim rebels. It was a troubling experience but the patience and commitment of the people and the Columbans in Mindanao to bring peace and understanding was inspiring. My classmate Michael Rufus Haley was based in the city of Marawi, a few hours drive into the mountains. Here there were armoured personnel carriers patrolling the streets. I saw too the extent of the rural poverty that was spreading under the rule of Marcos.

That year I also visited Negros Island in the central Philippines where the Columbans had being working since the 1950s. My friends Brian Gore, Niall O'Brien, Donal Hogan, Mickey Martin and many others were building up Christian communities in the remote parishes near Kabankalan, south of the provincial capital Bacolod. Niall O'Brien, from Blackrock in Dublin, was in the parish of Dakong-Kogan where the progressive and socially aware Bishop Antonio Fortich had erected a sugar mill to provide the small farmers a cost effective alternative to the mills owned by the wealthy elite who exploited the subsistence farmers and shamelessly exploited the factory workers who toiled for a pittance under harsh unbending conditions. The support of the church and the Columbans in helping the workers form a union earned them the ire of the powerful planters and the military. Here Catholic Christianity in action was what Jesus Christ would surely have approved. The unity and solidarity of the people and the risks taken by the lay leaders and the priests under the combat boot of oppression was remarkable. It was a community and a movement that anyone with a love of justice would want to belong to.

These communities were the result of restructuring and reorganising the traditional sprawling parish into smaller communities that had their own elected leaders and were self-managing. The leaders willingly and joyfully took full responsibility for the running of their own Christian community that was based on the Gospel values of community self-help and an unshakable commitment to justice and non-violence in the face of oppression and military harassment.

Many of the people were displaced tenant farmers or poor settlers who were run off their holdings by land-grabbing sugar planters backed by military force. They were exploiting their close ties with Marcos and were expanding their huge estates to cash in on the soaring price of sugar on the world market. Not content with taking the lowlands, they were now moving into the hills to grab even more. Greed has no bounds it seems.

Brian, Niall, John Brazil, and those risking themselves for their beliefs were an inspiration to all of us at PREDA. The faith of these pioneers was infectious. Their belief in the righteousness of their cause to defend and protect the dignity of the poorest and the weakness united people and empowered them to stand up for each other. There were rallies, marches and demonstrations protesting against torture, murder and oppression. The poor would hike across mountains and swamps, through valleys and rivers to support and help each other. All this had a profound influence on me and strengthened my own faith and in many ways guided my own social and spiritual awareness shared by the team at PREDA.

I heard that Brian and his community leaders were going to mobilise the entire population of the communities in response to a brutal killing carried out by a fanatical group called the Salvatores. I went back to Negros and on to Kabankalan and to the village of Orignao where Brian lived. I was riding on the roof of an overcrowded mini-bus with tussed up chickens and squealing pigs, fluttering among the crates and boxes and jostled side to side with the travellers on the roof. More people were perched on the rear bumper while others were hanging on to the sides, a common way to travel in the remote rural Philippines. We were bumping along the unpaved road between fields of tall sugar cane, across the rickety bridge and up the winding mountainous road to the village.

I was too late. The mobilisation had begun early that morning and thousands had trudged into the mountain lair of the fanatics to confront them and bury the community leader Lolito who had been murdered. I followed and set off alone along the unpaved logging road into the mountains. For an hour I hiked and climbed through the silent and eerie mountain passes. Here and there along the way I witnessed the incredible poverty of families living on the edges of what remained of the once lush forests. An hour later I heard singing ahead of me and then saw the huge crowd on their way back. They were in high spirits, brimming with confidence and a sense of unity was overpowering. I was swept along by their spirit. Brian was surrounded by the community leaders and welcomed me and told me of the success they were having in taming the ruthless Salvatores through the sheer moral power of a united community protecting their human rights. Their fear of these ruthless killers had dissipated as their numbers swelled. They had the courage to confront the leader in his own lair and demanded an end to the killings. He had capitulated and promised to change and stop the attacks on the members of the community. It was a remarkable non-violent approach. Others would have organised a retaliatory revenge seeking armed force to deal with them.

In the months and years ahead these communities of Brian and Niall would continue to grow stronger and more united and their huge numbers were so influential they brought many of the Salvatores killers to justice, halted some land grabbing in the area, stopped gambling and other social vices. In the absence of effective and incorrupt government the people had taken the initiative and the authority to themselves. It was this new reality of power to the people, a sense of dignity and non-submissive attitude that was flowing through the people and compelling them to take ownership of their own lives and a responsibility for the welfare of the community that angered the ruling elite. They had always controlled the lives of the people and now their sphere of influence and patronage was not only questioned but had been bypassed. People power had emerged in Negros, it confronted the social evils and demanded change. The authorities were not cooperative and soon retaliated.

It happened in March 1980 in the town of Kabankalan. It was one of the most significant and dramatic turning points in this part of Negros and was to have national and international repercussions. A huge protest was organised by the

Christian communities to protest the corruption of the local Mayor and the growing harshness of the military who were raiding isolated farm houses, looting and killing the tenant farmers and driving them off their plots. An estimated ten thousand people flooded the town, filled the plaza and spilled down the main road and into the side streets. Huge banners, flags and placards with messages in bright colours extolling social justice, Christian solidarity and demanding an end to abuse were everywhere.

Nothing had ever been seen like it before. Judging by their later action the Mayor and the military commander were awe-struck and frightened at the massive turn out and the fearless openness of those protesting and demanding justice. One after another the families of victims of physical abuse and murder took the microphone and spoke out defiantly and courageously, some in tears, others in anger. Fr Brian and Michael Martin also addressed the rally. A massive downpour brought the gathering to an early close and the Mayor believed that the rally was personally directed against him and his administration because there was no time to denounce the most important matter – the military abuses.

There were to be repercussions, a few days after Easter two leaders of the Christian communities in Brian's parish disappeared, Alex Garsales and Herman Muleta. Tension spread through the communities, instead of less oppression they were getting more.

Then a few weeks later seven more farmers mysteriously disappeared. There was suspicion that the Mayor of Kabankalan was involved. The wives of the disappeared appealed to Bishop Fortich for help and he demanded an investigation by the police. The bodies were dug up in the field close to the house of the Mayor. The hands were tied behind them and they had been shot, execution style. As a result, Mayor Sola was charged and brought to trial for the murder of the seven farmers.

In Olongapo 1980, our own efforts to bring the people

together was progressing slowly. The community organisers were training local leaders in Pag-asa where the people were living in the filth and dirt of the garbage dump. The children had running sores from malnutrition, infections from cuts from broken glass and sharp rusty nails. They were living off the trashed food and what they earned from selling the bits of wire, cardboard, bottles and tin cans they collected. One family living in a hovel made a living collecting and selling bones. This community was threatened with imminent demolition by the newly elected Mayor as were other communities where we helped the residents organise themselves. These groups began to demand basic rights from the city government like clean water connections. It was an uphill struggle and one day they marched down the main nightclubs area known as Magsaysay Drive to city hall. They were blocked along the way by police barricades but it was embarrassing to the city government which was sensitive to the image that the city projected to the US Navy personnel, no doubt to help them curry favour and get donations for the city projects. The march of the beggars and scavengers angered the new government administration and the residents were interrogated by the police about their leaders.

In the Lighthouse community close to Gordon Park, the people were trying to get the rights to the land they had settled on overlooking the US Naval Base just across the river estuary. But they had been blocked in their efforts by the city administration which was now more oppressive and unyielding. They had a good project going with the communal fishing boat and were now improving their homes using cinder block. They had been ordered to leave the place for no apparent reason. There were seventy families there and several had built small two-roomed houses. They too were clinging to life by fishing in Subic Bay and since organising themselves they had pressured the former city administration into making a water connection. We shared Bible and prayer sessions with the people. Our efforts had not gone unnoticed and the people were telling us of strangers hanging about when we had our meetings and even when we celebrated the Eucharist together. We felt we were under suspicion by Mayor Gordon

A young staff trainee, Conrado Villarez, came rushing into the centre one morning during that hot draught plagued June of 1980. He breathlessly announced that a bloodied body had been found along the roadside near our driveway. We hurried down to learn who it could be but the personnel of the Fernandez Funeral Home had removed the body. It was another unknown victim of the death squad, a shadowy group of armed men that had recently appeared picking up suspects, many of them young men. Some disappeared, others were found mutilated and dead. A reign of fear descended on the city. This was a new cruel face of Martial Law. Until then there was little evidence of the heavy hand of the Marcos regime in the city. Perhaps out of deference to the sensibilities of the American personnel at the US Navy Base the killing squads had spared the population. Perhaps the former city administration had been reluctant to allow it. But now there was a so-called crackdown on crime.

Later we held a meeting to discuss if dumping the body so close to the centre was some kind of warning to us from the authorities. In the following months many more mutilated bodies of young people were found dumped by the roadside or thrown over the cliff along the national highway. Mayor Gordon denied knowing anything about it and said that it was the result of gang warfare.

The following July we woke up to the roaring of a bulldozer and a back-hoe digging away at the bottom of our driveway making a huge excavation to the side of our driveway. We rushed down to learn that Mrs Amelia Gordon, mother of Richard, the new Mayor, had ordered the city engineer to prepare a grave site where a tomb and grotto was to be constructed right on the edge of our driveway. A young man, a godchild of the Gordon family, was killed by a snatcher in Manila and was to be buried there. However much we respected the dead and were sympathetic with the family of the boy, our driveway was not the most appropriate place to build a tomb.

I went to Mrs Gordon to discuss it but she would not talk to me. There was nothing we could do, her aides explained. They claimed rights over all property in the city. Our property line was in dispute so we had no cause to complain, they said. Later, because of our objections to the site of the tomb, I was accused with "throwing bodies from the cemetery onto the National Highway". This ridiculous allegation was to be repeated for years afterwards.

A few months later the son of a congressman, a friend of the Mayor, got a permit to hold a fashion show at the Marmont Hotel in Barrio Barretto, a nearby community. In order to get a permit he presented the show as a charity event with PREDA to be the so-called beneficiary. We were never informed about this and it turned out to be a nude show, nothing unusual in Olongapo where it was a common form of entertainment in the many bars and clubs that thrived on this dehumanising parade of young girls as a prelude to prostitution. To our amazement we were accused of conducting a lewd show and that was to be the basis of having our operating license as a rehabilitation revoked. Now we felt that we were being specifically targeted. I had to take a court action against the organiser to clear our name from this frame up. It never made it to court as our complaint was dismissed out of hand without even a preliminary hearing. But we made our point and that was to be important in the years to come.

Chapter Ten

The big event at PREDA in January 1981 was the wedding of our two co-founders and staffers, Merly Ramirez and Alex Corpus Hermoso. They had been working together at PREDA since 1974 and decided that they wanted to be together forever. I officiated the wedding ceremony at a beautiful simple resort on January 6, the Feast of the Three Kings. The green lawns spread beneath the coconut palms like a carpet, a cool breeze swept up from the sea, the sun lit the scene in its brilliance. There, under the coconut trees with all the families gathered around, we celebrated the wedding mass. After we retired to the clubhouse for celebrations. It was a blessed relationship that established a happy family of three children all named after Christ: Christine Rosa, Christopher Seamus, and Chrisanta.

The following month, I set out with camera and notebook to cover the papal visit of Pope John Paul II and write-up the visit for the Columban Mission magazines and UCAN, the Church news agency based in Hong Kong. I got a press pass and moved around with the Pope's press entourage when he visited the slums of Tondo, Baguio and Negros Island.

It was a magnificent and privileged experience to be so close to Pope John Paul; day after day, standing only metres from him, taking photographs and making notes. I made my own way to the site early knowing the way. I was deeply impressed with his simplicity and contentment to stand around without the usual extravagant pomp and ceremony that one sees on television lavished on the Pope in the Vatican, which I am sure that he disliked. In Tondo, an impoverished area of Manila near the docks there was a snafu the day he was to make an important speech on poverty and social issues. The Pope arrived without his usual entourage of media and police escort who got delayed. I thought that Marcos was trying to separate the media so that they would miss the important speech that some expected to be critical of the Martial Law regime. Pope John Paul was led up to a simple outdoor platform alone and only the barriers held back the crowds of impoverished slum dwellers. He was very much his non-ceremonial self, blessing and smiling at the crowd while the officials were running about looking for the master of ceremonies, then they arrived and the event begun.

It was a comic tragedy to see Marcos and his wife Imelda trying to grab the limelight to be seen with him whenever possible as to give the impression to the world that their regime was blessed and approved by the Pope. In fact, it was very much the opposite. There was to be no public appearances together save one. But the Bishops saw to it that it was a pastoral visit. Marcos was bitterly disappointed. Pope John Paul made a point of criticising the harsh regime and he highlighted the suffering of the people.

Nowhere else was this so clear or caused so much tension and anger between the local elite and the church than in Negros. The great outdoor mass and gathering of all the communities and parishioners was to be at a vast open space near the sea called the *Reclamation Area.* A huge stage was erected and sections marked off for the people.

They travelled from the furthest and remotest mountains to be there at enormous personal and material sacrifice. They were expecting something from the Pope, a word of encouragement, a sign that their resistance to oppression was legitimate and approved. Two media platforms were erected facing the stage and that is where I made my way early that bright sunny February morning. I was chatting with the local and foreign journalists bracing ourselves for the onslaught of the tropical sun as it climbed higher wondering if the Pope would arrive on time. A plane had flown overhead and landed.

The waiting crowds stirred and a loud murmur of excitement rose up as a limousine with escorts drove up the centre of the waiting multitudes and out stepped Imelda Marcos. We were amazed and disgusted at this brazen gate-crashing. She went up to the empty stage where a few workers were still preparing the altar and she took the microphone and launched into a harangue that was a kind of justification for Martial Law. She was countering a front page story in *Newsweek* that coincided with the visit of the Pope to Negros and called it, quoting Bishop Fortich, a "Social Volcano", and an "Island of Fear". There was nothing Marcos could do to cover up the shame that this social essay on the oppression of the poor brought to his regime. The story highlighted the murders of the Christian community leaders, Alex Garsales and Herman Muleta, and the discovery of the mutilated bodies and the bodies of the seven farmers buried in the fields of Mayor Sola of Kabankalan was in everybody's minds. The Mayor was on trial at this time for the murders of the farmers. All had been hog-tied and brutally murdered, some had been buried alive on the Mayor's farm.

It was a tension-filled morning after Imelda Marcos swept imperiously away after delivering her broadside against the *Newsweek* article. There was silence when she came, silence throughout and a vast silence as she left. It must have pained her much, accustomed as she was to the tumultuous cheering of the rented crowd that greeted her every appearance elsewhere. Silence had spoken so eloquently.

When the Pope did arrive that silence turned to joyous cheering. The long overnight journey, the fitful sleep on the ground, the early awaking and simple handful of fish and rice in the blistering sun was all forgotten in the elation and excitement. The fact that a Pope would come to such a remote island was for them a stupendous honour. The people had been well prepared on the significance of the visit. The diocese had held many seminars in all the parishes.

His coming gave prominence and importance to the changes that were occurring in the Church both the institutional and the church of the poor in the Philippines, its steadfast commitment to social justice, the value and worth of the poor, his presence affirmed their dignity and assured them and informed the world that demanding human rights, struggling for justice was right and moral and not subversive or illegal as the authorities charged.

They were not disappointed. The Pope stood firmly at the microphone and gave a stirring endorsement of the people's quest for justice and peace. My heart leapt with excitement when I heard his words. The moment the translation died away there was a huge cry of elation and cheering.

"The Church will not hesitate to take up the cause of the poor. She will be the voice of those who are not heard, not only when they demand charity, but when they ask for Justice," he said. They were at the heart of the strongest speech he gave in the whole of the Philippines and he had saved it for the right time and place.

During the offertory of the Papal Mass when gifts are presented, the widows of slain church leaders Herman and Alex brought, their laminated photographs to the Pope, he kissed them, it was a moment of extraordinary solidarity with these poorest of the poor, an endorsement of their struggle and encouraged the institutional church to stand with them. The wisdom and foresight of Bishop Fortich and the clergy of Negros were already far ahead in that commitment.

Marcos was furious with the way the visit had gone, instead of being a sign of approval of his regime it was a condemnation. The local elite were infuriated too. They had donated a lot of money to the preparation committee on which some of them and their wives had insisted of being a part, thinking it would give them a privileged place on the stage and be seen getting a special blessing from the Pope. But there was none, just a call for them to repent and do justice. From that day on, they had their knives out for the Bishop Antonio Fortich, the active priests and lay leaders and the organised Christian communities. Fathers Brian Gore, Niall O'Brien and Itik Dangan were on the top of their hit list. I left Negros with a powerful impression of the good and inspiration that John Paul's visit had planted among the poor.

Back at PREDA the typhoons were severe and they were something to behold as the might of nature hurtled itself against our flimsy metal Quonset building rattling and shaking every sheet of galvanized iron sheeting and bursting in the windows. We all gathered in the most sheltered place in the house, the corridor, and sat out the night with lighted candles. The power lines were down and the angry howling winds shrieked and moaned, rose and fell and then threw itself against us as if trying to throw us off the hillside. When it had passed the following day branches of trees and shredded foliage were scattered everywhere. We had several small landslides and soon after we had to spend every bit of extra money building the retaining walls. We could not afford to buy stones for the retaining wall so we arranged with a local contractor to borrow a truck for one trip to the riverbed every morning. We arose at 5:30, had breakfast of rice and fish and headed towards the river as soon as the raging waters had receded and the stones were exposed. The dump truck was waiting along the way and we went to the river. Then the twenty residents and myself began the picking of the boulders from the river bed and passing them hand to hand along the line until they were loaded over the side in the truck. An old oil drum served as a platform for us to reach the top of the dump truck. Then back to the centre for the rest of the day's activities.

Fr Eamon O'Brien was organising and managing a very successful three months workshop on justice and peace. It was to be held in Ireland that year and I was scheduled to attend. I left the Philippines on May 17. The three months was a renewal of faith and commitment. PREDA had been operating for five years and the workshop was a very useful time to think about the future and plan how the work could expand and be more effective.

When I was in Ireland, financial disaster struck at PREDA. To give some security and continuity to the work we had been slowly building up a trust fund from earnings from the sale of handicrafts. We invested this with a finance company, Commercial Credit Corporation (CCC), partially supporting the community at PREDA on the monthly interest. But the market collapsed with the weakening of the peso, the continual flood of wealth abroad and the embezzlement of many millions of pesos by a businessman named Dewey Dee who fled to Canada leaving banks and finance companies floundering with non-collectable loans.

I was in Ireland at the time and Merly tried to pre-terminate the deposit and withdraw it. She called me and I called the CCC. Between us we were able to get back a portion of the trust fund. It was enough to keep us afloat but life became more difficult. I felt helpless so far away but we had done all we could at the time. Before returning to the Philippines, I decided to use the super bargain round-the-world air ticket that the seminar organizers had purchased in Manila as part of the visit to Ireland for the justice and peace seminar. So on September 24, 1981, I set off on another overland adventure: this time to Central and South America.

After visiting my relatives in Canada I flew to Mexico City to visit the historical sites and from there set off by bus to Honduras. I hitch-hiked into the mountains to the border with El Salvador to visit the refugee camps. Guided by the staff of the Catholic charity Caritas who were protecting the refugees I heard first hand the harrowing accounts of brutality and savagery of that terrible struggle wherein no one who opposed the US-supported government was spared. The accounts of the refugees were horrific. Death squads were abducting, torturing and killing thousands of suspects every year, even the priests, sisters and Archbishop Romero were not spared. In a most brutal assassination he was shot to death while he was distributing communion during mass.

I crossed into Nicaragua. The Sandanistas had come to power just two years previously and were in the stages of trying to piece together the country after the ravages of civil war. The bus was fumigated at the border in their campaign to eradicate dengue fever and malaria.

They were facing a threatened blockade by the US and feared a possible invasion. Young people carrying sticks were drilling on the school grounds. The street corners of Managua had small plaques in commemoration of the young Sandanista freedom fighters who had fought Somoza's hardened troops in hand to hand combat and died heroic deaths. I felt sad and teary-eyed reading the names and ages of the teenagers who had given their lives to get rid of the Somoza the tyrant. It was no doubt one of the bravest struggles for liberation the century had seen.

I saw the devastation that was still unrepaired after the 1972 earthquake that had destroyed most of the city and learned how the Somoza regime had stolen most of the relief and rehabilitation funds that had poured in from around the world. It was this unrestrained corruption and plunder that ignited the spirit of revolt among the people. The old cathedral was an empty shell, surrounded by a landscape of overgrown empty lots where the hulks of Somoza's tanks were rusting in the tropical sun. A huge portrait of Sandinesta hung from the smoke blackened walls. The national treasury had been looted by Somoza before he fled and the nation was totally bankrupt.

I travelled about the country and met church lay workers, priests and sisters and they were unashamedly supportive of the revolution. There was excellent cooperation between the Sandanista government and the progressive church people in nation-building. There was little evidence of the atheistic Communism that I was told to expect. However the effort of building a just society was to be stymied by the rise of the US backed Contras and the nation was to be plunged once again into civil war. The comparison with the Philippines wasn't far from my mind if ever Marcos was to be toppled from power.

I went on to Panama, Ecuador and Peru. I stayed with the Columbans in Lima and saw their magnificent work with the poor and the homeless who had created "townships" for themselves by invading vacant lots on the city outskirts. In a single night, on a given signal thousands of slum dwellers would "invade" a vacant area and start to build a new town, neatly laid out and providing their own organisation, community discipline and development.

Fr Peter Hughes was the superior of the Columbans in Peru and he encouraged me to travel to the central highlands of the country. He gifted me with a plane ticket and so I went to Alto Plan and visited the historical Inca sites and witnessed the beginning of the fanatical movement of the "Shining Path" guerrillas. They were without compassion, dealt in cocaine and were a murderous movement, very different from the Sandanistas. The church was opposed to them and grenades were thrown at the bishop's house. I stayed with the Maryknoll Fathers there and they gave me a great welcome and a good background briefing about the dangerous situation. It was a great visit. I hiked in the hillside and saw the magnificent Inca towns and fortifications, every stone cut and fitted to perfection. I returned to the Philippines on Christmas Day 1982, my mind and heart still swirling from the experience of what I saw and felt in that unstable region.

On my return to PREDA, the financial crises was my first priority. The Commercial Credit Corporation had been taken over by Realty Finance headed by a rich tycoon named Leo B. Alejandro. His close contacts with the Marcos regime had secured him a sixty million pesos bail out by the Central Bank. The other reason he got this was because the Philippine Armed Forces Veterans Bank had a huge exposure with the CCC and the generals wanted to recoup their pension funds. They perhaps arranged the soft loan and got some seats on the board to be sure to recoup their money from the resurrected corporation now called the General Credit Corporation (GCC). A most appropriate name considering who controlled the board of directors.

They demanded the creditors agree to a write-off of fifteen percent of their deposit, forgo all interest payments past and future and accept a partial payment of the deposit after two years subject to the availability of funds and the decision of the board. This was gobbledygook to me, a devious way of saying that we would get nothing. I refused to sign the agreement and held that the company should pay back the principal with interest when it was financially sound. It was a dangerous position to take considering that the *Game of the Generals* was always one sided. We didn't have a chance.

The next phase of our existence began one day in June 1982.

Chapter Eleven

On June 5, 1982 the mother of Jenny, a nine-years-old Filipino-American child, went to St. Joseph's Community Centre to get help for her daughter who was showing signs of genital infection. The mother and child were referred to the Pope John XXIII Clinic, a church run clinic for the poor. The nine-years-old was found to have herpes, an incurable form of venereal disease.

Three days later, another child, fourteen-years old Annabel, was brought to the clinic with gonorrhoea. The girl told social workers that there were eighteen in their group and all had some form of venereal disease that was common among the prostituted women of the commercial sex industry, such as gonorrhoea, syphilis and herpes. Immediately the social workers began to look for the other children identified by Jenny and Annabel. We found twelve and brought them to the clinic, they were all infected. None of them were older than sixteen.

By June 16, Sr Maria – unable to treat so many children and knowing that serious crimes had been committed – reported the discovery to Mayor Gordon and to the City Social Hygiene Clinic funded by the US Navy. When the City Health Officer, Dr. Generoso Espinosa, confirmed the condition of the children, Gordon promptly ordered that they be locked away in a small room in the TB section of the ramshackle general hospital. They were warned not to talk about what had happened.

Dr Lydia Viray Zarbo, head of the Social Hygiene Clinic, gave them injections and had their lacerations and sores treated. There was a news blackout and the church social workers and Sr Maria were ordered to remain silent.

On July 11, 1982, Sr Maria came to the PREDA Centre and told me in a frightened voice what the city officials warned her to remain silent about. I decided to visit the children in the hospital. Unannounced, I went there the next day with Alex. It was three weeks since the children had been put into the hospital room. The city authorities didn't know what to do with them other than to keep the story under wraps. We found the room in the TB section and only seven children. Five had earlier pried open the window louvers and escaped.

The room was reeking with the smell of the long lingering sickness of half a century. It was dirty and threadbare, rumpled beds with old filthy blood stained navy mattresses were jammed together and the children were jumping up and down on them making a ruckus. They settled down to hungrily devour the cakes and drinks we had brought them.

The children were boisterous, excited. Visitors had not been allowed and we were surprised that there was no guard at the unlocked door. At that precise moment of our visit he had left for one reason or other. The kids were happy to have visitors to break their isolation. We introduced ourselves. Jenny was small, petite with long light hair. Her American father had long abandoned her. She was brushing her hair in a way that was mature beyond her years. Soon they were chattering on about all that had happened to them and pouring out their horrifying story. We recorded the accounts and they agreed to be photographed.

The prostituted children told us their story and said that they had told it all before to Gordon's investigators. They skipped school and frequented the streets most of the week begging from the sailors and went home about three times a week. *They were street children.* Pimps offered them money to go to the apartments and rented houses where US sailors had sex with them. None of the children being prostituted was older than sixteen. The pimps then gave them fifty pesos, about five dollars.

Three pimps were identified and named in the press. However, despite vows by Gordon to prosecute, nothing apparently was ever done to bring them to trial.

They told the investigators that they only knew one of their abusers – a fat man named "Doc". Jenny, the youngest, told us that she was bleeding after Dougherty had sex with her and she took his bowling shirt to stop the flow of blood when she left his rented house at Malagaya Hills on the outskirts of Olongapo. Crying in pain, she went to a friend's house until she stopped bleeding and then went home, according to social workers.

"Doc" turned out to be Daniel Dougherty, his name was on the laundry tag on the bowling shirt Jenny had taken with her. He was a US Navy Chief Petty Officer working in the electronics maintenance department of the US Naval Station. He was the only one of many paedophiles who was identified. We pieced together a horrific story of abuse and child prostitution on a scale that we had not imagined. It was education time for us.

We later discovered that Dougherty had been abusing children for several years and US Navy Investigators found pictures of nude children in his locker when he was living on the base. Later a military court marshal would hear evidence that his immediate officer knew that he was a paedophile but took no action. Another twelve-years-old, Anita, told authorities that Dougherty picked her up along the nightclub strip where they were selling chewing gum and took her to his place inside the base and abused her there.

Another child, Analiza, was brought by Doc to an area on the river bank near the bridge joining the city and base called Friendship Park across Lot 21. There, in public, he put her sitting on his lap, draped her dress over his knees and had sex with her while onlookers stared but did nothing.

The Dougherty case caused no social outcry, only a determined effort to sweep it under the carpet of ignorance and apathy. It was indicative of the overwhelming mental and social paralysis that then infected the population. The awe and fear of offending foreigners – the mental and emotional conditioning that brought many Filipinos in the areas surrounding the bases to treat them with deference4

and adopt a submissive and docile attitude towards them – had numbed the population to their own awareness of exploitation and loss of dignity and national pride. Attitudes successfully inculcated during the Spanish and American occupation and colonisation. So it was no great surprise that the sexual abuse of children by the foreign paedophiles was tolerated and ignored. There were few if any cases in the courts before 1995.

Many Filipinos were made to believe that everything in their lives depended on the Americans. Employment on the military bases and in American companies was the most treasured prize after that of getting a US visa. So many thousands of Filipinos have relatives in the US that immigration was the first option and any criticism of American policy would put an end to their hopes of joining them. Fear always muted any criticism.

One never knew when their son or any relative would be applying to join the US Navy, which was considered a "privilege", only allowed to Filipinos because of their perceived loyalty. The post war generation became so dependent on the US to rebuild the shattered economy and infrastructure that they allowed very unequal legislation to be enacted that gave exceptional economic rights to American citizens.

It was drilled into the children that the Americans, or the "Kano" as they were called, were not to be offended, confronted or obstructed in anyway. In fact they were seen as the source of the great and continual handout. Not only did children run after the sailors, begging for pesos, the national leadership was continually looking to the White House begging bowl in hand. It paid to give the foreigners what they wanted.

Dependency was inculcated, the elites were obsessed with the notion that if they pleased the tycoons of US business with legislation favourable to their interests they would get green cards and a share of the contracts. Philippine history is replete with examples of the political elites giving away the national heritage for their own personal gain. The most prized of all was US citizenship.

The concept of true patriotism, public accountability, transparency and honest governance is alien to many politicians. Those who have their integrity and conscience intact and operative stand out like a bright light on a dark night. With anything and everything from the US, Filipino self-image and sense of national pride was at an all time low during the American presence and it took the oppression of Marcos and his US backers to awaken a sense of nationalism and personal pride of the Filipino in his or her own identity.

Most Americans who lived in the Philippines for any length of time resented this very much. They found it difficult to break through to the real Filipino and relate on a genuine personal basis. They always felt that their relationships had ulterior motives and that the Filipino was always too eager to please, report only what the boss wanted to hear and bury deep inside resentment and anger. It was dangerous and unhealthy to show true thoughts or feelings. Besides if you had a business in Olongapo and critical of any person in authority, Filipino or American, you perished. A lesson that we were soon to learn.

Alex and myself left the hospital after interviewing the children and went back to PREDA shocked by what we had heard. Child prostitution was widespread, organised and had been going on for a long while. To learn that criminal gangs were supplying helpless Filipino children as young as nine-years-old to the US Navy personnel was astounding. A few years later we were to find out that children as young as four were being offered to sailors for sex too. Our visit to the hospital had been discovered and the news flashed to the office of Mayor Gordon. Damaged control measures were quickly underway.

That evening, July 12, Fr John Walsh, the parish priest at St Joseph's, came to see me. He had been urgently called over the phone by the secretary from Mayor Gordon's house on Gallagher Street, he said. Rear Admiral Richard Dunleavy, the base commander, came on the line and said that "they" wanted Fr John to get me to cooperate with them not giving him any details what it was about. Mystified, he came to see me right away.

I was surprised that the admiral and Mayor were working together to contain the unravelling scandal. They were both in danger of being accused of conspiring to obstruct justice. Both had much to lose. Gordon was creating a public image of a Mr Clean who was trying hard to play down the "Sin City" reputation, while allowing the sex industry to flourish by issuing permits and licenses to bars and clubs and at the same time creating the Mardi Gras festival, imitating the gaudy street carnivals of Rio complete with bikini-clad bar women, minors and gays.

The child prostitution scandal could swing the national mood against the bases. The review of the terms and conditions for continued unhampered access was scheduled for the following year.

The next day two Navy chaplains, a Catholic and Protestant, came to see me. There was a secret investigation into the alleged abuse and publicity was not welcome, they told me.

I felt the anger rising within me and I answered, "Investigation or not, I am not going to be part of any cover-up and you can tell that to the Admiral or I will tell him myself."

The chaplains left. Within an hour a Navy car arrived with a junior officer to arrange a meeting between Rear Admiral Dunleavy and myself.

I agreed and went alone. Later in the Naval Station conference room, the atmosphere was tense. Dunleavy and his staff officers dressed in white starched uniforms with gold braided shoulder boards sat around in silence, as if not knowing how to start. A civilian, Mr O'Reilly, from the Navy Investigative Office (NISRA) was there. I came to know him later as a professional investigator with a sceptical attitude to Navy officialdom and distaste for the Marcos dictatorship.

Dunleavy then came to the point abruptly. He said the Navy was trying to locate Dougherty who was in the US and any publicity would be detrimental to his arrest. I was surprised to learn that he left on July 6, three weeks after the children were first brought to the Social Hygiene Clinic. Presumably, he was flown out of the Philippines as soon as he was identified by the laundry tag.

"The Navy should have no difficulty in locating him and bringing him back for trial, one phone call should do it. How was he able to leave when he was a suspect in crimes against children?" I asked.

"It was a routine leave and reassignment," Dunleavy explained

"This is a serious case of organised child prostitution, there is nothing we can white-wash," I replied.

"There is no white-wash, it was routine. We are doing everything we can, we just don't want any publicity," he said.

"Well how long could it take you to pick him up. Four or five days should be enough time to bring him back."

Dunleavy was really annoyed. The other officers looked the same. Realising that I was not going to go along with their "no publicity" plan, Dunleavy said he had another appointment, stood up, and the officers who were standing snapped on their peaked caps and they all left in a huff.

A week later the story was published in the only independent Filipino newspaper that had survived the media takeover by Marcos. It was called *We Forum,* published by Jose Burgos, a gutsy oppositionist who had so far avoided prison and survived the media crackdown of Martial Law. He was later to have his presses confiscated after he published a story on the fake Marcos war medals.

The expose came out on the front page of its 1982 July 17-20 issue with photographs of the children, their eyes blocked out. *Prostitutes 9 to 14 hospitalised for VD,* the banner headline said. The story reported the child prostitution syndicate and alleged there was an attempted cover up. The story caused a sensation. I knew we were in for trouble when the story read:

City and base authorities have been trying to hide the story of the child prostitutes from the media. The government's reason is that expose of the crime would harm Olongapo which is being bandied about as a model city. Base officials on the other hand, said it would hamper investigation. The girls said they had been warned by Mayor Richard Gordon not to tell their experience to others. He also warned the social workers from talking to the media. The girls were told that if the vice-ring is exposed people will say children are not taken care of here and the Mayor will be affected.

Mayor Gordon was livid with anger. He went about brandishing the newspaper and telling various religious and civic groups on July 25 that I was irresponsible and ought to be deported for defaming the people of Olongapo. Mayor Gordon denied that there was any attempted cover-up. He made his position clear in an interview with a Sunday newspaper magazine, *Panorama*, the following week, the article stated:

"I never tried to cover up that story," said Gordon, face flushed, one could see his irritation with Cullen.... "The

admiral was concerned, I shared his view not to report it sensationally. We did not prevent Shay Cullen from writing the story but we asked him to hold its release until we catch this fellow or they'd be charged of letting the man go. And so because by that time he had not been captured, we wanted first and foremost to capture him."

Panorama: When the admiral told Gordon that Dougherty had left the country, had been out on leave during the investigation, did he (Gordon) ask for papers to show that the admiral was telling the truth?

Gordon : "I don't think I need to. I felt I had good rapport with the admiral enough. I've questioned him many times, but I don't think he's a liar. I was told that Dougherty had been there for two-and-a-half years, I suppose his duty was up and he was up for leave."

Dougherty was apprehended and brought to Guam, a US territory where he was to face a court martial. According to the Military Bases Agreement, jurisdiction fell to the US military and not the Philippines. This has always been a touchy issue in the Philippines. The bases' agreement always insisted that crimes against Filipinos by US personnel must be given over to the US military courts and not to the Philippine courts. Many believed this is an infringement of sovereignty, having sole jurisdiction over crimes against its citizens by foreigners being an indication of true independence and sovereignty.

In October 1982, the Military Bases Agreement was already in the news because it had been high on the agenda of the Marcos and Enrile visit to the US in September. Money was high on the agenda too. That eternal begging bowl was now waiting to be filled as Marcos accumulated his vast fortune. The US claimed that the US$500million was given for rent in return for "unhampered" use of the bases. Juan Ponce Enrile, the defence minister of Marcos, claimed that it was a payment, a consideration for the use of the bases. $50million was a grant, $200 million was for "security supporting assistance", presumably to keep the NPA rebels from disrupting US military operations. $500 million was foreign military sales credit, by which the Marcos regime could buy on credit all the weapons they needed to suppress the opposition. Marcos wanted this to be a direct payment. Not a loan, he wanted cash.

To increase that amount was uppermost in the mind of Marcos and his cronies. The "social cost of the bases", became a good reason as any to leverage more money from the US. The sexual abuse of women and children that we at PREDA were highlighting soon had supporters from an unexpected quarter – the national government itself, despite the fact that Gordon and Imelda Marcos were vehemently denying it. The renewal discussions were already underway.

That October of 1982, while the Dougherty case was being prepared in Guam, others were planning to get me and close the PREDA Centre. We had annoyed the authorities before. After the January 1980 local elections the newly elected Olongapo administration immediately began to look for ways of raising cash. The Mayor organised the Mardi Gras, a crude and paltry imitation of the famous carnival of Rio de Janeiro. It was crude in the extreme. Every bar and club was ordered to participate. The main street in the nightclub area was closed to traffic and a fee was charged to enter the carnival area. Even residents who lived there were forced to pay. The bars and clubs had to build platforms outside their clubs, vendors paid curb-side tolls and the bands played into the night. It attracted school kids, sailors and every undesirable sex tourist imaginable. The school kids were gyrating with US sailors on the streets and later in the clubs. It was like an introductory course for the youths to the commercial entertainment industry. They were being conditioned for life.

The gay community was dragooned into dressing in

sparkling and expensive costumes and parading down the street. Some protested at the cost and being forced to put themselves on public display during the opening parade. They were told that if they didn't like it then leave Olongapo.

Gays were not welcome in the Navy and any Caucasian seen in a gay bar was immediately tagged. Some of the cross-dressers made themselves into terrific looking women and some sailors fell for them under the influence of alcohol or drugs. When the moment of truth came they were infuriated and complaints reached the Mayor. No one could say who was responsible but gay people were mysteriously killed and mutilated. The gay community lived in fear along with everyone else.

I spoke out against the hedonistic festivities that were becoming a feature of city life and the brutal killings and the oppression of the gay community at some meetings and in church. The reaction was immediate. A very angry Mayor came on the phone demanding to know what did I think I was doing speaking against the economic development of the city? I proposed a meeting to talk over the moral and social impact the Mardi Gras had on the youth and families as promiscuity spread.

I refused an invitation to the Mayor's office or anywhere in the city because I would be surrounded by his ever-present heavily armed guards. I proposed we meet at the officers club inside the US Naval Base at 11:30 one morning. Gordon failed to show up. I waited in the lobby anyway. He arrived at 1:30 without the bodyguards who were not allowed to bring their guns on base. Gordon is a short stout man with round face and pouting lips, receding hairline and a slick smile that turned on and off like a light bulb as the occasion called for.

We sat alone in the empty restaurant. Nothing like dialogue, I thought. Gordon ordered a large chocolate sundae and he slurped with glee as he launched himself on a long-winded lecture about his great plans for the city and how he was going to change everything. I murmured how nice that would be if there were to be some factories and other forms of employment besides the bars.

"I am going to change the image of 'Sin City'," he said, adding that there would be no more talk of prostitution.

There was no dialogue, only monologue. When he had finished waving at the air around him, he stopped abruptly, as if somewhere an electric cord was pulled and his speaker went off. He starred at me across the table as if seeing me for the first time, and then told me to think about all he had said, abruptly got up and walked away.

It was now October 1982 and relations had not improved. A signed petition sent to the Columbans and to Bishop Henry Byrne from various Catholic church organisations, the local United Methodist Church and the Masons to have me removed from Olongapo appeared. I was an undesirable and must be banished.

The reasons given: *I abused the hospitality of the People of Olongapo!* As a journalist I had acted unethically and irresponsibly in exposing the prostitution of the children, I had allegedly accused the Mayor and the US Naval Base Commander of covering up the crimes against the children. "Fr Cullen should have been helping them (the children) in matters of faith, and virtue and spiritual guidance," the petition read. But worst of all I had failed to show priestly concern for the people of Olongapo, and I was a hindrance of the growth to the city.

Mayor Gordon took the position that the children were rape victims and not prostitutes as if this in some way changed the terrible reality. Dougherty was brought before a general Court Martial in Guam. The US Navy flew out the seven children to testify, but the Court Martial did not call them. Gordon went to Guam now loudly protesting the terrible crime that he failed to bring to trial. Later he lambasted the light sentence of the military court.

Dougherty was convicted on thirteen counts of criminal sexual misconduct that included sexual intercourse with seven minors, rape, sodomy, indecent assault and indecent liberties. Dougherty faced one hundred and forty-seven years in prison. Instead he received one-year hard labour and a bad conduct discharge and reduction in rank.

The editorial of the *Guam Tribune* called this a ridiculously light sentence which made a mockery of justice. Gordon came back echoing the same statement, but what can one expect when the military rules on the sexual conduct of one of its own?

The petition to have me transferred out of Olongapo was the start of an organised attempt by local politicians and community leaders to counter our outspoken denunciation of child prostitution and the human rights violations. This was answered by a letter of support signed by seventeen Columbans and published in the *Bulletin Today* Sunday magazine, *Panorama*, for which we were thankful. The letter expressed the "sense of horror and revulsion", that they all had at the extent of child prostitution in Olongapo and that they fully supported the expose made by the PREDA Centre.

Cardinal Jamie Sin, already an outspoken critic of the Marcos regime weighed in with his statement of support in a letter to Fr Nicholas Murray, the Columban Superior for the Philippines at the time. The Cardinal, always a good friend, never wavered in his support when we were under attack. The stand we at PREDA had taken was, "Priestly and Prophetic," he said.

Later Cardinal Sin would describe the rift between people and government in this way: "When people lose faith in their leaders, fear the military, and don't trust the courts, the only person left for them to go to with their grievances is the parish priest … and he cannot just file away their complaints like everyone else and pretend they do not exist. He has to act to do something or he too will lose all hope."

Bishop Henry Byrne and a few Columbans close to the local government (out of necessity) could not align themselves with that sentiment of Cardinal Sin. They did not sign the letter. The petition for my removal, signed by the heads of Catholic organisations, Protestant pastors and leaders of the local chapter of the Masons showed how politicians could politicise the church organisations and civic agencies and use them to counter critics and enhance their political power. The petition was sent to national government agencies and given to the military. They all ignored it.

There were government officials who supported our stand too. The Dangerous Drugs Board continued its moral and administrative support and ignored the petition and the threat of my deportation. They gave us the highest rating nation-wide for a successful recovery rate of the drug dependents and placed us as number one in the Philippines for a high retention rate of drug dependents in any centre. This proved that the open door system coupled with the persuasion and counselling techniques we were implementing with new arrivals was having positive effects. The primal community coupled with a multi-disciplined programme was showing impressive results. We decided to press on. It was the first of its kind in Asia.

We were greatly encouraged when the Zambales Provincial Board passed a resolution declaring their support for the work of PREDA. It barely stopped short of denouncing the alleged attempts of the Olongapo Mayor and US Navy to cover up the prostitution of children. Not all officials were corrupt or supporters of the Martial Law regime. We made a point of identifying the government officials who were covertly supportive of human rights and acting according to their moral conscience. Some church people collaborated with corrupt officials and politicians and cultivated close relationships with the rich and powerful who could give privileges and donations. The rich expected a compliant church in return. Some government administrations consider it a privilege for citizens to engage in business not a right to earn a livelihood.

The petition to have me removed from Olongapo failed. It was then turned into a complaint filed with the Bureau of Immigration and Deportation in Manila. The main deportation charge was that I had insulted the people of Olongapo by exposing the child prostitution. It seemed ridiculous but it was a baseless complaint that was repeated for many years. I faced an uncertain future as did the PREDA project.

It was clear that deportation was to be a way to get rid of missionaries troublesome to the regime by denouncing human rights violations, social injustice and now the sexual abuse of little children. My fellow Columbans came to my support with a strong letter to the leading broadsheet, published in the Sunday magazine *Panorama*:

We, the undersigned Columban priests, wish to express our full support for the action of our fellow Columban, Fr Shay Cullen, in bringing to the attention of the public the existence of child prostitution, (or abuse, or rape) in Olongapo City. The lurid details that came to light following the investigation – facts that the victims themselves substantiated-make this a particularly heinous crime against humanity

The youthful ages of the victims (ranging from 9 to 14), the acute forms of venereal disease contracted by the helpless girls, the sadistic forms of abuse used – these and other perversions fill us with a sense of horror and revulsion. Surely all men and women with Christian sensibilities share these feelings.

We feel that it was important that the public should have been made aware of the crime (and others of its type) within the community. Fr Cullen has courageously put himself on record on behalf of justice and truth by his publication of this evil. We fully support him in this act of Christian witness.

The petition was signed by seventeen priests.

The deportation charges were widely reported in the press. That September of 1982, the *We Forum* newspaper reported that the petition was in retaliation for exposing the ring prostituting children to the US sailors and the cover up. Another newspaper, the *Olongapo News*, reported the previous July the names of the pimps who had prostituted the children. They had never been charged or prosecuted, and it was rumoured that they had links to government officials. This was circulating and growing stronger and the deportation charges, much the same as in the petition for my removal, seemed to be an effort to deflect the criticism and distract the media.

The Catholic News of Singapore and a Hawaiian paper reported that the deportation charges were connected to the denunciation of the child abuse and the alleged cover up. *Midweek Magazine*, published in Manila, ran an interview with me around that time, titled *Prophets Are Not Political.* Not only did it cover the extent of child prostitution in Olongapo but went on to explore the emerging role of the priest as prophet.

It was an opportunity for me to explain to the public that Christianity is more than sacramental administration but a commitment to action, following the example of Jesus in his non-compromising commitment to the poor, and to lead them, like Moses, from every kind of slavery, be it sexual, economic or political, into freedom. While we, as priests, called to be prophets and disciples, are called to take a special role in proclaiming the gospel of justice and reconciliation, we are not involved in partisan politics, nor are we to be political activists. It is our job to prolong the presence and action of Christ into the modern age and like him, proclaim, without compromise, the Kingdom of love and reconciliation based on justice and non-violence.

The Marcos regime thought otherwise. The social encyclicals of the Church sounded too much like a socialist or communist manifesto to them. We were not officially informed of the charges and the threat hung for many months. The petition was now a formal complaint.

Chapter Twelve

Despite the fact that the military had already attributed the murder of Mayor Sola to the New People's Army (they had captured two rebels who admitted taking part in the ambush and the NPA Negros command acknowledged it), the military still used this years-old murder to frame up the priests and their lay-helpers.

On May 6, 1983 they were arrested, placed under house arrest in their parish houses for several weeks and a sham of a trial opened in Kabankalan. They were later brought to Bacolod City and placed in the military camp while the lay leaders were in the provincial jail across the city. The priests were determined to be with their co-workers and devised a stratagem with the help of fellow Columbans by which they escaped from the house in the camp and sped to the provincial jail and locked themselves inside with their lay workers.

The military commander was furious, but it was legal and it worked: all were safer together. There was an apparent attempt to assassinate them from the over the prison wall some months later when things began to look bad for the Prosecutors.

The farce of a trial was backfiring badly on the Marcos regime. International media attention was showing Marcos and his cronies for what they were: cruel henchmen of a tyrant killing and torturing their own people, persecuting the church and looting the national treasury. Protest demonstrations in Ireland during the visit of Ronald Reagan put further pressure on Marcos to bring the sham trial to an end. I was visiting them in the jail as frequently as I could get to Negros and I testified at the trial that I had clear proof that Fr Niall was in the PREDA Centre during the week that the Mayor was killed.

After a year of this mockery of justice, incredible hardship and deprivation, intense legal battling, the false charges against Fr Vincent Dangan were the first to be dismissed and then on June 24, 1984 the charges against Fathers Brian and Niall and the co-workers were also dropped.

It was a year-long campaign from behind bars and with their supporters they used their unjust imprisonment and false charges to alert the nation and the international community as to the iniquities of the regime. After that I was very careful to record my own movements, just in case anything happened to our Mayor, I would need to prove my whereabouts if framed for that.

There were dramatic happenings on the political scene in autumn of 1983. While the Negros Nine were on trial and we were helping the Lighthouse community set up their shacks and shanties on the hillsides above the centre, the exiled opposition leader Benigno "Ninoy" Aquino made a return to Manila. It was a city filled with rumours of President Marcos's ill health and official warnings of assassination. He ignored the threats and took the chance to come home to rally the opposition. He never made it beyond the steps of the plane. He was shot in the back of the head by the military as they led him down a flight of service stairs from the plane while hundreds of his supporters thronged the arrival area.

The so-called assassin, Rolando Galman, dressed in mechanics overalls was shot minutes later on the tarmac by another group of soldiers. The public were expected to believe that Galman, a lone assassin was responsible. It was a crudely staged tragedy that convinced few. Marcos and his wife denied any involvement. General Fabian Ver was suspected as the mastermind. Marcos was in bed recovering from a second kidney transplant operation. The outcry was nationwide and Marcos appointed a panel of five Judges to investigate the murder. As expected their deliberations came to nothing.

Despite his condition Marcos made a television appearance the next day to denounce the killing and in desperation blamed the Communists. Galman, the fall guy, was a member of a death squad organised by the army to counter the Communist liquidation units. Few doubted Ninoy had been killed by his military escorts on the orders of General Fabian Ver, a childhood friend of Marcos and allegations that Imelda Marcos was behind it were rampant and widely believed. A compliant court acquitted General Ver on December 2, 1985 after disregarding strong evidence on a technicality and ignoring the testimony of an eye witness.

There were over a million people on the streets following the cortege at Ninoy's funeral procession through the streets of Manila. His coffin was perched high on a big flat bed truck and covered in floral tributes. Thousands of mourners hung from balconies and windows, throwing yellow confetti (the colour of defiance) and waving flags and streamers.

A young, ambitious self-sacrificing politician died challenging a tyrant, and a martyr was born. For generations brought up on the life of Jose Rizal, the doctor and writer executed by the Spanish for his harsh criticism of them, Ninoy was for many the successor to this hero's mantel. He was seen by others as a Christ-figure so prevalent in popular Filipino religious culture, he was elevated to the suffering servant dying to save his people.

The following September 15 as many as five thousand students took to the streets and denounced Marcos as a tyrant and terrorist. Now hopes were rising that the massive show of opposition to Marcos might build into a movement for change. But a week or so later, Marcos retaliated with force and broke up a rally led by Corazon (Cory) Aquino, the wife of Ninoy Aquino. There was an uneasy standoff as the fractured opposition tried to settle their differences and present a solid front against Marcos.

The wealthy lost all confidence in the economy, already tottering on the edge of bankruptcy, and transferred half a billion dollars out of the country. Marcos, as was later discovered, had been transferring millions of dollars to private bank accounts scattered around the world, most of it into numbered Swiss accounts. Tons of gold had been stashed in a Zurich bonded warehouse where it still remains today. According to private investigators hired by government officials after the fall of Marcos, there was as much as thirteen billion US dollars in Swiss accounts and none was recovered.

It was a hard Christmas for all. The year 1984 began with mounting tension as to what turn the national situation would take. The young people at the PREDA therapeutic community were still recovering, the work of healing still went on. We had the primal sessions daily, the family meetings and the family counselling and reconciliation. But money was very short and there was little we had to offer the young people. But more still came in looking for shelter and help. One street boy, weak, skinny and desperate, collapsed as soon as he crossed the threshold. I later wrote a story that described a little of his personal experience of a life that led nowhere and shared by many thousands of young people today.

Yet we did manage to have a Christmas party for sixty or so children from the Lighthouse community now well settled in on the PREDA reforestation land. But there was trouble on the way.

Our finances had not greatly improved as sales of our handicraft products had not grown quickly enough for us to earn enough to support the growing community. We were paying out interest-free production loans to the producers, spending a certain percentage on community projects for them to improve the conditions of life, such as improving sanitation for the workers, seeing that the producers were getting a good wage and medical benefits. So there was little enough left for the drug abuse prevention and recovery programme.

At PREDA we were trying to be self-reliant and operate a sustainable project. We did try to make the parents of the teenagers responsible by asking them to contribute to their child's recovery. But most were very poor and those from a middleclass background were reluctant to help, preferring to exclude the child from the family and use PREDA as a human garbage heap for their family problems. All too frequently parents refused to accept their shortcomings and accept that they had a role in the problems that contributed to the drug addiction of their son.

At this time in 1984 we read in the newspaper that the General Credit Corporation had made a brilliant financial recovery and announced healthy profits, sixteen million pesos for the previous year. Now was the time to try and recover our deposits. We had nothing to lose and approached the corporation head Leo B. Alejandro asking for a repayment.

I went to this penthouse office atop the ACE building in Makati, the country's financial district. His office was plush, ornate but gaudy and he dripped with gold bracelet and watch. *No impoverished banker here,* I thought, but his reply was a downright refusal and an arrogant one at that. I felt he was telling me: "Who do you think you are, daring to ask for money? You should have joined the rehabilitation plan."

I was furious at this rebuff and returned to PREDA and had a meeting with the staff. There was a new spirit of freedom and protest in the air those days. We were less fearful of instant reprisals if we were to take daring action and so we explained the situation to the community and together planned to picket the offices of the General Credit Corporation. The boys in the community were all for it. It was action, excitement and a chance to do something positive in a different environment.

We prepared dozens of placards, posters and streamers demanding our money back. Then we headed for battle. There was a vacant lot across the road from the ACE building and there we parked the bus, hung out our streamers and posted our placards on every post we could find all over the district to create as much publicity as possible.

The employees were aghast as they rushed to the windows to see this previously unheard of spectacle. But protest was in the air and our streamers and placard demanded: "We want our money back", "Pay what you owe" and one more daring read, "General Credit Corporation, General Who?" referring to the fact that the military controlled a good number of the seats on the board.

Alejandro was furious and sent out an official to the picket line to tell us so and threatening dire consequences. With Alex and a small group of the senior boys from the centre we continued walking up and down with our placards held high. After four an official came out to say that they would discuss a settlement but it would have to be according to the rehabilitation plan. Alex made it clear that it was all or nothing, we wanted our deposit and the interest due.

The next day there was a rally along the streets as a group of protesters marched along the street calling for the restoration of democracy. There was a lighting attack on them as they approached the safe haven of the Cojuangco building two blocks away (This was owned by the brother of Cory Aquino). The group broke off the melee and retreated into the building.

Police in uniforms carrying truncheons and undercover agents came across an empty building site to look at our placards and to see if we were part of the demonstration. They took pictures and a few of the police came to talk to Alex to ask what exactly we were doing. He politely explained to them that it is a legitimate picket to get back PREDA's investment to support the children. Alex naturally got nervous. It was a frightening scene nearby and we were already threatened with violent dispersal but took the risk anyway. He saw the tear gas canisters fly and smoke and people running everywhere. He was afraid that they might take that opportunity to disperse our picket. He must have convinced them to just leave us alone since our protest was different and we were spared an attack. When the police and military agent left us, Alex moved to see what was going on at the other side to see if he could help any of the marchers who were bashed by the police.

A while later, Alex went over to make contact with the leaders. There was a photo and artefact exhibition on display commemorating the life and death of Ninoy Aquino. Alex met Cory Aquino and they chatted about the harassment and oppressive tactics of the Marcos police.

After about three weeks, GCC filed charges against us and got a court injunction to remove our picket. They were suing us for half a million pesos and fifty thousand a day, for every day of the picket. That was the amount that they claimed they were losing in new deposits because of the protest. We had made our point and were glad that it ended as it did. Several years later when GCC sold out to another company we reinstated our claims once again and fearful that we would launch another protest, they settled handsomely with us, returning the original deposit and ten years of interest at twenty-two percent. That fund helped to expand our work to help many more street children and sexually abused children.

A few months into 1984, new arrivals began setting up crude shacks and shanties inside the relocation area. They claimed they had permits from the city government and there was nothing we could do about it. The Mayor and his officials now saw it necessary to infiltrate the Lighthouse community and prevent if from becoming a centre of opposition. The trickle grew over the months and even relatives of public officials were grabbing portions of the area for themselves.

We were being overrun. We requested the Ministry of Natural Resources to intervene and restrict the number of people who could be permitted to dwell in the area. They were slow to move. By September our protests were falling on deaf ears. In December the people made a petition to Gordon and we wrote him asking him to stop the harassment of the residents and to improve the living conditions instead. There was a scarcity of water, no sanitation facilities and overcrowding.

Soon the newcomers were threatening the families of the Lighthouse community and the people's organisations were afraid to meet for fear of police action. One day the barangay captain, Jose Gonzales (Gordon's local district official) stormed into a community meeting waving his .45 automatic rifle and shouting that the meeting was illegal and subversive, he frightened so many of the settlers that they dared not meet again. The infiltrators were telling the military that there were Communist rebels hiding in the community. It was a scary time.

We continued holding seminars on the evils of child prostitution and the exploitation of women in the sex industry which still thrived and catered to the sexual demands of the US Seventh Fleet.

The problem was prevalent all over Asia. There were a number of foreign groups in constant communication with us on our campaign to remove the bases. Some groups from Canada, Japan and New Zealand came to visit for a period to study the issues, especially the plight of the children in prostitution and the Filipino-American children, many abandoned and taken to the streets to survive. Their mothers are virtual slaves of the bars and clubs, unable to rear them. In many cases, these children were either sold for adoption and there was a thriving trafficking of children in the city with prominent members of the political elite involved.

Sometimes the mother – when working in the bar met a steady American boyfriend and to bind him closer and try to make him responsible and marry her – allowed herself to get pregnant. More often than not, the boyfriend deserted her as soon as he found out. Rather than have an abortion, which was the common practice (despite it being illegal), she gave birth and then gave the baby to a squatter family to be taken care of. The women in prostitution gave what financial support they could to the family caring for the baby.

An Associated Press report, published by the Manila-based *Times Journal,* reported a conference on child abuse held in Jakarta with most South-east Asian countries attending. The absence of the Philippines was apparent, officialdom was in denial, for them child sexual abuse and child prostitution did not officially exist. The conference discussed the spreading child abuse and exploitation in South-east Asia. It was one of the first international gatherings that officially recognised the enormity of the problem, something that we had been trying to point out for years.

Our campaign against child prostitution was interpreted by the brothel and bar owners and their political protectors to be anti-base and by extension anti-American. It was a short step for them to wave the red rag and accuse us of being Communists. It was a crude but disconcerting way to discredit us and ignore the real problem.

There were many good American friends of PREDA on the military base and they worked with many members of the American peace, anti-nuclear, and military base conversion advocates in the US. The American Bishops had spoken out against US nuclear and military bases policy and human rights abuses in the Philippines.

In media interviews, we made it clear that the US military were not upholding the moral values and principles of the US Constitution and Bill of Rights in their personal behaviour and some aspects of US Navy policy. Their own young men, some as young as seventeen, were corrupted and morally perverted by their experiences in Olongapo and Angeles cities. There were countless victims on both sides.

I gave several television and radio interviews on the social and economic problems surrounding the bases and declaring that they had to go. The only alternative I could see then was to transform them into economic zones. Such enclaves for foreign companies were seen then by liberals as nests of exploitation. Yet, if they provided work with dignity and just wages and were a feasible alternative to the bases, then we would have to compromise.

Converting the military bases to economic production centres was by far the lesser of two evils from my point of view. The international media were taking greater interest in the pivotal role of the military bases in US foreign policy towards the Philippines and Asia as a whole. The bases were seen by US defence establishment as essential links in a chain of steel around Russia and China. The cold war dogma at that time was containment. The bases were a springboard for any military action into mainland Asia, as they had been for the Korean War and Vietnam. They were also a prime target for a retaliatory nuclear strike if the concept of a "limited nuclear exchange" ever materialised.

Washington's support for Marcos was based on their need to keep the bases, fearing that any weakening of Marcos would allow the Communist rebels to gain strength and then anything could happen. President Reagan was himself an "old friend" of Marcos since his visits to Manila and the lavish reception they received. Imelda had cultivated a close relationship with Nancy Reagan and kept feeding her with her propaganda.

Reagan was fully supportive of Marcos. After his planned stopover visit in Manila in November 1983 was cancelled, he wrote Marcos a personal letter reaffirming his friendship and telling him, "I've always had confidence in your ability to handle things."

Such personal affirmation from the US President was a heady tonic for an ailing strong man and stiffened his resolve to crush his enemies and survive. When the opposition grew stronger and the outpouring of resentment against Marcos filled the streets of Manila and the provinces, the state department was bothered. Primarily because of the possible loss of the bases, Reagan, ever the Republican hawk, was advocating a six hundred ship navy and believed that Marcos was his man to preserve Subic Bay and Clarke Air Force bases.

Under Marcos, criticism of these policies was muted but as his grip grew weaker the protest grew louder. Now Washington's affair with Marcos was dragging them to the edge but how could they escape his deathly embrace? Reagan had all but alienated the Philippine opposition by taking the position that Marcos was the only barrier to a Communist takeover. In February 1985, he was won around by the State Department and conceded in a *New York Times* interview that the Philippine opposition was also committed to democracy.

The Communists were a real threat. From a handful of teachers and students who had fled to the mountains in 1972, there was a robust insurrection with as many as ten thousand armed men and women and perhaps as many as a million supporters spread around sixty-two of the seventy-two provinces of the country. With opposition to Marcos growing stronger by the month, the danger that a power vacuum would be quickly filled by the increasingly popular rebel movement worried Washington.

The growing poverty and hardship swelled their ranks. US

support for Marcos was the biggest prop that kept him in power, remove that and he would fall. In September 1984, a US congressional report said that a Communist victory in the Philippines was a distinct possibility and that would mean the end of US bases. This would impair "our ability to preserve … the balance of power in Asia."

There was a growing disenchantment in the US State Department with Marcos. Many saw how he was becoming a liability rather than an asset to American interests in Asia. Washington had ignored the record of horrific human rights abuse, torture, economic plunder, social evil including the child prostitution that proliferated especially around the two giant US bases.

Marcos was desperate to improve his image with the American public and give himself the aura of being a democratic leader. The only way to do that was to hold a "snap" election. His plan was to win by a small margin, not a landslide, and convince Washington and the American people that he was lawfully elected and they would have no option but to continue their support. More and more he appeared to be that puppet of a foreign power that his left-wing critics accused him of. A vain, stubborn and cruel puppet at that.

Significantly, he announced his "snap election" not to the Philippine people but to an American audience on November 3, 1985 during an interview with David Brinkley on the ABC Sunday morning show.

Now elections in the Philippines loomed. The opposition was divided. Two main factions emerged to contest the election, Cory Aquino and Salvador Laurel, a traditional politician. Marcos was counting on the Filipino's inability to unite politically for a cause greater than personal ambition and a desire for power. But he did not foresee that Cardinal Sin, politically astute, influential, and knowing that the welfare of the people rested fundamentally in restoring democracy and ending the oppression and the looting of the national treasury, would bring them together. He directly intervened and persuaded Laurel to take second place.

By February 7, 1986, on the eve of the polling, the nation was in a fever of excitement. Marcos was against the wall; the fervour of the Aquino supporters, the presence of international observers and media, the massive turnout was astonishing. It seemed certain that Cory Aquino, the pious widow of the slain martyr, could not lose, if the counting was fair. But it wasn't. There was cheating, electrical failures during which Marcos's goons tried to steal the ballot boxes. There were dramatic television scenes of citizens physically holding the boxes, forming barricades outside the polling booths and risking physical harm to protect the ballots.

There were shootings, intimidation, and fraudulent tally sheets, fake ballot boxes already stuffed with votes for Marcos. The cheating was brazen and arrogant. In Olongapo, the entire process was under the control of the local government. There were some brave lawyers who tried to monitor the vote but as usual the ballot boxes were brought to the office of the local election official appointed by the Mayor. Few outsiders were allowed inside during the counting of the votes and they were unable to monitor the counting.

Gordon delivered a big majority for Marcos. In Manila the worst came when the final tally sheets from around the country came in. A church-based election monitoring group called NAMFREL (for National Movement for Free Elections) was tallying the votes at the same time as the government officials from the Commission on Elections (COMELEC).

The government officials stopped counting when the tally showed Aquino ahead, they tried to alter the total, the computer operators walked out in disgust. The official outcome was delayed, giving officials more opportunity to falsify the figures. US State Department officials in Washington had their people on the ground all over the Philippines and were closely following the vote, they knew it was Marcos who cheated. Ever true to his "friend", Reagan and his officials declared support for Marcos. US State Department officials were frustrated.

Reagan suggested that there was fraud on both sides, this infuriated Cory Aquino, and indicated that his interest was as much in democracy as in retaining the military bases. "I don't know of anything more important than those bases," he said. Again the nation's future was to be decided not in the Philippines by the people themselves but by a former movie actor thousands of miles away in a foreign capital. Reagan appeared to many Filipinos as an aging actor who treated the Philippines as a Hollywood movie lot, when the next episode of the movie script had to follow his plot and include his favourite lines.

Days later, on February 15, under pressure from George Shultz, Reagan backtracked from his partisan comments and acknowledged that the fraud had been mostly from Marcos. Marcos had already proclaimed himself the winner; Cory Aquino did likewise. The Catholic Bishops who had supported Aquino declared en masse that Marcos had "no moral basis" to rule.

According to the account of Stanley Karnov, Shultz sent Philip Habib, a forty-years veteran of the State Department, to Manila and made an assessment while Shultz looked for a way to influence the crises and ease Marcos from power. When Habib finished his exhaustive investigation of the situation he summed it up by saying: "Cory had won the election and deserved our support, Marcos was finished, and we ought to offer him asylum."

General Fabian Ver, the cousin and former bodyguard of Marcos had been consolidating his own power in the palace with the support of Marcos. The armed forces were placed under his direct command. Marcos was ill after two kidney transplant operations, one successful, but he needed dialysis. In the palace the jockeying for power and the succession was between Ver and Imelda Marcos. Ninoy Aquino had been the one threat to that power grab and he was already eliminated.

Ambition is seldom found alone. In the cabinet the defence secretary, Enrile, had plans of his own. A graduate of Harvard Law School, he became a close supporter of Marcos in 1965 and rose to power and influence thereafter. He became vastly wealthy through his association with Eduardo "Danding" Cojuangco, the estranged cousin of Cory Aquino. Cojuangco was one of the powerful sugar barons of Negros and is believed to have been one of the sugar tycoons behind the false charges brought against Fathers Gore, O'Brien and Dangan and their co-workers.

Enrile and Cojuangco got control of the revenues of a levy placed on the coconut farmers. The tax amounted to billions and it was suspected that the money was used to buy shares in the country's biggest company, San Miguel Corporation, most famous for its beer. It is still a controversial issue as the farmers claim that the levy is public money and was intended to improve the industry and the lives of the poor farmers.

Enrile was rapidly distancing himself from Marcos and eyed, perhaps, the presidency for himself. He formed within the defence department a group of young officers called the Reform the Armed Forces Movement (RAM). He was targeted by Ver as a possible rival and Enrile thwarted an assassination attempt. He also felt threatened by Cojuangco.

Enrile's group was led by a flamboyant young officer Gregorio "Gringo" Honasan (later a senator) and apparently their plan was to stage a coup against Marcos and install Enrile as president. The assassination of Ninoy Aquino and the rise to popularity of his wife Cory overshadowed that plan and the decision of Marcos to hold a "snap election" produced a new situation for which they were ill prepared. The RAM security was riddled with informers and Marcos came to know about their planned coup but took no immediate action to eliminate them.

The election of February 7, 1986 and the national uproar over the cheating created a very unstable political situation. Aquino was busy holding rallies calling for a boycott of business corporations associated with Marcos. The American public were enchanted with the popular Aquino and the morality play that was being staged on their television screens. Washington was distancing itself from Marcos by the day, but Reagan was still for Marcos.

After the departure of Philip Habib, the RAM Boys, as Enrile's group of officers came to be known, were emboldened and decided to make their move. Their original plan was to attack Malacañang Palace, the seat of power, and arrest Marcos. Their plan was blown and General Ver was about to arrest them all, including Enrile.

With no options left, on February 22, they retreated to the sprawling military compound named Camp Aguinaldo after General Emilio Aguinaldo, the young brash revolutionary leader of the uprising against Spain in 1896. That evening with about two hundred and fifty men, armed with automatic rifles and machine guns, the RAM group were joined by Enrile and a little later by General Fidel Ramos, a cousin of Marcos and head of the Philippine Constabulary. He was equally alienated by General Ver, disenchanted and continually blocked from promotion. But he too being a protégée of the US Military, a West Point graduate, gave rise to speculation that he was being secretly briefed by the CIA and the US military attaché in the embassy. While the US favoured Enrile as a possible replacement for Marcos, they didn't trust him and were hedging their bets and backed Ramos too and perhaps encouraged him to support the coup and bring over the main force of the Philippine Army.

The presence of Ramos improved their chances of surviving an attack by Ver's forces. But had the powerful tanks and armoured personnel carriers of Marcos come into action, there would have been little hope.

Millions across the nation were glued to television sets and radios. The live coverage dominated the airwaves. Then an extraordinary thing happened. Instead of the civilian population packing up their belongings and moving away from what was obviously to be the scene of a pitched battle, they milled around the gates of the huge military compound excited and thrilled at the open defiance of the rebel soldiers. General Ramos saw the difficulties of defending Camp Aguinaldo and, perhaps to assert his own independence, he decided to take his followers to Camp Crame on the other side of the eight lane highway that splits Camp Aguinaldo from its counterpart. Enrile had no option but to follow with his small contingent.

The media swarmed into the camp to get the first and perhaps last interviews before the death struggle began. Enrile gave interviews broadcast nationwide from the ministry of defence building inside the camp. He confessed to rampant cheating by Marcos, his own part in the rigging of thousands of votes and many other dirty tricks of the regime. He pledged his support for Aquino. It was electrifying to us who were witnessing this drama unfolding live.

The military were split. Many officers and men were angry at the deprivations they had to endure, the risks they took for low salaries. Millions of dollars for the Armed Forces were siphoned into private bank accounts of Marcos and his cronies. More army units followed Ramos and declared themselves for the failed coup plotters and joined them in Camp Aguinaldo.

Television reporters were hoarse with excitement as they announced each new development. A unit of helicopter gun ships came flying towards the rebel positions. Listening on the radio, we were breathless waiting for them to unleash their rockets into the RAM positions. Instead, amid emotional cheering from the crowds near the gates of the camp, the helicopters landed and declared themselves for the RAM Boys. It was a great relief.

Cory Aquino was in Cebu City about three hundred kilometres south of Manila campaigning for civil disobedience and a boycott. She retired to a convent to await the outcome. Her supporters advising her that it would be madness to return to Manila. She would be a prime target for the Marcos hit squads during the attack on the RAM rebels. Marcos would have then eliminated all his opponents in a single blow.

That week before the news of the pending arrest of Defence Secretary Enrile and the RAM boys, Alex had taken the PREDA community on a camping trip in the old bus to a tribal village in the mountains of San Marcelino. The Aeta tribes people were our friends with whom we had a small development project trading their rattan poles. There they followed the events over the radio. I was in PREDA with the rest of the staff listening and following developments.

News reached us that the local military units were aroused and split. Some were staying with Marcos, other units opposed. Road Blocks were set up, and battle stations were manned near the military camp in Barrio Barretto near us. Nobody knew who were who, although the pro-RAM were supposed to have reversed their arm patches.

As the tension mounted Marcos ordered his troops to silence the church radio station, Radio Veritas. His men burst into the transmitter station in Mololos, Bulacan about an hour north of Manila. The only source of credible information was off the air. The US government through its various departments was playing all sides.

According to the account of Stanley Karnov, the CIA provided access to an alternative radio transmitter so that the broadcasting of events could continue. The helicopter gun ships were refuelled in the US Clarke Air force Base. US electronic experts monitored General Ver's radio network and passed information to Ramos. It was not difficult to understand whom they wanted to see victorious, although defeat was inevitable, unless huge numbers of troops defected, then there was the likelihood of a full scale civil war.

But Marcos held back Ver from launching an attack. He had been cautioned by Reagan to avoid bloodshed. Reagan couldn't have his friend and ally slaughtering thousands of civilians on world television. Negotiation was one solution and everybody was calling everybody else over the phone and getting nowhere.

Television footage showed Ver demanding the order to attack and Marcos wavering. It was a costly delay. Enrile had acknowledged Aquino to be the rightfully elected leader and he called Cardinal Sin to ask his help. That afternoon Cardinal Sin, watching the crowds gathering around the entrance to Camp Crame, went on radio to encourage the people to gather on the highway known as Epifanio De Los Santos, or EDSA, that fronted the two military camps.

They came in the thousands and blocked the road, interposed themselves between the armoured personnel carriers and the troops that Ver had been drawn up waiting for the order to fire. The unit commander, who later was assigned to the security command of Subic Naval Base, was implored over the phone by his relatives not to fire. Marcos remained indecisive. The world media was showing the nuns and seminarians procession along the highway surrounded by crowds, offering rosary beads and flowers to the soldiers and kneeling before the armoured cars.

They then pulled back to roars of approval. Later they advanced again and were besieged by waves of people, pleading, imploring, offering food and drinks, kneeling and praying in front of the guns. This event was later called the Edsa revolution or the People's Power Revolution. The world watched, Reagan fretted, Washington sweated, and Marcos knew he could not launch an attack and survive the political fallout.

The stand off lasted two days. On February 24, one of the helicopter gun ships fired a few rockets into Malacañang. Rumours were spreading that Marcos and his family had fled the palace. But he was still there. The next day Enrile, relieved to be alive, had put aside his presidential ambitions, for the time being and proclaimed the formation of a provisional government with Aquino as president. Aquino returned to Manila, joined the crowds at the Camps and there were emotional scenes as the huge crowd sang "Ave Maria" in thanksgiving for victory.

But it was premature. The next day February 25, Marcos, still determined to hang onto power, encouraged by the tacit support of Reagan, took his oath of office appearing on the balcony of the palace and on TV. But he was cut off in the middle of the ceremony when the rebels took over the government television station. Aquino was advised to take the oath of office and was sworn in as president by Supreme Court Justice Claudio Teehankee, a one time loyal supporter of Marcos.

Marcos was prepared to stay on so long as he had the backing of Reagan. But the situation was desperate in Washington. Reagan could not be persuaded to tell him to quit. Finally in a meeting between Reagan, Shultz and Senator Laxalt, it was concluded that Marcos had to go and would be welcomed in America. Laxalt called Marcos and gave him the word. "I think you should cut and cut cleanly. I think the time has come." Again it was the word from Washington that determined the time of departure, the stepping down, the end of an era in Philippine politics.

On February 26,1986, pressured by Senator Laxalt, Marcos decided to leave. US helicopters took Marcos and his family and retainers to Clark Airfield North of Manila. They had hurriedly gathered up boxes of fabulous jewellery, bank certificates and other documents that gave them access to billions of dollars of ill-gotten wealth. When they arrived in Honolulu where they were flown, the US customs confiscated all of these. The money has not yet been recovered. More secret accounts were later discovered from documents found in the hastily abandoned palace together with the fabled thousand pairs of shoes of Imelda Marcos. Most of it is still stashed away in Swiss bank accounts – an astonishing thirteen billion US dollars. The secrets out in the open and, the Aquino government ready to lay claim to the ill-gotten wealth, the Swiss banks immediately put a freeze order on all the Marcos accounts to be sure no one could get them.

The emergence of the "People Power" phenomenon as a communal act of active non-violence to topple a tyrant did not bring about a radical social change or usher in an era of social justice to the Philippines. It brought about the flight of Marcos by delaying and blocking any serious assault on the besieged group of Enrile, Ramos and the Ram Boys surrounded in Camp Crame. It brought to power Cory Aquino as president based on the election held the previous February 7, during which more than thirty people were killed, and re-established a modicum of democratic rule. Her courage and resilience were already proven but there were more tests yet to come. There was a great sign of relief at the fall of Marcos. It was hard to believe and a great burden of fear and trepidation was lifted overnight.

At PREDA there were still problems that non-violent People's Power was unable to solve. The previous July 1985, a road improvement project of the national government funded by the Asian Development Bank began to excavate the cliffside under our centre, which is perched on a hill above the highway. The bulldozers and backhoes came during the night and woke us up. We were appalled to see them tearing down the cliffside under the building. The next day we protested and parked our pick-up truck to block the bulldozer but it just went around it cutting at the cliff.

I went to the construction office to protest the danger to our centre but the Korean contractor rebuffed my appeal and showed no interest in our plight. Furious, I stood in front of the exit of the cement batch plant. The trucks with the freshly mixed cement could not get out. The Korean contractor was really angry and there were heated words and I was threatened with a metal bar. Realising that they had the full backing of Mayor Gordon there was little chance to stop the excavations under our building. When they threatened to drive their dump truck straight at my pickup, I decided it was time to pull back.

Much to our anger, the rocks and soil that were been excavated from under the PREDA building was being dumped at the nearby Gordon Park making a new driveway for them. I appealed to the Asian Development Bank officials in Manila but they showed no interest and informed me that there was no money for such a project. I feared a huge landslide that would wipe us out and began to construct a retaining wall with the meagre funds on hand.

It had poor re-enforcement and a typhoon came in May 1986 before we were finished and we lost the whole construction that blocked the highway. We launched an appeal for protest letters to the President of the Asian Development Bank who were funding the road construction. One day, a few weeks after the campaign began, a limousine glided up to our door, and a British engineering consultant with the bank asked us what we wanted in order to stop the letter writing campaign.

The area damaged by the excavation was to be rebuilt with a huge retaining wall and for the bank to pay compensation for all our losses. He agreed and made out a cheque on the spot. We developed a construction design and with the help of a mining engineer the retaining walls were built. It was not our last encounter with the bank. Exactly ten years later, we were locked in another confrontation with the same bank and the Gordon dynasty over another environmental issue.

Chapter Thirteen

It was a new beginning. Aquino abolished the Marcos rubber stamp congress and set in motion the writing of a new constitution. The draft was approved October 1986. It set a single six years term of office for the president, a provision that succeeding presidents, Ramos and Estrada, would try to change to perpetuate themselves in office.

However, the dream of social transformation remained a dream. The problems were too vast and daunting for any meaningful change. There was no money in the coffers, most of it was deposited in foreign banks by Marcos and his cronies. Even a gifted charismatic leader with the highest levels of public support was up against an even greater and immovable force: the politics of patronage. Elected leaders in the Philippines have rarely had real democratic power or the desire to change a system that was tilted in their favour. Wealth has always been in the hands of the few landlords and industrial barons. The political and industrial dynasties that survived Marcos now returned to power and a new oligarchy was in place, ravenous to recoup their losses under Marcos.

President Aquino, a devoted Catholic, was no social reformer. She had political enemies on every side plotting her downfall from the beginning. It was not the beginning of a new era of true democracy, but a resurgence of a past era, where a ruling elite of aristocrats and business tycoons controlled and upheld a seriously flawed democratic process. It was a system shamelessly riddled with vote buying and patronage politics. For generations the small elite was able to hold the nation in poverty, stubbornly resisted social reform and left the field ripe for the likes of Marcos to take power. The election of Aquino, the fraud and cheating of Marcos aside, was the most genuine and sincere ever. Yet there was no major social transformation, no sweeping laws to redistribute land and wealth, to tax the rich and help the poor. In that regard little changed.

Aquino's greatest achievement was emerging from the shadows of her slain husband and taking on Marcos in a fervent emotional election campaign and winning. She was featured the "Person of the Year" by *Time* magazine and in 1999 was listed as among the one hundred most influential Asians of the century. A justly deserved title. She took upon herself to lead a nation that was in chaos. It was her leadership in the boycott of the Marcos crony businesses, her refusal to give up when cheated in the elections and her innate goodness as a person that brought her to power.

With the tyrant gone there was a period of relief and hopeful democratic rule. The fear of a jackboot army, arbitrary arrests and torture was eased for a while. Yet the provisional government of Aquino failed to act decisively and use wisely and swiftly the revolutionary powers that prevailed in the first months of her administration. A historical opportunity was lost to legislate by decree genuine land reform, a revamp of the corrupt judiciary and other vital changes that could have helped move the Philippines so much closer to being a more just society. She preferred to allow the democratic process to take its course and decreed a constitutional convention be held. Little did she realise just how perverse were the forces that were so undemocratic and they controlled the process.

The forces that surrounded her were not the kind that favoured revolutionary change or restructuring, they advised reform. Perhaps it was too much to expect considering that the corruption of twenty years of Marcos rule was still a powerful force. In Hawaii the Marcos millions were being readied to foment trouble and military revolt. Politically inexperienced, Aquino was swamped by the waves of contending interests that sought to gain favour, grab positions of influence and fill every vacant power slot.

There was little that the new administration could have done to reform the highly corrupt military and police much as it wanted to. They had had twenty years of unfettered power and a record of horrific human rights abuses. There was more to come. Aquino was the first woman president and commander-in-chief of the Armed Forces and the Marcos military were not about to obey a woman or accept civilian rule after years of suppressing their rights.

To keep them in check and reward the coup plotters, Enrile was appointed Minister of Defence and Fidel Ramos, became Chief of the Armed Forces. But a faction of the army that revolted with Enrile against Marcos when they sensed the end was near (called the Ram Boys) sensed all too keenly the weakness of the Aquino administration, and the lack of wholehearted support for Aquino from the US. The Republicans who were nervous and unsure about the left-of-centre advisors and officials, who were gaining positions of influence around the President, feared they would move her to take a position against the continuation of US military bases. Which she did.

The new constitution was approved by the people the following year on February 2, 1987. It gave the decision regarding the future of the US military bases over to the Senate. For a new military bases treaty to be approved a two-thirds majority was needed. The lease expired in 1991. Yet Aquino was believed to have such influence that her support for a new treaty allowing the extension of the bases was crucial. Her future hung on that single issue.

On this issue hung a vital link to the US military forward

deployment defence policy. Subic Naval Base was vital to that and Clark could be dispensed with. So when Aquino began to invite advisers considered radical by right wing forces in the Philippines and in the US, the enthusiastic emotional support for her began to wane. Aquino never forgot that Reagan was a fervent supporter of Marcos and did not recognise her election victory. During the campaign against Marcos, Aquino favoured the removal of the bases, which endeared her to the nationalists but alienated a lot of support among conservatives in the US. Under the influence of her advisors, she announced an open options policy regarding the future of the military bases. She didn't confirm or deny that she was favouring them to be removed. It infuriated the hawks in the US Congress. Sinister plots to undermine her and prepare for a successor were soon boiling in the cauldron of political intrigue.

As time progressed American right wing pressure and covert support for the rebels and fanatical anti-Communist militias would threaten her family and drive a wedge between her and her progressive supporters. In the end she turned to America for support and reversed her stand on the military bases and lobbied the Senate for the retention of the bases.

The forces of the Right had spread fears that the Communists would quickly dominate the Aquino government. There was little real likelihood of that occurring. The Communist movement had seriously miscalculated the forces at work that created the wave of popular support that swept Aquino to power. The Communists had stood back in disdain, aloof in a cloud of ideological self-righteousness.

The snap election of February 7 offered a unique opportunity for political participation by the Communists. Their party, Ang Bayan (The Nation) did not participate. It was a lost opportunity for the left. Had it done so it would have aligned itself with moderate forces and created for itself a pool of goodwill in the consciousness of the people power movement. They failed to join the crowds that marched and rallied for democracy and had physically and heroically defended the ballot boxes during the election. It was the non-political lower and middle class people who had rallied around the gates of the military camps defying the tanks and armoured cars of the Marcos regime.

The Communists stayed on the sidelines waiting for the civil war that was brewing and watched with dismay as the EDSA rallies and the people power movement toppled Marcos – a role that they had believed was their true destiny. Non-violence had achieved what armed revolution had not. They had missed a historical moment and, in later years, accepted their lost opportunity due to a lack of political savvy and analysis. Although Marcos had been removed, the centuries old system that enabled him and his oligarchy to rule with such cruelty and plunder was still very much alive.

One of the first things that Aquino did a few months after taking office in March 1986 was to replace all the Marcos era's city Mayors and Governors with temporary officers-in-charge. In Olongapo a lawyer, Teddy Macapagal, a distant relative of a former president, was appointed to replace Mayor Gordon who declared he would not leave without a fight. Gordon didn't recognise the Aquino government. He barricaded himself inside City Hall and surrounded himself with loyal policemen, bodyguards, goons and political supporters and, reportedly, some convicts released from the city jail.

There he stayed for about ten days. Outside his supporters surrounded the building and if the opposition approached there were fierce fights. At night the street was ablaze with burning car tyres, rock throwing gangs from both sides. One fourteen-years-old boy was killed. On one occasion the mob stormed across the street and attacked the office of civil rights lawyer Estanislao "Jun" Cesa, a governor of the

Integrated Bar of the Philippines. Cesa has represented PREDA in several human rights cases. Attorney Sergio Cruz and Cesa, both brilliant and lawyers of integrity, tried to stop the election fraud in the city. They questioned the late registration of voters at a local court; Gordon arrived with his bodyguards and there was a scuffle and grave threat of bodily harm before the Judge, who being an associate of Gordon, closed his eyes while all this was going on. Cesa filed a petition to the Supreme Court protesting the attempted fraud.

Gordon was cleared out of City Hall by troops sent from Pampanga and a local opposition politician, Teddy Macapagal, took over as acting Mayor. He immediately announced that he was setting up a board of investigation to look into the numerous killings by the shadowy death squad. The board was never formed and the killings were never investigated. For us there was a short respite from the constant threats and harassment that had emanated from City Hall during the previous six years.

For us the constitutional convention was an opportunity to change the course of history. The constitution banned all nuclear weapons from being transported into the Philippines and passed an article saying that no foreign military bases could remain on Philippine soil without a treaty approved by two-thirds of the Senate and recognised as a treaty by the other country. The existing agreement over the bases was due to expire in 1991.

The anti-bases coalition of non-government organisations (NGOs) was lobbying hard for the approval of anti-base provisions. At an important meeting held in St Joseph's College in Quezon City that year, different members of the coalition were assigned specific areas to work on. We at PREDA had introduced a military bases conversion plan a few years previously that would save the jobs of thousands of Filipinos if the Senate could be persuaded to reject a new treaty with the

US. At first it received scant attention or publicity but we presented it during seminars and forums. As the possibility that the constitution convention would ban foreign bases grew, so did the interest in the "life after the bases" concept, as the military base conversion idea came to be called.

The strongest pro-base lobby, led by former Mayor Gordon and his wife Kate, criticised the PREDA concept and claimed that the economy would collapse without the bases. We were determined to pursue this idea, realising that long-term planning had to be done or disaster would follow any military pull out.

That year, with the considerable help of the Mennonite Central Committee in the US, who were dedicated to peace and justice around the world, I made contact with Lloyd Jeffry Dumas, a renowned economist and author of several books and papers on economics. He held the position as Professor of Political Economy and Economics at the University of Texas. Professor Dumas was a leading peace economist with years of experience lecturing and writing about the effects of military spending and an expert on military base conversion in the US. With the help of the Mennonite Central Committee he came to visit us to discuss our urgent need for advice on what military base conversion could contribute to the future of the Philippines.

The American authorities were very sensitive about the future of the bases and with the issues hotly debated in the constitutional convention I expected it would be almost impossible to get Professor Dumas a pass to visit all the facilities at the bases. So I didn't bother to apply for such a pass but took Jeff around the Subic Bay base as a visitor. I bluffed my way into the ship repair facility and almost all other places including the high security area of the naval magazine where missiles were brought for repair and maintenance.

Although we were not able to enter into any of the strategic buildings I was able to give a good tour over a period of two days. Long discussions on all the possibilities of conversion to an economic zone followed. Jeff helped banish my self-doubts about such a farfetched plan.

Gordon later ridiculed the whole idea, claiming that he had a city development plan that would allow the city free use of some of the navy facilities. It was to be implemented from 1981 to 2000. The development planners made a survey of the city, pointing out the dependence on the military base and the entertainment industry, the absence of alternative industry, urban blight, inadequate public utilities, ecological destruction and social problems. The Plan also pointed out that "thirty percent of Olongapo residents inhabit dilapidated areas where conditions of life are far from satisfactory. School sites and appropriate educational facilities are likewise limited. Health and other social services still need upgrading, especially with regard to the improvement of delivery systems".

The report explained that the original inhabitants of Olongapo were displaced by the military bases and "as a means of compensation were allowed to scavenge at the base garbage dump". From being skilled hunters and gatherers, proud survivors of the tropical rain forests where few white people could survive alone for even a few days, they were made into garbage dump scavengers.

A few were selected to train the US Marines and airmen in jungle survival techniques. From the magnificence of the forest canopies where their ancestors lived with dignity in harmony with nature living on a healthy diet of wild fruit berries and fowls, they were reduced to eating throwaway junk food from military garbage. Everyday the truck of the junk dealer would bring them out the back gate not far from PREDA and they would be sitting on a pile of scrap metal and other junk they had scavenged. They got paid a pittance for the scraps they pulled from the rubbish, the scrap dealer made the real money. But it was a livelihood and that was later taken away by a political crony.

The plan proposed port development, conversion-based

tourism, expansion of the entertainment and recreational facilities, provided the US Naval Station would allow civilian flights. The introduction of a free port and tax-free goods would attract foreign tourists (sex tourism), Olongapo would join the free port belt, with Hong Kong to the North and Singapore to the south. Commercial fishing, industrial estate housing development and a polytechnic college, utilities development and help for the Negritos, reforestation and flood control were all suggested as important steps to be undertaken. None of the suggestions were implemented, instead the entertainment industry expanded.

The plan made it clear that these developments would have to take place with the US Navy Base as a "next-door neighbour". It did not imagine the possibility of removing the bases and implementing a conversion of the base facilities. This is what we at PREDA envisaged and planned for.

I accompanied Professor Dumas to Manila to meet Justice Reyes, personal advisor to the President and Joker Arroyo, an honest progressive congressman for much of his public life and then the executive secretary to Aquino. Both Reyes and Joker were very interested and supportive of the idea of creating an economic zone as a replacement for the military base. The free port concept was not part of our plan as it would create, we believed, a free trade environment where all barriers would be breached and tax-free goods would pour into the country through massive smuggling that would damage the local economy. The free port was later included and it had the predicted results that led to a massive campaign by Manila against the freely available duty free imports. Their availability was later curtailed. We discussed at length the need to prepare a military base conversion plan. This plan was vital to provide credibility for the concept of a military base phase out and the establishment of an economic zone.

We argued that such a plan would provide work with dignity for thousands more Filipinos. It would also spell the end of the prostitution industry on the scale as we knew it, and prevent the rapid spread of the HIV/AIDS epidemic that was already making inroads and ravaging the lives of women and children. Both Reyes and Joker agreed to broach the idea to Aquino and try to get a conversion committee started. This was an important meeting as it placed the conversion of the military bases firmly on the Aquino policy agenda.

We were working on this in anticipation that the constitutional convention might provide articles that would ban foreign military bases from Philippine territory and ban all nuclear weapons and nuclear powered ships. This would, we hoped, pave the way for the withdrawal of the US bases. I travelled to the convention hall several times to lobby delegates to vote for such measures. There we had a powerful and tireless advocate of military base conversion, Professor Roland Simbulan. He led the anti-bases movement in the Metro Manila area and lobbied for conversion when he was invited to address the delegates to constitutional convention. He was very persuasive.

By 1988, it was clear that a new treaty prolonging the military bases would have to be negotiated with the US and by 1991 if there was no approved treaty then the bases would have to close. Conversion plans had to be ready. The Aquino government, much to our delight, set up the Abueva Committee to study the possibilities of base conversion and prepare the legislation that would guide the administration of these economic zones. Jose Abueva, the President of the University of the Philippines, headed the committee and held meetings at the University. Alex and I had gathered maps and detailed plans from friendly navy engineers. We were invited on several occasions to make presentations to the committee on what facilities were in place and what conversion possibilities lay ahead.

Our presentations were interrupted with prolonged electrical blackouts. Metro Manila had a tottering infrastructure ravaged by the corruption and waste of the Marcos years. Billions had been spent on the corrupt loans for the Bataan Nuclear Power Plant and interest on the vastly overpriced facility was running at $300,000 a day. Despite the electrical failures we held the meetings outside the building and hung the maps and charts on the outside walls.

Denis Murphy and Ed Gerlock, former priests committed to social justice and both active in the social movement all their lives, attended some of the presentations. During the breaks they sat with Alex and myself and we joked and laughed at what we were trying to do. The removal of the huge US military bases and replacing them with economic zones seemed such an impossibility that we were laughing at our own audacity and wild idealism for even proposing such a thing. But they were days when we believed that anything was worth a shot. If we never tried then there was no possibility. To try and fail was nothing to be ashamed of, we believed.

The bases were an accepted and integral part of Philippine political and economic scene for the past fifty years and life without the American presence had been unthinkable. It was important to take the initiative and present new concepts of national life no matter how unacceptable they were to the majority. We were elated that the discussions on alternatives were taking place. They gave legitimacy and respect to the concept and the plan grew with every discussion. We felt we were participating in what might one day contribute to a change in Philippine history.

The following May a smouldering issue regarding the vastly overpriced Bataan Nuclear Power Plant, about forty kilometres across Subic Bay from the PREDA Centre, burst into the headlines. A major accident at the Russian Chernobyl Nuclear Plant caused a deadly radioactive cloud to drift across Europe. This ignited a heated debate about the safety of the plant under construction. The plant was started by Marcos in a swelter of allegations of corruption and bribery. It was on hold but lobbyists were trying to get the project completed and commissioned.

We joined this protest with church people. There were warnings not to interfere. The Chernobyl disaster was the clinching evidence that the project was a potential catastrophe. Eventually, the campaign was successful and the Bataan Nuclear Power Plant was shelved indefinitely.

One day our attention was drawn away from these issues to a very human drama that was unfolding on the hillsides above the PREDA centre where we had given over land to the people whose houses in the Lighthouse Community had been destroyed in 1983.

Two of the boys in the PREDA community came rushing to the centre to tell us excitedly that there was a bulldozer climbing the hill to demolish the houses. We had heard rumours that a brothel owner was claiming part of the hillside under the PREDA leasehold and was planning to build an exclusive villa there, no doubt another brothel.

I felt a stab of nausea in my stomach, a sickly feeling of anger and fear. There would be a nasty fight ahead against politicians and their land grabbing cronies running the sex industry. I wondered if the community leaders had been intimidated to the point of surrender of their new settled plots. They had not contacted us or asked any help.

Myself and Alex and some of the boys hurried up the hillside puffing and panting to see what was happening. I was furiously thinking what we could do to stop them. We heard the bulldozer before we saw it, its harsh engine coughed and roared across the normally peaceful hillside like an intruder from hell. Its dry metal tracks clanked and squealed, the whine of the engine, the high pitched squeal of the gears, sent shivers through me. It was like an advancing army, how could we stop it? We were unorganised, caught unaware, vulnerable and weak. I imagined the worst; another demolition, as had happened to the original community at the lighthouse. We topped the rise and looked across the hillside. There, its yellow cab and shiny blade, flashed like a sword glinting in the sunshine ready to cut all before it.

It was heaving its way up the steep slope coughing filthy black fumes against a blue sky on its way to sow havoc and destruction. A small group of men carrying sledge hammers and shovels walked behind it like a platoon on its way to war.

We shaded our eyes and gazed across a shallow valley between the residents and us. An amazing scene was taking place. About thirty-five women from the basket weaving project and their neighbours had gathered on the brow of the hillside. They stood in front of the first of the small houses in the path of the roaring mammoth of a bulldozer.

As it neared the group, I feared that the women would be hurt. But the women were ready for this monster and its followers. One of the women shouted something and they divided into two groups. One ran in front of the bulldozer and sat down, arms linked, forming a human barricade twenty metres ahead of its blade. The other group surrounded the machine shouting invective and waving their arms at the driver and the men following. They had brooms and canes and were waving them menacingly. Later, I heard that they had threatened to castrate all of them.

The men bunched together and were cowed by the onslaught of the angry and assertive women. So accustomed were they to ordering about submissive and docile women, they had no defence and turned and fled down the hillside to the rapturous roars and cheers of the crowds of residents who had gathered to watch and encourage the women.

We shouted and cheered, jumping up and down in excitement. The women, having seen the men off, ran back to join the other group around the bulldozer and joined them shouting invective. The barricade wasn't budging, the driver had stopped and realised he was alone. The engine began to splutter and falter and then cut out. The driver jumped down and ran after the others, leaving behind a cheering group of victorious women hugging and congratulating each other on their success.

We too were shouting and waving to them and they waved back. I felt so happy that these brave women had the courage to take on the bulldozer themselves. They had learned the tactics of non-violence, and had the intelligence to implement them. They had grown stronger, empowered and independent.

No one dared to come and rescue the bulldozer for three days. Eventually, a driver was sent with a police escort and took it away. I made a visit to the house of the brothel owner to find out what claim he had on the leasehold property. He did not show me any legal documents but I met his wife and explained to her that the land was under a leasehold agreement with the government and the people had every right to be there. They said they would make no further claims and send no more bulldozers. But the hostility was obvious, I felt there would be retaliation and with his political connection to the local administration I knew there would be trouble.

Soon after this incident it was noticed that more incursions of outsiders were moving into the Nagbaculao village. They took over empty lots and set up shacks and shanties. This would have been acceptable if they were really homeless people in need. These new arrivals were the goons of the politicians that ruled the city. They were hostile and rude to the original Lighthouse settlers and they began to set up squatter huts and shelters. It was an invasion. What they could not accomplish by threats and intimidation they were going to achieve by infiltration and take over. We feared the worst. The happy community was soon disrupted by the newcomers and fistfights broke out.

Among these newcomers were the relatives of the district official who had participated in the demolition of the Lighthouse Village. Other newcomers were the Alcantara family, twin brothers and their families, one of them a suspected hit man for a leading politician. We were to hear more from these in the months to come.

Chapter Fourteen

It looked like someone had dumped a sack of garbage among the bushes, fronting the Olongapo General Hospital, or so it seemed to the casual passer-by. But a more observant person would have noticed a human foot protruding from the bundle of rags and newspapers. The bundle stirred and turned over, revealing to the glimmer of an early dawn the American features that told of a night of momentary pleasure in the back of a bar about ten years previously. That was when Rogi came into this world, another living souvenir and reminder of the "love" between the colonial master and the colonised. The skinny legs moved, a small shrunken figure sat up. The large bones told one thing about Rogi: the fact that they were covered almost only by skin told another.

In Olongapo in 1989, there was an estimated three thousand children living part of their lives on the streets, many were school dropouts others attending infrequently. They were beggars, hustlers, prostitutes for the foreigners. They sold plastic bags, cigarettes, gum, cleaned cars, shined shoes, anything to earn money. Hunger drove most of them, others were drug addicts. They slept in doorways and allies, parked buses, everywhere and anywhere. They were the urchins of the streets, the abandoned, the throwaway, the outcasts of a lost generation, unknown, unwanted and unloved. Many were put in jail and held there until their parents or gang mates came to pay off the police who put them there. The jail cells were overcrowded, shared a bucket for a toilet, and the boys had to be slaves of the hardened criminals.

Many of them were fathered by US servicemen and left to their mother. Sometimes she could not cope and either descended to begging on the streets, selling the baby for adoption, or giving the child to another family to care for and going back to work in the bars. These were the "throwaway children", as we called them, the cast-offs of the sex industry, the flotsam of a huge navy that came and went and left behind abandoned children by the thousands. Yet whenever the mothers could support these children they did the best they could. Years later we helped them organise a mother association and lobby for their rights and provided a special assistance programme for them.

Many a young woman was given to the men for the night, a payment made to the warden in charge. The warden saw it as a source of income and a way to keep the inmates satisfied and reduce fights and riots. The Filipino-American children were more vulnerable than the other street kids, much less likely to have a biological parent and their Caucasian features were prized by paedophiles and child sex tourists. Many were sold into sexual slavery.

May 1986. Sr Eva Palencia, a religious nun of the Daughters of Charity, working in the St. Joseph's Community Centre related to me the horrific story of a street child. Rosario Baluyot, twelve-years-old, had been found with a severe infection of her vagina and had been brought to the Olongapo City General Hospital. There were no parents or family and an operation was the only thing that could save her, but with no money nothing could be done to save her life. Sr Eva guaranteed that she would get the donations to pay the expense of the operation. The surgeon operated and removed a broken piece of a sexual vibrator from her vaginal canal. The damage was profound, the infection had spread beyond control. It was too late to save her. Rosario endured intense pain alone, her only visitors were Sr Eva and the social workers of the St. Joseph's Community Centre. The operation was too late and on May 20, 1987 Rosario died. Whoever had done this terrible crime had to be brought to justice. Alex and our staffer at the time began an investigation. They went to the hospital and talked to the doctors and there he recovered the broken piece of the vibrator removed from Rosario. Alex photographed it realising that this would be important evidence in establishing what had caused her death. We were determined to find out and bring the abuser to justice. We found the boy, Jessie, the companion of Rosario, and brought him into the PREDA community for street children. Soon after the investigators came and said the Mayor had ordered he be in the custody of the investigators. This was strange and unusual and we wondered why. Only later I was to question really what had happened and if the accused Austrian Stephen Ritter was really the abuser.

Among the street children were several who were sexually abused by local paedophiles and sex tourists. Nothing much had changed since the Daniel Dougherty case in 1983. One day, on May 14, 1987, forty-five-years-old Gaspar Alcantara, one of the illegal squatters who moved into the relocation community on the PREDA leasehold, saw a young girl lying in the street along Magsaysay Avenue not far from the gate of the US Military base. She was in pain and her cotton dress was dirty, threadbare and covered in blood. There was a foul smell coming from her emaciated body. There were bystanders but they were doing nothing except gawking at her cramped body.

He walked her to a passing jeepney and brought her to the hospital. He pretended to the admitting clerk that he did not know the girl and gave her name as "Tomboy", and an address as Lower Kalaklan. He later admitted that he knew her well for over a year and that she was a child that was visiting a friend at the hillside shack of his twin brother at

Nagbaculao. According to neighbours, Alcantara was suspected of being her pimp.

The child was admitted to the emergency room and after a wait she was examined by Doctors Piga and Monzon. The Olongapo City General Hospital would give a medical examination and a bed to an impoverished patient and then expect some family member to pay later. The doctor made no medical report and the child was left to wait without treatment because Alcantara had left and there was no family member to pay for treatment or medicine.

The child still had not been treated and was vomiting and had diarrhoea. Two church workers from St Joseph's, Jessica Herrera and Fe Israel, were doing hospital visitation on May 14 and found the child sitting on the cement floor. They were able to get her name and age, but that was all she would divulge. She was in extreme pain and they went to the doctors to get the prescription and bought medicine and gave it to the nurse for Rosario.

The next day, they visited again with Sr Eva. She saw the terrible condition of the child who had not had a change of clothes, was in intense pain and had received no treatment. Sr Eva asked the doctors for a further examination of Rosario. On May 17, Doctor Val A. Barcinal, a gynaecologist, examined Rosario and asked her why there was a foreign object in her vagina.

Rosario answered: "A Negro used me and he is the one who put it there."

He then asked her when did it happen and she answered in Tagalog: "About three months ago."

He found a hard object lodged in the vaginal canal that was causing the massive infection and made the area intensely painful to touch. He tried to remove it but could not. This gave rise to the speculation in the community and media that it was a US serviceman who had abused Rosario. If this was so, and even the perception that it could be so, then the political implications for the renegotiation of the bases treaty would be devastating.

There had been one hundred and eight cases of sexual abuse filed against US servicemen in Olongapo between 1979 and 1989 and many more were unreported. Fifteen of these cases involved children between four and six years of age, several others involved girls aged up to seventeen. Most of the cases were either resolved in favour of the US sailors or settled out of court. Many of the cases were quashed before they were even filed; none ever came to trial as the vast majority were handed over to the US court martial under the immunity from prosecution agreement between the US and the Philippines.

Even though the church workers and Sr Eva said they would pay for the medicines needed for the operation, there was a further unexplained delay and no surgical intervention was made. Rosario was now writhing in pain and agony and started to deteriorate rapidly. She developed high fever and was at times delirious.

Eventually, the hospital director, Dr Rosete, learned about the case of Rosario after the appeal of Sr Eva and he decided to operate even though the child was now in an extreme condition. "It is the only way to save her life," he said.

He removed the hard object from the vaginal canal and Rosario was returned to the ward. Sr Eva and the church workers arrived and saw that Rosario's feet were tied to the end of the bed. No one was there to explain why. The next day, May 20, Jessica Herrera went to visit Rosario and found her dying. She stayed with her and at 1:45 pm she died. There was no autopsy.

The death of Rosario was a shock to all and Sr Eva was determined to do something about it. She went to the hospital and got a death certificate. Jessica went back to the hospital, talked to one of the doctors and was able to get the foreign object, which was about two-and-a-half inches long, rounded and as thick as a medium size banana. It was the head of a sexual vibrator. It was in a sealed bottle with the name Rosario Baluyot on it and given to Sr Eva.

The relatives of Rosario were still unknown. Sr Eva came to visit Lex, Merly and myself at PREDA to discuss the tragic events and to see if we could locate the house of Gaspar Alcantara who had known Rosario. Together we went across the rain-drenched hillside slipping and sliding to the shack in the Nagbaculao community. We met with Gaspar and his twin brother. They gave us a cool reception, especially as we had been trying to protect the members of the Lighthouse community from the new settlers who were harassing and intimidating them. We learned that Gaspar Alcantara had known Rosario for a long time and that she had a grandmother living in the city by the name of Maria Burgos Turla. We got the details of her address and went to tell her about the death of Rosario.

She called her son and they went to the funeral parlour. Later Rosario was buried at the Olongapo Cemetery. She was placed in a simple cemented tomb. There was no name plaque or marker until those of us at PREDA who went to visit her grave had one placed.

Sr Eva waited to see if the hospital authorities would report the matter to the police when it was clear that Rosario was a minor who had been raped with an instrument and had died as a result. It was a case of murder. But no action was taken by the hospital authorities and so Sr Eva on June 18 went directly to the Chief of Police, Colonel Nicadore Daos and demanded an investigation. She was told that there had to be a formal complaint charging murder before legal action could be taken.

Rosario's mother, Anita Burgos, died on January 18, 1982 and Rosario was brought up by the grandmother. There were three boys and one sister who was the eldest. Rosario's father had left the family and was living in Bulacan, a province fifty kilometres away. At the time, Rosario was restless, had no interest in school and took to the streets. Her grandmother made a living buying and selling old newspapers.

With suspicion falling on an unknown US serviceman the military base was very interested to be seen seeking the suspect. They appointed a detective from the Naval Intelligence Service Agency (NISA), a Filipino civilian employee Conrado (Bobby) Salonga to work with the local police and investigate the crime. It seemed impossible to find a suspect, a place or a time for the crime. But the media were growing critical of the US Military, the police and the terrible plight of the street children, which was reflecting badly on the newly appointed Mayor. He, in turn, blamed the administration of Gordon for his unquestioned support of the military bases, encouraging the sex industry, providing no alternative employment for the city of almost two hundred thousand people and providing little help for the children. The authorities were desperate.

On September 16, 1987, Conrado (Bobby) Salonga, the naval investigator, contacted some of the street children that knew Rosario and found three boys who said they knew her. According to Salonga, they were with Rosario when she was picked up by her customer and brought to the MGM Hotel on Magsaysay Avenue and that one of their gang mates was with her, Jessie Ramirez. It was an unbelievable breakthrough.

Jessie, according to Salonga, said that he actually went with Rosario and her abuser to the bedroom and their abuser made them undress, shower and lie on the bed. Then he took out objects like inhalers from a bag, left them on a table, sexually abused Jessie and then Rosario later. Jessie reported that Rosario told him that the customer put the inhaler-like object into her vagina. Then the next morning, he paid them and left.

The additional fact that the boys did not describe a black man, as Rosario told Doctor Val A. Barcinal before her operation, was of no doubt, a great relief to the authorities.

I met with Salonga several times and he had Jessie with him, keeping him close and they formed a close friendship which was natural since Jessie had no father image in his life and Bobby was like an elder brother to him. Someone at last who cared for him and provided his basic needs. This relationship lasted until after the trial and then when we at PREDA offered to care for him and send him to school, mysteriously the mother and boy disappeared. We later learned that they had been whisked off to a remote town of Samar province where his mother came from. We sent money to Jessie for his education through the parish priest.

The investigators had the boys describe the suspect and a composite picture was drawn. They described a fair haired blue-eyed person. This was passed around the military base and local police but no US serviceman was found matching the description. Together, with a US special agent Douglas Heinsell, Corporal Marino Victoria and policeman Andres Montano, Jessie and another boy Michael Johnson, Salonga went to Manila and wandered around the tourist area teeming with foreigners and then, according to the official record of the trial, it happened by chance that a blonde-haired man with blue eyes walked past them on the pavement and, according to Salonga, Jessie Ramirez said that he looked just like the man who took them into the hotel. He did not fit the composite picture because he had no beard but Jessie volunteered that he had shaved it off.

Unbelievably, they had found him and he wasn't an American serviceman but an Austrian. On September 24, without the benefit of a warrant or having his rights read to him, he was arrested and handcuffed and brought to his hotel room where his bag and belongings were searched and contents listed, again without the trouble of getting a search warrant. He was brought to Olongapo, detained and two days later was charged of the crime of rape with homicide. No doubt a collective sigh of relief went up from the US military base and the pro-base lobby. For us at PREDA we could only hope that they got the right person.

However, there was another problem for the investigators.

Could Ritter be reliably placed at the scene of the crime? It was found out that according to his passport he had visited the Philippines for only a few days in October 1986 and then unbelievably, as luck again would have it, the name *Ritter* was found in the MGM Hotel guest book written in block capitals with the date that perfectly matched his passport dates visiting the Philippines.

In the Philippines, to initiate the legal proceedings, a complaint has to be filed with the office of the public Prosecutor. This is an uncomplicated procedure. The complainant can make a statement to the police or to a lawyer or directly to the Prosecutor and swear to it there and then. Then it must be filed in the Complaints Receiving Office.

The Public Prosecutor will hold a preliminary hearing in his office and call the complainant and the accused to hear arguments, ask questions and receive a sworn counter statement from the accused. This can be responded to by the complainant and eventually the Prosecutor will set the matter for his study and resolution. The outcome of the Prosecutors resolution is to either dismiss the complaint as having no solid evidence or declare that there is *prima facie* evidence that is sufficient information about the alleged crime be elevated to the court. It is then sent for trial before a Judge.

Now that there was a suspect, it was necessary to have a formal complaint and the grandmother had to be persuaded to make it. Sr Eva, Salonga and myself went to the grandmother's small wooden house with dried sun-baked walls and a rusted tin roof. There were piles of old newspapers everywhere, most of them the *Pacific Stars and Stripes* valued for its strong recyclable paper. We successfully persuaded her to take legal action and brought her to the office of the public Prosecutor to make her formal sworn statement. This was given to the First Assistant City Prosecutor Dorentino Floresta who is a man of proven integrity and conducted the preliminary investigation. He was later given the inevitable task of prosecuting Ritter.

Prosecutor Floresta, based on the evidence presented to him, found probable cause that Ritter was guilty of the crime he allegedly committed against Rosario Baluyot and filed the information before the court while the American authorities were understandably relieved that it was not an American serviceman that was apprehended.

It was a case that exposed the viciousness of the child prostitution business, a social evil long denied by the administration of Gordon. The interim Mayor Teddy Macapagal did not take any major steps to close down the sex industry either or provide alternatives. In Philippine law there is no bail for crimes of rape and homicide but we were amazed and shocked when we learned that Ritter's attorney was Edmundo Legaspi, a close associate of the former Mayor Gordon. Ritter was held at the local police station but the Judge granted him bail for the equivalent of five thousand dollars of today's money. He was allowed to go free but not to leave Olongapo. He rented a room at the Royal Lodge.

I heard he had a twelve-years-old boy with him called Michael, a street kid who hung about the police station and shined boots, swept the offices and ran errands for the police in exchange for food. He met Ritter in the jail and moved with him to the Royal Lodge where he ran errands. I was able to persuade Michael to join the PREDA street child programme that we were starting at that time. Michael, a runaway, stayed for a year. His story was featured in a major Norwegian documentary on child prostitution called *Throwaway Children*, made by a famous director, Edward Hambro.

Prosecutor Floresta was able to persuade the court to cancel the bail bond and have him re-arrested. He was detained at the Olongapo City Jail. Then we heard that the grandmother of Rosario had been contacted by an assistant of Attorney Legaspi and brought to his office to sign an out-of-court settlement. According to the grandmother's testimony, Ritter came in to Legaspi's office and then left after talking with Legaspi. She was offered five hundred dollars to change her statement about the age of Rosario. She accepted and was brought to the office of the City Prosecutor and signed the affidavit they wanted.

The date of birth was considered crucial because if Rosario was below twelve-years-old, the crime would be rape (even with her consent) with homicide as charged. If she was older than twelve she would be considered over age and a prostitute freely giving her consent. The vibrator would not be a weapon but considered a pleasure toy and her death would be accidental or due to the incompetence of the hospital. This is how the defence argued.

The out-of-court settlement or the pay off is a common arrangement to have a case withdrawn or to change the facts of the case. But in a criminal case a payment of compensation can be considered evidence of guilt. Sr Eva and I went to the house of the grandmother and we sat among the piles of old newspapers stacked and tied with plastic straw. Two other women were sorting piles of papers sold to them by the street children who went about collecting scraps loading them in small push carts and delivering them to Mrs Burgos. It was during their deliveries that Rosario probably first met these wild kids who had a freedom of the streets and ran away with them from the harsh tongue and child labour in her grandmother's business.

She was an old woman who had had a hard and bitter life. That bitterness was etched on her heavily wrinkled face, her jowls and neck hanging like wet newspaper, her eyes deep set with black rings and eye-bags. Long hair, once black, was heavily streaked with grey, fell over her shoulders. She was a tough streetwise woman. We sat on a green vinyl-covered couch that was urgently in need of repair.

We hoped to persuade her to continue with the case and attend the next scheduled hearing. But the sum of money she received was huge and there was another five thousand pesos yet to come.

Mrs Burgos was irritated at our presence. She knew the reason for our visit and started telling us that the case was over and there was nothing more to be done. Speaking in Tagalog, we both explained that so long as there was no justice for children like Rosario the abuse and killing would go on. Perpetrators would know that they just had to make a pay off and there would be no punishment. Things had to change and she could make a difference if she would testify.

Making a payment to settle a case is a common practice in the Philippines. Social workers would tell me that the local police negotiated the price with the parents of the victim. The parents were told that the case would be impossible to prove, it would cost them a fortune in legal fees to fight in court so it was better to settle. The abuser was free to target other victims until caught again. Corrupt Prosecutors are also known to shelve or settle such cases under the table. In the years ahead this practice became a target for our publicity campaigns for children's rights.

We persuaded the grandmother by explaining that few people knew that such terrible things were happening to thousands of children and the trial could help bring justice and truth and knowledge to many. All she had to do was to testify in court to all that had taken place. I promised that I would get her a lawyer at no cost to her. She eventually agreed. I would pick her up on the morning when she was to testify.

And testify she did. A good friend and brilliant lawyer, Sergio Cruz (who fought many long and difficult legal battles with the Gordon administration and won a lot of them), agreed to come in as private Prosecutor. In court, during the next hearing he cross-examined the grandmother and exposed the payoff scandal. It was December 1987 and by now Attorney Legaspi, Ritter's lawyer, was appointed officer-in charge of Olongapo City as elections were scheduled for the following January 8, 1987 and the seat had to be left vacant. In the end the prosecution made a strong case and

Judge Alicia L. Santos found Ritter guilty as charged.

Ritter strongly maintained his innocence. He claimed he was a victim of mistaken identity, deplored the media's one sided reporting when it failed to air his denials, that his lawyers extorted money from him by delaying the case and he claimed that the US Navy had framed him.

The appeal took almost another year. The defence argued again that the length of time between the rape and insertion of the vibrator, October 1986 and the death of Rosario on May 20, 1987, a period of seven months without infection setting in, was medically unlikely and therefore the crime must have taken place much later, only weeks before Rosario was brought to the hospital. The correct age of Rosario was also a technical point and the defence claimed the proof of age was lacking. This was a terrible disappointment and all of us fighting for the victims of child sexual abuse could not understand the reversal of the guilty verdict. But never-the-less we were still determined to continue trying to bring about a climate where children were to be considered to have all the same rights as adults and even more so since they were so vulnerable and at risk.

Children's rights advocates redoubled their efforts to advance legislation to protect children. But it was not to be until 1992 that Republic Act No. 7610 would be enacted and signed into law by President Aquino on June 17 ,1992 and the implementing rules and regulations signed by the then Secretary of Justice Franklin M. Drilon the following October 1993.

There were reports that the sex mafia of Barrio Barretto, a suburb of Olongapo City, had set up a new form of exploitation of women boxing. I went with Alex to pay a visit. We went to the Casa Blanca, a sex bar and club. There was the usual raised mirrored stage behind the bar and a boxing ring in the centre of the club floor.

The brothel was operated by an American who specialised in putting on lewd sex shows to attract the servicemen. Olongapo had a wide selection of these lewd shows and clubs competed with each other in presenting the most lewd and dehumanising shows possible. Young girls and women were pressured into participating, not only for the money, which was little enough, but it was what they had to do to get the drugs their pimps supplied to them. Participation in the boxing was a condition of employment set by the operators. If the girl did not like it she was fired and blacklisted. No other foreign-owned club would hire her. The international sex mafia conspired to control the lives of the women as tightly as possible, especially to prevent the victims from making formal complaints of abuse and exploitation against the operators. Their lives are not their own. These impoverished youth have very few options in life.

There were depraved acts that they were forced to perform, advertised as demonstrating the supposedly "sexual prowess" of the women at that particular club. Thus they attracted more clients not only to see the shows but to pick up young girls, minors included, after the performance when their sexual appetites were suitably aroused. During the stage show, the women were trained to use their vagina to pickup objects placed on a small table on which they danced naked. There were the "banana cutters", "egg breakers", "the coin and bottle pickers" among others.

Oil and mud wrestling were popular. The women boxing bouts were especially favoured, perhaps the sight of bloody noses and the violence aroused the men's sexual aggression, who knows. These acts helped earn Olongapo's reputation as the "raunchiest liberty port in the world", in the words of a leading newspaper.

The Casa Blanca staged "female boxing" as it pulled in a lot of customers. The American owner told the girls to make a spectacle by boxing each other bloody and offering them financial rewards for the winner and something lesser for the looser. In the end it was severe punishment for a pittance while he earned thousands of dollars, the girls earned cents.

This is what we saw during our visit. Two young girls, with boxing gloves bigger than their heads in shorts and sweatshirts, were beating each other black and blue. No doubt the physical aggression became real and their anger at the injustice and suffering of life was transferred to her opponent and their fury was taken out on each other. The sailors loved this show of brutality and their screams and howls were accompanied by a ferocious banging of ash trays on the tables as they shouted for one or the other to "Kill her! Kill her"!

The other young women were paraded on a stage behind the bar in bikinis, some with miniature stars and stripes on the skimpy attire, in deference perhaps to the customers "patriotic" feelings. The customers picked out the girl of their choice like goodies in a market, paid the bar owner and took the girl to a room at the back of the bar or to a local cheap hotel for sex. In many cases the girls were as young as thirteen or fourteen-years-old. The customers are twice their size and weight and three times their age.

Fe Santos, who was one strong-minded girl who got a job at the Casa Blanca as a waitress, was willing to chat up the lonely customers but that was all. She never expected to be "bar fined", that is, a customer pays the bar owner a "fine" for taking her out of her job as waitress. Fe was not any ordinary girl, she refused to be bar fined or be a boxer. She was fired by the owner.

A very brave young man Dionisio (Dennis) Joaquin, from Santa Rita, Olongapo, was well known as a dedicated social worker and friend of mine. We met during his school days. He was in contact with the growing progressive labour unions and volunteered to help the women. One day, soon after Fe took her stand, she and Dennis came to see Alex and Merly and myself at PREDA and asked for our help. We were very glad for the chance to help these brave people who were taking on the same forces that we were already struggling against.

Dennis was active in labour issues when he was an employee at the US Naval Base. With forty-two other employees he tried to form an independent union inside the Navy Base. The admiral was not amused and unions were seen as fronts for Communists. Dennis and the forty-two were all fired. The group was led by Eddie Torres and he staged a hunger strike protest at the main gate of the base. We offered them help and support and they invited me to conduct a prayer service with them and I did. They were known as the "Subic 42".

Dennis with Fe organised a labour strike at the Casa Blanca brothel and set up a picket and small encampment outside the entrance along the national highway. We provided rice and cash for them to hold the picket line as long as they dared. Soon the other women were walking out of the club to join the picket. It was the first strike of its kind by bar women in the Philippines.

In the Philippines and in other Asian countries, many of the women are prostituted by deception, fraud and threats. As young teenagers in remote villages they are entrusted to some local recruiter who promises them jobs as domestic helpers in the big city. They give cash to the parents so that they are indebted and are like bonded workers who have to work to pay off the cash advance. Seldom do the parents know that their children will be prostituted by guile and skulduggery.

Many young women we rescued from brothels and bars told me they were sexually abused or raped in their own home or by a neighbour and ran away from home. They lose their self-esteem, feel useless and they easily fall for any empty promise. The young runaways are hungry, homeless and vulnerable. These young teenagers are picked up by pimps and sold to the bars and clubs. Then there was no enforceable law to prevent this but a few years later we would be lobbying vigorously for such legislation.

Prostitution is a crime under Philippine law but it is seldom enforced and many of the women are abused while in custody, the bar owners pay the police and the next day everything is back to normal. Other clever bar operators invite the chief of police to a party, there he "accidentally" meets a very young waitress who is then encouraged and paid to become his girlfriend. He is now involved sexually with a minor and has to protect the industry lest he be exposed. Not only police but even Prosecutors and Judges can fall into traps like these and are compromised and are easily blackmailed.

The striking women soon had placards and banners on display: STOP FORCED BOXING! one read. *We like Americans if they respect our rights*, read another.

The owner of Casa Blanca, Hoge erected a large sign board of his own: *Business as usual, pay no attention to Communist infiltrators (KMU)*, it declared, referring to the trade union movement know by it initials KMU. Hoge took in other desperate prostituted women to continue the boxing bouts and the sex trade.

I decided to write an article for my weekly newspaper column on the strike and went to talk with Hoge to get his views. I was astonished when he told me that he was a former assistant district attorney from Hawaii, a claim never confirmed. He owned two other clubs in Olongapo. He wasn't a sleazy pot bellied sex tourist type but educated, articulate and fully aware of what he was doing.

"I agree, it's an immoral business," he said, "but it's legal, when the girls come here to work we explain that boxing is a condition of employment."

And legal it was, since the bars and brothels had operating permits from the local government permit office.

I was standing by the roadside with Hoge, leaning on my car a distance from the picket line. "You may hate me for what has happened to Barretto, I was responsible for it," he said, referring perhaps to the fact that years previously Barrio Barretto, which straddles the national highway was a centre for wicker furniture and a quite residential suburb of Olongapo City proper. When the brothels and bars proliferated and the foreigners offered huge sums to rent building along the main road the property owners in Barretto threw out the small shop owners and wicker and cane furniture craft makers and many were unemployed. With official approval it became an extension of the Olongapo sex business along the infamous sex row leading up to the entrance of the military base. Some of the unemployed came to PREDA to find work. We were already forming small producer groups and engaging in Fair Trade.

While Dennis and the women were holding the picket line and receiving more and more threats we were doing our best to develop support for the issue. The fact that there were more friendly people in the city government encouraged us to try and get the lewd shows banned. Closing the sex clubs was impossible because there was as yet no alternative. Beside the family of the newly appointed Mayor had interests in restaurants and a beer garden along Rizal Avenue.

Our military bases conversion plan was still a dream, although it was taking on practical form with the Abueva Board preparing a conversion law and transition plan if ever such an unthinkable thing be possible. That January 14,1987 Alex and myself had joined up with a small group of religious sisters and went to the City Council during their monthly meeting. I read a proposal advocating an ordinance that would ban boxing and lewd shows. It was drafted by Assistant City Prosecutor Dorintino Floresta, a man of integrity and vision and a strong outspoken advocate of human rights.

"We have reached a point in our history when we, concerned Christians of Zambales, cannot simply close our eyes and seal our lips to all the violations committed against the human person that are continuously being perpetrated in our midst," read our opening statement.

The council took up the issue and tabled it for future deliberation and action. It helped that the session was being broadcast over local radio, a huge change from the days of dark secretive workings of the previous administration. I was soon leaving for a three-month justice and faith workshop in Ireland. With the new government in place I felt relaxed enough to undertake this course knowing that there would be no attempt to take over the centre or harass us. Merly and Alex were very capable to handle all contingencies and keep the work going and stand by Dennis and Fe on the ongoing picket by the roadside at Barretto.

After I left for Ireland, Alex borrowed a video camera and taped one of the bloody boxing bouts being staged by Hoge. Support began to grow slowly. After years of enforced silence several groups were becoming vocal and working openly to change the situation of the women and children. Brenda Stoltsfus and Mennonite missionaries had already joined the protest and being Americans they made a strong impression on the American community at the base.

The Mennonite Central Committee in the US had responded generously to our call for help in funding the visit of Dr Jeffrey Dumas as a consultant on the military base conversion plan we were working on. They responded years previously when I was trying to set up a team of women lay missionaries. I invited the Columban and the Maryknoll missionaries to train and support a team of women lay missionaries to provide a suitable service centre for the prostituted women and children. They responded enthusiastically as had the Mennonite Central Committee but – before the team was due to assemble the traditionalists in St Joseph's Parish, where I had begun my mission – stood against it. It was a sad day for us when the Columban and Maryknoll could not proceed but Mennonite Central Committee carried on and we welcomed Brenda to Olongapo and helped to get her settled. She soon had a contact mission underway to help the bar women in ways that we had not. The Buklod Centre (meaning "working together arm-in-arm") for former prostituted women was the result of courageous pioneering work which has endured to this day.

More support arrived with Adul De Leon, a well known actress and the charismatic leader of the Philippine Women's Coalition of Non-Government Organisations known as Gabriela, joined the picket and held a rally outside the Casa Blanca. Hoge was infuriated, his business had fallen off in all the clubs and he feared that his licenses could be cancelled as a result of our protests to the City Council. The issue of sex tourism was not then national in scope and it was around that time too that Adul played the role of a nun helping prostitutes in the film *American Dream,* part of which was filmed on location at PREDA. This film helped immeasurably to bring the issues of exploited women and children and the plight of the Filipino-American children to national prominence.

There was to be another Filipino feature film made in the city entitled *Sa Kuko ng Agila* (*In the Claws of the Eagle*). The story traced the life of an abandoned Filipino-American child abandoned by a US serviceman. It told the fate of the child's mother who became a bar woman. The leading man was screen idol of the decade, Joseph Estrada, who was then a Senator and was sure to vote against the upcoming treaty with the US to renew the bases treaty. He was to be elected as President of the Republic in 1998.

Nelia Sancho, a leading women's rights advocate also helped by organising a rally along Magsaysay Drive, the notorious red light district in the centre of the city. Dr Hector Ruiz, a long time opposition leader was then Vice Mayor, invited Alex to show the video of the women boxing to the City Council. It had an electrifying effect. The crescendo of screaming sailors demanding bloody faces and pulverized bodies and the cries of the beaten women, all showed the depravity and dehumanising, it had not only on the women but on the young sailors themselves. Imagining how th would treat their wives and children years later wa thing that sent shivers down the spine. God he often prayed.

The video made the case against the lewd shows. There was a loud and heated debate and in the end they passed the city ordinance banning boxing and all lewd shows. It was challenged in court by the club operators of the Casa Blanca and Casa Boom Boom, both owned by Hoge in July 1987. He claimed it was a sport and not a lewd show. Judge Esther Nobles Bans said in her decision the law was designed to promote and protect the dignity of women and that the "alleged sport" was a form of exploitation and total degradation of Filipino womanhood. The law was upheld but when the former administration came back into power a year later, it was seldom, if ever enforced.

Retaliation against the strikers had yet to come. I was still in Ireland as the women and their supporters demanded justice. Hoge would not budge. One night when Dennis was asleep near the picket line our worst fears were fulfilled. Two assassins crept up on Dennis. They shot him on the spot, got into a car and drove away. It was a brutal and vicious killing, all were shocked and outraged. When I received the news in Ireland I was very depressed. I had imagined, foolishly, that with the Aquino government there would be peace, order, and justice.

But that was to be a false hope. In fact the human rights abuses became worse and old scores were settled and new ones created. There was a growing paranoia among those with right wing anti-Communist fears. Unknown and unauthorised by the government, a shadowy hit squad associated with the military began a secret war against suspected Communists and their sympathisers. They were part of a destabilization force that was to attack the Aquino government from within.

There was a public outcry; Hoge was a suspected mastermind and he disappeared when five suspects were identified as the hit men and they were brought to trial. In June 1990, Judge Esther Nobel-Bans of the Regional Trial Court passed sentence on Nicomedes Fabro and four others (who were never caught) for the murder of Dionisio (Dennis) Joaquin. Fabro confessed to being paid ten thousand pesos (about $700) for the assassination.

It was just one more of the thousands of unsolved murders. The Casa Blanca closed soon after.

That March 1987, I left for a justice and peace workshop hosted by the Columban Fathers at Dalgan and organised and managed by Fr Eamon O'Brien, a classmate of mine at the seminary. It was excellent in every respect .

There were church lay people from many countries and all were involved with the work for social justice in their own countries. The workshop was intended to help all of us to reflect on what we were doing, give us an opportunity to rest and reflect on our work and how we were succeeding or not and it was a chance to recharge our spiritual batteries and plan for the future. It was also a great opportunity for me to have frequent home visits with my mother who was living alone but still well and active. We are a family of world travellers. My two sisters and my brother John had emigrated years before to Canada; my sister Sheila went to England and married there. John returned from Canada and settled down near home in Dublin. Michael, my other brother, emigrated to Australia, where he died in a car accident; his car was struck by a passing train at a remote rail crossing.

It took me time to adjust to life in Ireland. Church life was heavy with tradition and ritual and difficult to get excited about after the active and socially committed church of the Philippines where lay people, priests and nuns were risking their live daily for the poor. Many did lose their lives for their beliefs. I returned to the Philippines that June of 1987.

By the following August 1987, we felt a rising tide of resentment against us from the city administration. Philippine public opinion was changing. There was a rising tide of anti-US military bases sentiment. This communicated itself to the visiting servicemen and there was a fall off of customers to the bars and clubs. Since we were vocal and outspoken in our opposition to the bases and active in proposing the economic alternative plan it was not surprising that there would be a reaction.

It came in the form of a demonstration that August 1987 led by the infiltrators into the resettlement area provided by PREDA for the Lighthouse community that had their village totally demolished. This was well funded and organised by a politician opposed to our work.

The community relocated on the barren hillside leased to the PREDA Centre for reforestation had been infiltrated during the previous six months prior to the elections. Many we knew to be supporters of the city government and now that the ruling family was back in City Hall, we expected trouble. It was not long in coming.

There were some suspects from the criminal world setting up shanties on the hillside inside the PREDA lease area. The former district official who had helped demolish the Lighthouse community claimed a piece of land and set up a temporary shack. The original settlers whom we helped relocate after the demolition were now facing more trouble from their tormentors.

Their community meetings were broken up, sometimes at gunpoint. One woman described the local district official, who had led the demolition of their Lighthouse homes, as a gangster-like figure who called them Communists led by "that Communist priest". This was to become a familiar form of labelling and it was having sinister effects in other parts of the Philippines. The intruders took over the control of the community. We were powerless to stop them.

Perhaps it was on the instigation of their political boss that the new group began an agitation campaign against us demanding that they get rights to all the property. It was clear that they were fronting for somebody more powerful. It struck us that perhaps this was the plan of the nightclub owner and his political backer.

It was a serious setback for the original settlers and we decided to transfer land rights to them and block the land grabbers. When news of this leaked out the infiltrators staged a demonstration accusing us of driving out the squatters. The infiltrators' protest took the form of blocking our driveway with a small water tank and shouting slogans for me to get out. It fizzled out after a day when we showed them that we had formally turned over the rights of the land area to the Department of Natural Resources and Environment and they could apply for their rights to the government.

That August 28, we were shocked when we heard over the radio that there was a military coup taking place in Manila. Former military officers of the Marcos security group led by Col. Gregorio Honasan who had led a previous attempt was at it again. Honasan was a young officer with a history of turning against the ruling administration. In 1986, he revolted against Marcos together with his mentor, Defence Minister Juan Ponce Enrile.

Their plot was reported to Marcos who sent troops to wipe them out. Honasan and Enrile went to ground in Camp Aguinaldo, a military camp in the capitol, where they were joined by General Fidel Ramos. From this predicament of a failed revolt, they were rescued from Marcos' forces by a people's power movement supported by Cardinal Jamie Sin the previous February 1986. It was this people's power movement that quickly turned into a non-violent uprising that forced Marcos to flee.

The rebel officers and their political backers had imagined themselves the rightful victors over Marcos but had not reckoned with the democratic forces that swept Aquino to power. It was a frightening time for all who had thought the end of military dictatorships were over. Honasan and his fellow coup plotter, unabashed Marcos loyalist Reynaldo Cabauatan, were able to take control of three television stations and also Camp Aguinaldo. It looked like the government was going to fall.

One report claimed that the US Embassy had called up Cardinal Jamie Sin to ask him to advise Aquino to accept the formation of a junta wherein Aquino would have limited power. The Cardinal denied the report. The suspicion was rife that elements in the Pentagon were deeply worried about the future of the military bases and that a junta was the only way to preserve them.

The policy of Aquino up to this time was to keep her options open regarding the future of the bases. The US Military Bases Agreement was to expire in 1991. General Fidel Ramos, cousin and former supporter of Marcos who joined the rebels against Marcos and now the defence secretary to Aquino, rallied the government troops to beat back the military rebels.

The US was understandably nervous about the growing nationalistic sentiment sweeping the Philippines. For some right wing hawks in the Pentagon this was a front for Communist agitation and they believed that Aquino was soft on the Communists and the Left.

I was writing about the background to the growing harassment of progressive clergy and church workers by militias with rabid anti-Communist sentiments. Everyone who disagreed with them was branded subversive, anti-American and Communist. This was not lost on our local opponents in Olongapo who lost no opportunity to label all of us at PREDA as "Communist sympathisers".

General Fidel Ramos came under attack from a retired US Army General John Singulab who claimed that he should be replaced by "someone who knows how to fight" the Communist insurgency. At this time, the official newspaper of the Communist Party claimed that there were only seven thousand regulars under arms but "tens of thousands part-time farmer guerrillas". Singulab was a frequent visitor to the Philippines and suspected of laying the groundwork for the coup. This he denied.

It was at this time that a militant form of Christian fundamentalism was gaining political influence in provincial towns and villages. The movement was linked to the "new right" in the US and was seen as part of the "low intensity conflict" that was being waged at the village level by the anti-Communist groups. The Christian anti-Communist Crusade affiliated with the World Anti-Communist League of Singlaub and the Asian Ecumenical Inter-Faith Council, a regional affiliate of the Unification Church of the Rev. Sun Myung Moon.

Fanatical armed militia were the armed forces on the ground that set out to sow terror and fear among villagers who might harbour or help rebel groups. They worked on the vigilante principle, if you are pointed out as an enemy then you were an enemy and could be hacked to death on the spot. They had the support of local military commanders and committed barbaric acts and atrocities without control or restraint. The Philippine human rights group Task Force Detainees and other groups documented many of these heinous crimes.

In the Diocese of Kidapawan, North Cotabato Bishop Juan de Dios reported killings of church workers by a group called the Tadtad. In Davao City, Police Chief Lt. Col.Franco Calida said that he could call up two thousand Tatad fanatics also called the Alsa Masa. One group hacked to death Peter Alderite in public without any police response. Despite Church protest, President Aquino was helpless to control the groups and they expanded with her apparent blessing.

The church's social action had been dubbed by extremist right wing elements as subversive and priests and religious and church workers of several denominations were being physically attacked and some killed. The accusations that they were meddling in politics were sufficient to brand them as subversive. The Association of Major Religious Superiors of the Philippines had spoken out in November 1987 and condemned the growing violence and human rights violations and that it had "shattered hopes and dreams". The

Church hierarchy was not very outspoken against the spreading human rights violations.

Auxiliary Bishop Teodoro Bacani of the Archdiocese of Manila under Cardinal Jamie Sin said: "The Aquino government can afford that we (the Bishops) become critical, it needs more public criticism. The Bishops were silent in 1987 not because we were afraid to criticise the government but because we feared we might tend to dominate society."

We had all hoped and longed for a new Philippines under President Aquino with the fall of the Marcos regime but it was not to be. An entrenched right wing oligarchy still pulled the puppet strings of power. Cardinal Sin supported the involvement of church workers and lay people in politics. He told the bishops at a Synod in Rome that religion and politics cannot be divorced in an Asian setting. In the Philippines, he said, that to separate religion and politics would amount to schizophrenia. Catholic lay people had to act within Philippine politics.

A well known human rights advocate, Benedictine Sr Mary John Mananzan, told a newspaper "the rank and file members of the church have never given up the struggle for the poor" and said Bishops could find it hard to criticise a government they helped to install.

A socially active Good Shepherd Sr Christine Tan, a delegate to the commission that drafted the 1987 Constitution, was quoted as saying, "The gap between the moneyed rich and the masses will not only be wider but unbridgeable," and told reporters: "The Church will grow more rightist, more devotional and more worldly."

In September that year, I was invited to a meeting of writers and editors of various publications to reflect on the recent coup to analyse the role of the US. The coup plotters had been thwarted but the leaders had gone into hiding. I had noticed unusual convoys of military trucks coming out of the marine armoury and ammunition magazine on the base a few weeks before the coup and during the weeks after there was similar activity. The speculation was that the coup plotters had US backing and were hiding in the bases.

By October, that speculation came close to the truth. One of the renegade officers behind the coup, Reynaldo Cabauatan, called a press conference inside the Clark US Air Force Base in Pampanga, about ninety kilometres north of Manila. The cat was out of the bag, so to speak.

This was widely interpreted as a signal from the US Military that they were extremely displeased with President Aquino's sympathetic leaning to the Left and to the dismantling of the US bases that they espoused. Commenting on the press conference at Clark, an editorial in the *Inquirer* on October 9, 1989 ended with this comment: "The bottom line is evidently the bases. For as long as they are here, there will always be factions within the US government which, for one reason or another, will feel obliged to resort to interventionism in the Philippines."

The anti-Communist vigilantes proliferated in the countryside implementing what was believed to be a new US doctrine of low intensity conflict. This was a form of intervention wherein US troops would not be directly involved but local militias, army rebels and other anti-Communist organisation would be helped and assisted to achieve US foreign policy goals. This was the strategy that brought the Contras to prominence in Nicaragua and other Latin American countries and we were experiencing it here. Forcing Aquino to change her position on the bases was apparently one of the goals of this strategy.

In October, there was more evidence that elements of the US Military were out to destabilise the Aquino government while the US State Department continued to give reassurances that they were fully behind Aquino and the democratic process. On October 22, Malaya published the contents of an Army report that claimed US Embassy personnel had intervened on behalf of the coup plotters and tried to deflect the army from attacking them in Camp Aguinaldo. US

Assistant Military Attaché Major Victor Raphael was identified as the most active in helping to communicate the movements of the army troops to the plotters and in dissuading the army commanders from attacking. Fifty-three people were killed in the fighting and over three hundred others were wounded.

This became a major story and further inflamed a smouldering anti-American sentiment that had been long buried. Filipinos had resented the support that the US had given to the dictatorship of Marcos and how they had turned a blind eye to the long years of torture, murder and human rights violations by his regime. Nor had they been very supportive of the now slain Aquino who had spent three years in exile in the US.

We were all very depressed with this news. Our hopes for a new democratic government free from foreign interference was dashed. The legacy of Marcos was a bureaucracy riddled with graft and corruption that was next to impossible for Aquino to reform. She was considered to be weak and ineffectual during her first year and the coup attempts made her even more so.

However, we continued with our efforts to promote the plan to replace the bases with an economic zone. The anti-Communist fever was being stirred up by fanatics in the countryside backed, we suspected, by extreme rightwing elements. In those days of the Reagan administration, it was not surprising considering the policy of favouring non-democratic regimes that provided security to the interest of big business and military installations. The US Embassy denied involvement in the coup but conceded to the public outrage and Raphael was transferred out of the Philippines.

As if in response to this anti-Communist provocation and, which in turn further justified it, the shocking murders of four US personnel within a kilometre of Clarke heightened tensions on all sides. The sprawling 56, six and fifty hectare complex with almost ten thousand US servicemen and women, was on high security alert, intensified patrols were mounted. The killings were all within an hour of each other in a residential area outside the base perimeter fence. It was the first time that US servicemen had been targets of assassins. The Communists had issued warnings that US personnel would be targets if there was US involvement in counter-insurgency activities.

In Olongapo, as in Angeles City, the bars and clubs were deserted, the lights dimmed, the bands were subdued. The sex industry came to a whining standstill like an old gramophone running out of power. For the first time ever, US armed Marines patrolled the streets outside the bases to provide security to those living off base. President Aquino flew to Clark to attend the funeral of one of the victims and said that the patrols were justified.

The vigilante movement began to spread as a result. In Manila, Brigadier General Alfredo Lim organised a group of armed vigilantes to target suspected Communists even though they had little idea who they might be. Senator Wigberto Tañada, chairman of the Senate Committee on Justice and Peace, reported that as many as one hundred and thirty four well-organised vigilante groups were active in the Southern Philippines.

Richard Gordon returned to power following an election on January 18, 1988 that was mired in allegations of fraud, vote rigging and ballot box stuffing. None of it was ever proved of course. It was back to business as usual for the bar and brothel industry. The nightclub owners took heart that the industry would have renewed support and promotion from City Hall. Instead the Mayor announced that he was going to embark on a campaign to "clean up" the "sleazy city" image and to provide total protection for the military tourists. When the four US servicemen were killed in Angeles City the previous October, thousands of servicemen were confined to the base and it was a devastating blow for the Angeles and Olongapo sex industry.

The Manila Chronicle wrote that "Olongapo, the Sodom and Gomorrah of South East Asia isn't what it used to be". The city administration did not file libellous charges against the paper. During a press conference that January 1988, Mayor Gordon said he would be a strong leader, create a new image of Olongapo as the festival city with "Mardi Gras" on the streets. He clearly stated he had no policy on summary executions, called "salvaging", a euphemism. He declared war on drug pushers and criminals. He had a "no-work, no-pay policy", and that every one will help erase the "Sin City" image. The city would be a carnival town safe for tourists, in particular military tourists from the seventh fleet. We braced ourselves for some kind of crackdown.

In February 1988, the newly reorganised city demolition crews got ready for another demolition. The target was the shacks and shanties of the poor at the city dump behind the Pag-asa market. PREDA social workers were visiting the impoverished families that lived off the refuse of the clubs and restaurants. This was a person-to-person contact whereby first aid was administered to children with wounds and sores and others were referred to the charity clinics.

This area was situated behind the Pag-asa public market near the main gate of the Subic Bay US Naval Base. Just across the canal was the perimeter fence of the base. At night some of the residents sneaked across the canal, scaled the fence and scavenged at the navy dump. This was not unusual. Hundreds of intruders crossed into the base through holes in the huge security fence and sneaked through the forests. They walked several kilometres to get to the vast dump that leaked toxic chemicals into the nearby canal and into the Subic Bay. This was to become a serious issue in the years to come.

The US government withheld development funds to the local government because of the conditions in areas like Pag-asa which lined the perimeter of the canal that separated the squatter area from the base were considered a health threat to the base residents and an eyesore. Outright demolition was the answer, according to local officials. They were to be removed the same as the Lighthouse community.

At the Pag-asa dump, the people eked out a living savaging scraps from the piles of garbage that spilled from the back of dump trucks everyday. When the trucks arrived there was a wild scramble by the raggedly dressed scavengers, mostly women and children. They swarmed over the fresh garbage like hungry flies. Their weapons against want were empty sacks and bent pieces of wire. These they effectively used to scrape and sort the filthy garbage. They fought over found treasures that would mean a meal for the day. A piece of electric wire, a broken electric fan, a sack of old newspapers, a bag of bones, were all valuables that earned them a pittance but it meant a bowl of rice at least.

The ramshackle grubby shacks with rusted metal sheet roofs held down with rubber tyres were still home. There was no sanitation or toilets and the community had a few public faucets for water. Every morning and evening, long lines formed at the faucets to fill plastic buckets for their daily needs. I would visit from time to time and sit around on an upturned plastic bucket and discuss the community problems and the threatened demolition. The people were determined to resist. The Mayor was determined to clear them out and US Navy promised a school would be built there. The poor had little trust in the promised resettlement. Moved away form their daily course of livelihood, they would have nothing to eat. It was clear that the city and Navy authorities were working together to close the dump that was a ghastly eyesore on the edge of the pristine and manicured base. It was of course an unhealthy and dangerous place for any human to live but if there was no alternative work what would the people do?

It was a problem in thousands of urban communities everywhere in the Philippines and throughout Asia. The teeming poor were surviving on the margins of society without a daily income. Raking the dumps for food to live a day longer was their main preoccupation. The physical place where they continued to survive was determined by the proximity to the refuse of society. They put together cardboard and metal scraps to keep the sun and rain off them and that was home.

That February, a payloader suddenly came roaring into the dump scattering the people left and right and smashed into the first of the shacks before the people could form a human barricade to protect their homes. The media reported that as many as one hundred families lost their homes. The people had organised themselves as had the Lighthouse community and resisted demolition as long as they could. The city government established a remote landfill area in Cabalan, outside the city proper, and had stopped dumping rubbish in the Pag-asa area. Some scavengers moved to the new dumpsite on the city limits.

This was the local version of the infamous "Smoky Mountain" of Manila and the Payatas Dump in Quezon City that collapsed in July 2000 burying hundreds of men, women and children. The Olongapo scavengers were branded as illegal squatters and had to leave. Confrontation was inevitable.

There was a growing hostility and opposition to our efforts to help the deprived settlers and our campaign to replace the military base with an economic zone. Local politicians made critical remarks too about the PREDA campaign for children's rights. Some who had interests in the entertainment industry claimed that our campaign branded the city as a "Sin City", and gave it a bad reputation that kept away tourists. According to the politicians, there was no evidence that there was any child prostitution in the city.

We were still being pressured by the group of infiltrators who had come to dominate the hillside community at Nagbaculao. They were called out again in May 1988 to mount another concerted protest against us and develop as much bad publicity as possible for PREDA and to move for my deportation. There were calls to close down the PREDA Centre and turn it into a city training centre. Crudely made handbills calling for this were distributed around the market.

A coordinated black propaganda campaign in the tabloid media ran the false story that we were driving out squatters. The campaign was ignored by the Department of Environment and Natural Resources. At least they knew the truth of the situation. A few years later, the Secretary of the Department of Environment and National Resources granted our request to lease the land to the original evacuees from the Lighthouse community. They were granted land rights. However many of the infiltrators still stayed there.

The strategy was becoming clear. When we took a stand in support of the deprived and demolished squatters, then the politicians would conjure up a group of squatters who said we were the oppressors of squatters. This was a strategy that became standard procedure in the years ahead. When we helped abused children we were to be dubbed child abusers; when we rescued children, we were to be called kidnappers.

It was a difficult time for us and the original settlers from the Lighthouse community. Their efforts to organise themselves into a new self-sufficient village and reforest the hillside were wiped out. They had driven off the bulldozer and the land grabber but freedom was not yet to be.

The Mayor's main complaint against us was that we were insulting the people of Olongapo by making allegations of moral corruption that the sex industry was having on the community, something he denied. The Mayor denied, too, during a press conference that he had planned to demolish the PREDA Centre. "Not even in my wildest dreams had I ever planned to demolish Preda," he said.

Chapter Fifteen

The problem of child prostitution was growing, according to the reports reaching us from teachers and social workers. We felt helpless to do anything about it other than become more vocal and advocate change and action by the Philippine government. We were writing about the problem and networking with other childcare agencies.

A UN report said that based on research done by Norway, there were at least one million children trafficked for child prostitution everyday around the globe. I went to Hawaii early in 1988 to consult with friends and supporters. They arranged meetings for me with State Senators who were very concerned about the involvement of the US personnel in child prostitution. I stayed with Navy Commander Edward Robinson II, a good friend whom I met at the Subic Base and who helped us a lot.

The resolution was brought before the State legislator by Senator Ann Kobayashi which called for an investigation into the alleged "widespread and increasing child sex abuse being committed by US Navy and Department of Defence civilians" in Olongapo.

The US Navy Investigative Service conducted an undercover investigation into the allegations that a paedophile ring was selling children to servicemen. They mounted an undercover operation in Olongapo, posing as paedophiles to see if our allegations were true or not. Over a period of weeks, the agents were approached by pimps offering children.

The report confirmed that there was a paedophile ring operating in the city offering children for sex but that no US personnel were involved as clients, according to Tom Boyd, a US Pacific Command spokesman.

The evidence against the pimps was turned over to the city government, the report said, for the Philippine authorities to take the appropriate legal action, "since what was going on was being done by Filipinos."

When we heard about this investigation, we immediately tried to get a copy but were met with a stonewall of denial. However, City Assistant Prosecutor Dorentino Floresta, a man of principle, had briefly seen a copy of the report that had been accidentally left on his desk but later removed before he could secure or copy it. It was to prove to be a shocking document.

At PREDA, we decided that we had to try and get it from the US archives under the Freedom of Information Act. We contacted our friends at the Pacific Defence based in Dennan Island, British Columbia, Canada. They agreed to make the application. It took over a year to get some of the heavily censored reports of the undercover agents as they hung around the street corners where they were offered child sex.

They reported children as young as four-years-old were offered to them for sex and pornography by pimps. They played along with the offer and were brought to hotels and boarding houses. They photographed the children (and presumably some of the pimps) and eventually turned all the evidence over to the Olongapo City authorities in January 1989. The case against the pimps was prepared by Assistant City Prosecutor Nini Cruz but never prosecuted.

Later some government officials said the pimps escaped because I wrote about the investigation in my weekly column. That was long after the authorities had identified the suspects and they had disappeared. It was clear that a policy of cover up and denial by higher authorities had buried any prosecution. It would make the city look at itself and surely they would not like what they would see.

The Navy investigation uncovered the supply side but did not examine the customer base which had to be there if there was such a ready syndicate supplying children. That would have been extremely embarrassing to the US Navy and with the future of the base coming up it was time to put the responsibility on the local government to clean up the prostitution of children in the city.

Legal action against US servicemen was not encouraged by the authorities and most complaints were quickly settled out of court. Only one hundred and eight cases of sexual abuse against sailors were filed during the previous ten years. City prosecution records showed fifteen of these cases involved children between four and sixteen years of age. Most of the cases were either resolved in favour of the US sailors or settled out of court. Investigations into local paedophiles and pimps were largely unheard of. The results of the US Navy undercover investigation were not acted upon.

That February 1989, a retired forty-five-years-old US serviceman was charged for repeatedly raping a six-years-old child from Tabacuhan by the City Prosecutor Floresta but he was able to escape before he was arrested.

Around this time I made an extensive trip to the countryside of Mindanao and was appalled at the extent of military repression. I interviewed many victims of brutality and human rights violations and their relatives. Out of this, I wrote a series of articles about the mission of the Church to defend human rights and the extent of the "Dirty War", as it was called. The Philippine's *Daily Inquirer* published an editorial, on May 19, supporting the revelations that included the murder of church workers and priests.

The series mentioned the possibility of the involvement of US advisors in the counter-insurgency or low intensity conflict that was raging in the hinterlands of Mindanao. It provoked a strong response in the *Inquirer* from the US Embassy who denied any such involvement of US personnel. I concluded the series with the comment which the editorial quoted: "The more vocal the Church becomes in defending human rights and condemning violations of its own members, the more its priests and ministers become targets themselves."

Later that year, in August, I wrote in the *Inquirer* about the alleged anti-Communist campaign of John Whitehall who gave an address of a box number in Toongabbie, New South Wales, Australia and was active in distributing *The Pacific Newsletter*, a strong anti-Communist publication. Whitehall and his supporters denied the Christian Anti-Communism Crusade was to "whip up anti-Communist hysteria" as some human rights workers alleged.

In Manila that May, the First Asian Conference on Street Children sponsored by Child Hope International took place. Alex and myself attended and felt elated that, at long last, the serious problem of street children, especially sexually abused kids, was getting wide recognition and publicity. The previous one on sex trafficking was held in Indonesia a few years previously. After this we were greatly encouraged to intensify our lobbying for the passing of a child protection law, and support the other non-government agencies pushing this. We distributed copies of the video *Throwaway Children* to congress, people and Senators. I wrote to them and made personal visits to persuade them to enact the bill.

There was an estimated three thousand street children in Olongapo in 1989. Seventy-six percent of these children had conflict with the police. Jailing the children was routine then and children as young as six were to be found behind bars. Although we were visiting the jails and protested this to the authorities it fell on deaf ears. The police resorted to this when ordered to clear the street of the begging children and the roaming gangs of ragged kids that pestered the US sailors and tourists and even snatched from them. They were seen as pests.

Sometimes a police officer would have a scam whereby the children that were rounded up were the kids of street vendors. The vendors kept their children near them and spent their whole day walking the main street and standing near the gate of the military base selling cigarettes, gum, cheap sun glasses and other souvenirs to the sailors.

Others had small stalls where they barbecued chicken legs or claws over smoky eye-stinging charcoal braziers. At the end of the day, the police aides and a policemen would round up some of these children who had strayed from their parents side and bring them to the nearby police station. There they were put behind bars in a smelly cell without sanitation, beds or food. The small kids would cry for hours, some collapsed from exhaustion. The parents would then turn over their hard-earned takings for the day to *buy back* their kids. Other street children who had no parents to bail them out would help each other. Their hard earned money gleaned from guarding parked cars, selling plastic bags around the market, pushing huge wooden carts loaded with coconuts or vegetables is placed for safekeeping with a market vendor, a motherly image whom the street children trusted. From their earnings, they would pay a policeman to get their friends out of the jail.

Jail life was hard. The prisoners – so many crammed into small cells with practically no ventilation, bad food and violence – were in a constant state of anger and stress. Many could not pay bail and had to wait months before a court hearing.

The girls, some of them underage, were often raped and sexually molested by the male prisoners. A policeman tried to justify putting the girls in with the male prisoners by saying there would be a riot if they did not have sex from time to time.

The PREDA social workers, Alex, and myself would visit

the jails, record the names of the children and try to get them released if no charges had been brought against them. Usually they were not formally charged with vagrancy. We tried to get this practice of arbitrary detention stopped and offered to take them into the PREDA Centre but were refused. Local government cooperation was not forthcoming.

It was only some years later would we be more successful. The national Department of Social Welfare and Development opened the Lingap Centre for care of some of these children. UNICEF began an independent NGO community-based programme for street children that organised the children and got many of them going home and back to school. Yet the problem was never adequately addressed.

The vast majority of the citizens of Olongapo City would no doubt be deeply opposed to all the exploitation and child abuse if they only knew about it. But the media was tightly controlled. The business community was divided, too. Those in favour with the officials got contracts and privileges, usually relatives. Those who were independently minded or critical sought no privileges and were given none. Those opposed to government policies were frequently excluded and could be harassed with bloated utility bills or charged with minor infractions of the building code or fire regulations and denied permits and licenses. At PREDA, we were denied such permits to which we had a legal right.

This was a microcosm of the Philippines as a whole. The vast majority were excluded by the ruling elite. But there was resistance among the population to corruption and graft, and social evil. In 1988, there was a fine example of Olongapo citizens and young people who spoke for many. This organisation was dedicated to non-violent change in society and was called *Kasarinlan,* meaning "independence", and was opening up public debate on the root causes of the cultural and economic hardship that plagued the Filipino people. It [illegible] great sign of real democratic debate emergi[illegible] against the artificial semblance of democracy tha[illegible]

I remember their Second General Assembly on March 26, 1988 because Alex was a guest speaker. Their closing declaration expressed the heartfelt feelings and thinking of the vast majority of the upright citizens of Olongapo. The discussion centred on the social and cultural impact of the US military bases and a closing statement commenting on the colonial mentality described as a destructive influence. "It pervades every aspect of Philippine life so that for many Filipinos even memories of true freedom and independence are erased from their national consciousness. Self-identity is lost and sometimes even willingly suppressed. Filipinos have been led to envy the strength of this powerful nation (USA) and (are) overcome by the lure of Western materialism. Some collaborate in the exploitation of their own people for selfish gain."

It was a very significant statement that shows that the people were conscious and aware of the negative impact of the political system that allowed the bases to damage their culture and enslave their people. Another passage that impressed me greatly read: "In a starving world and a malnourished Philippines where thousands of children cry out with hunger and die of curable diseases surrounded by the incredible and obscene wealth as seen in the bases. This intensifies the insecurity of the poor, and many are driven by hunger and want to unknowingly collaborate in the process of their own oppression and economic bondage."

I felt so proud of these young people who had thought through the situation for themselves and were acutely aware that change had to come. I was very gratified that they accepted and supported the military bases economic conversion concept that Alex proposed to the assembly that weekend. We were strongly advocating this idea as an alternative to the jobs that would be lost if the military bases ever closed which was a far remote dream at that time.

But dream we did and whole0heartily campaigned against the bases. We were writing letters, joining meetings with the anti-bases coalition members in Manila, distributing videotapes to lawmakers to heighten their awareness and of course going to schools and churches to develop support for the military bases conversion plan.

That is why the support of the Kasarinlan group was so important to us. We felt that our ideas of base removal and replacement were not so eccentric and farfetched as our critics said.

It was not a safe time to be taking an anti-bases stance either. The previous week, Rey Franciso, was beaten up by a local neighbour patrol set up by the administration to police every district of the town. Their offence was sticking up anti-nuclear posters. In Manila, there was similar violence to quell protest and freedom of speech. Jon-Jon Bustamante was savagely beaten and tortured to death in Manila for distributing anti-bases materials in public. None of us knew who would be next. We just had to live with the consequences of our commitments whatever they might be. I was worried for Alex and Merly who noticed they were being tailed by a suspicious car all the way to their home in Manila. We prayed long and hard together for God's protection in those uncertain and dangerous times.

Cardinal Jamie Sin, who had played such a pivotal role in the non-violent uprising against the dictator Marcos in 1986, was being severely criticised by Right Wing politicians for his support of church groups protesting human rights abuses and vigilantism. He came to our support on several occasions when local politicians tried to end our work. On one occasion he declared that organised prostitution was "no more and no less than legalised rape (which) fosters corruption among officers of public order". Still we felt very much alone during these times in our advocacy campaign for children's rights.

That international report prepared by Anderson told of children being transported from Santo Domingo to sailors in the Caribbean as sex slaves, and the account of a fifteen-years-old Thai child who was a prisoner of a West German sex den for four years. It recounted how small boys in ar

Asian kindergarten bled on the floor after being tried out for sex by perverts from Australia. In California, the report described a syndicate that offered children for sex for $500 dollars an afternoon. In New York, a priest found a nine-years-old thrown from a ninth floor window after being forced to participate in a sex film and tried to run away. He described a seven-years-old with his arms cut off for talking to police about the child sex syndicates. Then in the Philippines we had the terrible story of Rosario Baluyot killed by a sexual deviant who inserted and broke a vibrator inside her vagina. But these were just a few of the horrific cases that came to light.

In the US, the report estimated that as many as a million children were prostituted out of 1.8 million children who run away from home; fifty thousand disappeared completely at that time. In India, a suspect religious sect prostituted children under the Devadasi-system where an estimated twenty thousand were supposed to be dedicated to a goddess but sold for sex. Every country was found to have child prostitution industries. In 1984, Defence of Children International said that the Philippines was one of the worst places of child sexual abuse and some of the worst places were the towns around the military bases.

"It is well known that prostitution in general, and child prostitution in particular, is controlled by the Philippine mafia. It is a flourishing industry. In the tourist area of Manila mafia networks provide every possible type of prostitution and in special areas deaf-mutes between the ages of ten and sixteen years, for example. On a still wider scale child prostitution is practiced near American bases and in tourist centres. The Philippine networks appear to have links with the American and Australian mafia and with the Japanese Yakusa," the report said.

ouraged to know that the international com-
ally waking up to this terrible organised abuse
his led to the drafting of the document that

Right: Street children who are arrested for petty crimes are forced to share inhuman conditions with adult prisoners. Unfortunately, many of the children are physically and sexually abused by the adult inmates.

Below: Fr Shay pictured with some of the rescued children at the PREDA Centre.

Above: Fr Shay leading a march to highlight exploitation.

Above: A young girl behind bars.

Left: Fr Shay attending the animals and friends for peace rally.

Above: Fr Shay in the US Congress with Rep. Chris Smith shaking hands, September 2005.

Above: Merly Ramirez.

Below: Fr Shay with the actor Martin Sheen.

Martin, Alex and Fr Shay went to the Payatas garbage dump to campaign for help and support for the redevelopment of the area as it was deadly and dangerous for the hundreds of people living and working there in sub-human conditions. Payatas, a giant heap of putrid stinking garbage where the poor suffer endlessly. The men, women and above all the children spend their lives scratching the garbage for scraps to live on.

Above: Annette Kinnie of ANDEC productions wins the Radharc best documentary award 2004 with her film "Fr Shay Cullen -Taking a Stand."

Below: Fr Shay laid a wreath at the Memorial stone in the former Nazi concentration camp of Buchenwald.

Below: Mayor Richard Gordon takes the salute a the US Naval Base at Subic Bay Olongapo is closed down and turned over to Philippine authorities for conversion to civilian development. Fr Shay campaigned ten years for the conversion of the U.S. military bases.

Fr Shay testified at the famous trial of Australian and Irish Columbans, Fathers Brian Gore and Niall O'Brien, falsely charged by President Marcos for murder. After nine months the charges were dropped and all were exonerated.

Right: Payatas, a giant heap of putrid stinking garbage where the poor suffer endlessly. The men, women and above all the children spend their lives scratching the garbage for scraps to live on.

Left: a street child sleeping outside a shop.

Below: the street children turn to drugs to help them deal with their misfortunes.

Above: Fr Shay and Bishop Casey at PREDA, July 1992. The head of Trocaire with him then was Brian McKeon.

Below: Victor Keith Fitzgerald convicted of child abuse. Fr Shay helped break up a syndicate selling children to sex tourists and paedophiles.

would become the famous Convention on the Rights of the Child. I was invited to attend the discussions in Finland.

Chapter Sixteen

Around this time, we began making more frequent direct street contact with the many street children and trying to discover their living conditions, where they hung out, slept and how they survived. Street children are wary of formal contacts and so we approached it by offering medical aid. The social workers were trained in basic first aid and went into the shantytowns and slums and were soon treating the children with open wounds and rashes. Those with more serious ailments were brought to the charity clinic operated by St Joseph's Parish.

After several weeks, a good rapport was established between the social workers and the children and they wanted to know where the social workers lived. They soon found out and began coming over to the PREDA Centre in the early hours of the morning in groups of about five or six boys and girls asking for breakfast. After we fed them, they played wildly around the centre and then collapsed on the couches and the floor and slept, exhausted. Nothing would wake them. By three in the afternoon, they were awake, demanding food and they would at once rush off back to the city streets to beg, or be prostituted.

We discussed what to do. A planned approach had to be worked out, funding had to be found and a community lifestyle had to be designed. Our experience working with drug dependents was a big help. There was a community of about twenty-four drug dependents still at the PREDA Centre during this time. All were recovering well and for most of them the family reconciliation process was working and they were being reconciled and reintegrated into their families.

The reconciliation was not easy. I remember the case of Andrew, a seventeen-years-old, with a deep anger towards his parents because they not only threw him out of the house for dropping out of school and taking drugs, but they eventually got the police to detain him without filing charges or having any evidence. In those days, civil and human rights were not respected.

The fact that the parents had requested his detention made it legitimate in the eyes of the local police. It was an example of the power and control of parental authority over their children and how the state supported that authority even if it was abused and the state concluded with the parents in violating the rights of the young person. He was held under the so-called protective custody in jail for six weeks.

Andrew was then brought to the PREDA Centre and as it was an open centre without fences or walls, no barbed wire, guards or gates, we had to persuade him to stay and try out the community life. What impressed Andrew was not what might become of him but what might be done to help his parents to accept their human weaknesses and the injustice they had done to him. He wanted the chance to air out his grievances against them. We promised to try and give him that chance. We assured him that we would do all we could to get his parents to attend parental therapy and counselling. And so he stayed, as did many others who longed for reconciliation and justice with their parents and family.

We had to persuade his parents to attend counselling and therapy sessions for parents only. They cooperated and gradually had a change of heart and came to realise that their dictatorial and excessive disciplinary style of parenting had alienated their children long before drug abuse became the crutch and escapism for Andrew. When they realised that he was escaping from them they were more understanding and willing to accept mistakes.

Visits between the parents and Andrew were always strained, awkward and uncomfortable. But there was a slow thaw and we could notice that they were more civil, patient and considerate with each other. Then the day arrived when we scheduled the first reconciliation session. The parents and Andrew were counselled separately. Each told the counsellor what they wanted to say and this was conveyed to the other party in another room. They gave their response and this was relayed.

In this way, both parties knew in advance what to expect from the other side so that when it came out the truth could be accepted, responses could be controlled and, if possible, forgiveness asked on both sides and freely given. And that is how it happened: Andrew was more mature, in control of himself, his hostility gone after many weeks of primal therapy and his grievances poured out of him in a quite measured tone that was not harsh and blaming but expressing his pain and hurt.

It had the desired effect as his parents shared their feelings and both asked forgiveness. It was a rewarding and happy time when they made up and embraced after five years of estrangement and bitterness. Andrew joined the family hardware business and today he has a hardware store of his own. We were hoping that we could have a similar kind of success with the street children, many of whom were alienated and throwaway children, as we called them. But how to start was the problem.

One day we had a visit from the representatives of a Swiss human development agency that represented Protestant churches in Switzerland, HEKS. Samuel Andres, who represented HEKS, was widely experienced and had dedicated his life to helping the oppressed and exploited farmers of developing countries. He encouraged us to set-up a project for the street children. He understood the situation of street children in the Philippines and offered to help. We formed a partnership to provide shelter, food, clothes, non-formal education, and to develop their self-esteem and feeling of self-worth. With street children, this is usually at an all time low. The abuse and lack of love and basic needs make them feel unwanted, worthless and a burden to the their parents. They usually grow up with daily scolding telling them that it would have been better had they not been born.

Soon we were working with the children and persuading them to leave the streets and settle down to a family lifestyle in the new community. This community was housed in a hilltop building with wide spaces to play among the trees and with a magnificent view of Subic Bay. But few settled down, they would still disappear back to the streets and reappear a day or two later. Little could be done to help them in the long term with this drop-in, drop-out behaviour.

They were healthier, better fed and clean and clothed. In fact we realised that they were more enticing victims of the pimps and the paedophiles. Were we helping or hindering their recovery? Some were calming down and staying for longer and longer periods at the centre. The healthy diet cleaned out the chemicals of the junk food they had been surviving on and that made them hyperactive until they grew exhausted. We observed that their sleeping pattern had been so altered by their lives on the streets that they could not lead a normal life and wake up and sleep with the sun.

So we arranged for a three-day beach camping event in a remoter part of the province from which they did not know the way back to the city. The social workers organised games, sports and swimming that carried them through the whole day without let up. They were too excited to sleep and we kept them awake around the campfire singing songs and telling jokes. Then when it was dark, they fell asleep. Three days of this and they were getting back to normal sleeping patterns.

Back at the PREDA Childhood for Children Centre we had to be openly honest with them and explain that they would have little chance of a good future if they did not get schooling and there was to be daily instruction at the centre and later, when they were capable, they would be enrolled at the local school.

The revolving door behaviour had to stop. It was disruptive to those children who were staying at the centre. When the drop-in began inviting the others to leave and join them on the streets again, we decided to draw the line. We would have a street based project and a residential based project for those who wanted to change and study.

After a clear explanation, we gave them the option to join the programme of their choice. Out of about thirty children, sixteen chose to stay and follow the residential formation and study programme. The others returned to the streets where we kept in contact with them. After a few weeks, some had a change of heart and they asked to join the residential community. Eventually it grew to be a community of thirty-five. Now the work of developing an effective therapeutic community for these children began. It was when we began to develop the trust and bonding of the children and write up their case histories that we learned that many of them had been sexually abused either in their home or by a neighbour.

Hilario was a twelve-years-old at the time we found him locked up in the Olongapo City Jail for over a week. His was a foul smelling cell at the back of the police station. The hardened criminals made him their slave. He had to wash their clothes, clean the faeces smeared corner where a hole in the floor served as a toilet and massage them on demand or else he would be left to starve.

A restaurant security guard found him scavenging for bottles and cans at the back of the restaurant and vented his anger by kicking the street boy around. Then to justify his brutality he told the police Hilario had been stealing. There was no evidence, his wooden pushcart with discarded ball bearing rings for wheels, had only bottles, tin cans and newspapers that the boy collected and resold. The absence of evidence was no impediment to having the kid thrown in jail. He was treated no better than the garbage that he collected.

Hilario had left home when he was eight to escape the beatings and abuse by his unemployed father. He followed his fifteen-years-old sister Melissa. She was sexually abused in the hovel by her father and she ran away to the streets. She was soon employed in a bar in the red light district of the city. He remembers most the hunger and beatings at home. Hilario told me this with tears streaming down his face.

"My parents always beat me and we had little food."

After a few months, this throwaway child was healthy, bright and going to school. We arranged for his mother to come to the PREDA Centre and they were soon reconciled. We did what we could to help her care for the rest of her children but we could never find Marissa. She had probably been sold out of the bar to a paedophile syndicate in Manila. Hilario grew up and today has a steady job.

I was invited as a delegate to the historical International Congress on the Rights of the Child held just outside Helsinki that was drafting the final version of the Convention on the Rights of the Child. This draft was the product of several years of consultation and discussion among various government and non-government agencies and organisations working for children's rights. The final version was to be presented to the UN the following October.

It was indicative of the growing awareness in the international community of the massive deprivation and suffering of children. It was rooted in the traditional thinking that children were the property of their parents, that they had no rights of their own. In most societies the state had limited power to interfere in domestic relationships. That is why sexual abuse in some countries was largely ignored and not even acknowledged to exist, as a consequence no laws protected children. In the Philippines before the 1990 Child Protection Law or Republic Act 7610, the Revised Penal Code only had "Acts of Lasciviousness" that refers to sexual abuse of minors. It was almost impossible to get a conviction in court.

That is why much of our public awareness work had been directed to supporting the passing of legislation and later its implementation. The convention of the rights of the child of 1989 was very important. It was a historical turning point as it gave international recognition to the child as an individual existing independently of his or her parents and with specific rights that have to be recognised and protected by law. It was also the basis for the introduction of new legislation.

I remember one of the most debated points was until what age did childhood reach. Many wanted it to be eighteen years, others said sixteen. The US delegation battled for sixteen as they believed that the congress would never ratify the convention if they could not recruit seventeen-years-old youths into the military. As of this writing, the US is the only country that has not ratified the convention. During that convention, another organisation was formed and I joined as a founding member, the International Forum for Child Welfare. This was the concept of Alan Davis, and it grew to be a large and influential organisation of child welfare organisations and was responsible for promoting the rights of the child. It was to become one of our many staunch supporters in the years to come.

After this, I travelled about giving talks and interviews and, on my way back to the Philippines that August, I made a visit to Honolulu to meet with the Inspector General and staff of Admiral David Jeremiah, commander-in-chief of the Pacific Fleet, to plead increased efforts to work against the child prostitution business that involved US sailors as customers. I was given assurances and then met with Senator Ann Kobayashi who was asking, unsuccessfully, for a congressional investigation into child sex business.

As soon as I arrived back in the Philippines, the PREDA children and staff joined the *National Campaign for Advocacy and Action* organised by Gabriela's Commission for Children and the Family. This opened with a rally before the Senate Building to call for the ratification of the UN Convention of the Rights of the Child, which was coming before the UN the following month. It was the start of a move to get children involved and empowered in advocating for their rights together with adults. It was felt that for too long children had been not allowed a voice of their own. They too had rights to speak out and demand their rights and participate in the decision making process that could profoundly affect their lives.

After workshops and seminars with the children on their dignity and rights, they were exhilarated at joining a rally with balloons, placards and streamers, music and singing. During that rally Senators Raul Roco and Joseph Estrada invited some of the adults and children into the Senate Building which was then at the Luneta. It was an indication that we were all being taken seriously. It was an opportunity to lobby for the Child Protection Law that was languishing in both the Congress and the Senate.

The situation of children in armed conflict was also a serious concern. The UNICEF and the Philippine Department of Social Welfare and Development held a consultation on "children in situations of armed conflict". UNICEF estimated that as many as four and a half million Filipino children were casualties of the guerrilla war during the past twenty years.

That October PREDA social workers were in contact with two children on the streets persuading them to come over to the centre. They did and told that they were child prostitutes and had been going with foreigners for sex since they had been eleven and twelve-years-old. They named one retired serviceman and another active one as those currently abusing them. The mother of one of the children, who was at this time fifteen, then filed a formal complaint with Prosecutor Dorentino Floresta and it became another indication of the extent of child prostitution.

At PREDA, we were not very knowledgeable as to the legal process necessary to monitor and help support the case for the children. Four days after making the complaint the mother of one of the children did an about turn and claimed she was "forced" into it and withdrew her charges. We were astounded. We heard later that the city legal officer ordered the police to bring the mother to her office and soon after she dropped her complaint. The authorities did not press any charge despite the testimony of the child. We were dumbfounded. Alex and myself and the social workers visited the mother at her home and found a very frightened and intimidated woman. There was nothing that we could do.

During this time the bases issue was heating in the public area. The first ever anti-bases rally was organised by a church group and was held beside the main gates of the base. Five priests from the neighbouring provinces came with busloads of supporters. There was also a big turn out of local anti-base supporters. We held a prayer rally and we dressed in our white soutane and prayed for peace and non-violence. The Association of Women Religious of Zambales were there in force with banners and placards.

The older children in the PREDA programme and the recovering drug dependents were there too and they brought doves and released them with a rousing hail of cheers. There was no interference by the local police or authorities much to our amazement. The Mayor was away in the US at the time. The authorities believed that we were the main organisers of the rally. In fact, the anti-bases coalition of non-government organisations were the real coordinators. It was historical in the sense that nothing like it had ever happened since the bases were first established almost fifty years before. We were to be made to pay the price however for that piece of history.

After the rally I met again two researchers that had been sent by a research group of the Navy in Washington to access the social conditions surrounding the bases. I wondered if my visit to Honolulu had contributed in some way to that research project. They told me "off the record" that the military were concerned about the situation – including the spreading of AIDS in the brothels in Olongapo and Angeles Cities. This was based on the screening and testing conducted by the US Navy in the social hygiene centres. What bothered the Navy was the international image as a service that tolerated and turned a blind eye to promiscuity and child abuse. It was also a serious issue in their military families. I heard from the researchers that the Navy was going to crack down on the drug and child prostitution syndicates by putting certain brothels and bars off limits. That was a threat of economic sanctions that would cripple the business overnight. Some of the operators were linked to city officials who issued permits for these establishments to operate. Ultimately the sex industry depends on the official approval of the city government. Blame for these sanctions were soon to be laid on my doorstep!

It seemed that city authorities laid the blame on me and the PREDA staff for anything unpleasant written about Olongapo, as if writers and journalists could not see the reality for themselves! Every regime needs a scapegoat and I was theirs. November 5, 1989 saw a series of explosive articles, called "Off Base" and filling three whole pages of the *San Diego Union* on Olongapo, written by Mike McIntyre who came to the city with photographer Jerry Rife and stayed for a few weeks. Mayor Gordon, a lawyer, was approached for his comments by the journalists but, according to an article in the Filipino community newspaper of California, the *Mabuhay Times* (November 26), Mayor Gordon refused to give the journalists his side. The paper reported: *Gordon cancelled two interviews for this story. Five seconds into the third interview – after he had been asked to comment on*

Olongap's dependence on the bases – Gordon dismissed the US reporter.

A press conference was organised and held at the Scottish Rites Temple in Mission Valley and Mayor Gordon who was in California at the time was the main speaker. He denied all the charges in the article. He denied the claim that one out of every five females was prostituted and said that there were no more than two hundred street children. The *Mabuhay Times* news article quoted Mayor Gordon: "The real prostitute, he continued, is the corrupt official, the lawyer who sells his case, the doctor who commits abortion (operations), the journalist who sensationalises a story in the paper called the San Diego Union. This article douses cold water, it kills the spirit of Olongapo moral boosting slogans of 'Duty Dignity, Integrity, Aim High Olongapo, Bawal ang Tamad sa Olongapo (Lazy people are forbidden in Olongapo)'. Mayor Gordon condemned the article as 'trash and yellow journalism, written by a snout-nosed amateurish, obnoxious reporter who does not even have the courage to appear tonight'."

The article continued: "Mayor Gordon further accused the writer of being one-sided relying solely on the information given him by Fr Shay Cullen. The said priest heads the PREDA Foundation designed for the care and therapy of sexually abused and neglected children. The Mayor of Olongapo also called the article a 'racist article', asserting that 'the real issue is not Olongapo, but the honour of the entire Filipino people'. Gordon promised to defend the Filipino people, ending on a note of firm belief in 'what the Filipino can achieve if he is determined'."

The *San Diego Asian Journal* reported that a demonstration would be held at the offices of the *San Diego Union* newspaper to protest the article and demand a retraction. It was to be led by Mayor Richard Gordon himself. They interviewed many people, among them a poor mother in rags living in a bamboo shack in the slums. Juanita, a former prostituted child typical of the castaways dumped on the garbage heap of used women.

The article read: "When the ships anchor at Subic Bay Naval Base, Juanita sells her only possession – her thirteen-years-old daughter. Sailors and Marines pay $5 a night to indulge their fantasies, using Christy as an erotic toy. In the morning, the girl slips into a blue-and-white uniform and walks to school, where her mental retardation has kept her in the first grade.

"'We are not bad people,' Juanita said, Christy at her side in their dirt-floor bamboo shack. 'We are poor people.' Christy, her mother said, is one of four illegitimate children of four different fathers – all of them US Sailors, all of them gone.

"The eldest daughter is married," Juanita said she sold her other two girls to an adoption broker for $50 dollars each. At forty-four, Juanita is no longer desirable as a prostitute - so she pimps Christy outside the main gate of the base. Subic Bay is home of the U.S. 7th Fleet which includes ships from San Diego. Juanita gave up her virginity to an American serviceman when she was fourteen. Christy whose tiny breasts are only now emerging lost her childhood at age ten to a sailor named Tony in the back seat of a car parked at the cemetery. 'Like mother, like daughter,' Juanita said smiling at Christy. 'If she follows me, she is going to be a good girl, I'm a good teacher.'

"In Olongapo, one in every five females – women and girls – is a prostitute," the article said. It was writing like that that inflamed the city authorities. The Mayor was in California at the time and he was understandably infuriated. The phrase, "One in every five females – women and girls – is a prostitute," was particularly galling and perhaps a grave and unjustified exaggeration. It also claimed that out of three thousand street children ten percent were prostituted. The journalist did not say we were the source of such information, nevertheless we were blamed. There were to be consequences for talking to the press at all.

"The prostitutes of Olongapo are not hardened cynics like the street walkers found on, say, El Cajon Boulevard in San Diego. They are primarily country girls, most of them running away from nothing but poverty. They are amateurs playing a professional sport."

PREDA social workers were informed about Juanita and Christy and located them and tried to get Juanita to bring Christy to the PREDA Centre for safety and recovery. It succeeded for a week but then Juanita kept coming to get her out and perhaps pimp her again. Christy left without permission and went back to Juanita. All our efforts to help the child came to nothing. We realised then that the child needed special protection from her own mother who could not be persuaded to let the child start a new life.

Many a night I roamed the streets looking for the runaway Christy. Once when I found Juanita and Christy standing near the gate of the Naval Base they ran away. I knew then that we needed a protected shelter for vulnerable children like Christy.

Then there was the story of Ching, a ten-years-old little boy with a baldhead. The article explained that some of the street kids have their hair shaved off by police to deter them from begging and pestering the sailors. Ching was a regular drop-in street child and we were trying to persuade him to stay and go to school. But the draw of the street was still in his bones. He was a glue-sniffer and when caught he was jailed. He was found with a group of other small boys there and once released he returned to PREDA to recover and eat a decent meal. These stories angered the Mayor who happened to be in San Diego at the time and it sparked a strong reaction and a movement to have the PREDA Centre closed and me deported.

On November 10, I received a phone call from the chief-of-staff of Senator Leticia Ramos-Shahani. He was in Olongapo, she said, with the senator and she was requesting that I attend a public meeting on the future of the military bases to be held in the Admiral Hotel (owned by the family of the Mayor). Politely, I refused but she was insistent and said she would send a car to bring me to the forum. I immediately had a meeting with Alex, Merly and the staff.

We knew about the forum but we did not intend to be present as it would be packed with pro-base supporters and we would be shouted down. There was no point. We discussed the possibilities and realised that it would most likely be a trap but then there would be no one to speak for the record that there were dissenting voices. Our stand was that silence in the face of injustice and the roots of immorality was tantamount to giving consent in certain circumstances. This seemed like one of them. We had to speak out and propose the economic conversion plan that would provide industry and jobs with dignity for the people of Olongapo.

It was decided – I would run the gauntlet. Alex was to drop me off near the hotel and stayed outside with the car to pick me up. A large crowd of demonstrators were outside and became hostile on cue when I approached the entrance. The Senator's guide steered me to a side entrance. The hotel conference hall was packed with administration employees and supporters and a gaggle of media people. The participants were made up of representatives of other Senators, local politicians, and others from neighbouring provinces. They were sitting around a square arrangement made up of tables with potted plants in the centre. There was a loud disapproving howl from the crowd when I entered but I took my place.

I knew it was the lion's den but it had to be done. The Senator called for calm and said that all voices had a right to be heard. One City Counsellor challenged my presence. He asked why should I be permitted to make any comments when I was a non-Filipino. I countered by asking if I was made a Filipino citizen would that change the truth of what I was to express? The Senator brushed aside the nationality objection and said I was her guest.

The discussion was no more than a series of prepared statements expressing the great economic advantages of retaining the bases and forecasting economic ruin and collapse if the bases were closed. Speaking in Filipino, I presented the PREDA concept of life after the bases. I proposed our alternative vision of military base conversion to high-tech non-polluting industries that would give many more dignified and better paying jobs. There were boos and jeers from the crowd who tried to drown me out. Senator Shahani had to call for order several times.

It seemed a fruitless debate as the majority were fixed on retention of the bases and the sex industry, which was the administration's position. A journalist I knew whispered that some members of the panel were telling reporters that I was a Communist and anti-Filipino and should be deported.

I wasn't surprised given the climate of hostility and anger. I never felt so alienated in my life until that moment of rejection. But I had prepared myself for it and had to accept the inevitable. After an hour, I announced that I had to leave. I submitted a paper on the military bases conversion plan that we had developed and written up and left. There were more jeers and cat calls as I made my way to the main exit.

Outside there was a staged demonstration. There was a crowd waiting in force with placards denouncing me by name, one read: *CULLEN, Journalist – NO, Opportunist – Yes!* Others had derogatory slogans. The media were following in hot pursuit and it was clear that this was staged for the media. The rent-a-rally crowd had been prepared and briefed in advance – a common phenomenon in political rallies and demonstrations. They were shouting invective insults and derogatory comments, as I tried to make my way out.

The police were ready too to "give protection" and to heighten the spectacle and impression that this was a person non-grata and all that I represented was totally rejected. They began throwing things at me: rotten vegetables and stones, I learned later. I walked directly away, ignoring the curses, taunts and shouts as the crowd broke and ran down the street after me waving placards. Alex was there. He had witnessed it all and, as soon as he saw a break in the crowd, he drove in, snapped open the door and we were away.

Surprisingly, the next day, the newspapers were critical of the staged and manipulated show of hatred. *Counsellor deplores stoning of priest by US supporters,* read the lead in the *Philippine's Daily Inquirer.* The lone opposition counsellor of Olongapo, Primo S. Galvez, who was a union leader of the base employees said the demonstration was "childish and unreasonable". He issued an apology to the senator and the other representatives of the Senate who were there.

All schools, business and market stalls were ordered closed that day to gather huge crowds on the streets as a sign of support for the retention of the bases. But the huge crowds were not there. One newspaper reported that vendors feared they would lose their licenses if they did not close and join the rally. Noli Capistrano, a local official told the *People's Journal* that the pro-bases would hold a vigil outside the PREDA Centre and gather signatures for my deportation.

They were as good as their word. The next day with an indefinite demonstration permit a group of pro-base loyalists gathered at the roadside at the bottom of the PREDA driveway. They set up a large amplifier and speakers under a tarpaulin and held a rally that shouted invective and insulting comments that accused priests and sisters of alleged sexual immorality. There were racist comments too against my being Irish. Another banner read: *Fr Cullen unwanted foreigner mudslinger.*

They were overlooking the fact that there were millions of Filipinos working in almost every country in the world and the city and sex industry depended on the money of foreigners in the bases. Their slurs and invective was recorded and when the main group of demonstrators left, the taped insults were then played at maximum volume over and over again while a group of ten demonstrators kept watch.

We had a meeting at PREDA and discussed the options.

The invective was very damaging to the children who could hear it. They played the taped obscenities at full volume late into the night. It was a psychological warfare tactic designed to humiliate, insult, frighten and intimidate us.

To spare the children and the staff, I volunteered to leave for Manila but the staff would not hear of it.

"It would be granting the opposition a victory and appear that you had been successfully driven out," said Alex.

We must endure it and outlast them, was our final resolve. Our opponents were also on the streets and standing at the gates of the base trying to gather signatures to present to the Bureau of Immigration to support a petition for my deportation. Not many signed it, we were glad to hear later.

The Olongapo City Vice Mayor, Cynthia Cajudo, told the *People's Journal* (November 15,1989) that the government were not officially supporting the demonstration in their official capacity. "But in our private capacity, yes, we support this campaign for the deportation of Fr Cullen and the closure of the PREDA Centre."

It was a serious situation. A crude leaflet was printed up and passed around. This called for the closure of the PREDA Centre and my deportation: *Join our crusade to eject Fr Cullen from Olongapo and deport him from the Philippines and convert his factory into a school of arts and trade for the people of Olongapo and Zambales.*

It was not surprising that behind the campaign there was another plan. The political land grabbers wanted to get the PREDA Centre and the prime property for themselves. They condemned our work as aimed at destroying the good name of the people of Olongapo. I commented at the time that the good we are trying to do, they call evil, and the evil that they do, they call good. It was a bizarre situation. But there was strong support too from other people in Olongapo and Manila who wrote letters to the editor supporting our stand and advising the people to listen to the message of truth that we were trying to get across.

Our work was to challenge the community to protect and defend the dignity of the women and children from the drug and sex trade. That appeal had to be based on the truth of the social and economic problems that resulted from the military base and the attendant sex industry. It was not criticising the people of Olongapo but a challenge to the civic leaders to take responsibility for the social evils that were proliferating and poisoning the minds and souls of the youth. Unfortunately, civil accountability was at a low ebb.

We had many reflections and discussions among ourselves at PREDA regarding our mission and the predicament to which it had led us. Thinking about it we realised that in order not to become a band-aid for government neglect, we had to help the victims of abuse and yet not remain silent. Our mission was prophetic too, even if they wanted to stomp out the message.

Some authorities want civil society to provide social services and humanitarian aid to the victims of the social and economic plunder and exploitation that they, the politicians, are responsible for creating. They expect us to heal their victims and to stay quiet or suffer the consequences. It seemed to us that some local authorities wanted us not only to say nothing but to prevent the victims for crying out too. Of the many comments that were written and published one that touched me in particular was that by Cita Soriente-Reyes writing in the *WE Forum* newspaper, when she described me as "perhaps more Filipino than his Filipino adversaries in government".

There was a motion of support too from nine members of the Australian Senate who were very much aware of our work and the causes of woman and child abuse. The statement of support read in part: *We decry the malicious propaganda and politicking being used to discredit him [Fr Shay]. To deport Fr Shay Cullen would show that there is a limit to freedom of speech, opinion and belief in the Philippines. We call on people of integrity in the Philippine Government and the Church to uphold Fr Shay Cullen's courage to stand against all those who want to betray the Filipino people and their sovereignty.*

In Olongapo, the social evil continued unabated. Drug abuse was spreading and the Navy was becoming ever more concerned because it affected their military performance. Who wanted a nuclear weapons operator secretly shooting heroin or getting high on drugs?

They ran an undercover operation in the bars and brothels and found big time pushers ready and willing to supply any prohibited drug for a price. The undercover agents risked their lives. They had learned from experience that there was no point in turning the suspects and evidence over to the local system for prosecution as it would go nowhere – the drug lords and their dealers were well protected. They remembered the undercover investigation of 1988 when children, as young as four, were offered for sexual abuse to undercover agents and no one was prosecuted.

So when they discovered that drug dealing was going on in seven particular clubs, the Subic Military Base Provost Marshal declared those clubs to be off-limits to the sailors. That was as good as closing them down. The owners were furious; a leading politician of Olongapo opposed the off-limits rule and declared there would be serious trouble if it was implemented. He was influential enough to have it held in abeyance on the promise that he would clean up the drug dealing and pushing.

A few months later, the undercover agents went at it again, posing as servicemen looking for drugs and they found plenty. Nothing had changed. The Provost Marshal called a meeting of the Base Disciplinary Control Board and the evidence was presented. The board recommended the clubs be off limits and the cases filed with the City Prosecutor's Office. Again the politician approached Rear Admiral Robert Rich and whatever passed between them we will never know but it wasn't pleasant and relations were strained for months. The off-limits rule was not imposed and no charges against the suspects were filed with the Department of Justice.

My weekly column, Reflections, in the *Philippine Daily Inquirer* exposed a lot of these social problems and frankly expressed anti-bases opinions. They were very unpopular with the authorities and the ruling elite and several attempts were made to have it dropped from the *Inquirer*. This campaign escalated and we were in for more attacks.

There was a positive turn of events in the case of then aged twelve and thirteen-years-olds who had been repeatedly sexually abused by two US servicemen (one of them retired). Two years previously, the abusers took them to local hotels, paid the mother and engaged in sexual acts with the children. Despite the withdrawal of the complaint by the mother, the two children decided to pursue the case on their own. We suspected that the mother was threatened and paid off. This was mainly due to the confidence the children had in their lawyer Attorney Sergio Cruz.

We realised that a successful prosecution was unlikely given the opposition of local politicians to putting US servicemen on trial. It was bad for business and the fact that, according to the records at the Prosecutor's office in the past decade to this time, only one hundred and eight complaints of sexual abuse were brought against US servicemen and fifteen of them were for the sexual abuse of children between the ages of four and sixteen. All were dismissed by local courts. Hundreds more were settled by payment in out-of-court settlements. This was and still is a common practice in the Philippines when complaints on the sexual abuse of children are brought to the police or Prosecutor.

The trafficking of minors was as rampant as ever. A Manila-based tabloid reported that young teenage girls were being picked up in Manila and sold into the bars and brothels of Olongapo.

There was no let up in the noise barrage from the picket at the bottom of our driveway. One morning as the noise barrage of obscenities continued, we noticed black ribbons tied to the bushes that lined our driveway, placed there during the night. That was a death threat of the first order. We began to take extra precautions. The senior boys at the centre stood guards on the hillside behind the PREDA centre and one night raised the alarm. A group of hooded men were seen making their way over the hill towards the centre. The boys shouted and it was enough to halt the intrusion but it put us all on edge.

The placards we had hung calling for peace and respect of our rights were torn down and the boys who went down the driveway to retrieve them were berated by a local official and threatened.

"We will shoot you," he warned them.

But support began pouring in. The Columban Superior Fr Charles Maegher came to visit and pledge his support as did many of the priests of the diocese including the Acting Bishop and Vicar General Christopher Cacho who all signed a letter of support.

Chapter Seventeen

A formal hearing by the Commission on Immigration and Deportation began on November 23. The list of unfounded complaints from seventeen Olongapo officials claimed that I was an "undesirable alien" and an enemy of the Filipino people. They alleged that I was portraying Olongapo as a crime city, engaging in business in violation of my vocation (handicraft training). They also absurdly claimed that I was abusing Filipino hospitality, attacking Filipino dignity and honour. The almost endless list of complaints also stated that I was usurping the drug rehabilitation centre and using it to solicit donations for the handicraft project. The complaint also said that I had continually criticised Olongapo for being a hovel of sinners and criminals. They even complained about some small construction project we made near the cemetery and, most weird of all, was a charge of sponsoring lewd shows!

With the help of human rights lawyer Sergio Cruz, we countered all the charges and presented our affidavit, refuting the false allegations. Support was growing and the Immigration Room was packed to capacity. Fr Brian Gore of the famous Negros Nine was there giving his support and advice. He had spent nine months with Fr Niall O'Brien and their six church workers in prison on false charges under the Marcos regime. Outside there were church groups chanting and singing hymns with colourful banners and placards demanding justice and an end to the exploitation of women and children in the sex industry of Olongapo.

That was the crux of the issue. The Olongapo officials behind the deportation campaign were incapable of accepting the terrible truth and the responsibility for the proliferation of the sex industry that exploited their own poor and most vulnerable women and children for the sexual gratification of the foreign sex tourist and US military.

Then on November 30, as if by design to further damage our credibility, the two US servicemen that we had helped bring to justice for sexual abuse of the two young teenagers came out with a statement in the press blaming me for their plight. They said, as was to be often repeated in years to come, that we at PREDA "had pulled the strings" to make the children testify. Attorney Cruz, who represented the children, told the media that the evidence against the accused was very strong. Our support for the victims was heavily criticised by the local authorities. It was another validation of our position that the military bases brought untold suffering to women and children. That the publicity would fuel resentment against the continuation of the bases was not lost on the pro-base authorities.

The industry was of course contributing to its own wealth. Our campaign was damaging that business and if successful the anti-bases campaign could shut it down completely. History has assigned the responsibility for this immense suffering and lives of mental, emotional and even physical torture and slavery to the bar owners, many of whom are foreigners, and to the officials who issued licenses and permits and collected taxes and fees.

They denied all responsibility, saying it is all lies and if not for the exposes of PREDA, there would be no problems. Life without criticism or accountability was their goal. What they wanted the nation and the world to believe was that if there was no criticism, no voice of protest, no evidence or documentation of abuse and human rights violations, then it didn't happen, there was no crime for which they could be held accountable.

The blaring noise at the picket continued at the bottom of our driveway and the invective still unnerved us. But by November 29 there was relief in sight with the approach of a super typhoon. Was this the answer to our prayer?

On December 1, it was another kind of super typhoon that ended the two-week long picket and obscenity barrage – a military coup. We woke up to the news over the radio that an attempt was being made to oust President Corazon Aquino to take over the government by a band of military adventurists. Lt. Col. Gregorio Honasan launched an attack more coordinated and better prepared than the previous attempt against the government of Aquino.

They attacked the Palace, the TV station, a military camp and the airport. They occupied part of Makati, the business centre of Metro Manila. They were far more successful than their attempt in August 1987. This time Honasan had infiltrated the Marines, the most disciplined and well trained soldiers of the armed forces. It seemed to us that the Aquino government was going to fall.

The rebels captured the airport and, with this air power, they sent light aircraft to bomb the Palace, hoping that this would force Aquino to surrender. But she bravely held on. While the rebels increased their foothold during the next nine days, Fidel Ramos, the Secretary of Defence, was organising a hasty counter attack against the rebels. The city was at a standstill, the North Expressway was closed and no one was allowed to travel.

In the morning of the coup, the picket on our centre suddenly disappeared. In a news report in *The Manila Chronicle* by Vic Vizcocho on December 5, one of the leaders of the picket, Dolores Legaspi, was asked if the pro-base demonstrators were joining the coup. She answered: "Even though we are Marcos loyalists, we will not be going there." The immigration hearings were postponed because of the coup attempt.

Finally, to regain control of the air over Manila, Aquino had to call on the US to send air power. Two jets eventually turned up to chase the rebel turbo props from the skies. Nine days later, after the economy and the city lay in smouldering ruins, over a hundred people, mostly civilians, were killed. The rebels were forced back and the coup attempt failed.

The connection between the coup attempt and the future of the military bases were crucial issues and hotly debated. Allegations that the US secretly supported the rebels were rife but constantly denied. It was well known that Aquino, while officially stating she was keeping her options open on the future of the bases, was influenced by the strong nationalist sentiments that had propelled her to power in the first place. This worried the Americans who saw that a new treaty securing the bases was far from certain. Only after the death threats from the rebels and the carrot of protection from the US did Aquino undergo a change of position in the bases. The existing agreement was due to expire on 18, 1991. For many, it seemed that the coup attempt had achieved one goal.

The coup attempt began on the eve of the joint US and Philippine military exercises and there were an additional twenty thousand US Marines stationed in Subic. Two US warships were stationed off Stanley point the morning of the coup, but moved away when the rebel soldiers passed by in a commercial boat and captured the small military air base from where they took control of the air over Manila. Rebel soldiers took over a Makati hotel where there was a contingent of US military officers staying. No definite evidence of any US involvement was apparent but the speculation raged in the media for months.

In January, a new Bishop, Reverend Deogracias S. Iñiguez Jr., was appointed to our Diocese of Iba, Zambales. He succeeded the Most Reverend Paciano Aniceto who was appointed as Archbishop of San Fernando, Pampanga. He was a strong and stalwart supporter of our apostolate. He had a wise and good understanding of the socio-economic roots of the poverty and prostitution and other social evils that beset the people.

By December 20, the hearings of our case were to resume again. Attorney Cruz, my defence lawyer, questioned the basis on which the immigration Prosecutor ordered the case to be sent for a trial, the charges were unspecific, vague and hazy and the affidavits which were the only evidence presented were signed after the complaint was filed. The hearing continued throughout January. There was continuing support and many letters backing our stand were published.

On January 24, when I was on my way to Manila, I read that there was an arrest warrant issued for me by the Acting Immigration Commissioner Andrea Domingo. This was a form of harassment as there was no danger I would fail to attend the hearings but it was manipulated to make me appear like a criminal. An arrest in the Philippines is often interpreted by the public as a sign of guilt no matter how innocent the accused might be.

That week, Fathers Brian Gore and Niall O'Brien of the Negros Nine fame came to visit me to discuss and advise what I should do about the arrest warrant, which had not yet been served. Bail was set but paying it was not a great option until I had at least been jailed. A decision was reached that it would be better to voluntarily surrender in the presence of the media to explain what the charges were about. Two days later, I went to the Manila Immigration Jail to surrender. I brought an overnight bag of personal effects. I took the liberty of calling the media before hand.

The personnel at the jail would not let me inside as they had no copy of the arrest warrant. I began to give a series of live radio and television interviews there and then. An immigration officer soon appeared to tell me that there was no arrest warrant and fearing that this was a gimmick to appease the media, I showed him the press reports and said I was staying.

After an hour, Commissioner Domingo arrived in her office and had a hurried meeting with her officials. Apparently, she knew nothing of the arrest warrant and invited me to her office. She assured me that there was no warrant and that I could remain in the custody of the Columban Fathers and of the Association of Major Religious Superiors of the Philippines. The drama of the arrest warrant was over but it generated a good deal of publicity in the Philippines and abroad for our cause.

The Catholic Bishops Conference of the Philippines that represents the Bishops all over the country were vocal in their support. On January 30, they held a meeting at the Betania Retreat house in Tagaytay City and expressed the social costs and moral implications of the military bases. They were divided on the issue where they should stay or be removed but they expressed support and solidarity for our position, according to Fr James Reuter. The one hundred and ten Bishops later issued a statement of support for what we were doing and said the work should continue. The Bishops statement was addressed to Fr Charles Meagher, the Columban Director.

Dear Father Meagher,

Peace!

I received approval on January 30, 1990 from the Catholic Bishops Conference of the Philippines to address to you a letter from the CBCP Permanent Committee on Public Affairs with regard to the case and ministry of Fr Shay Cullen.

I want to convey to you that the Bishops appreciate and support very much the ministry of Fr. Cullen in helping drug dependents and women and children who suffer from sexual exploitation. This ministry is very dear to the heart of Christ who ministered especially to the sinful and downtrodden.

We realise that Fr. Cullen's ministry will entail exposing situations that are contrary to the values of the gospel. It is our hope that his freedom to do this is not curtailed.

Please extend our words of support for Fr Cullen and his ministry.

With Best regards!
Fraternally,
Bishop Teodoro C. Bacani
Chairman of the CBCP
Public Affairs Committee

In the first week of February, Attorney Cruz presented a motion to dismiss the case based on the fact that no evidence was submitted to support the charges and the fact that our rights to due process had been violated. The Prosecutor had filed charges without having informed me and given me the opportunity of presenting my replies in writing. We also pointed out that the affidavits of the complainants had been signed after the charges had been filed by the Prosecutor. During the hearing, Attorney Ronaldo Ledesma ordered that all documents be submitted to him together with the motion to dismiss for his consideration and adjourned the hearing.

We also had Prosecutor Mabolo inhibited on February 15 from prosecuting the case and another was appointed who would start over again and who would give us due process and conduct a preliminary investigation, which should have been done in the first place before charges were filed. The effort of the officials to railroad the charges though without evidence and due process was defeated. We were confident that there would be a just review of the complaints and evidence if the complainants had any.

The handicraft training and production project was an apprenticeship-style project where out-of-school youths, over eighteen, could learn a trade and get well paid while learning and improving their skills in handicraft making. It was a "learn and earn" project. Any product of quality that was produced we tried to sell to have the capital to finance the project.

This was succeeding at PREDA under the guidance of Merly who had succeeded in building up a strong export market in Europe for the products. Merly had developed a strong presence in the Fair Trade market. It was very important to have livelihood projects that alleviated poverty, idleness and depression among the youth. Such situations contributed to crime, drug abuse and child prostitution.

The practical prevention projects were growing and expanding under Merly 's management. It was this that some officials were envious of and wanted to take over. There was no production or export manufacturing in the city on this scale. We were also supporting handicraft production in other provinces and exporting them. We provided interest-free production loans, design assistance, management advice and quality control.

Unknown to us, the opposition was busy trying to find witnesses against us. They apparently had none because if they had they would have filed their sworn testimonies together with the formal complaint with the Bureau of Immigration and Deportation. On February 5, we were shocked to read in two newspapers the same report, with no by-line, that said a vital witness was prepared to testify against me. He was named as a former staff member who resigned in 1984 after working for three years with PREDA. I confronted him after learning from the residents that unknown to us he was dictatorial and would punch the residents in the chest, curse them and threaten them to maintain his control over them. That was anathema to us and we could not tolerate it. He resigned rather than be fired. However, he had signed no affidavit, nor did he deny his quoted comments in the newspaper.

Then we heard that he had been given a job as city development officer. He had accompanied some government officials in visiting our other staff and tried to persuade them to make false statements against us. They refused and told us about the recruitment attempt. Yet with others they were successful.

Although he had made no sworn affidavit, he was quoted as supporting some of the charges that the government officials had levelled against us. The most serious of these were that the handicraft trainees were not being paid the correct allowance for on the job training. But Merly kept meticulous records of all costs, payments and cash advances that we gave to the trainees.

The training centre was organised around the casual nature of handicraft production. It was a drop-in centre for those who were willing to give the time to learn a trade. And since they were not all fully skilled and still learning, their work was frequently of poor quality and unsaleable. They were also organised on a piecework basis to encourage them to learn and earn. The trainees and apprentices were part-time, they came and went with no fixed hours, they were absent for days at a time because some had other part-time jobs elsewhere. When they did make quality products, they were well paid for each successful item.

It was six years since our former staff member was with us so what credibility would his testimony make without supporting documents or complaints from the trainees? We were to find out soon enough. Our opponents had been busy. They had infiltrated the training programme with a few of their supporters posing as trainees. Some of the other trainees reported secret meetings between the newcomers and two PREDA social workers, Maggie and Edison, were being held at night. We were shocked, disappointed and very worried. Had they been bribed to give false statements?

We were in the midst of the deportation case, bombarded with false and baseless and bizarre accusations, staffers being recruited to give false testimony and now this, another crisis that we could do without. There seemed to be no end to the plots, manipulations and intrigues deployed to destroy our work.

Maggie and Edison were our street contact workers and were only with us for a year. As many more children came to the centre, they were assigned to supervise the street child residential centre, which was housed in a separate building away from the residence of the recovering drug dependents. They both chose to live-in at the Childhood For Children Centre rather than live-out.

The children reported that their behaviour amounted to an intimate relationship scandalous to the children. I talked with them about this and they were immediately defensive, denied it, yet became hostile and took it as grievance. The statements of the children – their lack of any denial – was still insufficient evidence in my opinion to fire them. They were consenting adults but it was inappropriate for anyone to engage in intimate relations within the children's centre.

The two social workers could not explain abandoning the centre and leaving the children unsupervised and unprotected some nights. This we discovered one night when there was a serious fight amongst the children and some of them came running and crying to the main building. One of them had a nasty gash on his forehead. We rushed him to the hospital.

Maggie and Edison were nowhere to be found. The children told us that their absence was a frequent occurrence. When asked to explain this, Maggie and Edison became remote and hostile and felt threatened. Relations became strained and the trust and friendship we were building up with them suddenly evaporated. We suspected the worst: they had been recruited to testify against us.

We were determined not to retreat from these threats but to meet all attacks with the truth. Most nights we came together by candlelight, staff and residents together; we held hands in a circle and prayed for the strength and determination to overcome whatever they threw at us. We believed that we were called by God to do this work (that it had to be prophetic and unwavering) and no matter how impossible our task seemed, the Holy Spirit was with us and God would determine the outcome, not us. That was our prayer. If our work was from God then nothing could stop it. If it was really something else it would surely fail. With this belief that God was with us we stood firm and decided never to compromise.

It was then that we discovered where they had being going at night. The new infiltrated "trainees" had already persuaded them that the handicraft trainees should be convinced to quit the training programme and claim that they were regular full time employees and not casual trainees getting paid for successfully made crafts. They were encouraged to demand back wages and separation pay after they had voluntarily left the project.

Maggie and Edison had already persuaded some of the trainees to sue for huge financial compensation. With the help of a lawyer closely linked to the government officials who were bringing the deportation case against me, a labour union was instantly formed to give official standing to their claims. Most were pressured to join and to sign a formal complaint to be filed with the Department of Labour.

Those who refused were visited in their homes and warned that something would happen to them if they continued going to the training workshop at PREDA. The whole operation ceased. It was a terrible blow and Merly was especially devastated.

Some of the advanced trainees were becoming highly skilled and were earning monthly earnings much higher than many a casual employee at the nearby US Naval Base. Now with the training centre closed, they could earn nothing. They came secretly to meet with us and discuss what could be done.

The solution was simple and brilliant. Merly suggested that we help each trainee return to their home village and set them up there with their family to continue the production there. Each would receive financial assistance to buy a small electric motor, tools, raw materials and an order to make a certain number of products. Then, each family would become an independent producer group in their own right. Lastly, they would be helped to form their own association.

Not only would this help them preserve their newly found skills but would also remove them from the many temptations of the sex, drugs and gambling industries. It would remove them from the danger of contracting HIV, too.

Despite the many other problems that were swirling around us like a gathering storm, Merly planned the relocation project. We began to ask why we didn't think of this earlier. Many of the trainees were from the same province of Pangasinan, about six hours by road from PREDA. The implementation was not too difficult. They were all young men who had migrated from their villages to the city and the military base looking for work. Without connections, qualifications and skills, they could not be employed. Others lost their jobs when the bars took over the wicker furniture shops and that craft collapsed as some of the shop owners turned to the lucrative sex trade.

Merly led the relocation to Pangasinan of our truck with building materials, motors and all the personal belongings of the faithful trainees. It was a very happy time for them many of whom had not been home for two years with their families. They had been sending home money but this was a triumphal return. They had the construction materials for small workshops and orders for handicraft. They could start work at once and give their relatives employment. They were heroes in the village and very proud of themselves.

Merly advanced cash to them for raw materials and living expenses. She arranged for the connection for electricity to light the home and run the motors and drills, although the Philippines was suffering from a chronic shortage of electric power. Soon they had constructed small workshops adjacent to their simple rural homes made of bamboo and thatch and in a few days handicraft production was underway. The jobs and the market was saved.

Their relatives were tenant farmers who planted rice, coconut and vegetables. But it was a hard life and not sufficient to keep them healthy or enable all their children to go to school. If they did not have some member of the family working in the city or abroad, they could not survive. Their young teenagers would run away from the hardship and frequently end up in prostitution.

We discovered that some of their relatives were already skilled craft makers and so small producer groups began to form around these homes. When Merly was able to get increased orders, they all thrived and expanded. The young teenage boys and girls stayed at home, had enough money to go to school and the migration to the city from this village was stopped. We all realised that this was the ideal way to contribute to rural development and alleviate poverty and prevent child prostitution. So what at first seemed to be a disaster to our trainee programme turned out to be an opportunity to expand and improve the production abilities of the new formed village based producer groups.

Soon after this, Maggie and Edison resigned from PREDA and went their own ways. It became clear later that they had been influenced by the infiltrated agents posing as trainees. The formal complaint that was lodged with the Department of Labour was successfully answered by Attorney Cruz who proved that there was no violation of any labour laws and, in fact, the apprenticeship and training programme had not only given free education and skilled training but had paid the trainees highly for any product they made. He also pointed out that the training programme was open, had flexible and voluntary hours of participation and any products that were made anywhere, since the trainees could make the products whenever they chose and had the time, were well paid on a loose contractual basis. The case like many others was eventually dismissed as baseless.

The infiltration and land grabbing of the Nagbaculao community by the goons and hangers-on of local politicians was a shock in itself but when the women's weaving association, which we helped to establish, was disbanded by the infiltrators with threats and intimidation, we were very despondent.

Every project that succeeded in empowering the women to help themselves was dismantled before our eyes. It was as if everything good that the people tried to do for themselves was a sign of independence, and feared as a threat by the authorities. It was as if the ruling elite had only one role for women and that was prostitution. If we were helping them in any way, they were, it seemed, especially targeted for harassment and disempowerment.

The harassment and injustice of it became all the more apparent when the following April the Department of Labour and Employment, after a long investigation by the Secretary Ruben Torres, reported "widespread exploitation" of thousands of bar girls, together with hotel and restaurant workers. The violations in one hundred and fifty bars and clubs ranged from the non-payment of the minimum wage, overtime, holiday pay and other bonus payments required by law. Some of the bar girls were receiving only the tips they picked up from customers instead of wages. These women depended on getting picked up by a customer and taken out to a hotel for the night. The bar owner collects the payment in advance and keeps half of it for himself.

That March we helped finance a group of women, some former bar girls, to travel to Angeles City to join a women's rally against the bases. It was heartening to see over a thousand empowered women rallying against the exploitation of the sex industry and the bases. They demonstrated in front of Clarke Air Base in Angeles City, Pampnga, about an hour from Olongapo, and then moved to Manila for a demonstration outside the US Embassy.

The following May, another rally at the US Embassy was

organised by church, justice and peace agencies and human rights organisations. Religious women, priests, seminarians and women's rights campaigners, student groups were there. I, too, joined them and we marched along with our banners and streamers singing hymns and chanting slogans supporting the rights of women and children. Senator Wigberto Tañada was to address the rally but, before we reached Roxas Boulevard, a contingent of police suddenly appeared and blocked our advance towards the Embassy.

The leaders confronted the police and insisted on exercising constitutional rights to public assembly and freedom of speech. But the police dispersed the participants and arrested fifteen, among them was my friend Sr Carmen Balazo, a Franciscan, who was a member of the PREDA Board and had worked for many years organising, educating and empowering the Aeta people in Zambales to stand up for their rights. She succeeded in helping the indigenous people to unite and form their own organisation and get control of the rattan harvest from their ancestral forests, which was controlled by business traders and the military. Merly was working with the people, helping them to harvest their rattan and paying them a just price. They were thriving on this. Later, we began a craft training project in their villages.

Sr Carmen, known to everyone as Sr Mengay, and fourteen other demonstrators were taken to the Western Police District Station and held for nearly six hours. I was not arrested but stayed with them giving support while lawyers who arrived on the scene negotiated their release. The arrests generated a lot of ill feeling against the government and the police and the Embassy too since it was understood they had asked the demonstration be blocked.

In May, we were shocked by the terrible murder of a US Marine Sgt. John Fredette in Olongapo. He was shot dead on the street not far from the gates of the military base. There was an uproar, all military leave was cancelled and the gates were closed. The city ground to a standstill, thousands were out of work. At PREDA, we thought that this was going to lead to a series of attacks by the Communist hit squads to paralyse the city.

Desperate to solve the crime and have the gates opened, the police picked up three suspects. Assistant City Prosecutor Floresta demanded the police release the suspects since there was no credible evidence to link them to the crime and they were accusing the police of torturing them to confess. Other witnesses claimed that the sergeant was with other US servicemen and was seen quarrelling with them shortly before they left and he followed them. The murder was never solved.

A week later, the base commander relented and opened the gates but imposed a midnight curfew. The bar girls and jeepney drivers were called out by the business people to stage a protest rally and demand the curfew be lifted and the trade be allowed to continue. The Times of London reported that the lifting of the curfew, which was hurting Olongapo's only industry, known euphemistically as "entertainment with sex", was the main target of the rally, not the retention of the US bases.

The following June, another serviceman, Lt. Richard E. Brown, was stabbed and killed in nearby Barrio Barretto. This, too, was not solved but speculation ran high that the killings were linked to the Communists who were trying to create a crises of confidence in the government while the base talks were underway.

These incidents helped me realise just how dependent the city was on the sex industry and the military base. I was all the more convinced that the Senate had to reject any proposed treaty for the extension of the bases and adopt some version of the conversion plans that we and others were now proposing.

Chapter Eighteen

At the beginning of the 1990s, our efforts to get ratification of the Convention of the Rights of the Child took on a new momentum when the official campaign was launched at the Philippine International Convention Centre in Manila by UN Undersecretary-General for Human Rights, Jan Martenson. President Aquino was there and urged a speedy ratification that was strongly supported by Senators Wigberto Tañada and Joey Lina. We were hoping for a ratification by the end of June. For the convention to come into worldwide effect, it had to be ratified by at least one hundred and twenty countries. By January of 1990 sixty nations had already signed the declaration.

This was a momentous, historical occasion for the Philippines and millions of children the world over. Children were to be recognised as having special rights and needs. No longer could they be treated as the property of their parents or the state to be used and abused at will. The world community was now prepared to defend them and work to change people's attitudes that tended to despise and exploit them.

I was elated by the rising global public awareness of the plight of abused and exploited children. For years we were operating in a kind of isolation, advocating children's and women's human rights to a desensitised public. Local politicians were condemning our efforts. Our experience in Olongapo typified what was happening in many cities in the

Philippines and throughout Asia. Official denial of abuse was common and officials were shamed when confronted with evidence of abuse. It was a stark indictment of their disregard of the most vulnerable in society and their emotional and intellectual bankruptcy. As the frequent messenger of what bad things were happening to children, I felt the hard hand of denial and harassment. The deportation case against me was an indication of that. That is why the Convention is so important. It confirms what we were saying all along, recognises the correctness of our campaign and silenced our critics and opponents that preferred to cover up exploitation of children.

The UNICEF-assisted project called "Breaking Ground For Community Action On Child Labour" was led by a friend of ours, Leopoldo Moselina, who had made a famous research study into the social conditions in the bars and clubs of Olongapo years previously when he was a teacher in St Columban's College. His study helped motivate myself, Merly and Alex to set up the PREDA Foundation. The struggle for these rights was getting not only national recognition but international support.

Children's protection laws were being debated at the Senate and Congress at this time and the Department of Social Welfare and Development was taking new measures to curb the trafficking of children for adoption and sexual exploitation. In Australia, the *Catholic Weekly* ran an article expressing the concern of the Australian Church at the increasing involvement of Australian paedophiles in the child sex trade in the Philippines and singled out our efforts to stop it.

Pagsanjan is a small scenic town two hours south of Manila, famous for a deep gorge and shallow rapids that end at a towering waterfall. Thousands of tourists, mostly Japanese, enjoy the boat ride over the rapids in shallow dugouts. The famous scenery had become a cover for a shady business in the trafficking in children for sexual abuse and prostitution of small boys. The paedophiles were mostly Caucasian, wealthy and many of them took up residence in the town for a few months of the year. They gave lavish gifts to the family of the boys that they befriended and had the boys go live with them in rented apartments.

The wealthy ones built new houses for the family. Whether the parents knew that there was sexual abuse in the relationship or not, they went along with it, mesmerised by the flow of money and luxury gifts showered on them. Local politicians, who were themselves owners of hotels and apartments, prospered by renting rooms to the paedophiles. Many were their staunch protectors.

Two Senate committees (on women and family relations and local government) held a joint investigation into the Pagsanjan paedophilia problem and concluded that local officials had "failed to stop the proliferation" of paedophiles and their "nefarious activities". The report also said that there was a lack of interest of the local chief executives in curbing child sex trade activities of paedophiles and instead they made Pagsanjan "greatly comforting, attractive and actually advantageous" to paedophiles who want children as sex partners. In March, the Department of Tourism stopped all promotion of Pagsanjan as a tourist destination. The Secretary of Tourism said that she did it to protect the image of Philippine tourism and because of the "moral degeneration and apathy" in the town. The tourist industry was crippled.

Ronnie Velasco, whom I came to know during my research visits to Pagsanjan, was informative and very helpful. He is dedicated to stopping the spread of paedophilia. He helped establish the Council For The Protection of Children and vigorously advocated greater protection and rehabilitation for the estimated hundreds of children who were being sexually abused by local and foreign paedophiles.

In one report, he was quoted as describing it as a form of

abuse not very different to our situation in Olongapo and Angeles. "In Pagsanjan," he said, "we are not only talking about the corruption of minors but the corruption of entire families."

During a visit to the town, I heard about a group of about five Norwegian paedophiles that was planning to bring young boys to Norway. The parents of the five boys were separated and through a fake marriage the mother and the boys were brought to Oslo where they were housed in an apartment to be sexually abused. This group was still trafficking young boys to Norway. I brought this to the attention of the Norwegian authorities when I was in Oslo for the launching of the TV documentary *Throwaway Children* but no action was taken until some years later.

Many of the children abused in Pagsanjan developed severe psychological problems. They dropped out of school, took to alcohol and drugs. Others became boatmen or pimps when they were no longer attractive to the paedophiles who favoured younger children. Working as pimps, some even introduced their smaller brothers to the trade. Only years later when I made further appeals did we get an investigation going and that was to reveal surprises about the traffickers.

Ronnie told me about the arrest of Mark Harvey, an American paedophile who ran a worldwide pimping business from Pagsanjan. During and after his arrest, the immigration agents failed to look around his apartment. It was left open and abandoned. Some members of the Council for the Protection of Children asked the apartment owner permission to go there and they found index files naming as many as five hundred children Harvey had sexually abused. The index cards describe the sexual attributes that Harvey found attractive about them. He would pass on his recommendations to other paedophiles and had index cards for them, too. Harvey seemed to have the name of every single male he met on that list of shame.

Harvey was one of the most active paedophiles in the town

and kept an apartment near the river. He was arrested and deported in 1989 but he was never brought to trial much to our disgust, considering the strength of the evidence. I asked Ronnie if I could copy the files and other incriminating documents. Back in PREDA, I indexed them by country and crime and sent copies to the police in the US and other countries where it was likely that Harvey might set up a similar operation based on addresses found in his files.

The American Federal Bureau of Investigation (FBI) found him and put him under surveillance. After a year, he was arrested and charged for attempting to molest a child. The US District Attorney prosecuting the case submitted the files I sent him as evidence of Harvy's activities in the Philippines. Although I could not confirm the report, the Judge amended the sentence from one to three years as a result of this additional evidence, no doubt to keep Harvey away from children as long as possible.

The trafficking of children for illegal adoption to Germany was also coming to light at this time. The Secretary of Social Welfare and Development, Mita Pardo de Tavera, said that thirty-five children were discovered trafficked in January that year alone. We too began to look on the adoption of children in a new light. From seeing it as a pure act of care and sacrifice by childless parents, we realised there was a sinister profit making business behind it. New controls were introduced to limit the practice and today a prospective adopting couple have to be resident in the Philippines before they are eligible. A special travel permit for a minor is now required and this has to be checked by the Social Welfare Officer assigned to the airport.

In Olongapo, the Filipino-American or GI souvenir babies, as they were called, were much sought after for adoption and there was a strong trade going on. The mothers were mostly impoverished and indebted prostituted women. They were so vulnerable that they were quickly persuaded to sign adoption papers and part with their newly born child for a price. Some were admitted to a hospital to give birth and then saddled with the burden of payment. To free themselves from the threat of prosecution, they had to sign away their newborn.

Racism may have been behind some of the brisk trade in these fair skinned children fathered by Caucasian fathers. They were preferred to children born of Filipinos. Some people said the preference was not racist but because the children would blend into the culture and racial mix of the country of destination. But it is always a sensitive issue.

One day I had a visit from Tessie, a woman of about thirty-five years old, she was asking marriage advice. Her job in the bars and clubs was over. She was no longer "sexy" and attractive in a string bikini gyrating on a bar top and she had been unsuccessful in finding a serviceman willing to marry her and take her to the US – the dream of most bar women. She decided that I was her last sunset on a life of misery and failure and determinedly set her heart on appointing me her marriage broker.

Tessie had a proposal of marriage from an Australian. She was to meet him in Manila for the first time and travel to Australia. She was frightened that she would never be able to make contact with her family again. I was to be her guardian and point of contact when she went abroad. I did all I could to point out the dangerous and hard life that could result from such a deal. The trafficking of women willing or otherwise is a common practice in the Philippines, although outlawed. Tessie went away more enlightened, I think, and with a promise for further help if she needed it. There was no call for help. There were many women who came asking me to help them get birth certificates and even annulments from their previous marriages to a Filipino who had long abandoned them so they could marry some sex tourist. It was understandable when they endured poverty and abuse.

Alternative employment with a decent wage was not available. Not until the bases were closed and there was some kind of manufacturing or other jobs available. Our basket weaving project had been disbanded by the politicians' goons and the training workshop had to close down and be relocated to the distant villages. It was a desperate situation for many women. After every counselling session, I felt powerless and frustrated that I could do so little other than to give all the emotional and spiritual support and affirmation. I could help their children get to school and press some badly needed cash into her hand. Some we were able to persuade to abandon the mail-order bride business and join the Buklod Women's Centre that was offering dressmaking and manicuring training for women such as Tessie.

A legislative milestone was reached in the Philippines that month with the signing into law of Republic Act 6955, which outlawed the mail-order bride business. It prohibits all forms of arranged marriages, advertisements, publications or any offer to match a Filipina with a foreigner for marriage for a fee. It carries a penalty of six years in prison.

The trade is still thriving despite the efforts of women's rights groups to reduce the seedier, most shameful aspects. Women and children have become commodities to be traded not unlike the slave trade of the Eighteenth Century. Impoverished women, especially those prostituted by syndicates and, no longer attractive to the sex trade, are still offered for marriage by arrangement for a fee. They are offered for sale, body and soul, over the internet- picture supplied. Group of foreign tourists from the US are organised to find Filipino brides and introduce them to the members of the tour group. They advertise openly on the Internet.

We were aware of this going on in Olongapo as many bar women knew they could rely on us for help and asked me to help them get a birth certificate. A syndicate trafficking women to Hong Kong was uncovered in January 1990. A retired American serviceman was arrested by the Criminal Investigative Department of the US Navy and was accused of collaborating with a local government official who was providing false documents to the young women, some were minors. They were matched with US servicemen who declared the young women to be their legitimate fiancées. The women easily got visas to Hong Kong provided the US servicemen were travelling with them. There the relationship ended and the women were picked up by another syndicate and taken into the sex trade or married to a waiting customer.

My deportation case was still pending but then by August 1, 1990, the official decision from the Bureau of Immigration and Deportation was the best we could have hoped for. Attorney Cruz had made a strong and forceful presentation defending my rights to due process knowing that any preliminary investigation would show that there was nothing to support their accusations.

The complaints were dismissed as baseless and not matters to be considered for deportation. In fact, what they were accusing me of was not even considered a crime and the decision said that if the complainants could produce evidence to support their accusations they should file them with the Office of the City Prosecutor, not the Bureau of Immigration. In other words, they had nothing. But it had been eight months of stress and tension for all of us and every dirty trick was employed to have me deported.

Framing up innocent people who are critics or rivals is a common tactic in the Philippines. Writers, human rights advocates and troublesome clerics as well as opposition politicians are the main targets. I was to be one for many years to come. And much more lay ahead.

The dismissal of the charges also prevented a takeover of the PREDA Centre by the local government officials at that time. That was a goal that they never abandoned.

Free at last, I was able to leave for Australia where I was

invited to attend the International AIDS Conference in Canberra. Cardinal Jamie Sin, our friend and supporter, was a keynote speaker. I was invited to speak about our grass roots campaign to remove the stigma of AIDS and our preventive educational programmes.

The Philippines was emerging from a cloud of denial about AIDS as it had recently overcome extreme denial about the sexual abuse of children. Not only were officials reluctantly recognising the deadly threat that AIDS posed to the Philippines but the fact that the sex related industry near the military bases were high-risk areas and contributed to the rapid spread of the disease. A Philippine Senate Committee issued a report stating that there was a "definite link" between the bases and the spread of the virus.

The US Navy was conducting testing in Olongapo and Angeles not only on their own servicemen but on the bar women also. If they detected a case, the woman was reported to health officials and sent to the San Lazaro Hospital in Manila to be quarantined. It was devastating for them. They lost their income, could not help their family and were immediately branded and stigmatised and could never work again.

The city social hygiene centre conducted the testing for venereal disease and HIV, paid for by the US Navy and supported with navy equipment. This was more to protect the sailors than to help the women. Alternative work with dignity would have been the right thing to do. The hygiene centre collected a "Mayor's fee" for this service as indicated by a sign in the clinic. Instead of providing them with support and an alternative risk free employment, they were left on their own. Many escaped from the hospital or were discharged and with no alternative they returned to the streets or to illegal bars and back ally brothels.

Later, because of severe criticsm by the women's right groups and ourselves at PREDA, the city gave a few former bar women jobs in the city health centre as a publicity stunt.

A short term preventive education programme had begun under intense international pressure. The Government in Olongapo and Angeles were adamant in maintaining the fiction that there was no prostitution, only entertainment in their cities. AIDS-positive people were the unquestionable proof of uncaring and neglect and the consequence of the sex trade that they provided for their people. For them there was no money in sightseeing tourism as there was nothing to see. In Olongapo, the beaches are so filthy that no foreign tourist would go there.

The government's Department of Health admitted to diagnosing one hundred and seventy-two cases of AIDS in the Philippines that year but noted that this was double the figure of the previous year. Twenty people had already died. The World Health Organisation said the figures were understated and there were many unreported cases. The media sought me out in Canberra and gave good coverage to the problems we were facing in the Philippines. I expressed concern about the proliferation of AIDS in Perth where the US Navy ships made frequent visits to the port of Freemantel.

The Philippine Senate Committee on Health invited me to present a paper on the HIV/AIDS problem from our perspective. I pointed out the socio-economic conditions and unemployment that was behind the prostitution of impoverished women by the sex mafia. The demand for prostituted children was growing, I said, in the belief that they would be HIV-free and better for safe sex. I referred to the high numbers of infected servicemen in the US Armed Forces, twenty HIV-positive men could be in Olongapo during the visit of the US 7th Fleet. The statistics I quoted were from a study carried out by the Walter Reed Army Institute of Research that began in June 1986 and continued for three years. Our deepest concern for the people from the HIV/AIDS pandemic was heightened by the global political events. The Middle East was in crises. Saddam Hussein had invaded Kuwait and the US oil sources were threatened. The Gulf War was imminent.

Another row broke out when the Mayor was reported to have criticised us yet again for giving a bad image to the city in *Time* magazine. Jay Brannigan, a staff writer with *Time*, wrote a page-long article on Olongapo and its dependency on the military bases. He covered the sex industry and quoted what I had to say about the damage it does to family life. He wrote about our efforts to pursue an economic conversion plan based on the need to restore the personal dignity of the people. In that article, the Mayor is reported as telling *Time* that he wants to wean the city from complete reliance on the bases but he scoffed at the military base conversion plan we had put forward and that had been adopted by the national government.

Chapter Nineteen

The city was on a high, it was New Year's Eve and there had been nothing like it since the Vietnam War. Thirty-two US navy ships steamed into Subic Bay and dropped anchor and disgorged their troops. Tanks and personnel carriers were no longer the jungle green that we were accustomed to see but desert beige. The Marines were wearing similar camouflaged uniforms.

Dressed in shorts and t-shirts, thousands of servicemen streamed out of the main gates that night to enjoy the entertainment offered by the local industry. "Our prayers are answered," one businessman chortled on a local radio interview. War was what many in the brothel industry prayed for. Hundreds of additional women were brought in by the clubs and bars from Angeles City and Metro Manila to cope with the huge demand from the thousands of Marines and Sailors readying for their incursion to the Middle East and possible death from chemical or conventional weapons. Visiting the streets and the jail looking for kids in danger, I noticed an unusual uniform and insignia on a group of more sober looking Marines and asked who they were.

"They are the 'body-baggers'," explained a sergeant in starched white uniform of the Navy Shore Patrol. The Marine Corps Graves Registrations Specialists were in town on their way to the dying dunes of the Kuwait Desert where they expected to be busy bringing home the corpses. I learned too that the stand-off near the borders of Kuwait had resulted in the deaths of thirty-four US troops from accidents before a shot had ever been fired. The "body-baggers" would be busy.

The streets erupted before me in wild parties, blaring bands and drunken sailors waving beer bottles and dancing in the streets. Intoxicated young men, clutching small Filipino women like baby dolls under their arms, staggered down the centre of the streets now cleared of traffic for the occasion of the Mardi Gras-like celebration. Banners hung from brothel balconies welcoming the ships by name and number. Scantily clad women waved and called to the servicemen to come in for a "good time". Vendors touted sunglasses, gum and souvenirs.

In January, I visited Cebu City; there I met Danilo (twelve), Denis (ten), Lando (twelve), and many more street children all behind bars in the Lahug prison, mixed in with the hardened prisoners and working as prison janitors. Some of them had been arrested and beaten by the police, others had been held for weeks without being charged or brought to the children's rehabilitation centre. Others were actually sentenced to months in jail for attempted snatching. They had only a court appointed lawyer and there was no social worker to care for them. The absence of any juvenile justice law left these children in dire circumstances and thousands more were like them. It was to be years before services of any kind would be available to help children like these.

The human rights situation was not improving. Death squads were still active in the Philippines. Between January and August 1990, there were fifty-nine reported extra-judicial executions, thirty-six people were abducted and no report of them being found, almost two thousand people were arrested illegally and one hundred and forty-nine people were reported tortured.

At PREDA, I was growing apprehensive about the personal security of myself and the staff. They were feeling the pressure as much as I was and we could only pray and watch each other, taking no risks going out alone or having any regular schedules. There were sleepless nights filled with anxiety especially when we observed surveillance teams following us. It was a relief to get away for a while and do research in the provinces. I accepted more public speaking engagements on the bases issue and human rights. But that only drew me all the more into the spotlight of the authorities or, as I sometime saw in a nightmare, into the crosshairs of an assassin's bullet.

When I was visiting Negros in January, a priest of the Philippine Independent Church, Fr Narciso M. Pico of Kabankalan (where Fathers Brian Gore and Niall O'Brien were arrested and falsely accused of murder and subversion) was brutally murdered by assassins. He had consistently taken the side of the poor farmers protecting their human rights and helped them to appeal for more wages. Fr Pico had been threatened but bravely carried on his human rights advocacy.

On January 15, he was sitting at a roadside store close to his church when two assassins approached on a motorcycle and shot at him point blank range. He was gravely wounded and dropped to his knees."

"My God, have pity, that's enough," he cried out.

One of the assassins uttered a blasphemy and shouted to his companion, "Finish him off!"

A bullet to the head killed Fr Pico outright. In many places, Task Force Detainees of the Philippines reported that church workers, priests and nuns were being harassed and threatened. All were branded as subversives and the fanatical right wing anti-Communist cults were spreading the slogan "be a patriot and kill a priest". President Aquino didn't know what was happening and was prompted to give speeches encouraging the militias like the Alsa Masa groups in Davao City who were notorious killers. The Supreme Court issued an opinion legalising "warrant-less arrests". Mere suspicion was like a death sentence.

A day after the murder of Fr Pico, January 16, a columnist with the *Manila Chronicle* Antonio C. Abaya wrote that PREDA staff and myself were linked with the illegal National Democratic Front (NDF), an organisation declared subversive by the authorities. He quoted from a German church magazine, *Forum*, that reported our visit to the Evangelical Church of Westfallen the previous year, claiming that we were lecturing on the "social costs of the US bases which destroy the environment and lead to prostitution and drug abuse".

His article was entitled *NDF strengthens its shield in Europe*. He was insinuating that we were part of that organisation and doing their work. It could have been a death sentence for us. It was ammunition that our opponents in Olongapo seized upon with glee to brand us as subversives.

In Olongapo, we were feeling the hostility of the elite and the business community. Harassment was growing in reaction to the dismissal of the deportation charges against me and our exoneration. We worried that they would do something violent. We were all the more apprehensive with the growing persecution of church people and – despite the support of Bishop Paciano and the support letter of the Catholic Bishops Conference of the Philippines and the other religious organisations – we were encouraged by the example of so many courageous human rights workers in the Church risking their lives for the sake of the poor.

There was a growing gap between the church of the rich and that of the poor. Although prelates preached the need to preserve unity and bring reconciliation it was nevertheless a time of contradiction. Reconciliation could only be achieved where there was social justice and respect for human rights.

We were greatly encouraged with the stand taken by brave and outspoken Bishops.

A few months after the column of Mr Abaya, who wrote incorrectly that we were linked to the Communist National Democratic Front, there was another massacre in Negros. Bishop Antonio Fortich and Bishop Camilo Gregorio of Bacolod City, Negros, held a memorial service for a squatter family of five who had been mown down by police gunfire. They had dared to rebuild their typhoon damaged squatter hut on the city rubbish dump after being warned not to. The area was being claimed by a rich business family in the city. It was a killing that illustrated the power and ruthlessness of some rich people to have the police do their bidding. The force was like their own private army, a situation widely repeated throughout the Philippines and in Olongapo.

Bishop Fortich told a crowd of ten thousand: "We must try to be a church that defends and vindicates the rights of the poor even when doing so spells for herself alienation or persecution by the rich and the powerful." That was exactly what we were feeling in Olongapo.

A few weeks later, Archbishop Jesus Tuquib of Cagayan De Oro, the second largest city on the Island Of Mindoro, decreed that all church services be cancelled and the altars be stripped in the parish churches of Salay and Binuangan. This was an unprecedented and dramatic gesture.

The wealthy parishioners did not support their parish priest, Fr Mario Valmorida, when he was falsely accused by the military of helping Communists when in fact he was ministering to the refugees who had fled the military bombardment of their villages. He was criticised for not teaching the choir new hymns and instead spending most of his time in the refugee camps hastily set up in his parish.

"I cannot allow the Church to be just for the rich and the political leaders and the privileged of the town," he said.

The military claimed he was a subversive. His parish workers had been threatened and their houses fired on. One little child was killed. A grenade was thrown into the parish church of Fr Mario and his house riddled with machine gun fire. In ordering the closure of the churches, Archbishop Tuquib, referring to all the attacks, said: "In the midst of all this the people did not care, did not support their priest... because of all this I have decided to take away Father Mario Valmorida."

In Olongapo, we wondered if our situation would come to that level of violence and terror tactics. Time was to tell.

Back in Olongapo, the jail rescue work had brought us into contact with many young people held in jail without trial; a common situation. One was a youth, Raul Ganac Ramos, who had been active in the parish youth group of the Santa Rita Parish where Columban Fr Donal Bennett, from Ireland, was the parish priest. I was helping out the parish every Sunday celebrating the Eucharist with a church overflowing with parishioners. The young man was arrested for alleged stealing and held without charges for almost three months. There was a jailbreak on May 12 and he escaped with the other prisoners. The police traced Raul to a hillside squatter community where he was hiding and they surrounded the shanties and called on him to surrender. They promised he would not be hurt. Raul decided to surrender and came out with his hands held high and the squatters pressing closer as the drama unfolded. The police unit led him away about fifty metres from the gathering crowd and suddenly there was a loud single shot and Raul was executed. The death squad had done its work.

There was a huge funeral mass presided over by Fr Bennett who had many similar funerals when he was the parish priest of St. Joseph's during Martial Law. His sermon was strong and to the point. He expressed the feelings of many when he said that "because of this killing, all of us here at the Santa Rita Parish are in danger and afraid lest this happens to us also, to anyone, to me, to your children, to your brothers and sisters and to your friends and relatives".

"The boy was killed," he said, "as if he wasn't even human."

Respect for human rights was nonexistent in the community and we were living in a climate of terror and fear. He went on calling for all to unite and stand together to protest the injustice and to help each other oppose tyranny and oppression. It was a brave and outspoken sermon that was greatly needed in the city.

There was much disappointment and frustration the previous March when Heinrich Stefan Ritter, the suspect who allegedly abused the twelve-years-old Rosario Baluyot, who died from the infection caused by a broken vibrator that lodged in her vagina, was acquitted. He was convicted By Judge Alicia Santos of the Olongapo Regional Trial Court and sentenced to life imprisonment in March 1987.

He could not be convicted of rape, the Court of Appeals said, because the evidence tended to show that Rosario was over twelve-years-old and her participation was with consent. It also said that the homicide was not conclusively proven as the evidence was circumstantial. The court pointed to a statement of the doctor who attended to Rosario before she died who said Rosario told her that an African-American had inserted the vibrator into her vagina.

If it was not Ritter, then who had done this terrible deed? The finger of suspicion then pointed to the possibility that it was an American serviceman who had done the deed and Ritter was a pansy or a scapegoat to shield the US Navy from the allegations that one of their men had committed the crime. There was some suspicion about the authenticity of the identification of Ritter by Jessie Ramirez, the star witness, on the crowded streets of Manila months after the crime. It seemed like a miracle at the time that he would still be there and still recognised.

The other strong evidence against Ritter was the entry in the hotel register on the day the act was supposed to have happened. That, too, with hindsight seemed extraordinary luck since most customers using the sex hotels for short encounters do not register as they don't stay overnight. An enterprising investigator could arrange for a name to be inserted in the registration book. The fact that the US Navy had assigned its own detective to work on the case added further suspicion that perhaps Ritter was the fall guy with an elaborate array of circumstantial evidence manufactured to convict him. Ramirez was also kept away from us even after the trial. We could not question him privately and immediately after the trial he was spirited away with his mother to a distant province. When he came back years later to visit us at PREDA, he was on drugs or psychologically deranged, we couldn't tell which.

In no way do these speculations take away the sterling and honest work of the prosecution. They only had the evidence supplied by the police to go on and whatever other evidence that they could find themselves. However, it was much too late now to open another investigation. Rosario had been killed, she came to symbolise all that was wrong and evil about the prostitution of children and the system that covered it up.

In early June, 1991, before the eruption of Mt. Pinatubo, Roy Vidal, our staff in charge of the street children, brought the news that a police aide had raped a thirteen-years-old child and that he was not being investigated. Then a police captain was accused of the sexual abuse of a ten-years-old. That, too, was not under investigation. This was the same captain who routinely picked up street children and jailed them. Our worst fear was the city policy to keep the streets clear of street children was supplying victims to abusers.

The charges of sexual abuse of children against two retired US servicemen were dismissed despite strong evidence. The city Prosecutor, an appointee of the Mayor, was unreliable in pursuing justice. It was clear that the same mentality prevailed as in the past when we exposed the sexual abuse of the twelve children by US serviceman Daniel Dougherty. That was a simplistic form of cover-up. If it is not known, then it didn't happen, was the way of thinking. Denial and cover up of sexual abuse and sex tourism was what we were up against.

The image factor was a dominating concern of politicians. The campaign to have me condemned and deported by the city elite showed just how much they feared exposure of the truth. That is always a strong indication of corporate guilt. Even some of the clinics were involved in illegal abortions – and lawyers in fixing cases against innocent people with the connivance of corrupt Judges and officials. The attempt to have me deported and take over the PREDA Centre the previous year convinced us that there was a kind of mafia or syndicate operating behind the bar and brothel scenes. The trafficking of women and children was a hugely profitable business and the human commodities of this trade were the innocents lured from the rural villages and sold into sexual slavery. The evidence pointed to a massive cover up of sexual crimes against them.

I passed by the local jail on Magsaysay Drive that leads to the main gate of the Naval Base and noticed two street boys behind bars. I talked to the policeman on duty about releasing the children. He was irritated, his mind was on something else that New Year's Eve and it wasn't the release of kids to a pesky priest. But I persisted, and eventually he called the police van, an old converted jeep painted white with wire mesh for windows. The kids were bundled into it and sent over to the government-run Lingap Centre for Children. This was managed by the national government agency's Department of Social Welfare and Development (DSWD). The city government made a point of never referring any street children or abused children to the PREDA

Centre. They were under instructions from higher authorities not to do so. They feared that we would find evidence of many sexual assaults on the children and demand investigations. Soon the Lingap Centre was overcrowded with boys and girls.

That is when we increased our monitoring of the jails looking for children. It was inside the jail where children are most vulnerable to abuse. I went with Michael McCarthy, my cousin's husband, to the main nightclub scene on Magsaysay Drive. We witnessed the madness of the wild sex and alcohol industry bursting on to the streets as drunken American youths spilled from bars and clubs. Several had selected young teenagers from the platform where they had been gyrating and moving sensuously around a stainless steel post clad in a skimpy bikini or perhaps topless. In some bars, there were lewd shows where the sexual act was performed on stage.

The customer then paid the bar owner for the young girl of his choice, calling out the number of the girl he wanted. The young girls, who were no more than children, were sometimes numbered like merchandise with a price tag. On the streets, the intoxicated young men were to be seen pulling young girls by the arm towards a cheap hotel advertising rates by the hour.

One night I was escorting a group of social research students around the bars and clubs so they could witness and Judge for themselves the situation and understand the causes of many social problems. Suddenly there was a huge shout and people lined the streets as three or four young Caucasian men came streaking naked down the centre of the main street to the hoots and whistles of the onlookers. They disappeared into one of the bars further down the road. A Navy Shore Patrol jeep came after them with a siren blaring. It was ridiculous but just another typical scene from the streets of Olongapo or of Angeles City.

It turned midnight and we went to the local jail for a surprise visit. I greeted the policeman on duty and, as he nodded in return, I heard a child crying. I moved past the police desk down a corridor. A single dangling bulb gave a dim yellow light. The stench of urine, faeces and dried sweat assailed our nostrils as we walked down the narrow corridor of the police station. There were two cells, one left and another right. Four hard looking men were in the cell on the right, two were sleeping on the floor. The other two were watching the occupants of another cell and turned to look at us.

The source of the crying was a little girl not more than six years of age clutching the bars of the cell, tears streaming down her little face swollen with prolonged inconsolable crying. She turned her beseeching on us as if her only hope in her anguish and pain, "Mama why am I here? Please get me out!" she wailed over and over. She was holding an empty Coke can in her hand, clearly hungry and thirsty. A dozen other children were sprawled asleep on the floor. Others were piled on top of each other on a bunk bed at the back of the tiny cell, legs and arms intertwined, and hanging like lengths of brown rope.

I was speechless and felt a terrible anger rising in me at the sight. What kind of insensitive person could do this, someone devoid of human feeling, dead in the spirit, someone who looks on weak and vulnerable children as opportunities for profit and pleasure, unmoved by one of the most pitiful sights that would cause another species to fly into a frenzy of anger and concern. The police had come to look down the corridor and order us out. Perhaps it was dawning on them that this might be something for us to complain about to the higher authorities. I knew that this was not the time or place for a fit of anger. I asked Michael to give me the camera and I recorded the fact and then approached the policeman on duty to get the children released and brought to the children's centre.

The police had picked up the little girl during a sweep. Her parents were peanut vendors on the street curb. The idea was for this corrupt policeman to extort the day's hard earned money from them in exchange for releasing the child. It was a form of kidnapping. I talked to the sergeant on duty and strongly suggested that he release the children and bring them to the Lingap Centre. We knew that they would not bring them to PREDA Children's Home.

The politicians were trying to control the Lingap Centre for children. The courageous director, Adelina Apostol, was not intimidated and bravely resisted pressure and filed many charges against suspected sexual offenders, much to the annoyance of the city administration. Assistant City Prosecutor Dorentino Floresta was committed to bringing charges if the evidence was strong enough. That encouraged us to continue working for justice and trying to make the system work for children. The children were taken from the floor of the filthy holding cell, exhausted from pleading and crying and bundled into a police van for the short journey to the already overcrowded Lingap Centre.

It was a tense time in Olongapo city as the debate and battle for public opinion on the bases issues intensified. The factions working for the retention of the bases were lobbying the Philippine Senate to approve the proposed Treaty of Friendship, Cooperation and Security. They ballyhooed the negative impact that a withdrawal of the US Navy and Air Force would have on the economy. This was their main argument. The left or centre groups were arguing that sovereignty and freedom from political interference by the US would be the biggest benefits. Our main argument for the removal of the bases were the social and moral evils that they brought on both Filipinos and young American sailors hardly out of their teens and the alternative economic zones would bring work with dignity and more jobs and prosperity without a mafia run sex-based economy. We supported the freedom and sovereignty arguments also but the other groups were doing a fine job in the press in this important position and we focused on the economic and moral positions.

The anti-bases coalition had adopted and was promoting the economic zone alternative with us and it soon became a popular and welcome idea and a strong answer to the doom and gloom scenario promoted by the pro-US retention group led by Mayor Gordon. "You can't eat sovereignty," he would frequently bellow, and we would point out the advantages of conversion and the end to a nuclear threat to the region from the forward positioning of the US nuclear arsenal. In the end, it was these arguments that swung public opinion as well as the media support of these positions.

The *Philippine Daily Inquirer* was actively promoting the anti-bases agenda. I was still writing my weekly column and wrote frequently on this issue. Our position was supported and enhanced by the introduction of a free port concept into the conversion plan by a local businessman Conrad Tiu who was no friend of the city administration. One of his advisers was Assistant City Prosecutor Dorentino Floresa, a man of integrity and untainted by corruption. He was later to become the provincial Prosecutor of Zambales and a special Prosecutor for child abuse cases. We nominated him as the most outstanding Prosecutor of the Philippines award in 1996, which he won.

Mayor Gordon and his family still favoured the retention of the bases and warned of dire consequences if they closed. But the tide was turning against the retention factions despite the position of Aquino who was now for retention. This was probably out of gratitude to the US for saving her from the attempted coups. How much US support was behind those coups will perhaps never be revealed but they had their desired effect. Had the coups succeeded in toppling Aquino, the bases would have been safe, on the other hand, when they failed, they had the desired effect of pressuring her to opt for retention. Either way, they surely argued among themselves in Langely, they would emerge the winner. It was a million to one chance but we had faith that there was more at work than just human politics and manipulation. Olongapo residents could hardly believe that the only life of dependency on the US military for jobs and the bustling sex industry as the trade-off could now change.

By September 12, the tension was unbearable as the radio commentators breathlessly kept up a minute by minute account of everything they could think of, most of it gossip, rumours and speculation. The great secret to be unveiled was how five undecided Senators would vote. They would decide the fate of the nation and change Philippine history for the next generation and bring to an end the agonising wait that gripped us all. For us at PREDA, it was particularly tense. For ten years we had campaigned, lobbied and paid dearly for that anti-bases stance and now we waited with the rest of the anti-bases people to see the outcome of all our efforts.

It was a heart wringing half hour as the radio announcers counted off the votes as they came in. It was a quite tearful moment of indescribable relief and joy when the anti-base vote reached the magic eight needed to deny the pro-treaty the two-thirds majority they needed to carry the day. It was all the more stunning when the anti-treaty vote came to twelve.

There was consternation, anger, frustration and depression at the defeat and rejection among the pro-bases supporters as they were polled for their opinions by excited radio and television reporters. "It's a black day for the Philippines," said one pro-base leader. I could easily imagine the wailing and gnashing of teeth, as bar and brothel owners saw their empire of sex crumble like the walls of Sodom and Gomorrah and their human slaves running free.

All of us at PREDA were stunned. I strangely felt a wave of quiet elation and joy but no impulse to dance and party. I gave thanks to God for this immense breakthrough and victory of good over evil. We knew that thousands of innocents would be saved from trafficking into the sex trade for decades to come. We came together and celebrated a thanksgiving mass to the Almighty knowing that many previous years of work had been a channel of God's grace.

That somehow it had reached the conscience of those twelve Senators, God we believe, does not manipulate or negate free will, yet persuasion, reason, compassion, and perhaps for some very worldly interests all played their part in bringing about that vote that rejected a treaty to retain the US military bases. Yes, I felt an overwhelming sense of satisfaction and a strengthening of faith. The power of God's universal compassion and love had sustained and guided us in our Judgements and commitment. This historical change that would save thousands from exploitation and abuse came from the hand of God. The vote against the bases was for many the equivalent of the biblical parting of the Red Sea through which Moses lead his people to freedom from slavery and exploitation and then the waters closed in on the pursuing armies of Pharaoh.

The Filipino base workers, there were about twenty-two thousand in all, were busy working out the size of their separation pay and compensation and what small business they could start up. The separation pay was generous and just. For them, it was a windfall opportunity. Others were hoping they would be eligible to get a US green card and emigrate to California as promised by the US Navy if they fulfilled the required number of years of service and had turned down offers to work in the Middle East. The migration of Filipino base workers had threatened the efficiency of base operations and had undermined the efficiency of Subic Bay as a re-supply and repair station for the US Pacific Fleet. Those who would stay were promised green cards. For many, their loyalty was rewarded.

In the eyes of the local politicians and sex mafia, we at

PREDA were the troublemakers and to be blamed for their ignominious defeat. True, we were not popular with them for our role in ending the hundred-years history of US military presence in the Philippines yet we were happy and proud to have played an important role in the historic events of our day.

It was unbelievable that it could have happened and there was to be an end to much, although not all, US political and economic meddling and manipulation in the Philippines. The strategic value of the Philippines to the US had been primarily military and secondly economic.

A new era was indeed beginning and when President Aquino conceded defeat on the bases issue, we believe that she was secretly happy. The strong suspicion that the CIA had been the hidden hands on the puppet strings of the military coups behind the curtain of unrest would never leave her. She now delivered the required formal termination notice to the US as required by law. The Manglapus-Schulz of October 1988 had laid out the withdrawal procedures. The US had the right to remove all movable properties, the Philippine government would have first priority to buy excess property and they agreed to jointly secure and protect the facilities during the withdrawal period and minimize the disruption caused.

The US Navy decided to take back the three huge floating dry docks that were the mainstay of the ship repair facilities at Subic Bay. The smaller one was to be towed to Guam and the two monster ones would be towed to Pearl Harbor In Hawaii. Other valuable equipment from the machine shops and repair facilities were dismantled and shipped out by the end of March and civilian personnel were the first to pack-up and leave.

The gardeners, maids and drivers were the first employees to feel the impact. We had every sympathy for them and felt almost guilty that we had no immediate alternative for them. But Filipinos are masters of adaptability and have suffered life long hardships they have coping mechanisms within the extended family structure. In Western society where the extended family support system was given away to the cult of individualism, layoffs cause great psychological hurt but social welfare cushions the financial loss. In the Philippines, there is no such thing as unemployment benefits. The family and friends provide sustenance in times of financial crises.

One of the great strengths of Filipino society is the acceptance of mutual need and dependency in the struggle for survival. That willingness to help each other is what binds people closely in the essential human companionship that satisfies the longing and need of togetherness that is so natural of the human species as a social creature. I believe that the loss of this sense of community teamwork in the rush to loneliness and individualism is what contributes to so much unhappiness, exclusion and suicide among the young in modern society.

If there had ever been any doubt about the contention that some US Navy servicemen were paedophiles preying on the poverty stricken street children of Olongapo, it was forcibly dismissed by the case of Lawrence Venaska that surfaced in March 1992 as the preparations for the base withdrawal were getting under way. Venaska picked up street girls and took them to a rented apartment on Jones Street. There he performed perverted sexual acts on them over a period of several weeks. They were identified and taken in to the care of the Lingap Centre. The children were between the ages of eight and fourteen and the abuse went on from December 1991 to February 1992. He gave the children the equivalent of a dollar in Philippine pesos. The eight-years-old, who had been abandoned by her parents, lived in the house with him and was repeatedly abused. The director of the Lingap Centre Adelina Apostol brought in Prosecutor Dorentino Floresta to prepare the testimonies of the children against Venaska.

On March 24, Prosecutor Floresta reported the crime to the US Navy authorities and formally requested that Venaska be detained on an international hold order. There was no immediate response to this request but two months later on May 29, 1991, Navy Captain G. W. Kolarov wrote to Prosecutor Floresta requesting a formal waiver of jurisdiction over the case in favour of a US Court Martial citing that it would save the Philippines a lot of time and money. He cited Paragraph 3 (c) Article XIII of the Military Bases Agreement. It was also announced that unfortunately Venaska had disappeared and had somehow slipped out of the country and escaped.

The jurisdiction question was then referred to the Philippine Foreign Secretary Raul S. Manglapus by Acting Secretary of Justice Edwardo S. Montenegro in a letter dated June 25, 1992. Manglapus ruled that the jurisdiction question was to be decided by the implementing committee of the 1947 Military Bases agreement. On September 9, 1992 I wrote to Senior State Prosecutor Aurora Lagman bringing the case to her attention and pointed out the hideous perverted forms of abuse that was done to the children. They had been stripped naked, ravished, sodomized, raped, and demanded that action be taken.

Little did I know that behind closed doors the Philippine authorities were making a decision to drop the case into the jurisdiction of the US Navy knowing full well that the last thing the US government wanted as its last act in the Philippines was a case of child rape by one of their men with an eight-years-old and several others giving testimony. The committee wavered jurisdiction because the suspect was missing, there was no extradition with the United States and there was no way to have him returned for trial.

They must have known too that there was no way that the US government would bring him to trial and have the children testify in a US Court Marshal as was forced upon them in the Daniel Dougherty case of 1982. Then we exposed the sordid cover-up by the Navy and the local authorities and they were forced by public opinion to bring Dougherty to trial in Guam and have the victims testify. It was a great embarrassment to the Navy. It, too, was a travesty of justice. Although found guilty on thirteen counts of child sexual abuse, he received only one year in a mental home and a loss of benefits. "Boys will be boys, you know, just having a little fun," the verdict seemed to say.

I continued to follow-up the case of Venaska until February 1994 and was told by Navy sources that he was under surveillance in the US but fled the scene and eluded the police.

One morning in May 1992 as I stood on a hill I looked down on the still crumbled wreck of the PREDA Centre, like a toy building smashed by a great boot. Out across the turquoise blue of Subic Bay, a huge dry dock was starting its long journey across the Pacific to Hawaii. I couldn't help feel concerned for the workers who were losing their jobs. I talked to several and was assured by them that they had plans for their separation pay to buy a small farm, start a small business, buy a mini-bus or take that long awaited job in the Middle-east where they could earn twice as much as in Subic Naval Base.

The locals who had depended on the entertainment industry were hardest hit. The nightclubs, bars and brothels that had not already closed after the damage of the Pinatubo eruption along Magsaysay Drive were being boarded up with corrugated iron sheets. The buildings damaged by the ash fall of Pinatubo were abandoned. The answer had come, there would be no great future for the sex trade. That was the way we intended it to remain.

That had been the main goal of our campaign against the military bases, to end the enslavement of women and children for the gratification of the sex tourists local or foreign. Young American recruits barely seventeen or eighteen would also be spared the temptations, allurements and peer pressure to have sex with minors and take drugs and alcohol.

The Filipino pimps working for the Olongapo sex mafia were not the only links between the children and the sailors and sex tourists of other nationalities.

Some of the US retired servicemen could not forsake the joys and easy life in an enclave where they enjoyed the docility and submissive condescension of the enslaved women in the bar and brothel industry. The self-perpetuated myth of racial superiority, where might was right, was like a drug that they could not leave.

It was this easily available gratification of the need to dominate and control women and the immediate environment that led many to invest their savings, borrow money and spend their retirement funds on the survival of the bar and brothel industry in Olongapo and Angeles cities.

During the years of the frequent visits of the Pacific Fleet to Subic Bay, the retired servicemen who settled into running the sex industry had their friends still on the ships and aircraft carriers to bring in new recruits to empty their flush wallets of hundreds of dollars earned during many months of deprivation at sea. The recruiters earned rewards of free sex and a good time if they brought in new fresh faced kids from the ships many from an Iowa farm or small town. These young boys, many from God-fearing and religious homes, had their lives damaged, their spiritual and moral values destroyed and their health ruined with drugs, drink, hedonistic sex with minors and even HIV/AIDS.

The exceedingly high rates of suicide, broken marriages, child sexual abuse and divorce in military families has been seen as points of personal weakness by the Navy rather than the result of an institutional permissiveness of immorality and ignoring or failing to condemn the perversion and unnatural sexual practices such as child prostitution which the Navy failed to contain during its time in Subic Bay. The time, resources and effort committed to drug addiction and terrorism far surpass the meagre efforts to stamp out child abuse and child prostitution.

Our main goal was now within reach. The much hoped for but unexpected had happened, the bases were to close by December 1992 and the implementation of our conversion plan, which was once a fanciful dream and for which we were much ridiculed, was now a real possibility. But could the Filipinos do it? We learned that the political bickering and jockeying for political ascendancy and influence would be a decisive factor. The military base could become an alternative economic manufacturing zone yet it might not succeed if there was weak political backing from the central government.

Conversion was the dream of peace activists everywhere in the world, now it could be shown to be a viable alternative to wasteful military spending. The beating of swords into ploughs was no longer a fanciful unrealistic religious sentiment but it was a tenet of religious faith that was the driving force behind all our efforts. Peace was only possible in the world when there was global justice and the terror of violence and threatened annihilation was removed for antagonists to talk peace. Where the hand of the CIA had failed to win the day and keep the bases, the hand of God had seen them out.

A new era in Philippines and US relations had dawned. US President George Bush wrote the historic letter of acceptance to President Aquino. Losing the bases was one of the greatest failures of US foreign policy of the century. For over half a century, the US had ruled their former colony as a domineering and powerful force that shaped and manipulated laws and agreements to favour their interests. Filipinos had been generally docile and submissive. But new stronger feelings of national pride and resistance, stemming from the self-empowerment discovered at the popular non-violent uprising against Marcos, emboldened the Senators to say no. Perhaps they acted somewhat like a defiant child testing the waters of freedom.

President Bush had made the greatest blunder of his career

in regard to foreign policy when as vice-president under Reagan he praised the dictator Marcos and gushed on about how much he admired the tyrant's "adherence to democratic principle". This was at a time when there was more democratic principle among the sewer rats of Malacanang than the entire Marcos dictatorship that was steeped in the blood of thousands of victims of torture, foul murders, cruel executions and countless acts of injustice.

Bush's letter made it clear that any delay or temporary extension to the withdrawal period proposed by President Aquino was not feasible. They had to quit the bases and move on to a new partnership for the future. This he called the Second Century Partnership that would be marked by an "expansion of our economic relationship to our mutual benefit".

Proposals to leave the dry docks and facilities intact and for the Philippine private sector to provide ship repair and other services to the US Navy came to nothing. One had already been towed to Guam by the USS New Brunswick, the other two were towed to Pearl Harbour. After the Philippine Senate had voted against retention, the United States government was angry and annoyed at this monumental set back and they wanted no temporary interim measures. They wanted to get the withdrawal over with.

A power struggle now began to emerge as Mayor Gordon sought to find ways to gain control over the base facilities which he believed he was entitled to as Mayor of Olongapo City. He proposed and lobbied for the creation of an autonomous region comprising the greater territory of the Subic Bay complex, Olongapo City and the surrounding towns of Subic, Hermosa, Morong and Dinaluphian. This plan was called Autonomous Region of Greater Olongapo (ARGO). It was filed as proposed House Bill 35326 and was strongly opposed by the representative from the neighbouring province of Bataan Rep. Felicito Payumo. The proposal was to set up the autonomous region so that it would have its own banking and finance laws, manage all tax revenues, raise foreign loans, be free of any Central Bank supervision and have the power to acquire any private or public property.

The opposition to this was strong and critics claimed that it was practically establishing the Republic or Dictatorship of Olongapo, depending on the strength of their dislike of and disagreement with the Mayor. The fact that two-thirds of the land and sea mass of the huge former naval reservation being relinquished by the US Navy was inside the jurisdiction of the province of Bataan did not seem to bother the proponents.

The neighbours objected to the bill that would deprive them of their own authority in their province and towns. Finally, it fell flat and was ignored. There would be no independent autonomous region despite the rallies organised by Mayor Gordon at the Senate to press for the passing of the bill.

The Aeta, an ancestral tribal people of the Subic Reservation Area, spoke out and claimed their rights to return to their ancestral domain from where they had been removed by the US Navy in 1898. That was when the United States laid colonial claim to the Philippines after the Filipinos had defeated the Spanish on land and the US Navy had sunk the rag-a-tag Spanish fleet in Manila Bay. The most bloody and vicious war broke out between the Filipinos and the US that caused huge numbers of deaths and terrible atrocities perpetrated by both sides.

Chapter Twenty

One sweltering day, as the tropical sun reached its height, a group of Aeta tribal Filipinos came roaring up the driveway to attend a seminar that was being hosted by PREDA for tribal leaders from all over the Philippines. It was a great occasion and Sr Mengay Balaso was one of the principal organisers, together with the community leaders of various ethnic tribal groups.

They told us about the deep earth drilling of the National Power Corporation (NPC) on the slopes of Mount Pinatubo, their ancestral mountain, and how angry the elders were that the mountain gods were being disturbed. The NPC was drilling for geothermal sites to set up a thermal power generating station. The tribal people were very disturbed at this invasion of their sacred mountain and the habitat for the wild animals that they cherished and respected. The Aeta are traditionally a nomad people of hunters and gatherers. In recent years, to preserve their environment and save themselves from extinction, they had settled in small villages. Sr Mengay was helping them understand their ancestral rights to the forests and the mountains. They were fast learners and were now well organised.

They requested us to help them file their claims with the Department of Environment and Natural Resources and to verify the boundaries of their ancestral lands. We went together with them to the Manila government offices and helped them process their claims. It was one of the successful projects that we achieved together. Eventually, they were given the permits to harvest the forests. This is what they had been doing for over five thousand years; it was ironic that they needed a permit to exercise their rights on their own ancestral domain.

The recovering drug dependents went camping near the small village of the Aeta. The houses were small, low single room bamboo and thatched huts beside the river. There was always a warm happy welcome when we went to visit them. At night, a guard of tribal warriors armed with blowpipes and deadly bows and arrows took up their posts to guard their guests from possible intruders, bandits from the hills. How they endured the mosquitoes and insects on their practically naked bodies I will never understand.

During the national gathering of the tribal leaders, the Aeta told of rumbles and tremors from the extinct volcano and wisps of steam and smoke rising in ever stronger spirals day by day. They had informed the government agency of their observations. It was to prove timely and crucial in saving thousands of lives. Thanks to the warning, hundreds of people were able to evacuate days before the eruption. No more than an estimated five hundred people died in the ensuing volcanic eruption and the massive flows of "liquid cement" that rushed headlong down the valleys when the torrential rains swelled the blocked riverbeds and hundreds of tons of ash and sand were on the move. Some of the dead were the older tribes people who would not leave their jungle homes on the sacred slopes of Mount Pinatubo. The farmers and their families who died were trapped in their houses or swept away in their fields by sudden and unexpected mudslides and flash floods.

The following June 14 was a day of wonder and expectation. There was a mild explosion fifty kilometres north of the PREDA Centre and a pillar of grey clouds mushroomed into the clear blue summer sky. We went out and watched this spectacular display of nature's power and dangerous beauty. It was awesome and amazing. After six hundred years of lying dormant, the mountain had come alive. The evening sunset reflected off the billowing clouds that were spreading westwards and the entire sky glowed a magnificent red. The sea and mountain in the distance fogged in smoke was like a hazy Monet, bewitchingly beautiful and mysterious.

I was entranced by this magnificent wonder and felt the spectacular power of nature and reflected how weak and puny is our species in comparison. Yet, powerful as the erupting volcano was, I feared the growing power of human technology that was dominating our lives and destroying so much of the planet. It was clear that we would not, could not give up this technology when it conflicted with nature. It seems, even more so today, that nature is being forced to subject itself to the new powers of the modern economic juggernaut that is swiftly destroying the rain forests, polluting the atmosphere that we breath to live.

Looking at the awesome display of nature's terrible beauty I feared for humankind. I feel deeply about what happens to our planet and try to be at one with the universe. I love to think how we evolved from the great primeval eruption of which the boiling volcano was a consequence and a reminder. I imagined how we too came from that exploding stardust and evolved in God's plan to become its living self-awareness. How indeed we came to be the thinking consciousness of this universe, that through us, reflecting on its own power and magnificence, is the greatest mystery of life.

I turned away and went to bed worried at the destructiveness we are bringing on all life forms with the power of technology that we would never forsake no matter what harm it brings to nature and ourselves. Not only are we damaging our own offspring, I thought, but we have abandoned our close bonds with nature.

The next morning I had a headache from worry. There were indications that there would be further eruptions and all day we watched the sky and wondered what would happen. That night we were all shook awake by a mild earthquake at 2 in the morning. The building swayed and rattled and then the tremors subsided. We all ran outside, scared, knees weak and could hardly bring ourselves to lie down again. It was very tense.

The next morning, we gathered outside and watched in growing wonder as the smoking mountain continued to emit even greater columns of smoke that leaned to the west, like a smoke stack belching noxious fumes and spewing them out to sea. Alex and Merly left for Manila, according to the regular schedule, to be with their three children for the weekend.

At about 10am, there was the most spectacular explosion of all and a massive plume of black cloud, greater than anything that had gone before, could be seen rolling upward thousands of feet into the sky. More massive booms followed in quick succession like booming artillery and our windows rattled. Then as we looked an even greater cloud shot upwards at great speed, we jumped up in amazement with a cry of excitement. The sky could hardly contain the massive rolling black cloud that was like a great mushroom cloud, as if from a nuclear detonation. The clouds began to spread, advancing towards us like a scene from a Cecil B. De Mille's biblical spectacular, *The Ten Commandments.* It seemed the Almighty was about to appear amid thunder and lightning. The day was becoming night as the black cloud filled the sky and blocked the sun. The denser it became the greater the darkness. We were becoming really frightened.

The clouds were now overhead and white ash began falling like snow. It became thicker until inches began to build up around us. We were bewildered by this, as it seemed so gentle and harmless. Soon everything was covered with a ghostly shroud of fluffy and light ash. Then it began to rain. At 2.30 in the afternoon the sun was totally blocked and complete darkness fell on us. The dog was whimpering with terror; we were troubled.

Roy and myself went out to stand under the carport, a simple roof of galvanized sheets supported by wooden posts. We were trying to anticipate what might happen if this continued. I feared a deadly gas might descend from the black clouds like what happened at Pump and I thought of gas masks.

Junior, a former street boy who had grown up in the PREDA programme and was now employed as a house guardian, was standing at the side door of the centre. He suddenly shouted, "Takbo! Takbo! (Run! Run!) It's falling, it's falling!" We instantly sprang forward as we heard the loud crack of wooden posts giving out under some mighty weight. As I made a dash into the open yard, from the corner of my eye, I saw the roof swaying, leaning outward and suddenly crashing down. We propelled ourselves forward as if stuck with a needle. I sensed the structure falling on me, following me, reaching out to crush me in one massive smack like a fly swatter killing a fly.

My legs seemed to be running but I was terrified and felt I was stuck and couldn't move. I was about to be crushed and at the last second it hit the ground with a grinding crunch at our scampering heels. A grey cloud of ash puffed up all around us. We stopped staring in disbelief at the collapsed roofing. My body had scampered clear all of its own but my brains did not even register the fact, it was still thinking it was under the rubble. One minute we were alive and well and in a few seconds our lives were being crushed and snatched away. I was soaked with sweat and tottered back inside the centre on very wobbly legs. Roy was shocked too and silently he sat down, suddenly exhausted.

Junior and the other older residents took care of the children. I was dumbfounded and began to feel apprehensive. What was going to happen next if the rest of the building could not withstand the build up of sand and ash? I wondered. The rain had soaked the ash solid until it had the weight of cement. It was too risky to send the boys to sweep the curved roof and clear off the ash. They could easily slip and fall in the dark and there was just too much of it.

The electric power had failed. The ash had coated the terminals at the switching station a kilometre away and the rain soaked it, closing the circuit and shorting the entire system. The phone also was down but it mattered little as there was no one to call for help. We were on our own, we had to see it through.

Suddenly there was shaking of the earth and the building and ash fell in wet lumps from the roof. We ran out into the darkness holding flashlights and herding the children before us, telling them to hold hands and to get as far away as possible. The scary earth tremor lasted ten to twelve seconds. That was a long time for an earthquake and it must be the most primeval fear that painfully clutches the heart of every living creature. The falling ash and steady darkness made it all the more frightening. Some of the street kids were crying. The rest just held each other.

There was distant thunder and streaks of lightning began to slash through the day that had turned to night. The storm was swirling down from the mountain as the wind picked up and a storm was coming closer. I began to pray fervently that we would all be safe, unsure where escape and safety lay.

We looked up at a sudden massive flash of lighting streaked through the clouds like a burning rope, igniting the sulphuric gas and ash as it flashed to earth, the thunder rolled and boomed. We all gasped and jumped in fright, never having seen anything like it. Our wonder at nature's special effects was overwhelming our sense of fear and we stood unmindful of the rain and the wind, watching for the next spectacular fireball from heaven that would light up the sky like a blazing comet. Then to our delight another massive lightning bolt set the sky ablaze, with a fiery red flame that slashed through the darkness burning its way in a flash through the thick sulphuric atmosphere.

It was hard to comprehend that we were living witnesses to

such a mad magnificent chaos as the forces of nature clashed and collided. A massive boom signalled another round of terror as the volcano went off again and it was not hard to imagine it puking up six hundred years of accumulated rocks and debris. It was belching huge stones and burnt cinders of molten rock. Red glowing lava was surely being vomited left and right down the mountain into the valleys now filling with ash. The pumice stones, as big as cars, were blown thousands of feet high to land kilometres away like huge cannon balls. The massive jaws of the heaving bubbling crater was belching black fumes and poison gasses, millions of tons of it billowing skywards thirty thousand feet, turning day into night. It was incredible.

All of this was punctuated by earth tremors that came suddenly with a loud bang and a violent shaking of the earth under our feet. There was one every half hour or so and the lightning still crackled and shot burning streams of ash across the darkened sky. In the background over the horizon sheet lightning was ever present. We stood in the falling ash and waited for the next extraordinary heavenly show, forgetting for a while our predicament.

Our fear was overcome by the excitement of what we were experiencing. The rain had stopped and the kids were excitedly jumping up and down, shouting and pointing at the latest fireball of lightning to come hurtling through the darkness. It was a spectacular exhilarating experience, frightening, awesome and unexpectedly beautiful.

I felt so small and insignificant, completely humbled and overpowered by this gigantic upheaval of nature that was unfolding before my eyes, ringing in my ears, shaking under my feet, embracing me in a shroud of white ash, as if I was being readied for death and burial with great ceremony. It was exciting and thrilling and I felt a strange sense of being very much alive, perhaps because having been so close to death and strangely at one with this magnificent display of creation. It was an inescapable reminder of where the cosmos came from.

I was drawn to it. I could see that the energy and power and source of all life and creation was here, in the fire, the ash, in the earthquakes that shaped the planet and mixed those primordial components that gave rise to life itself. Call it the force of creation, the power of God, but it is present in everything and everyone, and was present in this catastrophic event. It was not the presence of a destroyer or a punishing God of vengeance, it was a glimpse of that powerful force of creation that enabled life on earth to emerge and evolve through the upheavals of nature. I like to think about where we came from as the only known intelligence and consciousness in the universe. I like to think that the whole universe itself is like one single living reality and we are part of its consciousness and because of us, it has self-awareness. In this terrifying yet magnificent volcanic eruption, I was looking at what I was made from. The universe was reflecting on its own primordial existence through me, and all of us, with intelligence. We must be the self-awareness of creation thinking about itself.

By 3pm, it was pitch dark, we could hardly recognise each other. Roy and myself assembled the children and residents in the main hall and counted them. They were all there. We stayed inside the main Quonset building with its rounded roof and lit the emergency gas lamps and had a late lunch.

We were still unaware that the ash on the roof was soaking up the rain and was becoming heavier by the minute. Then to our astonishment, we heard the grinding of an engine outside and hurried out to meet the headlights of a mini-van with four-wheel drive chugging up the driveway through the thickening bed of ash and came to a halt in the open space at the back of our large Quonset building. It was a TV crew from a Manila station. They had been filming the volcano and could go no further. The roads were becoming impassable, they said. It was total shutdown, there was nowhere to go. We invited them to come inside and join us for the meal we had managed to cook on gas rings and were eating. They had brought food and they stayed in the van. They shared our apprehensions about the build up of the ash.

Roy gathered all the children and residents in the main hall. There were about fifty-five in all. We still had a gas lamp and a few flash lights. We decided to get out and go to Olongapo about five kilometres away.

There was another powerful tremor with a loud boom that made us all jump with fright. The building shook, windows rattled, metal beams groaned and then steadied and it was deadly silent. Some of the smaller children began to cry in the silence. Roy went to calm and reassure them. We quickened our preparations to evacuate and hurried the kids through the remains of the meal. They were all standing around the gas lamp holding their plates and eating with their fingers, barely able to see the food by the spluttering light of the gas flame. It flared from time to time, it must have been the sulphuric gas from the falling ash that did it.

I had a sudden sense of danger. I was convinced that the building was no longer safe. We had to get out. I called to Roy, "Get the children together, we may have to get out quickly, I will get some things in my room."

There was sand and small pebbles falling from the sky like hailstones, clattering on the sloping sides of the roof where the ash had not stuck. I left the main hall and quickly grabbed some money, a jacket and cap, picked up the camera that was on the table and walked back a few meters towards the main hall and was about to enter when suddenly there was this mighty roar, clatter and screeching of collapsing metal that ended in a huge bang as the metal roof of galvanised iron sheets collapsed before my eyes.

I was stunned, one moment I was walking in the main hall as I had done for the past seventeen years and then in a second, it wasn't there. I was looking up into a dark sky from where the ash and sand was drifting steadily down into a great silence. A terrible fear shot through me, a giant hand squeezed my heart and a terrible pain. I had left them still inside standing around the gas lamp! My brain raced to take in what had just happened. *The children! Roy! The residents! They were all buried alive, they are all crushed and dead!*

I was filled with panic and shouted in Filipino, "Where are you, can you hear me? Roy, are you there?"

There was anger in my words to the jumbled mass of metal. My hands were trembling, I was sweating profusely, my shirt was soaked in an instant and the flashlight was shaking in my hands dancing over the wreckage of crumbled metal. My heart was thumping with the fright that I had narrowly missed being crushed myself, another near encounter with death by just a few steps, and the shock that the others were dead.

From beyond the jangled ruins, there was a distant voice, "We are here, over here!" It was Roy.

In desperation and with the panic rising, "Where? Where?" I shouted into the darkness.

The answer came: "Outside, we are outside, are all OK."

An inexpressible flood of relief swept over me. I still could not move, my legs were jelly. It was indescribable, as anguish turned to joy… they were safe. I could hardly believe it. But I forced myself to be cool and got my feelings under control. Having just believed they were all dead, I had to convince myself that they were alive.

I felt light-hearted all of a sudden. I didn't care that the building had just collapsed before my eyes, that I had almost stepped into it seconds before. We were all alive, that's all that mattered. I then hurried out by a side door. The kids and residents were huddled together with Roy in the scant shelter of a big pine tree. We all hugged each other to celebrate our lucky escape, so glad to be alive. The silence was only broken by the distant boom of the volcano still going off and the whimpering of a dog.

"It's Brownie!" the kids shouted.

We found Brownie caught under the metal unhurt and

pulled him out to the delight and cheers of the children. He ran around excitedly, delighted to be free and alive too. All anxiety lifted as I realised nothing worse could happen. The building had collapsed and we had survived what could have been a terrible tragedy. We gathered up the light cotton bed-covers so the kids and teenagers had a cover to ward off the ash and sand still drifting from the dark skies. It was about 4.30pm.

The TV crew were out of the van surveying the wrecked building and thanking God they had stayed in the van. I told them we were going to evacuate and they could stay. In the quiet of the darkness, we heard a strange sound. We were mystified at the loud snaps and cracks that came at us out of the dark hills surrounding the centre. We directed our beams towards the trees and saw that the branches were snapping off one by one under the weight of the ash that had stuck to them like snow. It seemed that all of nature was breaking up. It was like the end of the world.

The ash and sand was now ankle deep. I organised the children into two lines, side by side, and placed the older residents at the front and rear and got all to hold hands as we gathered up our pitiful bundles and headed off down the ash covered driveway. Our small pick-up truck was stranded at the bottom unable to climb from an earlier trip to Olongapo to buy emergency supplies. The road was deserted as we silently made our way past the hillside cemetery and closer to the town. Out of the darkness the occasional crash of a roof caving in and moans of alarm were heard. Men and boys were up on other rooftops sweeping the ash and sand away.

Vehicles sat isolated along the road like a deserted war convoy in a movie. We stopped from time to time to check that we had lost none of the kids. I led and Roy guarded the rear of our column. It was about six in the late afternoon. Our little band of children reached the city. There were queues forming outside a bakery, I told Roy to buy as much bread as he could for us and I shepherded the group on towards St

Joseph's Church and school compound. The buildings were solid concrete and would provide a safe haven for the children.

We had no sooner settled the children into the classroom when there was another mighty earthquake. A howl of fright went up from everyone. The ground shook, the building swayed, pictures fell from the walls, dry ash sand came spilling down from higher floors and the children rushed for the door and out into the basketball court where some squatted and started crying from the fright.

We gathered them together and many refused to go back inside. So we brought out the school desks into the basketball court and tied the blankets to them and made a simple shelter to protect them from the falling ash and sand. Roy arrived with the bread and drinks and that enticed the children to come into the car port which was a strong structure between the church wall and the rectory. But then the rain came and the children remained inside. That was where we spent the night.

I found old cardboard boxes and curtains and we spread them on the sidewalk under the carport and soon the children were asleep. The earth tremors continued during the night. Some of the children woke up startled but slept again. Foolishly, I laid down between two parked cars that were end-to-end. The earthquake started them rolling and I leapt up just in time before being run over. Another near escape, I led a charmed life! There was no sleep after that. The wind blew and howled bringing more ash and sand from the volcano and carried it as far south as Manila. The capital was covered with a fine coat of volcanic ash.

The following morning we woke at dawn to a strangely quiet city. The storm had passed, the tremors were less frequent, just a sudden jolt from time to time. There was no traffic. The Sisters of the Daughters of Charity had already set up an emergency food kitchen and were ladling out bowls of champarado, a combination of rice, condensed milk, sugar and cocoa. With a glass of juice it was an ideal fast food breakfast for all of us.

The skies had now cleared and a bright Sunday morning was dawning on the devastation of the eruption. Many buildings had collapsed roofs, it was a scene of devastation. Everything was covered in a thick layer of white ash glistening in the blinding sunlight.

Roy made his way back to PREDA with some of the older boys. They pushed our pick-up back down the driveway and miraculously it started. Soon we were bringing the exhausted but excited children back to PREDA in batches.

Amazing sights greeted us as we drove slowly along the road. It was a surreal landscape of houses and hills covered in white ash and trees twisted grotesquely. People were standing about aimlessly and forlorn surveying the damage to their houses, others were sitting in shock after a sleepless night of fear and worry. The hills looked like a snow-filled scene on a Christmas card. The coconut trees that once proudly flouted their waving palm branches were now humbled and subdued, their palms folded like a closed umbrella and laden with white ash.

The PREDA building was half-collapsed and the remainder was in a dangerous condition. There was one section of the dormitory that had been previously reinforced and it was safe.

In a few days, Alex and Merly were able to make it back to Olongapo from Manila. The roads were just opening up. It was a slow and tedious journey. I had already hired a small group of workers to start the clearing of the driveway and the area surrounding the centre of the sand and ash. We were now plagued by swirling, choking powdery ash whipped up by strong winds. The sun was blazing from a clear blue sky and away in the distance a huge westward leaning plume of smoke told us the volcano was still smoking. The ash and sand got into our eyes, noses, food and drink. It was everywhere. The children and staff were wearing facemasks to protect their lungs and plastic goggles for their eyes.

Merly and Alex described scenes of devastation around Angeles City and San Fernando as they came back from Manila. The ash-filled rivers had turned the waters to liquid cement that was still roaring onto the plains from Mount Pinatubo at terrifying speeds. Without warning a flash flood would unleash torrents of the ash filled waters (called lahars) and boulders from the mountainside would come tumbling along with the mudflows smashing everything in their path.

No human could outrun the torrent if it broke the banks which it was doing and spreading across the plains swamping and destroying the once lush green rice fields and turning them into a desert of grey mud. Houses and bridges were buried and the riverbanks collapsed and clogged the riverbeds. Everything that stood in the way of this unstoppable wave of destruction was demolished, flattened or buried. It was an all powerful force beyond the control and the ingenuity of humankind.

The once towering church at Bacolor was buried to the roof. Along the traffic clogged roads, refugees and homeless people were begging from the passing motorists who dropped donations into outstretched cups. It was the unstoppable mayhem of lahars on the move that was the most destructive of all.

Clarke Air Force Base, just three kilometres from the volcano, was effectively wiped out. The fall of ash and sand was so heavy that the clean-up and repairs were estimated at millions of dollars at a time when the installations were facing a very uncertain future. The US decided to abandon it. The day before the cataclysmic explosion, the last US servicemen and their families evacuated. A long convoy of military and private vehicles made their way to Subic.

On the eve of the eruption, there was frantic military activity at Clarke as the US Air Force removed in great secrecy and high security what we believed to be nuclear weapons, missiles and weapons from underground storage bunkers and shipped them to Subic. The US authorities denied there were nuclear weapons stockpiled there. Soon afterwards there was an invasion of the facilities by looters who carried away everything they could. Even pipes and underground electric cables were ripped up and carried away. Toilet bowls, faucets, doors and windows were even ripped out of the houses. The Philippine Air Force guards were suspected of complicity in the looting.

Subic itself had not been spared. Many buildings suffered crushed roofs and the runway was closed. The US evacuees from Clarke left for Manila and Cebu by ship where they took planes to the United States. The roads to Manila were covered with lahars at key points and made impassable for a few days but bulldozers and pay-loaders cleared the quick drying lahars until the next rainstorm and more flood deposited tons of mud on the new desert.

There would be no abandonment of Subic or the several other smaller bases unaffected by the volcanic eruption. The US wanted to retain the rest through a new agreement with the Philippine government. The new Philippine Constitution says that any extended lease on the bases had to be by a treaty recognised by both countries. The US wanted an executive agreement.

The negotiations over possible terms for such a treaty were still going on at this time. The US Navy worked around the clock to restore operations to full effectively and did a remarkable job. The runway at Cubi Point was cleared, roads cleared and swept, the damaged buildings were repaired and the base was back in full operation within weeks. Most Filipino employees were back at work.

The Olongapo City Mayor and the Admiral had a serious falling out during the height of the eruption. The row was over the refusal of Rear Admiral Rich to allow the Mayor and hundreds of his followers to evacuate the city through the base. The executive explained in a TV documentary later that he thought that the city would be completely destroyed. "It was like the end of the world," he said. They had to get out because everything was collapsing. But it sounded more like panic as fear gripped the executives and they wanted to flee for their lives. But the Admiral was having none of it. He expected the leader to stay at his post.

The Mayor had no choice, all escape routes were blocked. He now expressed disgust at being offered relief goods from the US Navy. However, a compromise was reached and the Navy Construction Battalion, the Seabees, were called out to clean the streets of Olongapo of the ash and sand.

The Church's Social Action Centre under the guidance of Fr Roque Villanueva mobilised dozens of volunteers and with emergency supplies from Caritas and Catholic Relief Services began to set up distribution centres for clothes and food. Our delivery truck was out on loan to the relief effort. We sent it to distant provinces to buy truck loads of rice and deliver the grain to the parish distribution centres.

Fr Roque borrowed a few army trucks to help reach the far flung areas most in need. In Zambales, the area closest to the volcano was devastated. The small town of Poonbato, not ten kilometres from Mount Pinatubo, where Columban Missionaries had built a school and a church for the tribal communities, was totally buried. Only the cross on the church roof was visible through the mountain of ash and sand when evacuees returned a week after the main eruption was over.

In San Marcelino, the home town of Alex, ten kilometres north of PREDA, where I was first assigned so many years previously, the huge copper mine was closed and the church spire was all that could be seen emerging from the centre of a huge lake. Parts of the market were destroyed and some people were tragically killed.

We turned the remaining part of the PREDA Centre into a distribution centre for relief goods. Merly applied her efficient business acumen and organising skills and soon had us and the recovering drug dependents well organised. Most of them had remained faithfully at our side throughout the crises. We spent hours together filling plastic bags with rice, canned fish and beans and sorting out relief clothes. These were then distributed three times a week when the people from the surrounding communities were gathered together at PREDA. We made special trips to the communities where our handicraft producer groups were and distributed relief goods to them and their neighbours.

It was a time when the best in the Filipino character came to the fore. The spirit of teamwork and cooperation is the strongest point in comparison to northern cultures of individualism. We were in ruins but we were happy and together we had survived, were alive and had much to do to help others. The spirit of community service was in evidence everywhere accept among the politicians who were looking for some way to make political capital out of the disaster. They rushed from one disaster area to another posing for the television cameras holding bags of relief goods while striking a ridiculous heroic pose. The wretched refugees, dressed in tattered clothes, smiled weakly their expected gratitude at this political gesture.

Streams of poverty stricken families loaded with what they could carry walked miles to relief centres for food and clothes, their bodies weak with hunger and babies crying constantly. At PREDA, we set up tents with the help of our friends and partners at the Community Crafts Association of the Philippines (CCAP). None of us could sleep in the remaining wing of the building on account of the earth tremors that continued from time to time. Sleep was impossible because of the fear of a collapse. We were refugees in our own home. A TV team came to visit and made a documentary for British television. They faithfully recorded the extent of the damage and the human suffering.

Everyday we were working non-stop to clean up what was left of the Centre. Alex, Roy and Tessie the social worker organised the residents and the children and assigned them to various tasks to uncover and rescue valuables from the wreckage and store them in the dormitory wing. Merly had a small team of the employees from the Fair Trade finishing and packing department of the warehouse working to distribute relief supplies. Some were former bar women and others recovered drug dependents, all of whom are now holding regular paid jobs.

Filipino resilience and good humour carried us forward and held us together. This remarkable gift of the Filipino to stand together for the common good in the face of adversity came to the fore during the crises of the volcanic eruption. They are a remarkable people of humour and can laugh and joke in times of hardship and calamity. It was a spirit of "never give up, there is always hope, plus a joke and a laugh". We were supported too by our faith as we prayed frequently, "Trust in God, do our best and all will be well." This spirit encouraged us to work on despite the enormity of the task ahead. Prayer, jokes, laughter, team spirit and camaraderie were the source of strength and resolve to make the best of our situation.

Seventeen years of endeavour developing the child protection and advocacy services, campaign for human rights and justice, sustaining educational programmes – it all lay in ruins around us symbolised by the collapsed building where we had shared life for so many years. But we were determined never to give up.

A shipment of baskets and assorted handicrafts was due to leave for the Fair Trade World Shops in Europe. Now more than ever, the producers needed delivery to the Fair Trade market. These products had been delivered from the producer groups in the distant villages that we help and support. It is part of the PREDA poverty alleviation programme and it is essential to help stem the flow of poor people to the cities in search of jobs. The neglect of the countryside has created untold poverty and many of the migrants' children end up as beggars, are recruited by pimps and turned into child prostitutes for local and wealthy foreign paedophiles.

Fair Trade pays just prices for produce and products, gives interest free cash advances for production, payment on delivery and a share of any profits for development project to benefit the whole community of producers. It is a movement that guarantees sustainable development and protection and improvement of the environment.

Failure to meet the shipping deadline would be another financial loss for PREDA and a possible loss of future orders for the crafts people too. Merly had already advanced an interest free production loan to the producers. When they had completed the order and delivered the products weeks previously they were paid the full balance. They were never kept waiting as the payments to them were always on time and in full measure.

Many of the baskets and handicraft had been damaged by the ash and sand from the Pinatubo eruption. The roof had collapsed burying a container-load of goods. It was heartbreaking to see so much lost. We worked late into the night, brushing, washing and drying the baskets and other products so that they would meet the high quality that we were proud of. About one third of the baskets were damaged beyond repair. Despite the very difficult conditions of living like refugees in tents without electricity, telephones or piped water, we all concentrated on saving the shipment from the ashes and the water. Within the week, Merly had a shipment in perfect condition for trucking to Manila. We were elated, it was a sign of recovery and resilience. We clapped and cheered and sang as we waved off that first delivery. I knew that our team would hold together and we would succeed.

I set-up a temporary living quarters in a small house at the back of the centre, rigged up a small generator and set up my Apple computer to continue writing my columns and preparing reports on the devastation caused by the eruption of the volcano. I sat near an open door and every time there was a sudden bang and a huge scary tremor, the house shook violently. I leapt from the chair and out the door like a scorched cat until the shaking stopped. It was a harrowing existence with many a sleepless night when we were shook out of our beds. I slept in a tent while the tremors continued. Writing from personal experience, I can tell you that the worst place to be during a tremor or earthquake is in the bathroom answering nature's call.

This being too dangerous, I set up home in a carport detached from the main building that had survived. I nailed plywood sheet around it and put in plastic windows. It had a lovely view of the bay and I put a toilet just outside. I moved into the small hut with the basics of life. I had a phone line rigged through the trees and moved in a bed and desk.

I was ready for work. I would be there for the next two years, during which time we lived in the makeshift "shanty town" and warehouse. The tremors became less frequent and we felt it safe to fold up the blue tents and the children were able to return to a building on the hill that had survived intact. When the warehouse was reconstructed, Merly and Alex made a room in there. The remaining part of the old building was used for storage and the recovering drug dependents.

Then it was time to revive our hopes and dreams for the future. We would overcome this disaster and rebuild. We dreamt of a new children's home providing protection, recovery and therapy for sexually abused children. The main building would house the administration office and a prevention educational centre. There, we would conduct youth development training and educational programmes to support children's and women's rights, HIV/AIDS and drug abuse prevention. We planned to expand our fair trading activities to reach more impoverished farmers and craft producers and start a low-cost loans project modelled on the Grameen Bank. We would rebuild the former training centre into a finishing and warehousing building.

However, with the financial ruin and loss of proper facilities, we were unable to continue the residential therapeutic community for the drug dependents. When each had experienced a good reconciliation with their parents and families, they were reintegrated. We were unable to accept new clients. But we did continue and expand the drug abuse preventive education programme.

Our dream became a reality when Misereor, the German Catholic church agency (an active supporter of thousands of projects around the world) approved our application for funds to rebuild the PREDA Centre. We were delighted and went back to our notebook sketches and scribbles that December 1991 and started to plan and sketch once again a building that would be both economical to construct yet have all the facilities to achieve the goals we had in mind.

When our friend Architect Antonio Balde had drawn up all the plans, we applied to the city authorities for a permit. Despite the terrible destruction as a result of the volcanic eruption, they refused to grant a permit. Two years previously, September 1989, we applied to the Olongapo City administration for a fencing permit to protect the children's home from intruders attempting to abduct the children or molest them but it was denied. No one cared what happened to the children. The City Council had issued a resolution claiming the PREDA area "for future government improvements" and because the city engineer said our leasehold agreement, which is up for renewal in 2008, does not allow construction projects. We challenged this and appealed to the higher authorities in Manila. The Secretary of Public Works and Highways, Franklin Drilon, who is now a Senator, rejected the arguments of the city authorities and ordered that the fencing permit should be issued. The city appealed that order to the office of the president and was rejected. The Department of Environment and Natural Resources also rejected the city's arguments that they had a claim over the area and supported our rights stating that jurisdiction lay with the national government and not the city. The Olongapo authorities, with usual arrogance, refused to comply with the order from the secretary or Malacañang. No permit was issued. Alex, who was handling the application, wrote to the Mayor's office: "It is clear that the City government has taken an active part in the denial of our permits and that constitutes harassment."

The city then took us to court that December 1991 and for Christmas I had an arrest warrant issued against me. I paid bail until we eventually won and the case was dismissed.

Following the destruction caused by the volcanic eruption, we applied for a construction permit to rebuild within our own destroyed walls, which strictly speaking, according to the building code, did not need a permit. Our application met all the building requirements and was still denied much to our disappointment. We believed the city authorities would relent, show compassion for the children and help the children's home. But it was not to be. Like the Pharaohs of Egypt, they were as hard-hearted as ever, never forgiving us for exposing the rampant exploitation of children in the sex industry that they allowed to grow and prosper.

Chapter Twenty-One

One evening after another hard day's work, distributing relief goods and managing the therapy for the children, Alex, Merly and myself sat outside on a mound of ash and sand watching the sunset. The red ball of fire was spectacular, filtering through the haze of volcanic dust that hung in the atmosphere like a veil deepening the red, yellow, blue of the evening sky tingling the wisps of clouds like an artist would to highlight the picture. The vast cloud of smoke and dust was to travel around the globe for two years lowering temperatures and delaying the ever increasing global warming.

The sun slowly extinguished itself, leaving a red glow behind the distant mountain across the bay. I felt that an immensely difficult part of our lives had gone with it. The worst, I felt, had to be over for us and that the next dawn would bring new promises and possibilities. We lived in the hope that we would rise out of the ruins and that somehow the future would be better than the past.

We quietly discussed our future work, which would be hampered by the lack of a good facility while we rebuilt, permit or not. Later the city took us to court for rebuilding the children's home without a building permit they had refused us for no legal reason. It was pure harassment. We fought back tenaciously and eventually won the case. They have issued the permit but are still determined, it seems, to close us down and drive us out.

We were feeling sad those days over the issues we were campaigning for. The audacity of our campaign to get rid of the US military bases was enormous, daunting and far-fetched for many. We were tilting at windmills to be sure but it was better than doing nothing to dig out the roots of the problem. Helping the victims is very important and must go on, yet prevention has to succeed. We were determined to keep trying. The hope that the Senate would reject a new military bases treaty was growing distant. *Surrounded by the ruins of our centre and eighteen years of work, where were we to begin again?* we asked ourselves. The city was against us and the majority of the population were still beguiled by the overwhelming influence of the US. The people could not imagine a Philippines without them.

The Mayor and his family had held political power in the city for the best part of thirty years and were campaigning hard for the retention of the bases from which much of the hotel and brothel industry drew its clientele. Bus loads of bar girls, political stalwarts and government employees were bussed to Manila to join pro-base rallies and demonstrate outside the Senate. The future of the bases would be decided by a two third vote of that body which drew its constituency from the whole population.

The Olongapo administration was angered by the decision of President Aquino and Foreign Secretary Raul Manglapus to give the historical one-year advance notice of termination to the US in May 1990, a legal requirement irrespective of any formal agreement being reached. The political drama was unfolding like the closing minutes of a tense football match that was to decide the fate of the country for the next generations. We had scored one goal, thanks to the moral pressure of Senator Wigberto (Bobby) Tanada who was guiding President Aquino towards a bases rejection policy. The US was applying a counter pressure, of course. Critics explained the several failed military coups as part of a destabilisation plan against Aquino to pressure her and the Senate to vote yes to the new agreement. Some suspected the US was playing her archrival, former Marcos's Defence Minister Juan Ponce Enrile, against her. He was being led along by false promises of succession as president, his long lost dream and the reason he turned against Marcos in the first place.

Our opposition to the bases was based on the dangers of nuclear accident or conflict that the bases attracted and the dehumanisation and sexual exploitation of the women and children caused by the government-supported sex tourist industry. Ten years previously, we discovered a syndicate of local pimps that were selling little children as young as nine-years-old to paedophiles in the US Navy. Under pressure from the local politician and the US Admiral not to reveal what we had discovered, nevertheless we did so. How could anyone be a part of a cover-up of any crime, especially the systematic sexual exploitation of children? We later learned just how common it was in many institutions, including the church, especially in the US.

We went to the press and exposed the syndicate. This drew an immediate angry denunciation of me by a leading official. I was accused of defaming the good name of the city and the administration. They tried to close down the children's home and silence us, a policy that endures to this day by the same city administration. Our determined campaign against the sexual exploitation and abuse of children began at that time. It was also the start of our campaign to close the bases and convert them into industrial parks to give work with dignity to many more Filipinos. In 1991 that campaign was coming to a climax.

The eruption of Mount Pinatubo closed Clarke Airbase but Subic was in the balance. The future of that and the continued US military presence had to be decided by the Philippine Senate. Following the non-violent uprising and the fall of the dictator President Marcos, a strong broad-based anti-bases campaign emerged. We found committed allies for our lonely and faltering struggle.

The anti-base movement had roots that went back to 1947 when the Military Bases Agreement was first approved by the Philippine Senate. Now it was experiencing a revival. The nationalist movement had resisted Martial Law and had never forgotten the long history of domination and exploitation by the colonial rulers at first by Spain and then the US. The Americanisation of the Filipino mind was due to television and the power of media. The post war period of reconstruction and the domination of the economy by US corporations created a humiliating dependence. This generation came to emulate everything American and looked, not to their own country for a better future, but abroad to America.

Young people longed to go to America and others made it their life's goal to join the US Navy, a privilege that was given to very few non-American citizens. There was a screening and recruitment centre at Subic Bay. The dream of every bar girl in Olongapo and Clarke was to marry a Marine and sail off to America. The majority of such marriages failed in misery.

The imposition of Martial Law gave rise to the Communist movement and the US support for Marcos fuelled anti-US bases feelings. Thousands of students fled to the hills in the early 1970s. Street assassinations, torture and imprisonment were the daily routine of the police and military under Marcos. I can recall many times when I went out to collect the bodies of the murdered youth around Olongapo and helped others to hide or escape. PREDA became a kind of sanctuary for those jailed and imprisoned children whenever we were able to get them released and accepted as drug dependents. It was the outright support of the US administration for Marcos that helped change the adulation for everything American to scepticism and eventually gave rise to a movement that made the removal of the US bases, symbols of occupation, a cherished goal.

The anti-bases movement had its modern roots in the statement called "Guiding principles, issues, basis of unity – A call for a sovereign Philippines" issued on December 26, 1984. The campaign for a sovereign Philippines grew from this and was supported by sixty-three civic and church organisations. The leading figures were Maria "Cooki" Diokno, daughter of famous nationalist hero and human rights lawyer Jose Diokno, a signatory of the Guiding Principles of 1984, and the Nuclear Free Philippines Coalition led by its dynamic new leader Professor Roland Simbulan of the University of the Philippines. He became chairman of the coalition in 1990 and the following year he was a senior political consultant and adviser to Senator Wigberto Tanada, a man greatly respected who belongs to a Filipino family that worked for a Philippines free from foreign political influence.

I was asked to be a speaker at many of the coalition's public meetings and rallies and I was elated to witness the growing support for the removal of the bases. Yet, this was a mere handful as the general public were feeling economically dependent on the earnings from the bases. There were about twenty-four thousand working at the bases. Millions of Filipinos have some relation living or working in America and their dream is to visit or to migrate. Any criticism of the US government would, in their mind at least, be a blow to such hopes. No matter what they personally believed many were inhibited from voicing opposition to the bases.

During the last days of the negotiations over the terms of the proposed new treaty, I was in Negros Island speaking at church-sponsored rallies. The day the terms of the proposed treaty was signed, I was at a meeting of the Negros Priests Forum and I was greatly encouraged by their support of our particular stand against the exploitation of women and children. The teachers told me that they were clipping my columns from the *Inquirer* and posting them on school notice boards. Some priests told me that they were using them in sermons and seminars. I was gratified to learn that so many benefited from my writings.

Many people in Negros were well aware that many young

women and teenagers were recruited from their villages for the bars and clubs of Manila, Angeles and Olongapo and destined as prostitutes. Their feelings ran deep. If there ever was a referendum on the bases issue, I knew that Negros Occidental would be strongly opposed.

The coming Senate debate on the proposed treaty was to be of enormous historical importance and would have long-term ramifications for the Philippines. The Senate debates were televised two weeks before the vote was taken. There were twenty-three Senators and a two-thirds majority was needed to pass a treaty. All that was needed to defeat the proposed treaty was for eight Senators to vote no. One of our strong points for rejection were the economic possibilities for the future of the facilities at Subic Bay and Clark in Angeles City. I came up with an economic conversion plan.

One day during a public talk, I was asked about the future of the forty thousand jobs, including those in Angeles and Olongapo Cities, that would be lost if the bases closed.

"Can they eat sovereignty?" the heckler taunted. That was the favourite line of the local politicians.

I replied in a moment of improvisation that there would be more jobs than that when the base facilities were converted to support manufacturing and services. The idea was born. It was so obvious, so necessary and so practical, yet no one had developed it as an important issue for the campaign. Its time had come.

I worked out the possibilities in a six-point economic conversion plan. This envisaged the airports being used as a South-East Asian trans-shipment hub. The huge military oil storage farms would be for commercial storage and distribution all over the Philippines. I proposed that the pipeline connecting Clarke Airbase sixty miles away would bring oil directly to the centre of Northern Luzon. The large empty spaces and military hangars would be ideal for business parks and manufacturing sites. The massive port, one of the best in the world, would be for shipping in raw materials and shipping out finished products and providing ship repair services. Economic zones with low tax brackets were not the ideal for sustainable development models but they were a better option than keeping the bases.

Another idea was the conversion of the military sports and recreation facilities to family tourism and the many barracks and administration buildings as offices, school and colleges. I imagined the rainforest-based building as being the centre for a World University of the Environment similar to the success of Costa Rica. All this would provide many more thousands with dignified work, I claimed. The raunchy sex industry depending on military prostitution would decline and go into total collapse.

I tried it out in public speeches to get the reaction. When it was well received, I wrote it up in my newspaper column and in an article for the *Manila Chronicle,* "Life after the Bases." This became a slogan of hope and promise for the anti-bases forces. It was not only a good positive idea but it was well received and became the bedrock of our campaign and gave the badly needed ammunition to the advocates of treaty rejection.

We scored another goal when the Bases Conversion and Development Authority and the Subic Bay Metropolitan Authority was established by the Bases Conversion Act. This grew out of the base conversion idea. We realised that there had to be a government entity in place to take control of the lands and facilities and to implement the conversion plan, if that ever came to be. During the preparation of the legal provisions, myself and Alex were travelling up and down to the University of the Philippines as consultants to the board of legal experts, headed by Prof. Jose Abueva, the president of the University, that was preparing the new law. The meetings were plagued by blackouts as the power failures were daily occurrences. We hung maps on the walls outside the steaming meeting rooms to give our presentations about the base facilities and the possibilities that lay ahead. This was visioning the future for the legal experts under the shade of a mango tree.

Two long-time friends, Denis Murphy from Ireland and Ed Gerlock, an American, came to support and be with us and share their own insights and offer ideas and encouragement during those briefings and take photographs. Ed is a superb photographer. Both are married and have lived in the Philippines all their adult lives, dedicated to working with the poor and the marginalized people of Metro Manila.

When Marcos exerted pressure on the US by demanding these changes to the status of the base lands in order to get more money from them, he unwittingly altered, however slightly, the perception of the Filipino people about themselves. The 1947 Military Bases Agreement expired in 1991 and, according to the new constitution, a treaty approved by two thirds of the Senate was necessary for any foreign military base to be on Philippine territory. It was the approval of that constitution on February 2, 1987 by seventy-six percent of the twenty-five million registered voters that effectively banned foreign military bases and declared the country to be nuclear weapons free. The declaration of principles and state policies in Article II, section 8 of the new Constitution states that "the Philippines, consistent with the national interest, adopts and pursues a policy of freedom from nuclear weapons in its territory".

There were twenty-three members of the Senate. In our optimistic way of thinking that meant only eight had to be persuaded to say no. There were four nationalistic Senators, names who were strongly opposed to the renewal of the treaty. Our hopes soared when we realised that we did not have to persuade the entire nation to reject the treaty, only five more Senators would be enough.

Many of those Senators had been arrested and detained by the US backed Martial Law regime. For some, it was payback time. This we reckoned was another big plus for our hopes of treaty rejection. Our hopes rose as the September 16, 1991 deadline drew closer. Our impossible dream of removing the bases and replacing them with a Philippine economic conversion plan seemed possible. I could hardly believe that this was becoming a real possibility. We lobbied the Senators everyday we could and joined petitions, live-in and every kind of rally. With our limited resources, we worked to secure the maximum number of votes against the treaty renewal.

President Aquino had by now changed her position. The US pressure was surely intense and she now favoured retaining the bases. Some Senators had veiled suspicions that the US were behind the coups to pressure Aquino to change her position. She had the public backing of the US and she had much influence in the Senate. Her weight could sway the vote.

Early in September 1991, the basic agreement between the Philippines and the US for the continuation of the military bases was agreed. Ironically it was titled "Treaty on Friendship Cooperation and Security". The Senate vote to approve or reject it was scheduled for September 16 and we were tense with anticipation. *The Inquirer* had published my investigative background article over three days on the chief negotiator for the US, Richard Armitage, the previous May 1990 when he first arrived to open the exploratory talks on the bases. He was US President George Bush's man in Manila and would shape the terms of the treaty that would be put to the Senate for approval or rejection. My comments on him were not flattering.

Armitage was our biggest ally. This brusque, overpowering former Special Forces officer was the picture of arrogance. His abrasive approach grated on every nerve of the harmony loving Filipino. The terms of the proposed treaty were humiliating. Instead of offering to increase humanitarian emergency aid to the Filipinos, who were suffering the aftermath of the worst volcanic eruption of the century, the US panel offered less.

The offer of humanitarian assistance was reduced from $700 to $203 million. Armitage said they were closing Clark Airbase and thus the financial compensation package should be reduced. This "cash register diplomacy", as it was called, associated the needs of hungry Filipinos with the approval of the terms of the proposed treaty. It was a sordid form of extortion and Armitage did no good for the US in proposing such terms. They betrayed the historical goodness and generosity of the American people. The fact that the US had bought over Egypt by forgiving its foreign debt of $20.2 billion and made it its major recipient of US foreign aid and at the same time gave Israel $3 billion annually cut into Filipino feelings. Neither of these countries hosted US military bases or had fought and died in World War II side by side with US soldiers.

The way Armitage presented the US position was as if to say, "You need us, we don't need you." The Senators and all Filipinos were told that they ought to be grateful to have the bases to protect them. These onerous and humiliating terms gave undecided Senators good reason to vote no. Several did admit the terms were atrocious and not beneficial to the Filipino people. Of course, most Filipinos were aware of the dangers of nuclear weapons and were afraid the bases might draw a nuclear strike in the event of war. The humiliating terms brought many into the anti-bases camp. Armitage and his negotiating team were completely out of touch with the real sentiments building up in the Senate.

On September 10, there was a huge rally with an estimated fifty thousand participants against the retention of the bases and an even bigger one the following week, on the day of the voting. The sky opened and torrents of rain drenched the crowds. Another rally supporting the bases was held in Luneta Park led by President Aquino with Mayor Richard Gordon by her side cheering on the pro-bases supporters. They then marched to the Senate to influence the vote.

I was listening to the continuous commentary on the radio

praying as we do at times like these, believing that there was a personal God who could influence the events of history to the good if there was enough positive good-will in the world to implement that good. It was like the story of Sodom and Gomorrah, if there were enough just people, evil things could certainly be prevented from happening. This, I believed, was one of them. Were there enough good people creating the universal good will to prevent a wrong decision and allow that continuation of the bases and all the human suffering they brought with them?

The answer came with the counting of the votes. I was sick with tension as one by one the votes for were called out, then one against, and then another. My hopes began to soar, could this be true? Senator Jovito Salonga, a true nationalist and the Senate leader guided the proceedings. Then, the vote of former Marcos and US stalwart Senator Juan Ponce Enrile was called out. It was an astonishing no! Senator Rene Saguisag listed the names.

The excitement grew per vote, I leapt for joy as every *no* vote landed with a mighty whack on my consciousness and that of every Filipino and US official watching the extraordinary event. One hundred years of history was being unravelled by the democratic process. In the US Embassy, there was surely an open phone line to Washington and the Pentagon. In the Presidential Palace, there were glum faces and an air of defeat as the Senators gave their little speech explaining their vote and left the rostrum tossing a *no* vote to Senate President Jovy Salonga.The tension was unbearable and finally the twenty-three has decided: twelve against, eleven for. A resounding victory to reject the treaty. It was over. Ten years of campaign, speechmaking, writing, seminars and rallies. We had made our little contribution. For us it had begun when that courageous religious sister of the Daughters of Charity came from the Pope John XXIII Clinic and told me about the little children who were prostituted to the US troops.

I was now filled with a great calm and inner happiness when the final vote was in. History was surely made that day. The twelve Senators, many with private reasons of their own for voting as they did, are still known as the magnificent twelve. Today in Subic Bay, standing before the administration building where once proud Rear Admirals commanded the US Navy's finest overseas base, a monument depicting the Philippines as a mother releasing the dove of peace is a fitting reminder. Below, on a long table is the sculptured imprint of their hands. Above against a blue sky, an enormous Philippine flag is making a statement.

The pro-bases camp were stunned and in disarray. The rejection of the so-called "Treaty of Friendship, Cooperation and Security" upset the pro-bases Senators that they declared: "This is not the end." The American military establishment and republican congressmen were outraged and needed to be mollified. President Aquino proposed a temporary extension for ten years by presidential agreement but quickly backed away from that when it was pointed out that it was unconstitutional to extend military bases without a treaty.

Then she proposed a national referendum on the issue to challenge the decision of the Senate but since there was no approved treaty, there was nothing to have a referendum about. There was nothing to present to the people. Senate President Salonga reminded President Aquino that the constitutional process had to be respected.

Then on October 2, 1991, the President said that the bases could have a three-year withdrawal period to ease the shock on the Philippine economy and enable the US to adjust its military presence in Southeast Asia. This, too, came under strong criticism. The withdrawal date determined by law was November 1992. This became the focus for the future.

There was an uneasy mood as elections were scheduled for the following May and it was feared that a pro-US Senate might be elected and reintroduce the bases treaty and approve it. Then all would have been lost. Then there was a move by the local government to set up an autonomous region covering Olongapo City, Subic town and the greater part of the bases area. It was to be called Autonomous Region of Greater Olongapo (ARGO). In the unlikely event that it would be approved by the Congress, it would give the ruling family vast powers for an area of about sixteen hectares and they could theoretically operate the base facilities under lease contract and lease it to the US military. There were desperate efforts to forestall the declared final withdrawal date of all US troops on November 22, 1992. The Bases Land Conversion Authority has already been set up and was soon to be voted on by the congress. The ARGO initiative was a futile attempt to forestall it.

We were deeply concerned about the Subic and Cubi rain forests. There was a heated battle going on in the country over illegal logging. Senator Franklin Drilon was then Secretary of the Environment and Natural Resources. He was under intense pressure and threats to approve logging permits all over the Philippines. He bravely resisted and instead began to cancel logging permits. I wrote to him some months previously suggesting that the Subic-Cubi rainforest be turned into a national park to help protect it. Although that was no guarantee. The Bicol National Park rainforest had been completely logged out.

I also suggested to Secretary Drilon that he promote the setting up of the World University of the Environment, an idea that I had lobbied for to protect the rainforest at Subic. I hoped that it would bring in local and international researchers and students who would be there to monitor and guard the trees from illegal loggers. But to no avail. We continued to worry about what would happen if the local government officials got control over the conversion process of the base when the American troops withdrew.

Chapter Twenty-Two

The sex industry was still thriving and US troops were carrying on as always. That Christmas I made a surprise jail visit to see if the city was still jailing the children and to my shock found several children, six and seven-years-olds behind bars and also a young woman and her baby.

The small cell had no beds or a proper toilet, instead there was a stinking hole in the corner that spread disease and nauseated anyone who came close. The crying children were on the concrete floor lying on newspaper. They were hungry, dirty and dressed in rags and bitten by cockroaches and mosquitoes. I went out and bought bread and drinks as they were dehydrated. Immediately, I complained to the officials and they were quickly transferred to the Lingap Centre run by the national government (the city had none). Officially, there were no street children because without birth certificates they didn't exist and were not a concern. The city has a standing policy of never referring any needy child to the PREDA Children's Home as it officially maintains that there are no such problems in the city. There is not a single record of a suffering, raped, abused or abandoned child referred to us by the city officials. Likewise, the sex industry did not exist – it was entertainment. HIV/AIDS was not there perhaps because the women that tested positive were immediately forcibly transferred out of the city. Denial was the only possible policy to cover all such social evils that were allowed to grow and fester.

It was a picture card washout but nevertheless a moment of history.

It was one of those mornings when you feel you are waking up in a dream and say to yourself this cannot really be happening. It was the last day that the US Navy would officially have a foothold at Subic Bay – ninety-two years after the US Marines landed in Manila as allies but within days became occupiers. It was now November 22, 1992 and the final step of the withdrawal was underway.

A few months previously, the US withdrew all their main forces, equipment, ships and aircraft. President Fidel Ramos, the cousin of Ferdinand Marcos, came to Subic Bay and received the formal agreement of withdrawal and the reservation was formally turned over to the Philippine government. Cubi point, the airport and pier would be the last areas from which the Marines would withdraw. Ramos made a speech that called on the Americans not to forget their duty to the women and children and he cited PREDA's work for the "throwaway children," as we had called them. That was the text of the official typewritten copy that we received. Just before Ramos read the speech, the Mayor created a scene demanding that the reference to us be eliminated. He succeeded, too.

Some weeks later there was a ceremony at Tappan Park in front of the old Spanish Church. This was the original Olongapo town plaza. This was a symbolic withdrawal and turn over of the Subic Bay Naval Station to the city. It was the moment of unwelcome truth dreaded by all involved. There was a band, a parade of flags, one for every decade of the special relationship, colonial and post colonial. Speeches were made praising the many years of co-operation from the days when Filipinos and Americans fought and died together in Bataan against the Japanese. Nothing was said about the horrors of the Filipino-American War or the human degradation caused by the sex industry that surrounded the military bases in Angeles and Olongapo Cities. That was indirectly praised when the "close co-operation over the years" between Olongapo officials and the Navy authorities was recalled.

The officers and their wives were eight rows thick dressed in their best. I climbed up on the covered press stand to get a better view of the affair. Mayor Gordon drew himself up to look proud, solemn and dignified. The base commander and his officers were smart in their starched navy whites, gold braid gleamed on epaulets and caps. A US Embassy official graced the occasion and was ready to make a speech. Then, as soon as the flags were mounted inside the bandstand and all were drawn-up in solemn salute in front of it, the band blared and the heavens were not pleased. A black cloud covered the sun, it was a bad omen. A great darkness descended, lightning flashed and the clouds thundered displeasure and released a torrent of unrelenting rain. No one could flee, they stood sadly in the downpour while aides rushed here and there with all too few umbrellas. Costly hairdos instantly became sopping sagging messes and everyone was soaked through from head to toe. The press box where I was safely ensconced was packed with sheltering newsmen. Misery ruled below.

The last day had arrived. The Marine force that secured the buildings, the airport and the wharf at Cubi Point were pulling out. There, on this sunny calm day, the USS Bellue Wood, a nuclear powered US Marine helicopter carrier lay quietly at anchor. Alex, Merly, myself and some of the staff went to the balcony at the top of the PREDA building to look out across the bay to see the historic withdrawal of the US military after ninety-three years of occupation. We felt it was in some small way the result of our part in the ten-year campaign to expose the syndicates selling children to Navy paedophiles. That fatal date in 1982 when Alex and myself found the twelve prostituted children abused by the sailors hidden in the back room of the Olongapo General Hospital. That changed everything. We exposed the botched cover up of the crimes against children by the local and US authorities and that set us on the precarious road campaigning for the removal of the military bases and their replacement with industrial parks. That defiant stand was to provoke vicious retaliation from the sex mafia and their political backers. It was the start of a counter-campaign to destroy our name and reputation by false charges of every kind based maliciously on manufactured so-called "evidence". There would be hard times ahead. Public exposure and speaking out was the only way to stop the abuse and save young Filipino girls who were as young as eight or nine when drawn into the sex trade. The American sailor boys, drafted as young as seventeen, were also lured and manipulated as sex customers into underage sex. No parent, Filipino or American, could tolerate that. Many of our friends on the base were shocked too and understood our good intentions and approved of them. There was nothing they could do.

Looking out across the bay towards Grande Island, I imagined the Filipino troops under General Emilo Aguinaldo in 1898 firing a salvo of shells from captured Spanish artillery at the US Navy ships that first entered Subic Bay. The US ships retreated to Manila believing Subic Bay was heavily fortified. They returned in greater force to mount a full-scale marine landing and capture the single artillery piece on the Kalaklan Ridge not far from where we were standing. Fittingly, it was the Marines that were first to arrive and the last to leave. There was more suffering and unnecessary dying and destruction packed into those years than ever before in recent history. It is difficult to acknowledge that the human species with intelligence is the most destructive of all. We are a species, driven it seems, more by greed and selfishness than by intelligence and love.

Watching the distant preparations for the last ship to leave

Subic Bay, I felt that I should be across the bay on the wharf to see them off. I took the Nissan pick-up and entered the Kalaklan Gate and was waved through by Philippine Marines who had now taken over the security of the base. It was the first time that the gate was unmanned by US Marines. A strange silence hung over the huge sprawling deserted base. I drove slowly, observing the empty posts and parade ground. The abandoned piers and lonely empty shops and offices gave the impression of a ghost town abandoned, lonely and inhospitable. This once bustling naval base that had launched armadas of countless troops and bombs on North Korea, Vietnam and later on Iraq during the first Gulf War had come to a standstill. There were still a dozen or so US Marines positioned along the road to the wharf providing an outer ring of security to the USS Bellue Wood. I stopped to take a photograph and was amazed to see a red Victory Liner bus come hurtling past me jam-packed with waving, cheering bar girls from the Olongapo bordellos and clubs.

I arrived on the Wharf at Cubi Point and was met by an extraordinary sight as Mayor Gordon and about twenty of his inner circle wandered about like lost souls not knowing what to do or where to go. They were a forlorn lot. It was poignant too as in 1904 when his grandfather, Jacob Gordon, from New York, stepped ashore at Subic Bay as a US Marine, married a local girl and founded the Gordon dynasty. The bar girls were the only constituents that had showed up to mourn the departure. Photographers clicked away at anything of interest. A few bargirls ran here and there to embrace a Marine before he climbed the ramp. A few Filipino base workers were on standby to help cast off the huge mooring cables. Although the Marines seemed to be doing this themselves as if to say, "We are leaving in an orderly fashion, no one is kicking us out."

There was no official ceremony here. The last of the Humbees with the security detail drove onto the pier with the security detail, up a ramp into the hold. A helicopter hovered overhead. The yellow ramp was hoisted aboard by a crane and the klaxons gave a mighty blast, a final fart to their most favoured port. The great screws churned the waters to a white foam and a tug boat, in a last embrace, pulled the great ship away from the pier. The USS Bellue Wood was underway. The group of girls in shorts and tight fitting t-shirts waved and jumped up and down with squeals of excitement. The Mayor and his group waved in a desultory fashion, looking depressed and defeated. It was the end of an era.

The last few US Marines that cast off the cables boarded a tender further along the pier and followed the carrier out into the blue waters of Subic Bay where it was hoisted aboard. I could clearly see the PREDA Centre on the hillside across the bay. There, a crowd was quietly watching with approval and some well-earned satisfaction. The carrier grew smaller in the distance as it passed Grande Island and soon disappeared over the horizon. I turned and drove away, wondering what would become of the remaining facilities. Clark Airbase was covered in ash and abandoned during the eruption of Mount Pinatubo and local gangs and Philippine Air force personnel were accused of wide scale looting. But I envisioned a booming prosperous industrial estate with hi-tech factories and many thousands of dignified jobs. I prayed that the politicians would see the possibilities and act on the recommendations on conversion we made to the Abueva Board.

I drove through the centre of Olongapo. It would never be the same again. Every bar and club was closed, shuttered and the hoarding of the buildings damaged during the volcanic eruption stood like broken teeth. The bands had packed up and the girls were gone. It was a ghost town overnight and the inhabitants were in a state of shock. There was no other industry or business in the city. The sex industry had totally collapsed. I walked through the deserted streets to savour the quiet reverie that had descended like a curtain on a noisy pantomime. Everything had been so unreal, so artificial and so dishonest. The greatest fake show had ended, the lies and manipulations had ended, the phoney smiles and insincere laughs were silent as the ghost town atmosphere descended and no flashy neon light cut through the gloom and darkness. There was hardly a jeepney moving along Magsaysay Drive that was once a bustling thoroughfare. While I was saddened by the loss of the jobs of so many workers in the US military base, I knew that many would take a generous retirement package and others would be well qualified to work abroad for a while and earn three times as much as they had at Subic Bay. Then, there was our vision of the conversion of the facilities to a thriving economic zone where many more jobs would be created.

Now was the crucial time for the implementation of the military base conversion plan. The Philippine Marines were guarding the facilities to prevent any looting and they were doing a good job. As the New Year approached, the Mayor realised that we were right. Converting the facilities was the way forward. He adroitly manoeuvred himself into a position to grab the chairmanship of the Subic Bay Metropolitan Authority that would take over the facilities and oversee the conversion plan that we had so laboriously worked for. Our greatest fear was that the conversion would be marred by corruption and nepotism. We were not to be disappointed.

In the UK, the public awareness campaign by the children's charities was on the rise. Jubilee Action, an active dynamic charity headed by Danny Smith, began to lobby for a change in the British laws so that British nationals who sexually abused children abroad could be charged in the UK. Danny asked me to make a report on the Philippine situation of children in abusive circumstances. This we did and highlighted the transcript of the Stephen Ritter trial that had convicted him for the death of Rosario Baluyot. The cover had the picture of Rosie, the five-years-old child behind bars in

Olongapo City, which I photographed in the Olongapo Police Station B on the nightclub strip at 1pm in the morning on Good Friday in 1991. Michael McCarthy, the cousin of my first cousin Rovena McEvoy, was visiting and I took him on one of my occasional surprise visits to the jails. Getting children from the jails was an ongoing and seemingly never ending task. The one hundred and thirty-five page report was presented to the Parliamentary All Party Group on street children in November. It was launched in the Jubilee Room in the House of Commons. I was there when the Members of Parliament, Nigel Griffith, later a minister in Tony Blair's cabinet, Ian Bruce and David Alton, took the lead in presenting the report to the media. David Alton is now Lord David Alton of Liverpool. The report had a huge impact and it helped to mobilise political will to do something about the situation in Britain where thousands of British men travelled to the developing world to have sex with minors.

The impact of the ratification of the Convention on the Rights of the Child by the Philippine government was also having a positive result. The Philippine children's rights charities and non-government agencies helped to prepare a new child protection law called "An Act Providing for Stranger Deterrence and Special Protection of Children against Child Abuse, Exploitation and Discrimination" and popularly known as Republic Act 7610. The law passed and was signed into law by President Aquino as her last official act in office. It was a powerful tool in protecting children and prosecuting offenders. Until then, the only law against child sexual abuse were acts loosely described as "lasciviousness". The law did not specify what these were and the punishment was minimal. The law penalises many kinds of sexual, physical and psychological abuse as well as forbidding the exploitation of children as workers and child soldiers. This was a major step forward. As a result the number of cases that came before the courts rose from a mere two cases to eighty-four cases in 1993, and six hundred and twenty-one by 1996.

With the new law we were able to bring charges against the suspected abusers and create greater public awareness of these crimes against children.

Another bill signed into law by President Aquino was the local government code. This recognised the place and the role of non-government agencies to organise and for their representatives to have positions on regional, provincial and municipal decision-making boards. Non-government organisations like PREDA had the opportunity to be advisors to government boards and monitor government contracts to curb corruption.

It was incredibly difficult to implement this, although later Alex was elected as a representative to the Central Luzon Regional Development Coordinating Council. Alex organised a coalition of the non-government organisations in Zambales and Olongapo. The coalition also had the right to monitor election procedures and results. As a consequence, the massive fraud in the Olongapo City elections was uncovered and the elections were suspended. The family dynasty that ruled the city was shaken to its roots. It was discovered that the number of registered voters far exceeded the number of eligible voters. Thirty-five percent of the population is the normal percentage of the population eligible to vote, according to figures from the Commission on Elections and the Supreme Court. The Olongapo voter registration was sixty percent of the city's population. There was a serious incident when Attorneys Sergio Cruz and Jun Cesa, official election monitors, were questioning the registration of additional voters that they believed were non-residents of the city. They took this to court and during the proceeding the incumbent candidate arrived with a troop of goons and unbelievably proceeded to threaten the lawyers in the courtroom. It reached such an emotional pitch the candidate threw the Judge's gavel at the lawyers while he cowered. Such was the wrath of the politician who was being challenged. Needless to say, the hearing was postponed and the lawyers made formal complaints to the Commission on Elections.

With the US Navy gone and the military base conversion plan still in the process of implementation, the plight of the thousands of abandoned Filipino women and their Filipino-American children came to our attention. Many of them came to us looking for help and we set about helping the mothers organise themselves into a mothers' association. Eventually, this organisation had five hundred and fifty members. Those worst affected were the common law wives who had lived with their American partners for a few years, had children and were then abandoned. The children were deeply disturbed and all were in dire straights. The PREDA staff helped them avail of small loans from our micro-lending project so they could start a small livelihood project. But we realised it called for a bigger effort and the rights of the mothers and children had to be recognised.

Belinda Rhodes, a freelance journalist, wrote a moving feature article about the lives of the Filipino-American children who were in the PREDA assistance project for the *San Francisco Chronicle*. Attorney Joseph Crotchet of the Crotchet, Illison and Pitre Law Firm contacted me and asked if we were interested in taking a class action suit seeking to redress the injustice suffered by the mothers and the children. I said yes and he dispatched one of his representatives, Mr West to visit us. I remember that he brought a gift of an Apple Macintosh Powerbook. We advised that Gabriela, a women's rights coalition, ought to be involved too because they best represented the women's rights. We arranged for him to meet the women at Buklod, the women's help centre in Olongapo. Then the hard work began in researching and getting hard evidence that there had been an unwritten contract between the US Navy and the women who provided services to the sailors based on the reality that the Navy provided venereal disease treatment, control drugs, the equipment and the training to the staff of the social hygiene centres in Olongapo. This made it possible for the Navy men to live off the ships and the base with these women as common law wives.

After a lot of work, we were able to get ID cards issued by the US Navy to the mothers of the children and other links showing the possible contract whereby the women provided services to the Navy men and in return the Navy made medical assistance available to them. When the Navy pulled out of Subic Bay Naval Station, these women and their children were all left impoverished and abandoned and deserved compensation of some kind for their children. Unlike in Vietnam and Korea where the children of the American military were granted US citizenship, Filipino children were not. In time three women from Buklod and their Filipino-American children and PREDA staff with four children in our care went to San Francisco for the formal press conference announcing the filing of the class action suit, which was to be heard in the Washington DC International Court of Complaints. The case was filed on March 4, 1993. Alex, Merly and Attorney Sergio Cruz and myself accompanied the children. They were Ruby and her brother Christopher, Francis and Hakim, fathered by an African-American sailor. The press conference was a big success and brought the issue of the abandoned women and children to the attention of the American public, short-lived as that always is.

I gave a brief but pointed message that opened with the call "Wake up America, these are the children you left behind!" The class action suit in the court was heard and the Navy responded to the arguments denying that they had any responsibility. Finally, the Judge ruled that the women were engaged in prostitution, this was illegal and they could make no valid claim for assistance based on illegal acts.

I had a good friend in the US Congress, Anna Eshoo from the 14th District in California, and I asked her to put the situation to the women's congressional caucus and she did.

They passed a resolution directing the US AID to design an assistance programme for the children and women worth two million dollars. We at PREDA had long announced that we were inhibiting ourselves from receiving any part of such financial compensation. The amount of $650,000 was finally released to the Pearl S. Buck Foundation for distribution in the Philippines. At PREDA, we continue to help the Filipino-American children and their mothers from our own resources and donors.

By 1991 the military base conversion plan that we were advocating was slowly becoming a reality with the establishment of the Subic Bay Metropolitan Authority (SBMA). The political battle for the chairmanship of this authority was brewing. Local opposition groups strongly opposed the candidacy of Mayor Gordon but this was eventually to prove insufficient and he soon held both offices, City Mayor and Chairman of the Converted Base. Sex tourism was suddenly seen to be on the rise again as foreign nationals began to get city permits and licenses to open the bars and clubs, most of them situated in the Barrio Barretto district along the beaches of Subic Bay. We were facing an influx of Australian, German, Swiss, British, and American sex tourists. The nightmare was back again and many youngsters on the streets were increasingly at risk.

A few years previously, I was invited by the International Federation for Alternative Trade to attend a conference in Kilkenny, Ireland. It was a pleasant trip to my other home for me. The PREDA Fair Trade Products Department was still thriving and growing under the guidance of Merly despite the restrictions we were experiencing. Merly, working with the producers, took care of the financing, training and production of the products and together with Alex and our staff, we initiated with the producer group development projects.

My responsibility was promoting the Fair Trade concept

and helping to strengthen our relations with the alternative trading organisations (ATOs). These are mostly in Europe and they import and distribute the handicrafts through the World Shops. The ATOs and civil society groups take active roles in campaigning for important issues such as the protection of the environment, a curb on the excesses of globalisation, and end to child labour and many more issues to uplift the dignity of those exploited by an unjust world economic order.

These shops are scattered in towns and communities throughout Europe and are set up and staffed mostly by volunteers who are dedicated to improving the lives of the poor through economic empowerment, self-help and community development projects. More professionally managed shops are spreading these days into the high streets and choice market locations as the Fair Trade movement is seen as an important influence and defender of the small community producers groups and cooperative in the developing world. They have all been strong supporters of PREDA over the years as we battled with the unjust social and economic system that created even greater poverty and exploitation of the disadvantaged.

Cooperatives and farmers associations producing coffee and food products are the most prominent producers supplying the World Shops. Handicrafts, jewellery, fashion accessories and clothing have always had a prominent place in Fair Trade. Product quality is greatly improving and the shops that displayed and sold the products are more professional, attractive and strong selling outlets and sources of information on the issues of the developing world.

But back in 1987, when I was in Kilkenny, there were no members in the federation from the developing world and the organisation was attempting to change the membership. The outcome of that conference was for producers to be represented on the executive committee of the Federation and I was elected by the delegates from Asia. A South American delegate was also elected and a delegate from Africa had observer status. There was a yearly meeting of the executive committee and one of the main topics was the biannual conference. It was decided that for the first time it should be held in a southern country.

PREDA was selected for the daunting task of hosting the conference in Manila. There were to be over one hundred and fifty delegates from all over the world and the Philippines was not the country with the best security and infrastructure. Electric supply was a major problem; we were living with constant power failures every day and the power was rationed and the telephone system was anything but efficient in those days. We hosted it in the Philippine Village Hotel from April 27 to May 2, 1992. President Aquino was so occupied with preserving her country from military coups that there was little done to solve the power problem.

Despite all of this it was considered a challenge and a matter of pride that we should have the conference for the first time in a developing country. It would be an opportunity for many delegates from the Northern Alternative Trading Organisations to visit the Asian producer groups. The biggest constraint was of course the budget. We were admonished to host the conference within a tight budget and this made it anything but lavish, yet the majority were well satisfied and appreciated the new experience and the opportunity to travel in Asia. We did everything we could to make it a success and had good speakers representing the causes of land reform and economic sovereignty.

It was only a few years since producers were invited to join the federation, which had been previously confined to the importer organisations. Producer groups insisted that their members be listened to and recognised. I was elected to be an Asian representative to the executive committee that met in Europe every year. It was time to have the meeting in the southern producer countries and, small as we at PREDA were as a producer organisation, we felt that we had to lead the way and show that producers had the capability and capacity to host the conference.

Our quality handicrafts were selling well in the World Shops and this was an essential part of our goal to contribute to the social development of the Philippines through Fair Trade. Not only had we to do all we could to alleviate poverty and injustice but this was prevention and that is always better than cure. We knew of course that the bars and clubs and streets were filled with teenagers and children running away from the hardships of rural poverty to the bright lights of the city. But there, their vulnerability to being lured or forced into child prostitution, was even worse. The village based livelihood projects helped families prosper and stay together and enabled the children to have a decent life even though they were still poor. When the sales of their crafts earned a surplus this was shared with the producers through a project beneficial to all the participants in the producer group and their neighbours, such as a well or building toilets.

Merly had worked hard to set up the dried mango production project. The goal of this was to help small farmers get higher farm-gate prices for all their mangos. The Philippine carabao mango grows on trees that can be the size of an oak tree. There are several varieties so mono cropping is not a problem. But grafted seedlings planted when two-years-old can produce a small harvest after five years and many more in the succeeding years bringing a bountiful harvest year after year. The fruit is heart shaped and soft yellow when ripe and is delicious, high in fibre and three times higher in vitamin C than oranges. It is ideal for drying because it stays soft and retains its natural sweetness mixed with a sharp tangy taste. The mango industry was mostly concentrated on the export of fresh mango to the prosperous Asia markets. It was controlled by as few as six wealthy families, mostly based in Cebu City, some three hundred kilometres south of Manila.

Some of them seemed to have formed an informal price fixing cartel to keep the farm-gate price of fresh fruit as low as possible. We aimed to change that one day. In the meantime we were helping mango cooperatives produce more efficiently and worked at developing a market among the world shops that paid a higher and fairer price of the dried mangos.

The benefit of drying the mangos was enormous. Farmers had huge losses because forty percent of their harvest could be rejected by the exporters of fresh fruit as below standard in size and looks. With the help of a professional fruit processor in Cebu, Profood International, we finally were able to dry the fruit without the use of any chemicals, preservatives or colouring additives. It was a hundred percent natural. We could arrange for all the farmers' mangos to be delivered to the processing factory where hundreds of young people had well paying jobs in the most advantageous and hygienic working conditions.

The processing was of superb quality in partnership with Profood Corporation of Cebu operated by Justin Uy and his wife Debbie. They reached the highest standard for quality production of dried mango in Asia. The unique drying technique without chemicals gave the dried mangos a long fresh tasting shelf life. They were practically organic in quality but not yet certified as such, that was to come later. Even the mangos too small for slicing and drying were turned into mango pulp for further processing into pulp called "puree" and then into concentrate. This went to the juice making companies in Germany and brought more benefits to the farmers. In 2002, our partner Dritte Welt Patners, German Fair Trade procuts importer, directed by a dynamic young director Thomas Hoyer, developed an apple-mango drink that combined organic apples from German apple growers and mango puree from the Filipino farmers. It won a prestigious award in Germany.

The Fair Trade movement was becoming stronger and more important year by year. Not only was this putting into practice the calls for justice in international trading, it was a movement that was showing the most effective way to reduce poverty by helping people to work with dignity and support themselves. All they asked was a fair price for their products. It was a powerful and influential lobbying body that worked to persuade the rich countries to stop their unfair practices of imposing tariffs and restrictions on imports from the Third World while subsidising their own producers. The rich used strong bullyboy methods to pressure developing countries to open their markets to western goods by threatening or bribing their political and business leaders. This is the bad side of globalisation, a grand concept that promised to change the world trade practices by creating an equal playing field for all in the global markets. It promised equality access to western markets yet it has seldom delivered on that promise.

The poor nations could never compete fairly. They were frequently controlled by dictators or corrupt regimes with whom the multinational corporations gladly did business to their own advantage. Western government officials allowed arms to be sold at inflated prices so they could suppress and control their own people when hunger and want caused them to protest. These corporations with loans from the World Bank or the Asian Development Bank got huge contracts at inflated prices that crippled the economies and left them crushed under huge foreign debts for decades to come. Huge farming subsidies in the EU countries and in the US effectively blocked the poor countries from exporting their more competitively priced products. Migration of the poor from the countryside in the poor nations to the cities was the inevitable result. We saw in Manila and in Olongapo the spread of slums and the images of Smokey Mountain, a garbage dump where hundreds of urban poor raked the garbage for a living, came to dominate the world media as the symbol of Philippine poverty. Hundreds of small children took to the streets to beg, sell trinkets or flowers or even be sold by pimps to the sex tourists.

Chapter Twenty-Three

I was busy too helping raise public awareness in other countries about the extent of child sexual abuse in every country and the roots of sex tourism. Ron O'Grady and his wife were the most inspiring and supportive people I had ever met. Ron was the visionary behind the famous international movement called ECPAT (End Child Prostitution in Asian Tourism). In 1991, an inter-church conference on children in prostitution was held in Chiang Mai in Thailand and came to disturbing conclusions about the extent of commercial sexual exploitation of children in the tourism industry. The church groups decided to do something significant about it. ECPAT was born and set goals to campaign worldwide and challenge and persuade governments everywhere to introduce legislation to protect children and curb sex tourism. It has achieved extraordinary success and changed the culture of unknowing and apathy among officials in the international community. It has persuaded governments to set standards and implement resolutions to protect children. Ron O'Grady gave us great affirmation and support and invited me to Auckland, New Zealand to speak at the ECPAT International Conference.

One day in January 1994, I was standing on the balcony of the newly constructed PREDA Centre overlooking the playground where there was a children's party underway and taking a video of the scene below. The children from the surrounding community were playing games and it was a babble of excitement and delight as they scrambled for prizes and treats. I panned across the playground and noticed a yacht moored on the blue water of Subic Bay below. Out of curiosity, I zoomed on to the deck of the yacht and I was surprised to see three Filipino children playing on the deck and a single Caucasian man moving about the wheelhouse. Unless the children were his own, then the presence of the children on his secluded boat would be a violation of the Special Child Protection Act of 1992 or RA 7610.

I went into the centre and got the binoculars for a better look and it became clear that there was no Filipino adult on board. The next day, I assigned Rolly Bessara, the paralegal officer and researcher, to conduct a surveillance of the boat from a close location and again the children were clearly seen alone with the Caucasian. There was certainly something suspicious going on and I contacted the National Bureau of Investigation (NBI) and asked for a surveillance team be sent to observe the boat and to investigate. I was now convinced that those children were likely to be at risk.

An NBI officer, Magno Britanico, was assigned and came to visit us. He left his assistant outside and with some of the PREDA staff I described the situation and pointed out that it was a direct violation of RA 7610 and expected that we should proceed directly to the yacht to investigate and question the Caucasian. Brittanico was reluctant to act and gave lots of reasons why PREDA should not interfere and if anything would be done he would do it alone. In other words, he didn't want us around. This was suspicious behaviour as the suspect might offer some temptation. Besides, we had to be there with a social worker to see that the children were safe and cared for as the law mandated.

This did not seem to bother Officer Britanico very much. After some argument, which we recorded with his knowledge, I explained that we would go to higher authority to get action and save the children. He reluctantly agreed and I took the PREDA pickup and drove down to Ocean View, a nearby beach resort where we could get to the Nagbaculao beach. The yacht was moored about a hundred metres off the beach and there was a rubber dinghy with an outboard engine tied to it. I stayed on the beach and sent a staff member with the video camera to accompany the two agents as they got a small outrigger from a fisherman and went out to the boat. They found three little girls on board with the youngest being only seven-years-old. The owner of the yacht was an Australian tourist named Victor Keith Fitzgerald from Darwin. He was arrested on January 21, 1994 and brought to the office of the NBI and held there for investigation. PREDA social workers located the parents of the children and they were brought to Officer Brittanico.

We were not permitted to participate in any part of the investigation or get a copy of the NBI report that was sent to the local Prosecutor. I was really upset when we learned that a deal had been made and Fitzgerald was released despite the clear wording of the law that a violation was committed if a minor was taken to a secluded place such as an apartment, car or boat with a non-relative. Even though I was the official complainant and a witness, I was not allowed to participate in the preliminary investigation. The video evidence showed the law had been violated. The next day we observed Fitzgerald making preparations to sail away.

In the meantime, we had learned that other children had been brought on that boat on other days and they had sailed around the bay with Fitzgerald. They were Gloria Limpat, Jacqueline Purificacion, and Marlyn Dionido. They revealed to Rolly Bessara and the PREDA social workers how they were sexually molested by Fitzgerald. I called a senior official of the NBI in Manila and asked for help. Fitzgerald had made his escape but a week later he was located sailing off the Southern Luzon Island and was arrested and brought to

Manila. He put his boat under the protection of some security agency. I wrote to the Secretary of Justice Hon. Ramon Esguerra. He responded without delay and immediately ordered a re-investigation of the case against Fitzgerald. To be sure that the investigation would be impartial and transparent for all, on April 22 we took the children to the senior female Prosecutors at the Department of Justice in Manila with their parents and they were carefully interviewed in a friendly way and they freely described what Fitzgerald had done to them on board of his yacht in Subic Bay. This was to prove crucial later when we were falsely accused of having interviewed them and influenced them unduly to give false statements. They were Jacquelyn Purificacion (13), Gloria Limpat (13) Daybie Perez (14), April Alcantara (11). They complained of having been sexually molested and some said they were given tablets that made them drowsy. Daybie and April were children who lived at the Nagbaculao beach not far from Gordon Park and with whom Fitzgerald had regular contact. The other children were picked up by Fitzgerald on the streets of Olongapo and brought to his boat on the back of a motorbike he kept at a nearby beach. He was well settled in the area.

We realised that this was the first time that a foreigner suspected of child sexual abuse was charged in this way. Unknown to us, it was the opening of a war against the sex mafia that was to continue indefinitely and involve us in a confrontation with leaders and customers of the sex mafia, a bishop, priests, politicians and government officials in the years to come. There was retribution and threats from the organised sex mafia to frame us with false charges to have our licence to operate withdrawn and close the PREDA Centre once and for all. That would end any opposition to their trafficking of women and children. The press were soon onto the story and the news of the pending trial was widely reported in the Australian media and elsewhere. The video footage of the arrest of Fitzgerald on the boat with the three children was used in many documentary video reports. The publicity was already having its effect and we hoped it was keeping away the less determined sex tourists. The operators of the bars and brothels were uneasy and we began to receive nasty phone calls of a threatening nature. It turned out that Fitzgerald had been in Olongapo and Subic for many months previous to his arrest and had friends in the bars and brothels.

Fitzgerald was a retired building contractor who had left his wife and family to cruise the islands alone on his yacht, the Mariposa, which is Spanish for Butterfly. Little else was known about his past. Surveillance photographs taken by PREDA weeks previously during another operation showed a small boat named the Whaler with a person fitting the description of Fitzgerald contacting children. This boat was traced to a Swiss man living in a rented house on the beach who later died of AIDS.

On April 22, 1994, the charges of rape and child abuse were filed against Fitzgerald. There was a reaction at once from Fitzgerald's backers. Who these unknown backers were had yet to be discovered. But they were clearly well connected and had lots of influence.

The following May, Merlita Perez and Violeta Alcantara, the mothers of Daybie and April, brought the two children to the Prosecutor in Manila and formally withdrew the rape complaint. We were really worried that Jacquelyn and Gloria would be abducted and forced to do the same. The parents were desperately poor and that was one of the reasons that they allowed their children to go with Fitzgerald on his yacht. He was giving them money, as he admitted later in court. He claimed in his defence that he hired the children, with their parents consent, to clean his boat and cook for him but there was no witnesses or proof of that and it was highly unlikely that children that small could cook food for a Caucasian taste. We suspected that the forces behind the scenes were doing everything to protect the image of what remained of the once thriving sex industry. Since the closure of the US Naval Station, the local tourist or "entertainment" industry was a shadow of its former self but a deadly one as sex tourists still frequented the beaches and brothels. The parents of the small children more than likely had been paid off to retract the complaint. This was a common defence tactic widely used until the Supreme Court ruled that such withdrawals were inadmissible. They made a mockery of justice and encouraged people to file false charges and damage an opponent's reputation then withdraw for a price. It was a way to extort money or threaten an opponent. The two other children, Gloria Limpat and Jacquelyn Purificacion, were thirteen-years-old and had willingly asked to stay in the PREDA Children's Home that offered therapy and recovery to abused children. Their parents were not co-operative and were under pressure, too, to withdraw the charges and get their children to sign the statements of withdrawal.

After some time in the PREDA Children's Home, we arranged for Gloria to study in the therapeutic community and daily returned to the home. She had been badly treated by her family and frequently ran away and lived on the streets. When she was found on Fitzgerald's yacht, she had been already shaven bald by her brother to punish her for running away from their hillside shack. There was more food to be had by begging on the street. One afternoon, unknown to us, Gloria's mother showed up at the school and, exercising her parental rights, demanded the child to go with her. She took Gloria to the small grass-roofed bamboo house on the hillside and chained her to a post. Gloria was then slapped and beaten. She was left hungry and thirsty for days. We went looking for her but could not find the hut. They were slapping and kicking Gloria to get her to agree to withdraw her complaint against Fitzgerald. But bravely she refused and one day when her mother and brother were out, she managed to escape with the chain still attached to one foot. She made her way back to PREDA and told us what they had done to her. Gloria had suffered much in her short life and wanted justice. She asked me if she could make a formal complaint against them and I told her she could.

We went to the NBI's office in Olongapo. This had a positive impact on the other parents of Daybie and April and perhaps they were advised by the NBI that they might be charged with obstruction of justice so they went to Manila, how we don't know, and reinstated their complaint against Fitzgerald. However, this never came to trial because the two children "disappeared". We presume that the parents were given money to return to their distant provinces and warned never to return to Olongapo City.

Two separate charges were brought to court against Fitzgerald. One for his alleged acts against Jacqueline Purificacion and another for his acts against Gloria Limpat. On August 30, 1994, seven months after his arrest, the Department of Justice filed the evidence of abuse against Fitzgerald in the Olongapo Regional Trial Court. The charges in the case of Jacquelyn Purificacion were for rape and violation of the child protection act or RA 7610 in the court of Judge Eliodoro Ubiadas, Branch 72. Fitzgerald was arraigned on September 21 for these offences.

The following October 1994, he was arraigned for similar offences against Gloria Limpat in the court of Judge Leopoldo Calderon Jr at Branch 75. The children testified to the same events consistently in both courts, which added to the authenticity of their testimony. Fitzgerald was held in the Olongapo City Jail in Barrio Barretto without bail. The cases made little progress as the delaying tactics of the defence lawyers ensured that there would be ample opportunity for them to influence the witnesses and use their parents to persuade or threaten them to withdraw their charges. So long as they were safely in the PREDA Children's Home that would not happen. Gloria was not going out to school but we arranged for home classes. Jacquelyn had dropped out of school a long time previously and did not want to study.

Every day, they had values training and therapeutic sessions to help them mature and develop. The mother of Jacqueline was visiting her daughter from time to time and despite the presence of a social worker at every meeting the mother was having a negative influence on her. By December 10, Jacquelyn was making repeated requests to visit her mother at home.

It was now almost one year since the investigation had begun and the long drawn out trial caused witness fatigue to set in. The artificial delays and the constant postponements drive witnesses away from the judicial system. At PREDA, we assist many children to testify against their abusers in distant provinces and cities. Many a day we travelled hours to a hearing at much expense only to be informed on arrival that the case was postponed for some ridiculous reason. The lawyer for the defence was absent, the Judge was sick or at a seminar, the accused did not appear, there was no Prosecutor and so on. When the Judge or Prosecutor does not show up, then the twenty or so cases scheduled for that day's hearing are automatically postponed. Dozens of people who travelled long distances and took leave of their jobs or borrowed money to come from a distant province are just sent away. It is a sad and bitter reality of the judicial system. With some serious misgivings, we gave in to the repeated requests of Jacquelyn to visit her mother in nearby Subic town. We allowed a day visit and when she returned she was excited and very secretive. She was seen having long talks with Gloria. The following day, both disappeared. That was November 1994. We were greatly upset as they were the prime witnesses in the cases. It was clear that someone, presumably Fitzgerald's friends in the sex mafia, had promised Jacquelyn rewards and treats to leave the centre and bring Gloria with her. The prime witnesses were gone and unless we could recover them, the case would collapse. We were deeply disturbed at the manipulation of the witnesses behind the scenes. We were appalled at the extent of their efforts to have the accused acquitted; whereas no one seemed to care the slightest about the thousands of child victims of abuse that cry out for justice other than the committed Prosecutors like Dorentino Floresta who was the biggest headache to the government officials because he was incorruptible. That was the biggest sin of all in eyes of our local regime.

Later, we learned from government social workers that the two children were promised a trip to the movies, pocket money and treats if they left for the weekend. Judge Leopoldo Calderon Jr issued a bench warrant for their recovery. In desperation to recover them, we circulated a missing child notice. Two days later, we received a tip-off that the children were seen being escorted into the office of the City Mayor by Kate Gordon, the wife of the former Mayor who was the controversial chairman of the Subic Bay Metropolitan Authority. I called our human rights lawyer Sergio Cruz and together we hurried to City Hall with a copy of the bench warrant. They were in the office of the city legal officer with their mothers. As we were climbing the stairs, there was a mad rush of people out the other door in the room above. Nobody wanted to be seen with the children when they should have been immediately brought to the Judge. They could have been cited for contempt of court. The city legal officer rushed over almost shouting that she had nothing to do with anything that might have happened in her office that day and fled down the stairs. We went back down and passed the police station just outside the City Hall and saw the two children and their mothers in the foyer. We learned that they had been brought to the City Legal Office and signed a prepared statement withdrawing their charges against Fitzgerald and another making a counter charge against me. Another common tactic designed to delay the progress of justice and damage our good name.

We were flabbergasted with this blatant obstruction of justice. The Fitzgerald case was very highly politicised. It was fair to presume that the city authorities were desperate to end it and have Fitzgerald declared innocent. As if in some way this would be exoneration for the town and its officials that child prostitution did not exist. To their way of thinking, if it was not proven in a court of law, it did not exist. The negative publicity abroad must have been driving away sex tourists and causing a loss to the entertainment and hotel business. The families of the local politicians were in the hotel business themselves. Sadly, under the circumstances, we had to refer the two children to the Lingap Children's Centre on Gordon Avenue as a precaution that they would not be lured away again as they were being influenced to accuse us. This centre was operated by the Department of Social Welfare and Development. It was independent from the city government and was a more secure centre. Despite overcrowding, a low budget and being understaffed, it did a remarkable job protecting the children and helping them to recover from abuse. It was small but surrounded by a high wall and fenced in. The special therapeutic and spiritual development programme that Gloria and Jacqueline were receiving at PREDA was ended. They were sacrificial pawns in a game to deny and cover up corruption. We were determined to battle on despite the odds and the growing conspiracy to crush us and our efforts to help the abused children.

The following January 3, 1995 I received the subpoena from the Office of the City Prosecutor to answer the complaint of the parents of Jacqueline and Gloria which they too were pressured to join. The complaint accused me of exerting grave coercion, subordination of perjury, child abuse, and interference in the administration of justice. It was clearly prepared professionally, they had astute lawyers working for them. We suspected that someone in City Hall was using the children to get at us. Some local correspondents called me to ask my comments about being charged with "child abuse". I was shaken at first but when I read the complaint sheet I realised that it was a dirty trick. The printing and circulating of the missing-child poster when Jacquelyn and Gloria went missing is what they labelled "child abuse". I was quickly learning that such an allegation had the potential to generate screaming headlines in some tabloids but there were none. The editors realised it was a tactic to draw them into a smear campaign they wanted no part of. I was thankful for their decency.

On the advice of Attorney Sergio Cruz, I filed a motion to the Department of Justice in Manila to have the Prosecutor in Olongapo inhibited from investigating the case as one of the appointees of the city was sure to be biased against me. The Department of Justice approved my request and the preliminary hearing of the complaint and my rebuttal was assigned to Regional State Prosecutor Glenn Palubon in San Fernando, Pampanga about one and half hours drive from Olongapo.

While our enemies were manipulating the girls and their mothers and using them to put me on trial for child abuse, the case against Fitzgerald slowly got underway. Another witness Marlyn Dionido, an eleven-years-old who had also been abused by Fitzgerald and was present when the other two were molested, testified in open court on February 11 to the acts of abuse she witnessed on the boat. This was vital evidence and corroborated the testimonies of Jacquelyn and Gloria. Marlyn was staying at PREDA and going to school daily. She was an intelligent student and had resented what Fitzgerald had tried to do to her. She was open and frank in her testimony. Her mother lived in a shack on the hillside at Gordon Heights on the outskirts of the city. We were worried that she too would be abducted and brainwashed to testify against us. We took every precaution to protect her and give no pretext to the enemy on which they could make a frame up.

On February 25,1995, Marlyn was severely cross examined by Fitzgerald's defence lawyer and the thirteen-years-old bravely stood against the intimidating questioning that tried, but failed, to catch her in a lie. She was consistently clear and her testimony stood without contradiction. On February 24,

I was in the witness box and testified to the events surrounding the surveillance and the arrest of Fitzgerald. We carried the television and the video player into the courtroom and set it up as the Judge asked to see it even though the defence tried to exclude it. The Judge and all the court personnel crowded around to see the tape. There is a long shot of the boat moored off the shore, thus establishing that it was in an isolated place. The next footage shows the outrigger with the two NBI agents approaching the yacht and tying up to the side and going aboard. The first image is of two very small children, one sitting on the pilot's seat and then an older child, Gloria, appearing with her head covered. That was because her head had been shaved by her brother. On the tape, the voice of Fitzgerald is heard asking what is the purpose of the visit and the police say because of a complaint made by PREDA. Then the footage shows Fitzgerald and the three children climbing down into the rubber dingy. The next shots are on the beach when the little children are brought to the social worker. It made a very clear testimony that the children were alone on the boat – a violation in itself and puts the lie to the testimony of one defence witness that the parents were always on the boat. During the hearings, our friend and supporter Danny Smith, the founder and director of jubilee Campaign based in Sussex, England, came to visit and monitor the case. He has an interesting and vivid personal account in his book, *Who Says You Cannot Change The World?* While waiting for the case to be called, Danny stood around the snack bar outside the courtroom. Fitzgerald was wandering about, his guard was taking a drink. Danny writes:

Fitzgerald sauntered over to me and started a conversation, while I played the part of a curious onlooker. Nothing he said was surprising and, predictably, he blamed everything on Shay, whom he cursed frequently, while referring to him as a "correspondent from Time magazine". We talked for about forty minutes and he let slip that he had a daughter studying in London. He mumbled, "But they don't want to know me. That bastard has ruined my life." He cut a forlorn and dishevelled figure, and a twinge of sympathy hit me while a shadow of doubt crept in. I wondered if this apparently kindly old man could have been misunderstood... Meanwhile, Gloria came out of the courtroom. She was a slim, elegant girl, about fourteen-years-old. Fitzgerald was facing a charge of attempted rape against her, and he watched her intensively as she walked across our path and climbed into a maroon Space Wagon-type vehicle. As the vehicle pulled out, I observed Fitzgerald closely. The body language and facial expression were unmistakable. He was enraptured, almost mesmerised, and followed her movements, barely blinking, completely obsessed, watching the Space Wagon till it was out of sight. It was this eerie spectacle, captured in a private moment that convinced me that his look of affection was not one of a parent but of a lover.

Danny did not come out to the Philippines for the Fitzgerald case alone. He had been involved with another undercover investigation in Britain with the television reporter for the News at Ten in the trafficking of children to Britons travelling abroad as sex tourists. In April 1995, he worked with Adam Holloway of ITV and they had uncovered a suspicious travel advisory agency called *Paradise Express* advertised in the *Exchange & Mart* that was advertising a trip to the Philippines billed as visit to an "Adult Disneyland". Another charity group had embarked on the same undercover operation and had video from a hidden camera showing the operator offering minors for sex in the Philippines to an undercover researcher. Danny and the other group agreed to work together and follow wherever it would lead.

Adam Holloway and Danny joined the tour offered by the operator named Michael Clarke of Eastbourne. When the day of departure came, Danny wisely pulled out. The other charity, despite the best will in the world, were going about it without the PREDA undercover team and the social workers necessary to be on hand in case any minor was offered for sex trafficking. Our priority was not to get some story but to rescue the children and bring them to safety, gather the evidence and with trusted police officers arrest the criminals and bring them to trial. That whole process was, in our understanding, what the media ought to be following and videotaping with hidden cameras if necessary. But they were going to "go it alone". The camera team went for the story and flew into the Philippines with the researcher from the charitable organisation. They called me from Manila and I advised them of the proper procedures to follow and offered our team. They said they would call on us if needed. They then drove to Angeles City about three hours north of Manila and checked into the Southern Star Hotel as instructed by Michael Clarke. He offered them twelve-years-old girls and brought them to the sex spots of Angeles City; then on May 3 Clarke was about to leave for Olongapo city when he showed the undercover researcher a handgun that was in a cotton bag and hidden in the hotel safe. He sent them a fax from Olongapo and offered them underage children. However, they did not have social workers with them and had not asked for our help. Had they contacted minors, they would have been obliged to report to the police at once and get social workers to rescue the children.

On May 7, Adam Holloway and the researcher went to Baloy Beach and met with Clarke. When Clarke was at the water's edge, he was openly confronted by Adam Holloway on camera and asked why he was offering children for sex. He stammered and denied it. The report was aired on the ITV news before the end of May showing the system that allowed children to be sold into prostitution by sex traffickers poising as travel agents. There was an interview with Danny and he gave some background and explained the work of Jubilee in combating the trade. It was an important public awareness building and helped our campaign to get the British government to work harder to bring such traffickers to justice in Britain when they escaped the jurisdiction of the Philippines. It was also aired on CNN's *Inside Asia* report on May 16 and Senator Ernesto Herrera led the public reaction of shame and shock as the country realised the extent of the exploitation of children in a huge sex industry thriving on sex dollars with the complicity of local police and politicians. It was a huge international embarrassment to the government.

Senator Herrera called for the arrest of Clarke claiming that his admission on the report was sufficient evidence to arrest him. He berated the National Bureau of Investigation for being unable to find Clarke. He called me on June 5 asking if we could help find Clarke. The Senator was the best publicist that we could have hoped for. He brought to the surface the sense of shame and called it a "national disgrace" that the likes of Clarke should be selling children for sex with impunity. Little did he know how much of it was really going on. I had hardly hung up the phone but it rang again with the NBI in Manila headquarters asking if we had any leads as to the whereabouts of Clarke. I thought it ironic that with all the obstruction of justice going in Olongapo over our efforts to bring Fitzgerald to trial and see justice done, here was a well-known Senator and the NBI asking for assistance from us. I began to put out word to all our contacts in the bar industry to be on the look out for him.

The tip off came the day Danny Smith arrived in Manila for a visit. I just had a phone call from a German who ran a bar and restaurant on Baloy Beach, a known sex tourist destination and just across the bay from PREDA. Hartmut "Harry" Joost had come to the PREDA Centre previously to get my support in some complaint against him. I had felt that he was not telling me the truth and there was something suspicious about him. I was unable to help him then and now he was on the phone. He volunteered information about the whereabouts of Clarke. He told me that Clarke was engaged in some dirty business and was staying in a house of the Perez family near his bar that was named Pumpernickels, German for "Brown Bread". He requested me not to tell the police the source of the information which I thought strange considering he ought to be taking the credit for catching Clarke and getting the appreciation of Senator Herrera and the Filipino people. I wondered why. Anyway, I immediately contacted the local office of the NBI and who do you think was assigned to make the arrest but Britanico, the agent reluctant to arrest Fitzgerald. With the request coming to me from the NBI director in Manila, Britanico had to comply and although he said that he would go there alone and didn't need my assistance, I was again suspicious and insisted that I would lead him to the place and I would bring a vehicle to assist in the arrest and take a staff member with me from the PREDA surveillance team. The NBI had no vehicle for such purposes. We went to the beach, it was already dark and saw the small house where Clarke had rented a room but he was not there, according to the owner who lived at the back of the house. Britanico seemed reluctant to cover the back exit. I checked the clothesline and saw Caucasian size clothes. I watched the backdoor from a doorway nearby and to my surprise noticed a poster on the wall of the neighbouring house beside me advertising a sex orgy on the beach signed by "Crazy Doctor Clarke". I realised it was crucial evidence and photographed it.

The next day, fearing that it might disappear if I left it there, I went back and brought it to the Prosecutor as evidence. Britanico wanted to go but I insisted on waiting and an hour later my patience was rewarded and we saw Clarke coming down the dirt pathway that ran parallel to the beach. Then Britanico had him identify himself and since there was no arrest warrant, invited Clarke to voluntarily go with him to answer some questions. I had the feeling that Clarke recognised him and that they had previously met and to my surprise agreed to go along. I did not show myself but slipped around the corner and brought the van around. They boarded the back and I drove straight to the NBI office in Olongapo city. I contacted Senator Herrera and the NBI headquarters to report that Michael Clarke was apprehended.

Before the arrest of Clark, there was the preliminary hearing into the complaint made by the parents of Gloria and Jacquelyn. I drove down to San Fernando, about an hour from Olongapo City. The preliminary hearing is the first step in any judicial process to determine if there was any basis to the complaint. On the advice of Attorney Cruz, I had submitted a detailed legal reply to the complaints and pointed out that issuing a handbill looking for the missing children couldn't be harmful and was not "child abuse".

The following March 30, 1995 State Prosecutor Glenn Palubon issued a ten-page resolution that examined in detail the complaints one by one and discussed the arguments for and against to see if it was possible to establish probable cause and thus have a basis to send the case to the court and for me to stand trial. He concluded that there was no credibility to the complaint and it was a baseless accusation. He said that circulating the poster to find the missing children based on a bench order could not be called child abuse. Nor was the help given to the children in anyway obstruction of justice but, in fact the opposite, it promoted the cause of justice for the children. He dismissed the complaints outright. In other words, they were fabricated. I was lucky that the Prosecutor was a person of integrity and honesty. If he were not, there was nothing one could do to stop a critic or opponent from filing a malicious and false case. It is sufficient for anyone to make a written statement, swear that it is true before a Prosecutor and then it can be filed as a formal legal complaint. No police investigation is necessary or serious evidence needs to be produced at the time of making the complaint.

The judicial system is like a swamp, even if you are sure you are on firm legal ground, it frequently gives away beneath you for no apparent reason and against all expectations. Bribery is a common cause of inexplicable court decisions. The innocent can be accused without credible evidence, the guilty acquitted. In one notorious incident, a woman Judge in Caloocan City, Metro Manila, asked a fourteen-years-old child, who had been seriously raped twice by her father, could she forgive him. The Prosecutor failed to say anything to protect the child's rights, and she answered yes. The Judge asked the father if that was accepted and having already pleaded not guilty, he said yes, he accepted the forgiveness not realising that he was admitting his need of it. It was an admission of guilt. The Judge thereupon said he could go home and if he raped her again she could file the complaint again. With that she declared the case dismissed. We were fuming and the child realising how she had been tricked was deeply upset and retreated into depression.

We learned too there was no way to prevent a Prosecutor who has been suitably influenced with an inducement given by an accused from deciding that there is no case to be answered. Likewise, the Prosecutor frequently decides there is a case to be answered when there is no evidence to support it. Should that have happened, we would have had to file a motion for reconsideration with the regional Prosecutor or directly with the Department of Justice in Manila. If that failed, then it would surely go to trial. I thanked God for the fair and just dismissal of the false charges by Prosecutor Palubon. I was certain that the sex mafia and their political backers would never stop until they successfully framed me for something. But not this time. Prosecutor Glenn Palubon was a good upright person and public servant. Later, he left the government for private practice.

The sex bar and brothel operators were annoyed with us for spoiling their orgies and cosy protection arrangements with the police. For the first time they were scared of being investigated and charged for child prostitution. They were out for revenge and they were going to make us pay.

The Fitzgerald trial dragged on slowly with frequent postponements and delays as is usual in the Philippine judicial system. Then on April 27, there was an important testimony given by an expert witness for the prosecution. A psychiatrist, Dr Moncada, had been assigned to examine the children and testified that they had all the indications of having been sexually abused and said that they had freely disclosed to her the way Fitzgerald had abused them. Her testimony carried no indication that they had been pressured or coerced in any way to make up the story as the defence would claim. The version recounted by the children to the psychiatrist was consistent with the details of their earlier versions. Usually, if witnesses are lying they tend to forget the details of their first lie when they tell it again and again without having been coached.

Fitzgerald took the witness stand in his own defence on June 7 and recounted his side of the story. He denied abusing the children and said that he was just helping them by giving food, clothes and medicine. The children had testified that he had given them money too. This was important evidence as it helped build the case against him. When he continued on June 14, he accused me of having concocted the complaints against him. This was the main part of his defence. The children had been out of the PREDA Children's Home (and under the custody of the government social workers since December 1994) and they had not changed their testimony during that time when they could have easily done so. He denied bringing the children onto his boat during the days he was under surveillance. He could not explain how the children got onto his boat since he denied bringing them there in his rubber dinghy. It was already established that he was picking up kids on the streets. He brought Jacquelyn, Gloria and Marlyn to his boat on a motorbike. He claimed they were cleaning the big yacht yet during the surveillance the PREDA staff or the NBI had not seen any cleaning going on. The head social worker and director of the government-run

Lingap Centre that had custody of the children testified on June 16 that they had disclosed that Fitzgerald had abused them. This account was also consistent with that of Dr Moncada and the earlier detailed accounts of the children.

On the following July 11, Fitzgerald said that the children came on board themselves, but didn't explain how. He said that he was treating their wounds with medicine he happened to be carrying on board. On July 27, 1995, Fitzgerald admitted on cross-examination that he gave money, food and clothes to the children because the children cooked and cleaned for him. He admitted to picking up Gloria and Jacqueline at the supermarket on Magsaysay Drive and bringing them to his boat moored at White Rock Beach Resort owned by the sister of the former Mayor Gordon. It was during that trip that the children said he gave them tablets that made them drowsy and it was then that he molested them. So from January 1994 until April 1996, the children were giving the same detailed testimony and it stood up to severe cross-examination. But that was to change.

While all of this was going on, Clarke was brought to Manila for further investigation. Before leaving Olongapo, he had asked permission to go with the NBI agents to his room on Baloy Beach and get his personal things. This consisted mainly of a cheap shiny pinstripe suit and to our amazement a large chart with the same advertisement for the sex orgy to be held on Baloy Beach.

In a room next to the office of the director of the NBI, the media were having a field day with Clarke, photographing him holding up what he believed a great opportunity to advertise his upcoming sex party. For us, it was incriminating evidence and the more he associated himself with that in public before the cameras the better. We planned to file charges against him. I picked up Danny Smith, Roger Insall, the famous reporter from *News of the World*, and equally famous photographer Alistair Pullen and brought them to the NBI to interview Clarke. They were soon getting an exclusive interview and photographs. Soon, the local media arrived in force and Danny tried to hold them at bay while Roger and Alistair finished their work. It was incredible that he still did not realise the furore he had caused with his sex tours. He held up the orgy poster proud as punch, sitting there, a sleazy businessman in his pinstriped suit. The stripes like his ego were just a bit too big. For him, it was an opportunity to promote his sex tours and the Philippines as a sex tourist destination. So what if the sexy prostitutes were as young as twelve-years-old? For him, that made it all the more attractive. Many in the industry perhaps felt the same way and that is why they were angry at us for "making it a crime". We had spoiled their party once again and the publicity over Clarke's arrest was another nightmare and loss of business for the brothel and bar operators.

On July 9, I filed the formal complaint against Clarke for violation of Article 3, Section 5, paragraph A subpart 2 of Republic Act 7610, the child protection law. It stated that "those who engage in or promote, facilitate or induce child prostitution which include, but are not limited to the following…(2) inducing a person to be a client of the child prostitute by means of written or oral advertisement or other similar means..." shall be meted the penalty of reclusion temporal in its medium period to reclusion perpetual.

We prepared all the evidence we could including the videotape of the CNN broadcast and poster we recovered from the beach. The preliminary hearing of Clarke's case was set for July 25 but he did not show up. It was August 1 before he appeared and then admitted to the Prosecutor that he owned a gun, which he claimed he gave to an NBI investigator, Attorney Mamerto Espartero, who was called in to investigate his activities. The gun disappeared and Mamerto denied having received it. Clarke waived any further preliminary hearing and the case was filed in court. He was soon arraigned and pleaded not guilty.

Gloria's case against Fitzgerald moved slowly in the court

of Judge Calderon. That August 29, 1995 we were deeply worried and tense. I waited with Alex for the trial to open and the witnesses to be called. Prosecutor Floresta had heard that Gloria had been forced to sign an Affidavit of Desistance that would be her formal withdrawal of the charges against Fitzgerald. It was a black moment. I wondered sadly at how they had threatened or pressured her and how they could have reached her when she was under the protection of the Lingap Centre. It was a clear case of witness tampering but we couldn't prove it. Then, the dreaded moment came when the defence counsel presented to the court the Affidavit of Desistance of Gloria. Prosecutor Floresta made a strong protest and argued brilliantly as to why the affidavit could not be accepted by the court. He cited the opinion of the Supreme Court that urged such affidavits to be rejected by the court because they were usually offered in exchange for money and brought the court into disrepute and gave the impression that justice was for sale, which it was at times. To his everlasting credit, Judge Leopoldo Calderon weighed both sides and ruled that it was inadmissible. A huge sigh of relief went up from the children's rights supporters. I had a lump in my throat with emotion. The evidence that he had heard so far was credible and that a mere piece of paper declaring the opposite could not remove the record of testimony already given, he said. I was elated. It was brilliant and an important legal precedent had been made by the senior justice of the regional trial courts. The defence was shattered, they had believed that they had won the case and now their balloon had burst. Another just Judge had just proven himself.

The trial continued with the prosecution cross-examining Victor Fitzgerald and pointing out contradictions in the evidence his defence had presented. When questioned about the discrepancy between his affidavit regarding the arrival at the Subic Bay Metropolitan Authority Marina (where he disclosed that he arrived at the middle of July 1993) and the certification issued by the Marina authority where it certified that Fitzgerald arrived at the Marina on May 1993, Fitzgerald said it was due to the pressure of the case.

In the court of Judge Asdala, Prosecutor Floresta was making a strong, well-presented case against Clarke. Prosecutor Floresta had been appointed in 1995 as special Prosecutor for child abuse cases in Olongapo City by the then Secretary of Justice Teofisto Guingona, a liberal and very patriotic and popular politician from Mindanao. Later, he was to become a senator and then vice president. In 1996, he appointed me to the Presidential Committee for Child Protection.

Prosecutor Floresta in his first year as special Prosecutor took one hundred and eighty-one suspected child abusers to court, a staggering number considering that only a handful were ever referred to trial and few convictions. We nominated him for the Supreme Court prize as the most outstanding Prosecutor of the Philippines and he won. This was terrific as it strengthened his work as special Prosecutor. The city Prosecutor is usually recommended for the position by the Mayor and was in the habit of dismissing almost all complaints against suspected child sexual abusers. Local officials and police were privately instructed to keep any abuse victims from coming to the PREDA Centre. The city then set up a residential house where victims were locked up and their complaints against the abusers were seldom acted upon. Not even the national inspectors of the Department of Social Welfare and Development could get in there. Church workers could seldom get inside.

At that time, we made complaints against the city Prosecutor for being prejudiced against us. He was recommending the complaints made against our social workers and myself by members of the sex mafia to go to trial without sufficient evidence. Frequently, we had to appeal those decisions to the Department of Justice and we were upheld in almost all cases. We had to ask him to be inhibited and another state Prosecutor to decide the case. The cases were then given a fair hearing and we could present our side and expose the lies and motives. The cases were justly decided and the baseless allegations were dismissed. One opponent alone made twenty-six baseless charges against me. All were dismissed as groundless. But they all took up many hours of work as we had to prepare our own defence affidavits before giving them to our lawyer for the final rewrite and submission to answer the false charges. The city Prosecutor was angry at us for calling on the Department of Justice to investigate allegations of child abuse against him. He was suspended from office but reappointed at the Department of Justice in Manila and we had reason to believe that he continued to work against us from there as we were to find out in years to come.

When he was suspended from his post in Olongapo many cases of child abuse began flowing through the system to the courts with the excellent work of Prosecutor Floresta. He was later made a Judge in another city as the powerful political clan of the city opposed him being made the new City Prosecutor and they prevailed. Soon after, the former City Prosecutor was re-appointed. Then to our dismay and frustration, the dismissal of child abuse cases continued.

I wrote to the British charity that had sent the undercover researcher, let's call him Jerry, asking them to supply any evidence available and for Jerry to testify that Clarke offered him children as young as twelve-years-old as prostitutes. The charity was reluctant to become involved and I knew it would be a difficult ordeal for Jerry. The ITV offered no evidence although Jubilee tried to get it from them. Eventually, Jerry came on October 16, 1995 and told the court of his undercover operation with Adam Holloway of ITV. He showed a fax message sent by Clarke to him offering the sex tour. By now Clarke had come to realise that this could mean a long prison sentence and he was in an ugly and angry mood. Clarke went up to Jerry inside the courtroom and threatened to have him beaten up when he returned to England. He was badly shaken because Clarke had let it slip that his brother was a tough guy and would take revenge. The next day, Jerry was cross-examined and his evidence stood firm.

I was then called to the witness stand and I presented the poster and described how it came into my possession. I pointed out that it was the same one Clarke had proudly showed to the media in Manila. There were photographs to prove it and I had really obscene brochures sent by Clarke to Jerry. The magazine with the advertisement of Clarke and the ITV videotape was shown in the court. Clarke had a difficult time refuting the evidence and his denials were the only defence he had. Almost one year after I testified, the case was decided on October 11, 1996 by Judge Fatima Asdala of Branch 74 Regional Trial Court who found him guilty beyond reasonable doubt. He was sentenced to a maximum sixteen years, four months and one day of imprisonment.

Real pressure was mounting on the children to deny their previous testimony. Gloria had been reached and persuaded to sign withdrawal statements and we expected the same from Jacquelyn. It came on November 8, almost one year after she had disappeared with Gloria from the PREDA Children's Home. Jacquelyn sat in the witness box and was asked by the defence counsel who had told her to make up the false story and she had been coached to say it had been me. But Prosecutor Floresta, while objecting to the leading questions, could not persuade Judge Ubiadas to have it struck off but later asked her where was her original complaint made and she had to admit that it was in Manila and it was given to the female Prosecutor Attorney Emily Santos. Asked if she was forced by anyone to do it, she answered no. Jacquelyn admitted too that she had signed the statement of her own free will. So there was no coercion after all. Two of the other Prosecutors, who had taken the other testimonies, came to the hearing from Manila to supposedly strengthen the prosecution in this high profile case and also to do a bit of grandstanding. They attended the hearings and for a while they cross-examined Gloria. We were shocked when one of them began leading her to give contradictory statements. I urged Prosecutor Floresta to intervene and stop this subversion of the case.

On November 21, the defence rested its case and Prosecutor Floresta began his rebuttal. Prosecutor Glenn Palubon, the inquest fiscal who investigated the complaints filed by the two victims, testified as a rebuttal witness of the prosecution. He said that the two victims confirmed to him that Fitzgerald had sexually abused them and this was one of the reasons he dismissed their complaints against me. He told the court that he suspected that the complaint against me was just a defence ploy to acquit Fitzgerald. His powerful testimony terminated the rebuttal of the prosecution. Prosecutor Floresta was confident that he had done everything he could with the available evidence. We were very surprised when Attorney Manuhig, the defence lawyer for Fitzgerald, was joined by Attorney Mario Leyco from Iba, the provincial capital of Zambales (Leyco was then the diocesan lawyer of Bishop Deogracias Iniquez Jr). I then remembered that he was also the best friend of Mayor Gordon, his political adviser and election campaign manager.

Right away, I suspected something big was afoot for them to bring in such a legal and political heavyweight with close church connections. Church and State had come together wonderfully in the brilliant person of Leyco. For Fitzgerald to be able to afford such additional legal counsel was extraordinary. I doubted if he was actually paying the legal fees from his pension. What was even more extraordinary was the nasty bombastic presentation he made before Judge Eliodoro Ubiadas. Leyco was really angry about something. He turned on us in the public gallery with a fuming red face and a rhetoric of unrestrained criticism of those who had brought the charges in the first place.

Afterwards, he turned on Alex and berated him for his involvement in the case. As if helping children find justice was a crime. Nor did the good attorney refrain from frequently looking at me and aiming a few broadsides my way during his tirade. I thought he was grandstanding but he was setting the ground for his next courtroom bombshell – the dramatic presentation of a document signed by Jacquelyn withdrawing her case. There were gasps from around the courtroom. This was devastating; it was unbelievable that anyone would try such a tactic at this late stage in the trial after clear and unequivocal testimony had been given. But there it was. We waited with bated breath as Judge Ubiadas took the document without any great surprise as if he was expecting it. He accepted it and entered it into the record despite protests from Prosecutor Floresta who had battled for months to get a conviction. Now he was sure it was clear that the case was being manipulated. I really felt shattered not so much that the case had fallen through so shamefully but the course of justice seemed to have been so easily thwarted and manipulated. What hope was there for the children if they could never really get justice? This was our first well-prepared case, supported by strong and articulate witnesses whose testimony had been corroborated by each other, and held up under cross examination and, while they were in the government centre, supported each other over a drawn out period of almost two years. The PREDA social worker Mary David testified that the children had recounted the same detailed account of the abuse over a period of almost nine months without wavering. It was only during the trial when they suddenly changed their testimony and said they were forced to make up the story.

On April 25,1996, Judge Ubiadas acquitted Fitzgerald in the case filed by Jacquelyn. There was a travesty of justice here and many were disturbed that the course of justice could be so changed, especially when the court had heard the clear explicit testimony of Jacquelyn supported by that of Gloria and Marlyn. The acquittal by Judge Ubiadas was frustrating and it highlighted the long history of acquittals of cases against suspected child sexual abusers in the past. It was rare that a child could ever speak out and make a complaint about being abused by an adult. That same testimony had been presented in the case filed by Gloria against Fitzgerald and Judge Calderon had rejected the attempt to have the testimony withdrawn. We now placed our hope on this second case before Judge Calderon.

That fateful day was another tense and drama filled morning as we all trooped to the courtroom, once again, to hear the final decision. Fitzgerald and his backers were looking smug as a smirking cat under an empty birdcage. We feared the worst. The Judge appeared and we waited. They must have had a tip-off that it was an acquittal. The long document was read and first spelled out the evidence and arguments that pointed to the possible guilt of Fitzgerald and then the defence arguments and rebuttals, then the conclusion. Then the crucial last paragraph and, finally, the verdict: he was *guilty* as charged beyond reasonable doubt! We had expected an acquittal and had resigned ourselves to it. This was a shock, the unimaginable had happened, a foreign tourist convicted of child abuse! It was the first major conviction in the Philippines under the child protection law. We were delighted! All the children's right advocates, Attorney Cruz and Prosecutor Floresta were elated. A wave of emotion and excited chatter ran through the courtroom. His defence lawyer was totally off balance. He looked confused, irritated and very annoyed. He had probably been told that special inducements were offered the Judge. Fitzgerald was slumped in his seat and looked dumbfounded and dejected. I genuinely felt sorry for him. His acts of abuse against the children were severe. They were not isolated acts of passion in a moment of weakness, rather they were planned and calculated. He had stalked the children on the streets of Olongapo, induced and attracted them from the beaches. Then, he lured them with gifts and money to the isolation of his boat to prevent detection while he molested them. But as chance would have it, his lust was so strong he anchored his boat too close to his impoverished victims and that was his downfall. He was sentenced to eight to seventeen years in prison for Violation of Art. III, Sec 5, Par (a) of RA 7610 in the case filed by Gloria Limpat. He was acquitted of the rape charge.

The conviction made the headlines and we hoped that it would deter other would-be sex tourists and paedophiles from visiting the Philippines. The guilty verdict broke an invisible psychological barrier that somehow gave deference to foreigners. Payoffs and cover up were the common practices. Their crimes somehow were rarely brought to court and then frequently they were acquitted. Was this the result of a colonial hangover growing out of a sense of inferiority or fear of retaliation by foreign governments against Filipinos? We had a lot to think about. Politics really do influence the judiciary who have to keep in mind the impact of their decisions on the greater good of the community. For them, that is part of administering justice. As public opinion had changed both in the Philippines and abroad against the tolerant attitude towards child sexual abusers, the judiciary had perhaps taken note. The dependence of the country on the foreign earnings of overseas workers that reached $8 billion a year and millions of Filipinos vulnerable abroad and millions more applying to work there made the authorities hesitant to arrest foreigners, Caucasians that is. The tourism industry may have lobbied for a "go-easy-on-tourists policy". We will never know. Whatever, the convictions of Fitzgerald and Clarke were a breakthrough.

Chapter Twenty-Four

Early in June 1995, on a hot scorching day, a shiny Toyota drove up the driveway to the PREDA centre and out stepped Superintendent Kevin MacTavish, one of the most highly rated Australian federal police investigators in Asia. This must be something important, I thought.

"I am assisting the British police to track down a dangerous paedophile, Brett Tyler, who with Timothy Morss, had brutally kidnapped, raped and strangled an eleven-years-old blonde boy from East London by the name of Daniel Handley," he informed me.

We sat under the shade of a tree overlooking Subic Bay, Grande Island, lay off in the distance and beyond that the South China Sea. It was hard to believe that such wickedness was rampant in the midst of Gods beautiful creation.

The boy had been abducted on October 2, 1994 by Tyler (30) and his sex partner Timothy Morss (33), as they cruised through Beckton, East London in a minicab from Guys garage where Morss worked. The business was owned by another sex partner of Morss, David Guttridge (59) from Bristol. Morss and Tyler showed Daniel a map as if asking directions and then pushed him into the minicab. His bike was left thrown on the roadside. They sped off with their victim to the seedy garage where Morss had an apartment on the upper floor. Morss, a former soldier, was cold blooded and brutal, Tyler, who was feminine in demeanour, was in awe of him and totally dependent.

They began to act out their sexual and vicious fantasy dreamed up in Wormwood Scrubs prison where they had met up while serving four and five year prison sentences for sexually molesting boys. Previous to this, they had been to Olongapo City and abused many children there, which doubtlessly whetted their appetite to abuse more children when they returned to England in April 1994. They were caught and convicted but despite therapy never cured. When they were released they began to implement their perverted fantasy.

Tyler himself had been sexually abused as a four-years-old child. He was placed in an orphanage when his mother abandoned him. Morss had a similar abusive childhood. They began abusing others when they became adults.

In the apartment, they raped Daniel and video taped each other doing their vile acts. Then they dragged him into a car and drove him towards Bristol where Guttridge lived and Morss had a florists shop. On the way they pulled into roadside rest stop. Daniel knew what they would do. "You are going to kill me now?" he asked. They did by wrapping a rope around Daniels neck and together pulling one end each the murdering paedophiles strangled him. They then drove to Bradley Strokes and dug a shallow grave on the edge of a golf course.

The disappearance and search for Daniel Handley created immense publicity and remained a mystery. One day six months later an extraordinary, a once in a million event took place. It was as if his spirit was crying to heaven for justice and reaching out from the grave. Animals disturbed his bones and his skull rolled down an embankment to the side of the road. He was found. Immediately the hunt for his killers was on again and they fled back to the Philippines with the help of Guttridge and returned to Olongapo, a haven and protectorate for foreign paedophiles.

After the remains had been found the BBC Crime Watch

programme described Daniel and reconstructed the probable scenario of the crime by paedophiles. A psychiatrist and a prison officer, Edward Cook, recalled overhearing Morss describing to Tyler his wildest sexual fantasy during a group dynamic therapy session in the prison. They reported their suspicions and immediately the police linked them to Guttridge because of the proximity of the buried remains of Daniel to Bristol where Guttridge lived and the fact that Guttridge was their former prison mate.

Guttridge admitted he had helped them flee to the Philippines and revealed that Morss had returned. Arrested and interviewed Morss told police that Tyler was still in Olongapo. They called Mathew Gould at the British Embassy who contacted Kevin MacTavish and he turned to PREDA for help.

This shocking story of rape and abuse of an innocent boy and his killer hiding out in Olongapo moved the PREDA child protection team to action. We followed the information that Morss had given the police and, piecing it together, identified the area where Tyler was likely to be hiding. Going undercover with a good cover story the PREDA detective team identified a likely house and put it under surveillance. Soon, with the help of a photograph faxed to us, Brett Tyler was spotted at the window of a house on Waterdam Road on the outskirts of Olongapo. With these photographs we confirmed it was him and contacted the office of Kevin MacTavish and described the location of the hideout. We stayed on the quarry day and night lest Tyler escape waiting for the police to contact us so we could confirm he was still there and lead them to the house when he was inside.

Inexplicably, they never contacted us again. A few days after I had faxed a sketch of the house to Supt. MacTavish, he and two British police and two Filipino NBI arrived and following our sketch they found the house that was inside a walled compound . The PREDA team called me and reported what was happening and the fact that Tyler had left earlier that morning. One of the PREDA team had followed him to the market. Now with the bungling police barging in he would know they were onto him and go into hiding, we might never get him. As sheer luck would have it Tyler returned to the house and bumped into the police party. They were as surprised as he was. Our team that had shadowed him for days quietly pulled back. We had done our part.

The police bundled Tyler into a car and drove away. A while later I arrived with our team unhappy that we had not beeg contacted to coordinate the apprehension. The house was a rundown, unkempt place but spacious .The housekeeper was there and very nervous and afraid. I talked with her and learned that Tyler and Morss had many boys into the house where they slept with the paedophiles and no doubt were abused. The house was rented by a boy friend of Tyler, Rolando Reyes. He was away at the time. To our amazement we discovered two very small children five and six-years-old in the compound. The housekeeper said they had been adopted by Tyler from very poor families in the nearby mountains.

I called the government Social welfare officers and waited until they came to take them into care. Several years later I received an unusual e-mail from a mother in Australia who had read an article about the work of PREDA in rescuing the two children from the clutches of Brett Tyler before any harm could come to them. She had adopted the little boy and he was now a teenager, bright, intelligent and a loving son.

That was the only happy part of this story. Morss and Tyler were convicted of the crime of kidnapping, grave sexual assault and murder. They received two life sentences without parole. Guttridge was sentenced to thirty months in jail for perverting the course of justice. He had helped them escape to the Philippines and hide, the one place where I happened to be with the PREDA team to help bring him, and hopefully, many more to justice.

Chapter Twenty-Five

Easter of 1996 was one of the most exciting times after the long build up of tension during the courtroom drama in the Fitzgerald case. We needed a bit of excitement. In June, we began our protest against the erection of an electric power line of dangerous dimensions outside the children's home. This was to be a back-up power line for the Asia-Pacific Economic Conference to be held at Subic Bay Freeport.

Richard Gordon, the chairman of the Subic Bay Metropolitan Authority (SBMA) that managed the Freeport and all the economic estates inside the former military base, was in his element. He lobbied with President Fidel Ramos to host it in the Freeport. The juicy prospect of many new lucrative projects, no doubt, brought out the best in all the politicians eager to serve their country and make a profit! It was a golden opportunity by the diligent exercise of hypocrisy and lots of people made loads of money from the event. The APEC meeting was the most prestigious meeting a nation could host in Asia. US President Clinton and many other heads of State would attend. The world media would cover every aspect of it and no expense would be spared to make it the greatest Philippine show on earth, a farcical one at that, if it were not for the serious questions about where millions of dollars went.

Money making scams were everywhere, justified because they were deemed essential for the success of the APEC meeting. A string of luxury toilets were to be constructed along the highway coming from Manila to allow the important people relieve themselves along the way. A huge luxury housing estate was funded on borrowed millions guaranteed by the government. It was supposed to be an overnight villa for the heads of State but none stayed there and it became a private country club. The loan as expected was defaulted and the taxpayers had to pay the bill. Those behind it were of course politically well-connected. Another wasteful and unnecessary project was the erection of additional electric power line from the sub-station at the Half-Moon Hotel along the highway to the entrance to the Freeport over the Kalaklan bridge. The huge towers were to pass in front of the PREDA Children's Home. The existing power line was a 96 kv power line and came from the same substation and passed safely over the hills and the cemetery.

When we saw the foundations being dug and learned that the cables would be 250 kv, we were really worried because we knew that they gave off a powerful electromagnetic radiation that would possibly have serious health consequences on humans especially children. Evidence showed higher rates of leukaemia among children in communities close to high powered cables. That April 1996, Alex, Robert, Lowell, myself and other staff had a meeting to plan the protest. It was justified in the name of the APEC meeting from November 24 to 25. This was another cause of protest in itself because it promoted unrestrained economic globalisation. This is the reality of the economic system that demanded all nations lower or remove completely import taxes and tariffs and open their markets. The power line was a danger to children and just another waste of public money to support the APEC meeting which was a rich men's club.

The National Power Corporation agreed to our proposal to re-route the last section of the cables up and over the hill as early as February 28 but there was a strong objection from Mayor Kate Gordon, the iron lady, who said it would disrupt the peace of the dead in the cemetery. The fact that a 69 kv power line already crossed the cemetery did not seem to have crossed her mind. She denied the power company a permit. Our plan was to symbolically capture one of the pylons near our centre and use this to protest and raise public awareness. We intended to build and attach a small 5x6 foot covered balcony or covered platform high up on the pylon and attach a billboard to it with our messages. At the base of the pylon, we planned to set up a tent and a supporting picket line. More placards, streamers and banners would get the attention of the passing public as it was the main road to the north. It would be a good media story too during the run up to the November APEC meeting.

The pylon we choose to "capture" was the one directly across the road from the PREDA building. Our centre is about thirty metres above the road and so the platform on the pylon would be almost at the same level, directly across from us.

The platform or balcony was made in our own workshop by welding pipes and angle bars into a sturdy frame with a handrail and plywood sides waist high. There was a strong plywood floor and a light plywood roof from which curtains could hang down to the handrail. The little balcony could be curtained off for privacy, or to provide shade from the direct sun. The back of the metal frame would rest against the pylon and a heavy duty chain wrapped around the pylon would hold it in place. The pylon tapered upwards.

We kept the project a secret, the welders didn't know the real purpose of what they were constructing. The last thing we wanted was to be blocked by the police from erecting the balcony. A long removable ladder was also constructed but this was kept at the centre for emergency use. The plan was for me to take up residence on the balcony for as many days as possible until the authorities negotiated with us to end the protest. So it was equipped with a sleeping mat, a portable toilet and an icebox. An electric wire and telephone line strung across the road from our centre on the cliff side opposite.

We made a long rope with a hook on it and cooked food and water could be lifted up from ground level. We had two-way radios for constant communication. All was ready by April 6.

Early that Easter morning, we prayed fervently to the Risen Lord and set about implementing our plan. The PREDA's team was ready and well-trained. They drove down the driveway then a short distance to the base of the pylon. The scaffolding was already assembled on the back of a light truck and swayed precariously until it was secured to the pylon to prevent it from toppling over. The workmen realised for the first time the true purpose of their creation and were happy and excited at the adventure of it all. They scaled the tall scaffolding and passed up the pieces of balcony which our carpenter and welder bolted together and then tightly chained to the pylon. The second team was ready with the equipment I would need. As soon as all was in place, I was ready with my survival pack and went down to the base of the pylon and began to climb up to the balcony high above.

It was a fresh, crisp Easter morning on April 7 as the sun was peeping over the ridge and sending golden shafts of light to pinpoint my progress. I looked down and froze. I was suddenly seized with a fear of heights as nervous as I began setting up home. I lashed the foam sleeping mat against the steel pylon at my back that would serve to insulate me from the heat that radiated from the steel pylon. Robert was in charge of electric supply and communications and he soon had a line for me to haul up and into the box. This was the electric and telephone connection. I would have light at night and a phone and internet connections.

We set up some placards and banners with our messages. The balcony had a large sign board attached to the front with the message:

APEC, GORDON, SBMA, NAPOCOR – Stop causing

cancer to children!

Re-route the two electric posts!

End the oppression, serve the people, not yourselves!

PEOPLE OF THE WORLD, UNITE AGAINST EVIL!

The following days we set up a tent and hung more colourful signboards, streamers and banners left and right of the pylon. It was a carnival atmosphere, too. Motorists drove past and blew their horns. We had a notice saying *blow your horn if you support.* That we regretted after sometime because it got very noisy with all the horn blowing so we removed it, elated as we were with the show of solidarity. The jeepney and bus drivers on a regular run who saw it the first few days continued the practice. We were delighted with the wide range of support that it had generated. There was no reaction from the authorities to our picket during the following days and our information office. There were more caustic comments from the local politicians. Mayor Kate Gordon said I was sick in the mind and was quoted as asking, "Do you think I am stupid enough to take action to harm people?" The public utilities department then announced to the media that the planned power line was to carry only 69kv, not 230kv. How true this was we could not be sure. It was a 230kv cable that they were using with the pylons to match so it was over designed by 330 percent and presumably 330 percent of the cost too, according to Congressman Tony Diaz. He asked if the proponents had perhaps misled the World Bank when it applied for US$1.3 million by not informing them that there was a sturdy operational 69kv line in place. The issue really heated up in the press with letters of support. *The Tribune* and *The Manila Times* published letters from Ameth dela Llana-Concepcion of a people's organisation called "Sandigan". She said that Mayor Gordon's disregard of the plight of the people on Kalaklan ridge and at PREDA was "highly irresponsible and childish". Senator Juan Flavier, a highly respected former health minister, sponsored Resolution 381 calling for a Senate investigation into the health dangers of electromagnetic radiation from cables close to human habitation. The tactic of "capturing" the pylon was very effective and was to last almost two weeks more than we ever had anticipated. There was a lot of attention also in the international media, so within a period of one week we had raised the issues of corruption in infrastructure projects associated with the upcoming APEC meeting and the health dangers of cables. I was constantly getting media calls from around the world. The BBC World Service and other radio called me for a live interview from the balcony asking to describe what was going around.

The European Parliament called on the Philippine government to respect human rights and the rule of law in a resolution sponsored by Irish politician, Mary Banotti. The statement declared: "The European Parliament welcomes the action of Fr Shay Cullen and colleagues in the war against child prostitution."

It was blistering hot as the balcony was exposed all day to the hot sun. I had some insulation sheets attached to the top of the flat plywood roof and that eased the heat a bit. The cool breeze from Subic Bay helped too. I still sweltered and drank gallons of water. The cramped accommodation helped me understand what it is like for prisoners in tiny cells or squatters crushed together sleeping, eating and answering natures call. Down below the picket line was cheerful and we organised games and events at the base of the pylon for children who came to visit and get drinks and snacks.

The police vans were constantly passing by and we were wary of them knowing that they were very frustrated in not being able to attack the picket line or get at me high up the pylon because of publicity. The teenagers came and helped to pass out car stickers. Then one morning, a jeep pulled up and two men jumped out and grabbed three of the small boys standing near the picket line and hustled them into the van and drove towards Olongapo. We demanded the release of the children but it took several hours to get them out. We then discovered that the police that picked up the children were led by an Olongapo district official from Barrio Barretto, a Mrs Nafarete. She was in the van with two barangay police. Three days later, our friend and supporter Fr James Laquindanum came and climbed the pylon to spend time and lend support. We were his partner in the big protest against the Masinloc coal-fired power plant at Bani in his parish the previous two years.

By now, we had a ladder fixed at the back of the pylon in case it became necessary for me to exit the platform quickly or for visitors to come and visit. The support group was at the base guarding the access. Fr Roque Villanueva, the diocesan social action director, also took a stand.

Three days after the children were picked up at dusk, a police jeep passed by with armed police and then we heard automatic gunfire. I immediately ducked down but the only protection I had was a sheet of plywood. We had not anticipated that it would come to this and they would fire at me. I felt scared at that point. Over the two-way radio, we asked if anybody had been hit at the picket line below by the hail of gunfire. But all were safe. Then I realised that no bullets hit my balcony – an open and easy target – so these were warning and threatening shots to scare me into coming down and ending the protest. It worked because I was feeling frightened, but I had no intention of quitting. I took my chances that they wouldn't go that far. If they had intended, my balcony would be riddled with bullet holes and I would be dead. Firing shots in the air by police or military is nothing new in the Philippines.

The next day, attorney Cruz, our human rights lawyer, came to the picket line and there was some dialogue with the chief of police about a compromise. We wanted the Mayor to lift her objection to the approved plan of the National Power Corporation to re-route the last few pylons over the hill rather than in front of it. She was not willing to make any compromise and grant a single concession. The iron lady ruled.

The final day came on June 13. That morning we knew something was up. The crane had already begun hauling the big cables into place and our former staff member Lowell Maglaqui came to visit and joined me in the box. The police were gathering in bigger numbers and at about 6:30 two more vans of police arrived and swarmed all over the place. The streetlight showed them tearing down the remainder of the streamers and the crane began to lift up a railed box with three policemen on board. They were coming to get us.

On the street below, a policeman walked up to Alex with gun drawn and pointed it at him, ordering him to hand over all his valuables. He grabbed the camera, radio and a cell phone.

He was there to direct the operation but to avoid taking responsibility for the illegality of their actions. They had no authority to disband a *peaceful* picket line – our constitutional right – nor to rob people. Several of the police had removed their nametags. By now, the support team led by Alex had retreated to the top of the PREDA driveway overlooking the road and across from my balcony. They were watching anxiously to see what the police in the crane box would do.

As soon as they reached our level, myself and Lowell were bracing ourselves for their onslaught. I immediately feared that the additional weight of three men would cause the balcony to collapse and we would be flung down forty feet to the ground below. As they drew level, I asked them what they wanted.

"I order you to come down," barked the chief police officer.

"This is a peaceful protest action," I replied. "We are doing nothing illegal."

They jumped over the railing into our box, one by one, and pushed us both against the pylon. As soon as the three were in the box, they began punching and grabbing our arms. Suddenly the streetlight went out. It was total darkness. This was planned and, in my head, I felt disaster coming. They were going to throw us off the balcony and make it look like an accident as we were resisting arrest. The darkness was the cover for their evil plan to be sure. But Alex and Robert and the PREDA support team swung into action too. The police pulled the curtain over so that they would not be seen beating us up. But the witnesses gathered on the hillside saw everything. That struggle gave the team the vital minutes to get the emergency lights on and saved our lives. Instead of dropping us over the side, we were lifted into the box on top of the crane. It then began to bring down the box with all of us in it. When we reached the group, Fr Sean Connaughton was there. He was flabbergasted. "What is happening," was all he could say.

I tried to twist myself around but with two sets of handcuffs cutting into my wrist behind my back it was difficult. They were cut red and raw, my leg was swelling where Radovan had kicked me and my head was bruised from hitting and bouncing off the floor like a basketball. We were both brought to the police station.

"Did she tell you to do this? You follow everything she says, right or wrong. Do you think I am a *criminal*? We have done nothing illegal," I asked the chef of police.

He was looking ashamed of himself.

I was brought into an investigation room and left sitting there handcuffed and feeling battered and hurting all over. A policeman in a t-shirt was sitting at a typewriter ignoring me, not knowing what he was supposed to do. Still handcuffed I walked out of the room to look for Lowell and see if he was all right. He too was still handcuffed and sitting in another room. But he had not been further harmed. A policeman came and I demanded the handcuffs be removed from my wrists. No one seemed to have keys.

"I demand to see a doctor. It is a basic human right," I told them. "You have to call a doctor."

Soon after, a medical doctor from the Gordon Memorial Hospital arrived to examine me. I refused and wanted my own doctor. Attorney Leyco arrived and he had that gleam of triumph in his eye. He began to ask stupid questions about who did we think we were making such a protest and if we have a permit to do so.

"What right do you have to interrogate me? Are you in the pay of the Mayor or what? Don't you know any law?" I asked. "Can't you see that my rights are being abused and the police beat me up and Mr Maglaqui too. Are you a part of this...this corruption? You will answer for this," I told him.

The look of triumph on his face quickly turned to frustration. He was the political campaign manager of Mayor Gordon and he intervened to defend paedophiles we had on trial. Inexplicably, he was also the diocesan lawyer

I was as defiant as ever and vowed to file charges of human rights violations. He became angry and stamped out with the doctor from Gordon's Memorial Hospital in tow.

Soon, attorney Sergio Cruz was at the jail demanding that I be released. Immediately (although it was 9pm) we drove directly to a provincial hospital at San Marcelino to get a legal-medical examination of our cuts and bruises of physical injury. No hospital in Olongapo was ready to do it out of fear of the city authorities. To go against the city officials meant bringing down retaliation in the form of perhaps a double electric bill, cut off our water, or a loss of an operating permit. Conrad Tui, a critic of the city, suffered huge electric charges. That was the cost of taking a stand. We suffer the highest electric and water rates at the children's home to this day. It's a kind of punishment for being so critical of the regime. They severely overcharge us as a charity, we asked for a reduced rate to no avail. They ignored our request and slapped us full charges. We can do little about it without going to court, which would be costly and hard to win.

The news about my protest, arrest and maltreatment had already travelled around the world. In Ireland, Fianna Fail TD for Dublin South East, Eoin Ryan, called on the Tanaiste, Dick Spring to intervene and protest the police brutality. Danny Smith, the director of Jubilee Campaign in Surrey,

England, called for an international protest. The Mayor Katherine Gordon and her police said we were arrested for public disorder and grave threats and grave coercion. Within days, we had filed charges of violations of human rights and physical injury against the Mayor and police with the local prosecution office. They exonerated the Mayor of course and ruled that the case was against the police for arbitrary detention. Years later when detailed eye witness testimony was given day after day in the court of Judge Dee in Quezon City we were sure we would see justice. This lady Judge is the daughter of a famous Judge known for honesty and integrity and never having taken a kickback. With the testimony and supporting medical evidence we were sure we could get a win. To our bitter disappointment the defence declined to present a single witness to rebut our testimony and the Judge accepted that and set the case for her immediate decision. We then knew it was cooked, within weeks, a record for a decision (which in some courts can take six months to a year to allow for a negotiation), Radovan was summarily acquitted and the case dismissed. He immediately got a lucrative promotion when the case was cleared. If that how it is for us what chance have little children got without good lawyers and evidence to clear them? The camera, radio and cell phone the police robbed from Alex were never returned.

Chapter Twenty-Six

I am fortunate to count the Irish-American actor Martin Sheen as a close friend. That staunch catholic actor and hero of the West Wing Television series in which he portrays a liberal democratic US president.

He is also renowned for his famous role in Apocalypse Now and many more great films. He came to visit me in the early 1990s when he was playing a small role in a war film that was being shot at the nearby Subic Bay, a former military base. This was a favourite location of movie making and the vision I proposed promoted for its phase out and conversion to a hi-tech and ecological protected area succeeded spectacularly despite much political corruption and exploitation in the first five or six years. Today it is a Freeport and hundreds of factories and small businesses are thriving. As many as fifty thousand Filipinos are employed today and the same number in Clarke, the former US Air Force base now connected to Subic Bay by a spanking new highway. We at PREDA may have been like a flea on an elephants back but a flea with a bite nevertheless.

The former Mayor Richard Gordon, who was now a senator, supported the US bases and marched with president Corazon Aquino and Bishop Teddy Bacani from the Luneta Park to the Philippine Senate to oppose the phase out of the bases and the conversion plan is one and the same that claims credit for the campaign to remove them. Such flip flop twists and turns are a feature of Philippine Political life.

Martin came to PREDA and joined the children at the Sunday mass and then came again in November 1997 to support the Urban poor and their campaign for social justice in Manila. Martin is well known for his Christian activism for justice in the US and is proud to say he has been arrested more than fifty times for taking a stand for peace and human rights mostly in front of the US Congress.

Alex Hermoso, Martin and myself went to the Payatas garbage dump to campaign for help and support for the redevelopment of the area as it was deadly and dangerous for the hundreds of people living and working there in sub-human conditions. Payatas, a giant heap of putrid stinking garbage where the poor suffer endlessly. The men, women and above all the children spend their lives scratching the garbage for scraps to live on. The acrid smoke that covers the dump comes from the smouldering toxic waste. It causes lung diseases and asthma and endless ill health. Martin trudged silently through this garbage tip of hopelessness. His inner anger was controlled as he surveyed the depths of human misery. His face expressed feelings of pain and frustration that humans should be forced in such inhuman conditions. Here, the poverty is profound. He showed only compassion and caring, no revulsion at the nauseating stench that clung to our hair and clothes. The people were covered with the filth and the smell, the dirt and dust of the garbage. To the world of the well off they are outcasts, untouchables, lepers, but to Martin they were just people that were happy and feeling privileged in his presence. He embraced an old woman, held the hands of the children, called them God's people and asked me to give his apologies for intruding on their lives. He told me that he felt he was in a holy place, unworthy to be where God is present in the poorest of the poor asking us to be with them to help, in any small way to change their suffering into joy. After his visit to the Philippines Martin became more committed to the peace movement and joined more campaigns for human rights and social justice.

All we could do was support the campaign of the peoples organisations at the Payatas dump for the huge mountain of rubbish to be flattened and redeveloped and a decent life be given to the hundreds of poor. This went unheeded – despite the publicity Martin's visit brought. This trip was organised by Dennis Murphy and Ed Gerlock, two former priests who have dedicated their lives to helping empower the Filipino poor and elderly in Metro Manila. The people's concerns were well founded and they needed the publicity to get the government attention. The government ignored them. Then three years later on in 2000, after a week of torrential rain, the great mount of garbage was saturated and began to move. Slowly at first and then with unstoppable force a million tones of compressed garbage came avalanching into the village of scavengers squatting at it base. More than five hundred garbage pickers and their families were buried alive under the decomposing stinking mass. Only one hundred and fifty bodies were recovered, the rest were left buried under the mountain where they had the daily struggle of food and holding on to the barest thread of life.

Martin Sheen supported the PREDA Children's project and when we were nominated for the Nobel Peace Prize he was quoted as saying he would love to make a movie about the children helped by PREDA. Dozens of television documentaries were made about its work but no film yet.

Chapter Twenty-Seven

When the law creating the Subic Bay Metropolitan Authority (SBMA) in 1992 and establishing the Subic Bay Freeport came up in congress, Kate Gordon, being a congressional representative, was one of the sponsors and had an influential say in including a provision that set a six year fixed term for the chairman that would run the Subic Bay Freeport. In the committee discussions that worked to reconcile the congressional and Senate versions of the law, a few crucial words were included. After intense lobbying, the Gordon lawyers got wording that said that the Mayor of Olongapo may be the Chairman of the SBMA. Later in the final draft that was placed before the President for signing it was mysteriously changed to shall be chairman of the SBMA. By this means, Gordon, who had opposed the bases phase out became the government official mandated to implement the conversion plan that we, Conrad Tiu and many other truly patriotic Filipinos, had envisioned and helped bring about. Soon Gordon presented himself to the media as the champion of the conversion plan and claimed that it had been his idea all along. Well, he would wouldn't he?

I was not made welcome at the SBMA while Gordon was chairman so I rarely went there. Soon he was challenged for holding the double offices of both Mayor and chairman. He fought for both powerful positions but in the end lost and choose to be chairman of the SBMA. That's where the money was. Olongapo city was impoverished despite decades of Gordon rule and a thriving sex industry. No one knew where the millions had gone.

Sometimes with Merly and Alex I did some shopping inside the SBMA. We were followed about and photographed by security people wherever we went. My picture was pinned at the guard house like a wanted criminal. Paranoia reigned. Everyone was suspect and cars were searched and people needed special ID cards.

Later I discovered documents that showed how millions of missing pesos had been spent on buying leg irons, batons shields, riot equipment, guns, payrolls of volunteers, the leasing of houses and granting of business permits were all personally approved by the Chairman himself. A gigantic task that would have exhausted a lesser man. Indeed strange things were going on inside the SBMA, it became like an armed camp and little was leaked. I exposed some of the allegations in my column in the Philippine *Daily Inquirer*, the biggest daily newspaper where I had a Sunday column on the editorial page for eight years. Gordon objected vehemently to the editors and I was advised to cool the exposes. When a relative of the Gordon dynasty married a relative of one of the newspaper owners there was a change at the newspaper. My column was the first to be cancelled and how many items were shelved is only speculation.It was a board decision, not an editorial one I was told. Today my column is published in the Manila Times and several other newspapers from Hong Kong to England and on the Internet.

Gordon wanted to hold onto the job as chairman so he pressured president Fidel Ramos to appointment him for another six-year term in a midnight appointment just before his term of office expired and the elections began. Then as fate would have it film star Senator Joseph Estrada who was stoned and driven out of Olongapo in 1989 became the champion of the poor and was elected president on June 30, 1998 with a big majority. Money played a big role as it always does but those with most of it wins. There was consternation at the SBMA and in Olongapo city. Gordon was on the wrong side yet again.

Gordon was ordered out from the Chairmanship overnight. Felicito Payumo was to be the new chairman. Gordon was understandably apoplectic with rage and refused point blank to obey the direct decree of the President. If he succeeded it would be a humiliating defeat for the new president who would be seen as a weak and powerless, a lame duck from the start.

Gordon barricaded himself in Building 229 and called on the families of the unpaid volunteers, three thousand of them, to surround the building and act as a human shield in a last heroic act. Cowardly as this might seem to some it was for him a good move. I went there to see the situation for myself. It was unreal, everything was quite and picnic-like. Hundreds of people were sitting on the grass with umbrellas and hastily erected tarpaulins for shade from the blistering sun. Restaurants in Olongapo were delivering packed lunches. I believed the radio reports that negations were resolving the stand off.

The siege of building 229 began. Gordon was sure the police would not harm the women and children protecting him. He bought time by filing a petition before the Supreme Court asking them to confirm the legitimacy of his six-year fixed term. The court took a week to deliberate and ruled against Gordon. The position was a political appointment and ended with the term of the appointing president.

The police drafted in from other districts were unmindful of the women and children and launched an attack to break into the building. The women and children ran crying and screaming in fear and scattered in the grounds. The police drove out the goons inside and captured the building. I was called by a member of the dispensary to come and help bring out the wounded women and children as the main gate was closed and they could not get to the hospital. Many were hurt by flying glass and God knows how I rushed to the back gate in the PREDA van but it was blocked by vehicles and troops and there was no way I could pass.

Within an hour, the goons counterattacked the police and set on fire two fire engines. They mauled, stabbed and injured twenty-two police .Among Gordon's protectors seventy-three were hurt in the melee; then they fled into the main administration building where Gordon had transferred for a last stand. Here, another bloody confrontation ensued but finally the police prevailed and Gordon and his goons were evicted. All computer data about the leasehold deals negotiated by Gordon were mysteriously erased.

The international image of the Philippines as a secure and intelligently managed country plummeted as business at the Freeport stopped and an estimated US$3.5 million a day was lost. This penchant for violence and reckless disregard for the well being of the country to serve personal ambition has no precedent. For years Gordon accused me of damaging the image of Olongapo and the Philippines by speaking out against the child prostitution and branding the country as a haven for paedophiles, which was the true state of affair s because of the sex industry he encouraged and supported. Now in a few days of defiance he was causing untold damage to the vision we had of a prosperous and dignified Philippines that all could admire and respect. Instead of street fighter Gordon, we got a professional business manager in the person of the new chairman Felicito Payumo. A new era for the better at the SBMA had begun. But it was a sad day for us at PREDA. Thinking we had a great friend and supporter in the new chairman, we planned a new home for the children. After months of research preparation and having verbally won the approval of a majority of the board members to approve the project, Chairman Payumo brought it all crashing down when I addressed the board meeting. "The site is not suitable I have to disallow it," he said, "there is a place in the Navy Magazine that you could apply for." Everyone was in shock that turned to disgust. Now I understood why my power point presentation could not be played through the beamer, it was blocked. Payumo had made up his mind that democratic elections could be bypassed. The board, I realised, was just a front. The navy magazine area is ten kilometres from a school hospital or market and is surrounded by dense jungle. How could children be dumped in such isolation? We hoped that the future government would have compassion on the kids and give help and support for the children's home.

Chapter Twenty-Eight

It was a letter dated August 19, 1999 that started another campaign to help endangered children.

Dear Father Cullen,

A death threat looms over our children and youths in the streets of Davao City. The deliverer of doom is called a death squad disguised as a group of concerned vigilante citizens who promote peace and order. Some of our children and youth considered an unsightly nuisance to our community, have been killed in mysterious circumstances and this has endangered the lives of their friends.

We need your support to stop these senseless deaths and harassment inflicted on our children and youth in the streets of this so-called Child Friendly City. Please express your urgent concern by sending letters of protest to the City Mayor through this address: Hon. Mayor de Guzman, City Mayor, 8000 Davao City, Philippines. We call on you to urgently respond to this situation. We believe that it is only through our concerted actions that we can ensure the protection of the rights of our children and youth.

The letterwas signed by a very courageous leader of a children's rights group in Davao City, Pilgrim Bliss Gayo-Guasa.

Death squads are not new to the city of Davao. There is a history going back to the Alsa Masa and other fascist groups that unleashed a reign of terror on the city residents in 1988 to combat communist infiltration. Davao is a wealthy city in Southern Mindanao, (Mindanao is the second to the largest island of the Philippines), that thrives on tourism and the fruit industry.

The majority of the residents are impoverished and many fled there from the countryside. Government statistics showed that in 2006, Davao Del Sure had 24.2 per cent of families below the poverty line. Hundreds of hungry street children scrape a living from collecting recyclable junks from the garbage dumps and around the city streets. Their emaciated scarred and unwashed bodies, gaunt faces and tattered clothes are silent condemnations of the selfishness of those who have it all. Now they were being targeted by an assassination squad, out to cleanse the streets of their unwelcome presence.

Their unwanted existence is a living reminder that the power and property grabbing families have much to answer for. Their total power and domination of the political structure and the economy is the root cause of poverty and rebellion. These elite two hundred families, which make up the oligarchy, dominate Philippine politics and the government. Government resources and the opportunities such power enlarges their personal fortunes and keeps them in control. The opposition is another group of jealous clans seeking the top posts for themselves.

The dispossessed and land-less are left to die in disease-ridden slums. The street children are a constant reminder to the rich of their enormous guilt and assassination is their chosen method to get rid of them. By branding all as drug addicts and criminals they justify the killings and make them appear as necessary to maintain law and order. They present the executions as an exercise in civil virtue.

On July 6, 1999, two men in dark clothes riding on motor

bikes without plate numbers, equipped with radios and guns pulled up at the Galaxy cinema and levelled their weapons at two street kids. Two fearful shots rang out and Royroy and Mamay fell spurting blood on to the street. Another boy, Roger, ran as fast as he could and escaped into the crowds. He had recognised one of the killers. Many more youth had been shot, threatened and intimidated and a cloud of fear hung over the hundreds of street children. Nine days later, on July 19, a group of eleven children went with social workers to the City Hall to report the harassment and threats. Standing near the Mayor office was one of the hit men who had killed Royroy and Mamay. Terrified the children fled and hid. According to the human rights workers there was a total of one hundred and four children murdered on the streets since 1998. In 2002 the figure had risen to forty-six assassinated that year.

I wrote a letter dated September 8 1999 to the Mayor describing the killings and quoting a national newspaper article which said Mayor Benjamin de Guzman supported "secret marshals". I was leaving for abroad and arranged with the PREDA staff that the letter be sent a few days after I left. My letter explained:

This shooting and harassment of street children must stop. It is a direct violation of Philippine law, international law and the Convention on the Rights of the Child. As a city Mayor you will be held responsible before the International community for these atrocities against children. It is for this very reason that in my keynote speech before the World Forum on Children's Rights this September 5 (in Stockholm) I am calling for the establishment of an International Court of Children's Rights. Like the officials who allow, order or approve, by act or omission, the violation of human rights, are brought to trial at the International Court of Human Rights in the Hague, Netherlands, likewise higher leaders and civil authorities who cause, allow or approve the execu-

tion of impoverished street children by hit squads must be brought to trial.

I am appealing to the International Community and the Presidential Committee for the protection of children for direct action to stop these murders since you are unable to do so. I will appeal to the world community of child advocates to demand the killers be brought to trial.

They are known and have been identified; it is your duty to bring them to justice for the murders of these children. Denial and claims of ignorance about these murders have no credibility. The evidence is clear; children are being murdered on the streets by an organised squad of motorcycle riding gunmen.

If this is a method of curbing crime in your city then it is the cowardly and dastardly action heard of. Picking on malnourished, abandoned, vulnerable and defenceless children, is the worst of crimes.

Signed, Sincerely,
Fr Shay Cullen.

When I was in Stockholm that September at an International Conference on Children's Right I presented a paper at the World Forum calling for a special court to bring to justice those responsible for the mass killing, torture and abuse of children. My letter became part of our international letter writing campaign that asked our friends and supporters to write to the Mayor. Many quoted my letter and apparently this infuriated him. He set up a special response desk to answer the hundreds of letters pouring in and promptly sued me and the Child Advocacy Team of PREDA for libel.

Mayor De Guzman claimed that my letter was defamatory and said that "the whole scope and apparent object or motive of respondents – in that I, as Mayor of Davao city, harbour vigilantes out to murder street children and that the killing of malnourished, abandoned, vulnerable and defenceless street children by organised crime of motorcycle riding gunmen is a daily occurrence in Davao City under my administration..."

Of course I had made no such accusation but just pointed out the reality and the need of him, as the Mayor and most authoritative and duty bound to protect the children ought to do so and bring the criminals to justice. Perhaps painful to the Mayor was the statement I made saying that all high officials that allow the abuses ought to be accountable to the international community and international court of human rights. I never said that he had actually allowed or was behind the death squads.

Like most of the fifty-four or more court cases filed against me and the PREDA human rights advocates I answered this myself point by point in a long counter affidavit. I couldn't afford to hire a lawyer then. What I had written was not libellous, that it was a letter challenging the city official to do his duty or be held accountable. There was nothing wrong in saying that unless you say it to a powerful politician who doesn't like being held accountable for public safety. A long list of the newspaper articles had reported the many killings by the death squad. Most were shot in the head with the same .45 calibre weapon.

One point was that should a libel case like this be sent to court for trial then the law would be used as a weapon to instil fear in critics. It would restrain and inhibit the constitutional right to speak out and would silence the voice of the innocent who cry out for justice. This was especially true for advocates and defenders of children's rights. And according to Philippine court procedure that can issue an arrest warrant at once. The accused has to pay bail or go to jail and await trial. With a death squad around me I paid the bail. With the help of Robert Garcia our paralegal officer at PREDA and Alex, I responded and appealed the resolution of the Prosecutor all the way to the Department of Justice in Manila. Before that office gave an answer it was already February 2001 and the case had to be called in the Davao regional trial court where I was to be arraigned. We couldn't have it postponed any longer. I flew to Davao City wondering if the death squad would meet me at the airport and get it over with. I had been warned.

There was a welcome committee all right but it was a big group of street children with welcoming banners and placards calling for justice for children; the kids surrounded me and escorted me to a jeepney organised by Tambayan. As I was about to board the jeepney I noticed a huge billboard announcing Davao as the winner of *The Most Child Friendly City* in the Philippines. I should have known.

I stayed as a guest of the Maryknoll Fathers who were very supportive and encouraging. They too had been active behind the scenes and working with Fr Pete Lamata and Fr Paul Cunanan of the diocesan justice and peace to reach some kind of compromise.

The Mayor wanted a public apology from me and the PREDA team, which would have been tantamount to an admission of guilt. That I could never agree too. Once you stand up for something it's not wise to sit down again just because of threats. I told Fr Paul and Pete that there would be no apology and if convicted of libel for standing for children's rights, so be it, I would serve my sentence. I had no defence lawyer in Davao other than hiring a lady lawyer to file motions and get copies of court documents.

It was getting tense because the arrangement was the following day, February 14, 2001. Once arranged it would be very difficult to withdraw the information from the court and drop the case. There would be huge loss of face too. Something had to be done now. I suggested to my friends that if the Mayor failed to show up in court the case could be dismissed.

The next day the pavements were packed with supporters and well-wishers and street kids. I was surprised at the big number of supporters. I took it as a silent protest against the death squad. The courtroom was packed with media people, sisters, fathers and well-wishers. The heat was stifling and there were just two lazy fans churning the humid air. I sat with one of the Maryknoll Fathers, no Columban could make it, to my disappointment. Nevertheless the tension mounted as the time came to call the case and still the Mayor didn't show up. I felt there was a chance he world drop it and admit we were right. Suddenly there was a commotion by the door, the crowds parted as Mayor de Guzman's lawyer walked in. He was the Mayor's private Prosecutor and took his place at the crowded table before the Judge. The Judge ordered the case to be called: *The People of the Philippines versus Father Shay Cullen.*

The lawyer for the Mayor stood up and passed a letter to the clerk of court. The Judge read it and gave it back. Suddenly the buzz stopped and there was silence, all were straining to hear, microphones were outstretched, tape recorders were piled in front of the clerk as he began to read. The cameras were clicking, video cameras pointing and zooming to catch every movement and facial expression. The clerk of court stood and read the following: *Heeding the appeal of the religious led by Archbishop of Davao, Fernando R. Capalla, thru his emissaries, Fr Pete Lamata and Fr Paul Cunanan, and other Non-Governmental Organisations and well meaning Davaoenos, Mayor Benjamin C. De Guzman, in the spirit of genuine reconciliation and unity, has decided to forego the prosecution of Fr Shay Cullen and place all issues to rest so that he can attend to more pressing demands of the City. With this, Davaoenos can move on and look forward to a better and meaningful life ahead of them.*

The media people exploded, some rushed out talking to their mobile phones, cameras flashed. Applause was heard out in the corridor as the magic word spread: withdraw. Judge Robillo banged his gravel for order and ordered the clerk to continue. He looked very relieved. I was quietly delighted and quickly sent a text message to Alex and the team back at PREDA. We had won.

Judge Robillo gave his decision dismissing the case outright. Several months later the Department of Justice also ruled in our favour recognising the validity and correctness of our legal arguments. We, the children and the brave social workers of Davao got more publicity for the cause than we had ever dreamed of.

Mayor de Guzman lost the next election and his rival, Rodrigo Duterte, was elected. The death squad became more active and the killings increased. President Gloria Macapagal Arroyo appointed Duterte as crisis manager for Southern and Central Mindanao. A crises allegedly created by the rampant killing for which no one was arrested or brought to justice.

Chapter Twenty-Nine

Child pornography is the propaganda arm of sex tourism and goes beyond the computer or the television screen. For many, it incites the sex tourist and the paedophile to groom and seduce children to meet and abuse them. It fuels their imagination and their twisted sexual fantasies and can propel them to hunt and abduct, rape and murder children like Anthony Morss and Brett Tyler did. It also has a damaging life long impact on children themselves. Not only when they are used and abused in the process of making the child pornography, they are defiled every time it is replayed and shown. The abuse goes further.

Child pornography is used as a visual aid in grooming and training young children to overcome their instinctive reluctance and intense discomfort when they are sexually touched and made to perform sexual acts on adults. I was called to investigate reports of a foreign paedophile ring in the sex tourist destination, Puerto Galera in Mindoro, using child pornography to seduce little children. Investigators found a community of foreign men living in beach cottages and apartments luring children into their doorways with a promise to buy the trinkets and sea shells that the children were vending to the tourists. The kids, girls as young as eight to eleven years, were brought in to the beach houses, given lemonade while watching videos of children performing oral sex and then they were coached to do it on the "big daddies" and were rewarded with candies and money. They were told that the children on the TV were stars and everybody applauded what they were doing. The pimps and traffickers, some of them women, were waiting near by to get the children and the money. It came to light when a teacher noticed the unusual disturbed behaviour of one child in her class and with gentle coaxing succeeded in getting her to tell everything. Then the others told too.

Some of the suspects were arrested and jailed. One German got out after paying a lot of money. He mysteriously died the next day in his rented house. Other suspects fled with their appetites aroused and whetted to stalk and abuse more children in their own countries. Child sex tourism does not end at the airport after the holiday, it is just beginning. Police or politicians think it is better if their paedophiles abuse abroad there will be less of it in their own territory. But not so, it only becomes worse. The child sex abuser is insatiable. He has an uncontrollable appetite to abuse. That's why they are addicted like collectors of thousands of child pornographic photos and images. Some settle abroad to have constant satisfaction of their desires.

Like the one-time rock star Gary Glitter. Like many others, he went to Vietnam and Cambodia after he was arrested, convicted of possessing child pornography in 1999. He moved to V ng Tàu in Vietnam in March 2005 and sexually abused two children (10 and 11) and was jailed for two years in November 2005. It is a sentence that did not fit the crime. It is too light and inadequate for such a horrendous crime against helpless and impoverished children. Perhaps the Vietnamese have been desensitised to child abuse and prostitution by the long American military presence in their country during the Vietnam War when it became an accepted practice.

In Puerto Galera, there was a big cover up of the abuse of the beach babies by the public officials. They were more intent on protecting their foreign high paying customers and sex tourist business than the children. The child victims were hidden away. Not even the DSWD social workers could find and bring them into care. Two were eventually found and they were brought to the DSWD children's centre in Laguna. Statements were taken, charges were filed but that was an end to it. Even the US Embassy investigators met a stone wall of indifference and non-cooperation when they followed up leads I gave them about an American national abusing children there. No suspect was ever brought to trial. They had easily escaped. A few years later I found one of them, a German national, hiding in Austria and gave all the pinpoint information to the German Federal Police and promised to help them gather more evidence. What they did to bring him to justice I was not told.

Alex was invited by UNESCO to a conference in Paris in January to share with the delegates from all over the world our experiences and the efforts to track down the cyber-sex operators and porno kings that were making child pornography in the Philippines and selling it over the internet. By the year 2000, cyber sex operations were being set up all over the Philippines. Some were simple cubicles where pimps and even mothers would bring a young child to have her undress and gyrate in front of a camera connected to a computer. These images are then sold. The cyber dens were at the back of the sex clubs, internet shops and then in private houses. The young boys and girls were made to perform lewd acts in front of a video camera connected to an internet linked computer. The customer whether in Britain, Ireland or anywhere in the world could connect to the studio and request the sex act he preferred and then select the age of the performers and the sex acts live on his computer. The customer paid by credit card into some remote and untraceable account.

I was invited to a conference in Sweden the following March 2000 to talk to the Network of World Shops on the importance of campaigning in Fair Trade to bring trade justice and more equality into the world. It's a strategy that I promote as a vital positive way to combat trafficking and trading of children and young girls as commodities in brothels and cyber sex shops. We have to promote dignified work for their parents and education for the teenagers. PREDA Fair Trade provides dignified employment to hundreds of once impoverished people who are now prospering and protecting their children, preventing them from migrating to the cities and inevitably becoming victims in the sex industry.

It is extremely difficult to detect a cyber-sex child porn operation and the police do not think it is a crime. Many go to sex bars and some even operate their own using underage girls to attract the customers and usually inviting other police officers and government officials for a party and getting them involved with underage girls. The officials are then compromised by consorting with an underage girl and the sex club can get away with anything after that. There was a bar in Subic town. I was there to find minors and document their exploitation and then rescue them. On hidden camera, I asked the Mamasan if we were safe from the police since we were talking to underage girls. "You are very safe. No police will touch you here, you can do what you like with them,",she said motioning to the children.

"Why is that?" I asked. The owner of this bar is a policeman, and she threw back her head and roared with laughter.

Many police and local officials think that sexual abuse of women and children in the home is a domestic matter and they negotiate an amicable settlement. A compensation payment is made to the parents of the victim by the abuser. The officials get a hefty percentage from the paedophile, for being so helpful in arranging the pay off. The child is traumatized and left without help, the parents end up pimping their own child and the paedophile goes free to abuse other children. This corrupt practice in the system of local government is what we tackled through our human rights education seminars as part of the project funded by Irish Aid abroad. This is a project to strengthen human rights in developing countries. It was very effective in alerting the people to their rights and many more came to report child abuse and bring their children into the care of the PREDA Children's Home.

The police like to imitate the action movies where the police heroes are inevitably in fast car chases going after drug pushers, kidnappers and bank robbers and ending up in a bloody shoot out. I was almost shot myself in one keystone cop like fiasco.

I was on another undercover operation in Manila to arrest two pimps selling minors for sex. Craig Kilburger, the young Canadian advocate against child labour was with me learning about the exploitation and slavery of the child prostitutes. We had what we believed was a professional police unit surrounding the McDonalds in Manila where the pimps pick up and sell the kids like Michael Clarke did for the price of a hamburger. I had the camera crew hidden in a van and I wore a hidden camera. The social workers were waiting in another van nearby to take the minors into care. As soon as the pimps brought the girls and offered them for sex, on camera, I gave the signal for the police to move in and cuff the two traffickers. Instead of a quiet arrest, the undercover cops came rushing from all directions shouting and screaming with guns drawn. For a moment I thought they would open fire. We all froze with fright and the first four policemen grabbed the two terrified pimps and pushed them to the car park. I thought they were going to grab me and Craig too. The TV camera was out of the van and immediately every one of them wanted to be an action hero. Those who had no suspect to cuff ran off to get one and came back with our two drivers and cuffed them too. They were like the keystone cops running all over the place.

At least the children were saved. The pimps were charged

(although they bought their way out later) and Craig had important documentary evidence of the worst form of child labour. It was a moving experience that helped him raise public awareness in Canada about enslavement of children in brothels for years to come.

The work of "Onechild", another youth led Canadian organisation fighting the trafficking of sexually exploited children came to PREDA to learn about the situation and make a highly acclaimed documentary. Cheryl Perera, who started "Onechild", helped influence public opinion and strengthen the political will to make Canada more child protective and responsive to trafficking and abuse. Today Canadian police operate the world's most sophisticated integrated computer tracking and identification system. Wanted paedophiles and missing children are being found in record numbers. Later in 2006, Onechild formed a partnership and made a commitment to help PREDA combat the trafficking and help in the recovery of the victims.

At PREDA, the daily work saving children taking them into care in the PREDA Children's Home and bringing their abusers to justice went on. The death penalty was one of the major obstacle to getting children to testify against their abusers especially parents or relatives who had raped them. PREDA social workers could not ask young children to testify, even in a child friendly way, when it might result in the execution of their own father. Their brothers and sisters would blame them for the rest of their lives. We campaigned against the death penalty with other human rights organisation and the Christian churches were very outspoken against it. Eventually in 2006, it was abolished by an act of Congress.

We had some terrible cases in Olongapo at this time. A three-years-old girl was raped and murdered by a sixteen-years-old on drugs in Barrio Barretto, not far from the PREDA Centre. Then a six-year old girl was gang raped in Gordon heights, a residential part of the town and there were several more serious cases that were evidence of the long -

term damage done to the moral fabric of the city by the sex industry. Young people grew up influenced by the tolerance of promiscuous sexual behaviour.

The growing number of broken homes, abandoned children and wives jettisoned for underage girls is evidence of moral breakdown. The number of sexually abused children under twelve was growing alarmingly and the press was warned not to report such sensationalism, it made the city look bad, besides the energetic and highly organised Mayor kept insisting it was the cleanest in the entire Philippines.

Little of this reached the tightly controlled media. Journalists lives were always under threat if they wrote stories critical of the administration. Throughout the Philippines it was similar. The one thing that proud Filipino politicians can't endure is the shame of the truth. They hate being exposed. Over a hundred journalists have been killed in the recent years and in 2006 alone ten were brutally murdered. Most were radio reporters and commentators and they invariably exposed some corrupt practice of a politician or local mafia boss. I was nervous myself during all these killings and they are still going on as state sanctioned death squads kill at will. It was enough to make any writer or journalist practice restraint and self-censorship.

When I wrote about the alleged crimes of the sex mafia in the Philippines, I always had to be careful. I had my share of death threats and had to watch my back. I was scared at times too. Threats work but we can't give in to them because that's a green light for the politicians, abusers and criminals to silence the media and bury the truth.

There were so many new cases coming to PREDA that we had to build a new home for the rescued children with the continuous help of Kindernothilfe, the leading child support agency in Germany. We built and opened the new home in March 2001. We needed a safer and more spacious home and it came just in time. We lost that week our special Prosecutor for child abuse cases when the awarded Prosecutor Dorintino

Floresta was appointed as a Judge in another province and this opened the way for the former City Prosecutor to return who dismissed almost every child abuse case against suspected paedophiles so other cities would look child friendly and get the big money prize as most child friendly city in the Philippines as I wrote earlier. However, frame ups and false charges against us by the sex mafia were allowed to prosper and we had a hard fight every time to show they were fabricated.

The previous year, the sex mafia and those politicians protecting the paedophiles used dummies to file twenty-seven complaints against me and the PREDA staff. The year before, they filed seventeen complaints. Most of them charged me with libel for what I wrote in my weekly column published in newspapers and on newly opened PREDA website. The website receives thousands of visitors and they can download huge amounts of information. Advocacy through the internet is hugely important.

The website is managed by two of our own student graduates, Filipino-American brothers, left behind by their American father, and whom we helped through computer school. They do amazing work and the PREDA website was one of the twelve finalists from a world-wide selection by the committee of Bettinhoe Media Award. This is a Canadian Association for ProgressiveCommunications. The PREDA website was cited for its excellence in campaigning for human rights using modern communications in 2002.

The complaints were varied; grave oral defamation when we asked questions, obstruction of justice when we prevented a child witness from being abducted, slander when we counter charged, and kidnapping when we rescued a child from an abuser. When another journal published the name of a minor involved in a court case we were charged with child abuse. The sex mafia tried every dirty trick to blacken and smear our name and failed. We defended ourselves and showed that the so-called evidence was false and fabricated.

We won almost every single case at the preliminary stages and the few that reached court were allegedly helped along with a generous gratuity to the Prosecutor. They too were dismissed by the Judge as lacking merit.

The worst frame up of all was by one of the Mafias dummies. A middle aged American whom we suspected of child abuse, American Joe we call him, is a former employee of the US Air force that retired in Olongapo city. He bought a house in the nearby province and set up home with a middle aged Filipino woman called Fat Mama as his housekeeper and mother image. He brought her two children, a boy Arnold, and girl Alice into the house and sent them to school. American Joe became intimate with the twelve-years-old Alice. He put the house in her name perhaps in exchange for her daughter. In an amazingly frank interview at PREDA taped with American Joe's permission, he admitted being with the twelve-years-old in bed and he wanted to marry her. That is what her mother wanted too. The child didn't. He admitted too that he had shown her pornography videos and she confirmed our worst fears and disclosed that after that he lay with her in the bed. Her brother Arnold confirmed that they went to bed together.

American Joe's adopted fourteen-years-old son Reggie and Arnold watched American Joe's pornographic videos when he was away then they tried to practice what they saw on the screen and sexually abused American Joe's adopted six-years-old daughter Daisy several times. She fought back and loudly complained to Fat Mama and American Joe but they did nothing about it, smacked her and told her to shut up. But the brave child wouldn't be intimidated, instead she told her classmates and her teachers. When the PREDA social workers heard from Daisy's teachers about the abuse, they alerted the government social worker and police and the child was taken into care at the PREDA Children's Home. When Arnold was questioned by the investigating Prosecutor he admitted he and Reggie had abused Daisy several times and he willingly signed an affidavit. When American Joe learned Arnold had told all about his intimacies with Alice and confessed to his own abuse of Daisy, he went apoplectic . He knew we had the evidence that might put him on trial and in prison. He ran to the sex mafia boss, a German paedophile protector to get help and advice. With the German's sleazy lawyer, American Joe filed against us numerous charges of kidnapping, grave oral defamation, libel and blamed me for the abuse of Daisy no less. He was furious and unrelenting to get back at us. All these baseless charges were proven false and dismissed. American Joe had an overpowering belief in his own superiority and was affronted that his secret was out. He vowed to get even with everybody who thwarted him.

He succeed with the help of the mafia lawyer and a dodgy Judge to get Daisy out of the custody and safety of the PREDA Children's Home into the government child care centre. There she continued to accuse the two boys and charges were prepared against them by government lawyer and the social workers. American Joe was infuriated and filed charges against the government social workers, the regional director of the DSWD and against the Prosecutor who had been especially appointed by the Secretary of Justice to stem the non-stop dismissal of child abuse complaints by the city Prosecutor.

In response to another pleading by American Joe, the dodgy Judge returned Daisy to his house where the two abusers were staying. It was a disaster for justice. Daisy was in his power. She was now terrified and intimidated and silenced. She could never testify against her two abusers who still had access to her. We hope Daisy was able to fight them off. They were silenced too and would never testify against American Joe. The charges against the two boys were archived by the court because Daisy was not available to testify. There would be no court case, just more non-stop filing of charges against us to harass and try to discredit us. There were fifty-two in all and all but an oral defamation case and libel were dismissed as baseless fabrications. American Joe had the help of the German paedophile protector and was seen as an eccentric troublesome crank. It was a hard two years but in the end we won out and the truth was exposed. The harassment didn't end on the courtroom steps, it continues to this day.

Our children's rights advocacy campaign was expanding too. A PREDA staffer went to Yokohama to the World Congress on the sexual exploitation of children and brought back many important insights and contacts. Then eight of the PREDA recovering children went to Kufou City in Japan to visit a children's centre there directed by Mr. Masao Tagaya, a very progressive and dedicated children's rights advocate and teacher. He pioneered new approaches to helping disabled and retarded children in Japan. The "Free The Children" group in Japan funded a new jeepney for the children at PREDA to get them to school safely. We launched the Angel Annie campaign in November to raise public awareness about the rights of children to be free from sexual exploitation. We launched it with a big rock concert at the Subic Bay Free Port and the logo of the sketch of a child with a broken wing and a tear. We opened our mobile phone hot line for receiving reports of abused children by text messages and distributed thousand of stickers and information pamphlets. More children were referred for protection and care and more abusers were charged and, eventually, jailed.

Chapter Thirty

The historical German City of Weimar gave me its prestigious Human Rights Award in 2000 but a German national, Hartmut Joost, based at Baloy Beach in Olongapo City, wrote to the selection committee to block the award. He submitted a list of reasons why I or PREDA did not deserve to win the prestigious award which was to be approved that June and present on Human Rights Day on December 10. Mr. Joost is from the German district of Verden, near Bremen, North Germany. He lived in the Philippines for more than sixteen years and married a Filipino, Zenaida Joost, and had one son. Mr. Joost has always been most helpful to foreign tourists when they are accused of sexually abusing children. His closeness to the distinguished politicians of the city earned him the position of Liaison Officer of the foreign community. Several thousand are residents, retirees or overstaying tourists of all nationalities. Many are retired US Navy men. More are investors in the tourist business providing rest and young female companionship to the weary and worn international travellers.

For example in October and November 1997, Mr. Joost hurried to the side of Victor Keith Fitzgerald to help him appeal his conviction for child abuse to the Court of Appeals. After his trial and conviction in the Regional Trial Court, the two child victims were taken by their parents from the PREDA Children's Home and were found later to be working at the Tahiti sex bar in Subic town. American citizen Bill McCune, a retired pilot and friend of Mr. Joost e-mailed me to explain why he was with the child in the sex bar – to rescue her of course. He failed to report this serious crime of a prostituted child to the authorities, however. It made me wonder. The prepared affidavits that the children were made sign recanted their court testimony and claimed that they had been forced to lie by the PREDA staff. Mr Joost, as the record shows, was as helpful as ever and brought the young victims from their place of work at Tahiti with the help of McCune to the office of the Solicitor General to make a sworn statement. The petition to reverse the conviction then went to the Court of Appeals.

After two years of due deliberation, the court on September 27, 1999 denied that appeal and said it was absurd that I or the PREDA staff would influence the children. They recanted their testimony for monetary consideration, the three Judges unanimously said. We were completely exonerated of any wrongdoing. The unfortunate Fitzgerald was not so lucky: the Court increased his sentence from eight years to fourteen-to-twenty years. He was almost bankrupt as a result.

Mr. Joost, as helpful as ever, had friends among the Diocesan clergy and tried to make up for his blunder with the help of his close friend and adviser, Australian Fr Michael Duffin. Fr Michael, uncomfortable in Australia, became permanently attached to the Diocese of Iba, Zambales. Father Michael, like his fellow Australian was a sailing enthusiast with his own yacht and Baloy Beach was his favourite anchorage when he came to Subic Bay. The mothers and the girls were brought to Bishop Deogracias Iniguez, Jr. and were encouraged to tell their well rehearsed tearful story of how they were forced to lie and sin against the eighth commandment, "thou shalt not give false testimony against thy neighbour", but now they were sorry and repented. Good Bishop Iniguez was deeply moved and signed an affidavit on

February 2, 2000 supporting Fitzgerald and said PREDA might have exceeded bounds in influencing the children to give false testimony and called for a retrial. A serious allegation, unfounded and damaging to our reputations and credibility. If the bishop was telling the world in a public testimony in court that we were likely to have framed up suspects then if it stood unchallenged how about all the other suspected paedophiles, traffickers and child abusers we brought to court when we rescued their sex enslaved child victims? The bishop overstepped the mark himself. He acknowledged but, for some unknown reason, ignored the decision of the Court of Appeals that exonerated us.

The diocesan clergy also heard the sorrowful tale during their monthly meeting on February 7, 2000 and were so emotionally touched. Some clergy of delicate nature reportedly held hands and were teary eyed. From a total of forty-three clergy, twenty-seven signed the appeal letter there and then to support a retrial for the convicted paedophile and questioning our integrity. No one thought of asking our side as natural justice would demand.

Later in open court, the good Bishop Iniguez testified to what he had signed despite our explanation that the Court of Appeals had already exonerated PREDA and our appeal for fairness. The fact that PREDA therapists were assisting victims of clerical sexual abuse in the diocese at the time might have influenced the outcome. More astoundingly, one of the accused clergy was the god-son of the diocesan attorney who had defended Fitzgerald at the trial and berated Alex and myself in the courtroom. His dual position as a political manager of Mayor Richard Gordon gave added weight to his opinions, apparently shared with the bishop. The separation of Church and State was difficult to see. The attempt of politicians to compromise the bishops is not an isolated practice. In 2006, at the annual meeting of the Catholics Bishops Conference of the Philippines whether the church ought to support or not, the impeachment of President Macapagal-

Arroyo, for cheating in the elections and other high crimes, they were given envelops stuffed with cash and free air tickets and lavish dinner parties. This attempted corruption of the bishops was revealed by those bishops who had the courage to speak out and condemn it. Others did not.

There was no time for our side to be heard, we were later told. Fitzgerald had to be freed without delay. There was no rush, he was not lonely in the Olongapo City jail either because the prison visitors' book shows that the children he was infatuated with and had abused were brought to him in his cell several times. According to the prisoners, Fitzgerald had the cell to himself and they could see and hear everything. The children were prompted by their mothers to ask his forgiveness and he forgave them and then he hugged and cuddled them and made up. The children happily received monetary gifts. The acting prison chaplain, Fr. Duffin and the warden were pleased with the reconciliation they helped bring about. We brought the whole matter to the attention of the Papal Nuncio at the time. The Bishop was promoted to a diocese in Metro Manila.

The Court of Appeals made no further ruling for or against Fitzgerald, it refused to act. The original sentence still stands. A local Judge however was persuaded to grant Fitzgerald bail and he was joyfully met and welcomed at the prison gate by his friends Hartmut Joost and Fr Michael Duffin who had stood by his fellow Australian throughout the whole ordeal. The happy group then posed for a media photograph outside the jail. Months later after being released, Fitzgerald was caught on a surveillance video through an open door in a beach house with younger girls he seemed to love so much. The police made no investigation.

Then I had the unpleasant duty to bring a formal charge against Mr. Joost regarding the sudden disappearance of a child witness, thirteen-years-old Maria, a child complainant under the care of PREDA who had also accused Mr. Fitzgerald of abusing her on his yacht. The case had to be archived by Judge Santos because the child disappeared on November 3, 1997 during a home visit and could not appear in court. To get her out of the legal custody of PREDA, friends of Fitzgerald, unknown to us, had her legally adopted by an American couple in a court in another town. In a statement to the National Bureau of Investigation, Mr. Joost said she was with a diplomatic couple in Manila. He knew of her whereabouts but refused to tell the investigators where and was then a prime suspect linked to her disappearance. The NBI agent testified in court on March 20, 2001 to this. When removed from the protection and care of the PREDA Children's Home she could never testify against Fitzgerald. Mr. Joost was then charged by me in court in Olongapo for the Obstruction of Justice Violation of Presidential Decree 1829. The case still drags on, unresolved still, nine-years later such is his mastery of the judicial system. Mr. Joost denies all the charges.

At that time Mr. Joost was so upset that he wrote to the awarding committee of the City of Weimar to try to block the Human Rights Award that was to be given to PREDA. The support for PREDA was overwhelming and the research done by a distinguished panel of experts on the awarding committee proved the allegations to be false and trumped-up and they voted overwhelmingly to give the award to PREDA much to the disappointment of Mr. Joost and the other politicians, paedophiles and sex tourists that detest our work.

It is hard for ranking government officials not to fall into temptation of honey traps placed in front of them by the pimps and traffickers of children. Once they fall into such a forbidden relationship with a minor they are trapped in the blackmail and extortion ring of the sex mafia. They have to cooperate with the mafia and give protection and allow them to act with impunity or else be exposed and charged with child rape. That is how it works, they have to protect each other. Some lawyers are also on the municipal or city council and members of town or city, women and child protection committees but they also give legal service to defend accused traffickers and paedophiles at the same time. No one other than the social workers defending child victims raises even a question. This and the "areglo" system where officials arrange a pay off with the paedophile for the parents when the child has been raped must be the inherent signs of a failed state or at least a very corrupt one.

Even though Mr. Joost was a respected member of that group and helped the tourists in trouble with the law we had to take further action and file deportation charges against him with the Commissioner of Immigration in Manila where his impunity hopefully would not extend. It was a dangerous move as he had many influential friends and had close contacts to certain judicial personalities, some since exposed, disgraced and removed by the Supreme Court and Department of Justice. Like rotten apples, more are sure to fall as the good and dedicated people in government and the judiciary get the upper hand.

The deportation resolution signed by the Commissioner Andrea Domingo and three other associate commissioners on December 2, 2002 was evidence of good people doing their best. The resolution alleged that Hartmut Joost was accused of being a supporter and protector of a paedophile support ring, a group of suspected child abusers and he was charged with obstruction of justice. But still Mr. Joost denied all the charges.

Commissioner Domingo noted in her resolution the evidence that Mr. Joost was instrumental in trying to reverse the conviction of Fitzgerald. He allegedly persuaded the complaining witnesses to retract their testimony to falsely blame the PREDA staff and officers for inducing them to give false testimony and led the conviction of Fitzgerald. The commissioner also noted another case in which he allegedly gave false testimony against the commissioner and associates that signed the deportation order. Being a man of contacts in influential circles allegedly with some power over them and they beholden to him, he was able to circumvent the deportation order.

Then, three years later, on October 5, 2005, the *Manila Bulletin* and the Philippine's *Daily Inquirer*, leading newspapers, reported that Mr. Joost had been arrested in Olongapo. The story told about a German fugitive wanted in Germany for allegedly kidnapping and robbery and extortion of a German couple, Norly and Wilko Klauenberg over a decade ago. Hartmut Edward Joost (65) was arrested on Baloy beach. The international arrest warrant was issued by a German Court in March 2005 and the European Union issued one in December. He was to be immediately deported back to Germany. The arrest warrant said that Joost had allegedly conspired with two others, Swiss nationals, Cyril End and Regula Muller and two agents of the National Bureau of Investigation (NBI) to kidnap and force the couple to sign blank sheets of paper and these were later used to have the Klauenbergs' beach resort property turned over to the name of Zenaida Joost. The official record shows that the gang of five got an arrest warrant based on false charges against the Klauenberg couple filed in the Olongapo court accusing them of illegal recruitment of overseas workers. They flew to Busuanga, Palawan Island on November 24, 1994 with the arrest warrant that ordered the NBI agent David Golla to bring them (Klauenbergs) to the Olongapo Court. They found Norly there. The husband Wilko was in Manila that time. They took her by force, ransacked the house, robbed a safe deposit box with twenty-five thousand Deutschmarks and all the documents to the land and property. Norly was stripped of her jewellery and forced onto the light plane and flown to Manila.

There, she was taken to a restaurant and allegedly forced to sign the blank sheets. Wilko was picked up at a hotel where he was staying while buying materials for the resort. He was forced at gunpoint to sign blank sheets of paper too. He was robbed of cash and jewellery. Joost allegedly threatened to kill him if he made reports to the police according to the official documents filed in the German Court. The arrest warrant was served on November 24, 1994 and what has confounded investigators is how the deed of sale putting the land and beach resort into the name of Zenaida Joost is signed and dated November 25, 1994 when they were both supposed to be in the Olongapo jail. Despite an investigation by the NBI and the serious amount of evidence that would lead to a conviction, no charges were brought against Mr. Joost who denied all the allegations. When the Klauenberg couple asked me to help them get more evidence, I did my best to help them and went with other NBI agents to Palawan to interview more witnesses. These were employees of the resort who saw the gang allegedly kidnap Norly and bring the safe with the money to the plane. This apparently convinced the German Court to issue the arrest warrant and the EU to do the same and, as a result, Mr. Joost was detained at the Bicutan Immigration Jail in October 2005 and was not immediately deported.

Then astoundingly, the following January, he was released under circumstances no one could explain. Senator Jamby Madrigal, a human rights advocate in the Senate, conducted an investigation into the Joost affair but the authorities were baffled and could not explain why the German Court reversed its arrest warrant. No one knows who is blocking the prosecution of these suspects in Germany. Joost made the authorities look incredibly foolish by beating deportation a second time. The indefatigable Philippine Senator M.A. Consuelo "Jamby" Madrigal in the course of investigating the impunity of suspected women and child traffickers uncovered the corruption and injustice of this case – put it on the public record.

Chapter Thirty-One

Two years after Joseph Estrada was elected president and fired Dick Gordon as chairman of the Subic Bay Metropolitan Authority that administered the Subic bay Freeport there was a massive political upheaval and a fever of high hope ran through the country that a truly democratic society might be at hand if Estrada resigned. He was under pressure to do so because of mounting allegations of corruption and cronyism and inefficiency. He struck back and took on the prestigious *Manila Times* and forced it into virtual bankruptcy and a forced takeover to silence it. He tried the same on the Philippine's *Daily Inquirer* but was unable to take it over. Hoping to divert the media and improve his image as being tough on insurgency Estrada declared all out war on Muslim Mindanao. He ran afoul of the church with his alleged heavy gambling, drinking and womanising. Eventually lavish houses and resorts where his mistresses were kept were exposed by the media. In October 2000, Cardinal Jaime Sin called on him to resign as being morally unfit to hold office. Then a gambling crony Governor Chavit Singson from Cagayan Del Norte was almost ambushed in Manila by Estrada military over a money dispute. Singson went public and confessed he was giving Estrada monthly millions of pesos payoffs from illegal gambling syndicates that he controlled. That is the usual source of political funds that keeps politicians in power. The opposition filed impeachment charges and prevailed by

December 7, 2000. Supreme Court Justice Hilario G. Davide Jr. presided over the impeachment trial held before the Senate in the full glare of the TV cameras. The nation sat glued to the television as the drama unfolded and most popular movie hero, defender of the poor, was accused of amassing 3.3 billion pesos in eighteen months.

The showdown came when the Senators loyal to Estrada refused to allow crucial evidence to be presented that would reveal this money in a bank account traceable to President Estrada. The presidency of Joseph Estrada hung on the evidence that was in an envelope. The Senate, acting as a Judge, said it must be put to a vote whether to open the envelope or not. The voting began and it was split evenly between loyalists and opposition. The Leader of the Senate, Pimentel, loyal to Estrada, voted last and it was decided in favour of Estrada. The prosecution panel resigned and left the chamber. There was widespread disgust at the Senators who refused to admit the evidence and thousands of people began to gather at the EDSA shrine where the mass demonstrations brought down the tyrant president Ferdinand Marcos years before. The Estrada cabinet resigned and the second People's Power Revolution had begun. The huge crowds paralysed the metropolis and the military withdrew support form Estrada. He was isolated and word spread that he had fled the palace. On January 19, 2001 the mass demonstrators began to march on the palace and loyalist supporters massed there dispersed before a confrontation could develop. The Supreme Court Justice Hilario Davide Jr. declared Estrada incapacitated to rule and swore in to office the Vice President Gloria Macapaga–Arroyo the next day.

I arrived in Manila from Germany where I had just received a civic reception in connection with the awarding of the Human Rights award from the City of Weimar and laid a wreath at the Memorial stone in the former Nazi concentration camp of Buchenwald. The stone is always maintained at the exact temperature of a human body, one thing that all humanity has in common. Here, political prisoners were detained, tortured and executed by a bullet at the back of the head or by strangulation by being hung up on metal hooks high on the wall with wire around their necks. Then the bodies were put into an elevator and brought to the crematorium. Their body parts were looted and they were shoved into the oven to burn. Outside was a huge photo showing the piles of skeletal bodies found by allied troops. I felt sick in my stomach as I looked on the stark evidence of what evil humans do to each other. Humans are the only species that kill and murder and systematically sexually abuse their own children and turn many more into slaves of paedophiles and pimps. If the abuse of children and women is about power, domination and control of others, I had seen enough for one lifetime. The taste of political power that oppresses innocent people and allowed abuse must cast a dark question about the personal lives and practices of those who held power with such irresponsibility. What twisted deviant people could do this to other humans because they disagreed with them? The paedophiles, some say, are incapable of relating emotionally or sexually to adults in a mature relationship because of childhood neglect, rejection, harsh treatment and being unloved as children. They grow up isolated and powerless before adults and can only relate to other children, especially younger ones over whom they can exercise control and power.

In the next few years in the Philippines we were to see the rise of similar Nazi-like practices of torture, executions, and beheadings as President Arroyo consolidated her power. Many journalists, broadcasters, human right workers and farmers organisers were assassinated almost daily, allegedly by military intelligence hit squads. The international sex tourists and child exploiters continued their activities with impunity threatening and harassing us in our work protecting abused children. I had a number of death treats in my time and one was more bizarre than another.

One day a fax arrived advising me to be careful, people were concerned for me because they heard a big sum of money was paid to have me shot. Unlike anonymous untraceable phone calls and text messages, this had a return fax number on the heading. I noticed it was a local number. I called that number hoping it was a phone/fax as is frequently the case in the Philippines. It was and the owner of a gasoline station in Subic Town ten minutes away answered. Together with Robert, our paralegal officer, I went there and asked about the fax. The owner was shocked.

"How could you know about it so quickly?" she asked. But then she would not tell me who had sent it.

"My life is in danger," I said. " I want to know or I will call the police."

That did it.

"It was sent by the Carmelite Sisters," she said.

I was shocked at first then I understood they really had insider information and were genuinely warning me. With Robert I went to the Carmelite convent where I celebrated the mass from time to time. They knew me well and I talked to the External Sister. She was doubly shocked and ran inside the cloister to speak to the Reverend Mother. When she returned, she told me that a penitent had confided and the sisters were under an oath of secrecy not to tell me the source until they were safe. But it was true, an insider had overheard a late night conversation. A foreigner had conspired with a powerful politician to hire a local to do it and they discussed the cost – a mere thousand dollars for the job. I was humiliated to learn I was only worth a thousand dollars. Now I was really scared. I had to take precautions. I learned never to go the same way to the same place at the same time with the same vehicle and never to be alone in an isolated place. I watched all cars following behind mine and so on. We were accustomed to being under surveillance by the authorities and one agent of the SBMA during the time of Chairman Gordon gave me a copy of the official surveillance reports.

Another time during Martial Law when priests and pastors were being targeted by assassination squads and Fr Romero, a human rights activist disappeared after the military picked him up, a group of three men and two women came to me at PREDA. They said they were members of the Communist Party and the New Peoples Army (NPA) and wanted me to contact the military and help them surrender. *Who were they in truth?* I asked myself. *Were they government agents testing me to see if I would or wouldn't assist them surrender?* I was being tested or trapped. If I said yes and went to the military then I ran the risk of being tagged as an agent of the repressive government and an informer. If I advised against surrender and they were undercover military intelligence out to entrap me I was done for. Jesus himself must have felt trapped too when they asked him if it was right to pay taxes to the repressive Romans or not, either way he answered he would be denounced. His answer was perfect. My answer was that they needed good legal advice and representation. I would refer them to a good human rights lawyer the next day and pay him to represent them. That was the last I saw of them. They were military intelligence undercover agents in my opinion. Anyway, the women had traces of nail varnish, the men too soft of hand and face to be mountain living NPA's and the imitation Gucci shoes of one woman was a real giveaway. It could have been the end for me had I put my foot in it. The election 2001 was coming the following May and already the political climate was heating up.

In Olongapo, the progressive clergy with a love of human rights organised a rally for just and peaceful elections and invited Fr Robert Reyes, a nationally known advocate for human rights and clean elections. He is a kind of folk hero with strong media support for opposing oppressive government and human rights violations. His campaign was against Trapos, a common term for traditional politicians who form family dynasties and alliances that rule the nation by controlling the congress and making laws and legislation that benefit their economic interests. They had no interest in new laws protecting children from abuse and children being imprisoned. Fr Robert is called the "Running Priest" and does jogging runs for justice and peace. He mobilizes the youth and public to get healthy exercise and healthy politics too. The morning of March 21 was blistering hot and I was togged out to join the run from PREDA into the city, a good three kilometres. I still play half-court basketball at sixty-four-years-of-age with the staff and boys and go swimming to stay fit but this would be a challenge, I was fifty-nine then. The caravan of pickup trucks and vans with flags, music, balloons and cheering riders led by Fr Robert and about thirty joggers arrived along the highway passing below the PREDA Centre on the way to the city. Our group joined in and off we went, I was wheezy keeping pace with Fr Robert (half my age). He set a tough pace and as joggers everywhere know it has to be steady and maintained. At the city we marched with banners and flags to the roundabout with the warriors head and the PREDA youth organisation staged a street theatre skit on human rights issues. Then the skit against sex tourism and child exploitation was played out in front of the City Hall. The officials of Kate Gordon, the wife of former Mayor Richard, now a senator, came out and berated the youth. Alex, never one to back off a confrontation over human rights, engaged them in robust argument.

Later there was a Eucharistic celebration of life and human dignity on a flatbed truck near the circle with ten priests concelebrating. There was a huge crowd. Later at Rizal Park, Alex and Fr Robert made impassioned speeches calling for fair elections and an end to tyrannical trapos, oppressive government and domineering dynasties. The Gordon administration officials looked out from their office windows and were not amused. They were restrained from unleashing their goons by the presence of media that Fr Robert always attracts. This was the first opposition rally in many years and the people flocked to hear the message. It was not likely to influence the election outcome because most people were afraid to vote against the powerful family dynasty. Retaliation could be swift and deadly when a district voted against them. However, it is always better to light the proverbial candle of truth than curse the darkness of ignorance and oppression.

In 2001 it was very different. Many were being killed day after day by men riding motor bikes or vans. No entrapment was needed; just a hail of gun fire and it was over. Like in Davao, the street kids got it full in the face. Journalists and broadcasters got it in the chest or head as they stepped out of the radio station or office. The killers attacked without fear of apprehension or identification. After the faxed warning from the Carmelite Sisters I became watchful and suspicious of motorbikes idling outside the house or on street corners when I was in Manila. An innocent ice-cream cart I imagined hid an assassin.

One day a tough looking man drove up to the PREDA centre on a Saturday when there were few about and talked to the social worker on duty. He had two girls with him that wanted to escape the sex clubs, he said. When the social worker was interviewing them he asked for the bathroom but instead he went fearlessly around the house up to the second floor and asked a student where my room was. He was told I was in Manila. Hearing this he quickly left with the girls. That was the scariest incident of all. I immediately got more students to live-in and keep tight security. Nowadays it is more necessary to watch out for accused paedophiles or their agents coming in to get one of our children during their time in the playground.

The news of the assassination of my friend and classmate Fr Rufus Hally shocked me to the core; I still can't get over it. He was a martyr for peace. Fr Rufus was brutally gunned down on his way back to his parish on August 28, 2001 by unidentified killers. I was stunned. We were good friends and he was a man of deep spirituality and close to God with such sympathy and understanding of the Filipino Muslims that he was loved and respected by them in their thousands. Parts of Mindanao are areas of conflict between Muslims and the national government troops. Estrada declared war on them when they resisted oppressive policies that only impoverished them. Rufus spoke out against the military shelling and burning of Muslim villages and he gave his life for them. His school had eighty percent Muslim children and he refused to say mass at the military camp so as not to offend the Muslims by showing solidarity with their enemies. Besides they had their own chaplain. He tried to stand on neutral ground but it was tilting to the side of the victims of atrocities. He had caused the military commander to loose face and had tried to expose the human rights violations in the press.

Then one day when he was riding his motorbike to the outlying villages a truck of armed men forced him to stop before he could turn around the motorbike. It was the executioners. They shot him to the head and it ended his beautiful life. A tragic loss of a good and loving person. He was filled with a consuming love of God in people and was with them heart and soul, mind and spirit, day and night. His friends were the weak, the dispossessed, and the discriminated against, the wretched of the earth, the unwanted and forgotten. His cruel vicious killing is a hurt that I still carry with me, a wound that will not yet heal.

Everyone who knew him mourn the loss of a terrific person. Rufus was a deeply spiritual person, he prayed longer and harder than I ever have. His life and love were for the people of Mindanao, Christians and Muslims alike. His commitment to peace and reconciliation between the communities is a lasting legacy of heroic sacrifice. His life was frequently on the line as he risked himself to bring the presence and peace of Christ to communities racked by family feuds and military oppression. He stood with the Muslim families that suffered from the atrocities committed by the Philippine military. He was respected by them and would be at his ease with them, he spoke the languages with fluency and could even turn the situation to his advantage. He would see it as a God sent opportunity to integrate himself into their lives, persuade them of the value of reconciliation and peace.

The death of Fr Rufus is a terrible crime and a great loss to all of us. I have felt the fear brought by death threats myself and do my best to keep out of harms way. Rufus courageously went back to a dangerous situation to be with his people. He returned to the simplicity of serving the poor, standing with the oppressed and being a happy and fulfilled human being. He had nothing of his own but a powerful faith and consuming love of God which he shared with all the wretched of the earth, the throwaway people, the poor and forgotten. He will never be forgotten; his life and dedication will be forever remembered.

It took months to overcome the worry and ease back to normality. Since 2001 there have been one hundred and forty-four killings of progressive community leaders, journalists and even pastors. Amnesty International issued a report on August 16, 2006 saying there were one hundred and fourteen killings recorded since 2001 by Task Force Usig – the unit that coordinates investigations into political killings. The police have arrested suspects in just three cases and no convictions have been reported.

Reverend Edison Lapuz, a member of his church's national council, worked for the rights of farmers and fisher folk and served as a regional co-ordinator for the Bayan Muna political party. He was active in seeking justice for the killing of a local human rights lawyer, Felidito Dacut, who had been shot dead by two men riding a motorcycle. On May 12, 2005, Reverend Lapuz was killed by two unidentified men in the house of his father-in-law (province of Leyte), whose funeral he had been attending earlier that day. Local residents said they had seen four men on motorcycles parked at a nearby store before the shooting, wearing their helmets. Before his death, Reverend Lapuz had complained to fellow church workers in Manila that he was under surveillance by the military. His sister said that uniformed military personnel had come to their father's house and asked for detailed information about her brother the previous October.

There are serious concerns about police investigations into Reverend Lapuz's death, with witnesses not being offered adequate protection. The investigation remains stalled, and over a year since the attack, no charges have been filed or arrests made.

"The failure to identify and investigate suspects is fuelling a lack of trust in the police and aggravating the lack of convictions. Witnesses are afraid to come forward. Victims' families are liable to refuse to involve themselves in police investigations or to withdraw from court proceedings," said Tim Parritt of Amnesty.

The increasing killings have contributed to the breakdown of the peace process with the Communists. Amnesty International believes that only when the government takes decisive steps to prevent and prosecute political killings can any hope for peace be realised.

Chapter Thirty-Two

The following June, I was invited to Germany to give a presentation to the great assembly of the Evangelical Church held at the football stadium in Frankfurt. It was astounding. The stadium was filled to capacity and the centre field was filled with massed brass bands from every church group in Germany and Austria. It was an inspiring moment when they struck up together Amazing Grace. There were about fifty thousand people, the biggest live audience I have ever addressed. They gave a standing scarf waving reception after my short message appealing for solidarity with the poor, struggling for human rights and an end to sex tourism. It was translated line by line.

In London, I had a meeting with Scotland Yard Senior Chief inspector Bob McLachlan, the Interpol liaison officer with the team investigating paedophiles. Annette Kinnie was there with her film crew making a documentary on the campaign of PREDA to focus public attention on the plight of the women and children exploited by sex tourism. Then I met with Lord David Alton at the Parliament House, the co-founder of Jubilee Campaign and later with Nigel Griffith, now Assistant Parliamentary Secretary who nominated me for the Nobel Peace Prize. Then I went back to Dublin to be with my mother. She had not been very well and I was worried about her. I had been able to spend time with her earlier in the year too. She was a strong and inspiring woman and had a devoted interest in the work of PREDA and had come twice to visit in previous years. Despite wanting me to be with her as much as possible, she insisted that I keep on with the work for children. The many invitations to give talks and presentations at international conferences gave me a great opportunity to be with her several times a year. That September after being invited to a conference in Germany I was in Ireland again to visit mother. Then sitting in the living room of Rosetta in Glenageary at 2.20pm exactly together we witnessed the terrible terrorist attack on the Twin Towers. It was a shocking and disturbing moment as I felt the horror and fear that filled the hearts and minds of the people trapped in the towers as the fire raged all around them. Questions invaded my mind and I couldn't fathom the feelings and fanatical anger and hatred that drove the perpetrators to such mass murder. The sadness of this gave away for a while when we celebrated the ninety-third birthday of my mother at a local hotel mid-September with a small group of family and friends.

That week, there was a memorial mass for my friend and classmate Fr Rufus Halley who I had last seen in Manila only weeks before he was brutally gunned down in his parish in Mindanao on August 28. A week after the mass in his memory, I set off on an advocacy tour to promote the campaign against sex tourism. This was to support Fair Trade as a means to promote prosperity for the poor and reduce migration of the rural population to the cities where children were easily prostituted. I was calling home daily as mother had taken ill. She was admitted to hospital for tests. I flew back to Dublin to be with her in the hospital and discuss it with the doctors.The rest of the family was informed and gathered around.

I had to be in Manila for a series of court appearances. The sex mafia was doing all it could to get me convicted of anything and to slow down or stop our investigations and cases against them. If I failed to appear in court, they could get an arrest warrant against me. I would have to pay another big sum of money for bail or they might influence some dodgy Judge to deny it and I would have to fight them for justice from behind bars. That was unthinkable with mother so sick. A tumour had been discovered. It was not big but at her age an operation was very risky. The alternative, the doctors explained, would be to leave it and she would face a long, slow, painful death. It was a terrible time for me.

I had to leave for Manila. I arrived back in PREDA and attended the court hearings day after day. They were over by October 26 and I could get back to Dublin to be with mother. With so many court cases I had to get clearance from the courts and the Bureau of Immigration. I was desperate to get the "free to travel papers" signed. There was no commissioner to sign the papers, the legal office was closed, the assistant commissioner was out of town, one obstacle after another blocked my departure and mother was becoming critical. I was never so angry at the corrupt bureaucracy all my life as I was that week. It took five days to process all the travel clearances and then I got on the plane, exhausted, tired and worried.

My mother was a spiritual woman, well-read, strongly-opinionated, wise, and compassionate and nobody's fool. She could read the hearts and minds of all of her children and told us her thoughts or wrote them down for posterity as she saw fit and appropriate. I felt close to her and spent as much time every year with her as I could, especially in the last five years. The many invitations to speak at international conferences brought me home frequently. It was a blessing and a time she looked forward to. In her last years, despite fragility and against all advice I brought her and her sister to the Holy Land. It was the dream of her lifetime and there, despite the oppressive heat, she had more resilience and determination to visit every holy site than the rest of us on the pilgrimage. She and my Aunt Aileen were truly amazing. Then a year after that we went to Fatima, another dream fulfilled.

Needless to say, mother organised all of these trips herself over the phone, her lifeline to the world.

I had a long talk with the doctors and with Ma, my brother and sisters. She was amazingly healthy at ninety-three, except for that tumour. We all feared the complications but no one wanted to prolong a well-lived, long life and have intense suffering and long drawn out uncontrolled pain. The doctors at St. Michael's Hospital, Dun Laoghaire, gave us the odds. They looked good despite her age. Ma said she would do it. She was ready to go to God if the operation failed. Her courage was incredible, when I quaked, she laughed, when I was at the verge of tears, she smiled, when I thought all was lost, she told me: "I have nothing to fear. I did the best with what I had in this life. I am ready for the next. God will welcome me," these were her last words as I held her hand and the trolley passed through the swing doors of the operating room. Her faith never wavered but mine faltered, I feared the worst but knew we had made the best possible decision.

The next I saw her she was propped up in the ICU. The operation had been straight forward and no complication. She was smiling, it was a beautiful morning and after a few days she was well enough to be moved to the ward from the ICU. That could have been too soon. She was chatting with visitors after a day making an astonishing recovery to the wonder of all. Two days later, I got an urgent call on my mobile and rushed to the hospital. Ma was back in the ICU. There was only one problem, the kidneys were faltering and then began to fail. This is what I had feared, the side effect, and the weakness of age. The family was there at her bedside in the ICU, the hospital staff of St. Michaels was superb and many Filipino nurses were giving extraordinary service far beyond the call of duty. We took it in turns to keep vigil. We all knew it was a matter of time, the kidneys were not recovering. Ma was serene and accepting and at peace. We looked at each other and knew it was the end this side of eternity and we would always be together in spirit here and on the other side in time. It was 4.30am on November 12. I was holding her hand and she appeared to be asleep. Her hand fell away from mine ever so gently, I looked at the monitor and knew the moment had come and passed. Later I left the hospital and drove to our favourite place overlooking the sea and wept.

Then there was a cold Christmas in Ireland. All the while I was in close contact with PREDA by mobile phone texting and e-mailing. I was visiting our friend and supporter Christina Farmington in Sligo, discussing plans for awareness building seminars when the mobile phone rang. I was speechless. Merly, the wife of Alex, had collapsed withan aneurysm, a brain haemorrhage. It was such a shock. She was still alive in the hospital in a coma. I packed immediately, said my goodbye and drove through the night to Dublin, finished up all business at Rosetta through the night and next day took a flight to Frankfurt. I was in Manila in two days on a Lufthansa flight, they were terrific to get me a seat at last minute notice. I went straight to the hospital.

It was a sad and emotional scene. Alex and the three children were waiting just outside the ICU. They were tired from lack of sleep and stress. The doctor explained that an aneurysm, the bursting of a blood vessel in the brain, occurs in about one in ten thousand people and there is almost no way of detecting it unless there are brain scans when severe prolonged headaches occur. Merly was in a coma. Believing that some people can hear faintly when in a coma each of us talked to her to reassure her everything was being done, we were there and that all were praying for her. Yet after two weeks without any indication of brain activity and increasingly frequently recurring heart attacks, she would eventually be beyond saving.

While I kept vigil once again by the bedside of another woman who had been a great influence and supported me in my life and work, I recalled the day twenty eight years ago when I walked into a small dingy office at the Dare

Foundation in Metro Manila to collect some documents and met Merly who told me if I was starting a centre in Olongapo and if I needed anybody she would be the first to join the new staff. Well I didn't have any money at the time and it was still a dream I had then. But the day came when I began to make the dream a reality. Merly, a woman of great determination and extraordinary faith, said she was ready to leave the Dare Foundation and start out on a new adventure into the unknown, for almost no pay whatsoever. "God will make it happen, we just have to do what we can," was her inspiring and encouraging answer.

It was hard those first days, as I wrote earlier, and the iron-fisted jackboot tyranny of the Marcos regime made us cautious and fearful of being arrested and accused of subversion. The social issues that plagued Olongapo were like a swarm of locusts eating the heart and soul of the Filipinos leaving a moral wasteland and we had to confront that from the earliest days and plant the seeds of dignity, freedom and hope. Merly was undaunted at the challenge we faced. "When I have to walk on water I want it to be frozen over." Her cheerful faith, optimism and trust in the power of God carried me and Alex along when the going was difficult especially when we were challenged legally by the powerful politically well-connected Dare Foundation. Her skills as a graduate of business got us started in Fair Trade and her management ability got the occupational training up and running and she developed a market for sales of handicraft furniture and woven baskets. Within months we were breaking even. When many others shrank from the challenge Merly clearly understood her mission was to bring God's Kingdom of justice and love to the poorest of the poor even if it meant defying the authorities that allowed evil to proliferate unchecked. She could have been a successful professional in a big corporation but instead she joined PREDA, a simple struggling organisation with a daunting mission ahead of it.

When Alex Corpus Hermoso, a young, handsome, intelligent sociology graduate joined the fledgling team just as we were starting up, friendship blossomed and a spirit of teamwork grew into love and marriage and then three beautiful intelligent children. Today they are studying law and medicine and are imbued with that same sense of dedication and commitment to do as well as their parents. Their names Christina, Christopher and Chrisanta reflect that single hearted commitment to Jesus Christ and all He lived and died for.

Today the Fair Trade projects that Merly began have flourished and a little planted garden of goodness that has grown into a field of plenty. Plenty of poor people, not so poor anymore, plenty of artisans busy making patio bamboo furniture, plenty of mothers sewing recycled drink pouches into fashionable bags and wallets and carrying cases. The dried mango fruit project was a great success too and today thousands of farmers and their families are benefiting from the high prices we pay for the delicious healthy fruits that are naturally turned into dried fruits and are chemical-free and sugar-free and environmentally beneficial.

This success also brought more income to the PREDA social services that were rescuing the children and youth from exploitation. We were then able to help many more victims of sexual abuse and provide them with protection, therapy and education. Merly was by now the senior administrator and general manager of PREDA. When the evil-minded officials conspired to close the training workshop and handicraft centre to their everlasting shame we faced ruin and closure. But Merly was undaunted and she made contact with the Fair Trade organisations overseas in Europe and the US. Although the manufacturing workshop was to be closed because the city denied us an operating license, (the sex clubs and brothels had licenses galore) Merly had the brilliant idea to relocate the workers to their home villages in the countryside. The men and women were far from temptations and were with their families in a healthy environment. From potential disaster she made miracles happen. She made crossing of the Red Sea look like a picnic by the lake. Today these craft and food manufacturing and agricultural projects are flourishing, every year dozens of Filipino youth and overseas visitors from the Fair Trade movement meet the crafts people and have fun joining the activities and happily joining indigenous people in tree planting in their natural mountain environment. It is a kind of eco-and Fair-Trade tourism that is an authentic alternative to the fake resort tourism. It is also an antidote to sex tourism.

Merly persevered and worked to make this a more just and happy world. It was a life well lived, true and honest, unblemished and full of goodness. What better life could one live, but for others, seeking no selfish reward, putting others above self and giving encouragement to all. Her passing that January 27 was a terrible loss and grief to us all. Her mission is our mission and it goes on. Her life was well lived for others, her spirit is still with us and will endure forever. None of us can have dry eyes when a friend like Merly dies and I wept frequently. It is what makes us realise how fragile we are and yet through our emotional vulnerability and faith in infinite goodness we can be strong again and make that goodness present to all in need.

Chapter Thirty-Three

On Holy Thursday night 1991, I was walking along the streets of Olongapo infamous night club strip with Michael McCarthy, my cousin's husband from Ireland. I was keeping an eye out for any street children in need of shelter and I was showing Michael the social situation caused by the US Military and why we were proposing it be closed and converted to provide work with dignity for the Filipino people.

We walked along the strip past the American Legion with a WW II relic anti-aircraft gun outside – a reminder of the one hundred years of US military presence. Women offered themselves as we walked along. Behind the thick mascara and make up some appeared mere teenagers. The shops offered T-shirts with obscene messages. For some people it was no place for me, a priest, to be on a Holy Thursday night, for others who believe God is everywhere there was no better place.

We came to the police station "B" and walked straight past the police desk and down a short corridor to the holding cells. There was Rosie. She was about seven-years-old, crying her heart out for her mother, hungry and terrified, not knowing if she would ever see her mama again. The guards ignored her pitiful crying. I was cut to the heart. I'd seen a lot of human misery and degradation but had never seen anything like this. A stench of faeces and urine hung in the humid air. Several other children were sprawled in utter exhaustion on the floor and a few more lay unconscious on a shelf at the back of the tiny cell. The smell of industrial glue stung my nostrils and I knew they had eased their hunger with the mind numbing substance. There had been a round up that afternoon to remove eye sores and preserve the sensibilities of the visiting sailors. I asked Michael for the camera and took the photograph. It has become a powerful image and a reminder of how children are made suffer by an uncaring pleasure seeking adult world driven by passion and power.

It was past midnight, Good Friday had arrived. Jesus was already betrayed and jailed. He was here, present in the poor, inviting us to find him there, looking up from behind the cruel iron bars, eyes filled with tears. I recalled his words: "What you do, the smallest of all you do to me, stern words of rebuke to the jailers but empowering for us whom are out to save the children."

I confronted the police and demanded to know why the children were treated like criminals. "What was their crime?" I asked.

"Vagrancy would be the charge," they said. They felt my anger and radioed for a police van. Michael and I waited until it arrived and we saw the children safely brought to the city children's centre. The police said they were under orders never to bring such jailed children to the PREDA Children's Home. I presumed that the city officials were afraid we might find that the children had been abused.

There was an American ship in port that week when we rescued Rosie and the other children. Thousands of servicemen had come to spend unholy hours in the sex bars and clubs, the streets were in an uproar of carousing merry making men. They received a great welcome from the hotel and bar owning officials who built their political careers on the exploitation of the women and children. They provided what they called fresh clean women and even minors, reassuring the American admiral that they would be tested and screened for the deadly HIV/AIDS and other sexually transmitted diseases.

The US Navy dispensary provided the training and the equipment for the testing. Those tested positive were taken out of the clubs and treated with US supplied drugs. Although some times, those drugs disappeared and were then sold out of private clinics to the unfortunate women suffering disease. This was so repulsive and dehumanising that we were still campaigning to have US military facilities closed and converted to industrial parks, family recreations areas, schools and colleges.

Mayor Gordon was a great organiser and manager who used the sheer power of personality to impose outward cleanliness, discipline and order. He was a man to be respected and feared. The round up of street children was a cosmetic gesture, a window dressing exercise to appease the international agencies concerned about the non-compliance of the Philippines with child protection laws and the UN Convention on the Rights of the Child. I was invited to a conference in Helsinki, Finland in 1988 to help finalise some provisions to that convention drawn up by the child protection agencies world-wide. It was adopted by the UN in 1998, ratified by all nations except the United States and Somalia. Sections 34 and 36 are especially relevant as they instruct governments to protect the children from all forms of sexual exploitation and pornography. We lobbied hard with leading NGOs (Non-Governmental Organisation) to have the Philippine Child Protection Law, Republic Act 7610, successfully passed several years previously. Strong as it, implementation is weak; few paedophiles, child traffickers and sex tourists are ever tried and convicted. Laws are like traffic lights, the moneyed big shots can drive straight through. Laws achieve little if not implemented equally to all.

The Mayor and his cousin, his wife and brother, all who succeeded him as Mayor, had good intentions perhaps when they put the little children behind bars instead of the pimps and paedophiles. It was the common practice all over the Philippines. Sadly, the rounding up of street children to punish them as suspected criminals continues to this day but now PREDA human rights workers are there to protect and defend them for being jailed and beaten. We provide them with a daily meal, medical and educational help. But they need much more. Some of them live up a sewer pipe, others live under a bridge by the river. I appealed to the government to let us use an abandoned government building in the city as a home for the street kids but they immediately found a new use for it. Kids were still being jailed and most were homeless.

I began to think more deeply about how many children were being abused and traumatized in cells like this all over the Philippines and how many of the little girls and boys were sexually assaulted inside, overpowered and helpless. Meeting Rosie was a turning point for me and all of us at PREDA. After she was rescued and returned to her parents we learned that she was in the jail as a hostage of station "B" until the impoverished parents turned over their earnings from a hard days work selling peanuts to the sailors. With that kind of police corruption it is little wonder that pimps could easily sell children to the sailors and sex tourists with impunity.

I knew then that we had to do something more. We began by visiting more prisons to see the conditions and try to have children released to our custody. But it was almost impossible then. They were treated as adult criminals and could only be released to government centres, but these were too few and overcrowded. So the children remained in jail in horrific conditions with adult criminals.

There was Jamie, whose story I have told elsewhere; it's so typical and terrible it needs retelling. He was a little boy, twelve-years-old and jailed with the rapists and murderers of Metro Manila. He was frail, skinny and very frightened when I found him shivering in a dark corner of an overcrowded cell crammed with half naked sweating criminals. He was but one of thousands of children that are behind bars in the Philippines.

Jamie's crime was playing cards on a street corner after school. The police said it was gambling, the family said it was child's play. The Prosecutor never saw him and the Judge never heard him. He was forgotten because the family could not afford to pay the bribe to have him released or dare to challenge the power of the authorities. The family brought him food just once a week. They had to pay the warden to get in. Jamie needed more than the daily handful of jail rice and a spoon of vegetable, it left him weak and hungry. Tuberculosis was rife sucked in on every breath, it was only a matter of time and he would receive his death sentence. In the jail sick room, twenty prisoners with TB lay on the concrete floor on straw mats spitting blood untreated. This was total neglect of the sick and the dying. Scabies spread like a bushfire. Sores broke out all over and brought an agonising itch. AIDS was an ever present danger. Jamie was desperate, locked in behind bars alone against the world and defeated, vulnerable and powerless. He was dragged into the toilet at night and repeatedly raped, he tried to resist and fight them off, he told me later, but they were too powerful for him. Later he was crying with the pain and they beat him to make him shut up, and then starved him until he let them do it again. It reminded me of the scandal of the UN run African refugee camps, no sex, no food. Like thousands of others, Jamie was abused and exploited. It was slavery of the worst kind and we thought that was long abolished. He was forced to wash the adult prisoners clothes so they wouldn't beat him. He massaged their backs and sex organs so they would feed him, he cleaned the excrement-filled toilet and they would give him a space to lie down. It was survival and they made him a girlie boy, passed from one prisoner to another in the darkness of the overcrowded prison cell. It was the Philippine gulag for him and as many as twenty thousand more children all over the country.

He scratched the itch of the scabies and the mosquito bites until he bled and the wounds became infected. There was no doctor or nurse, no medical treatment. He couldn't get out into the yard to feel the sun and enjoy the light. He became pale and his eyes sunk into his head as if retreating from the evil of the world. You could count his ribs by the time I found him, skeletal almost, like a famine victim. He cried when the cockroach bit him, cried with the hunger and the fear and the loneliness. He prayed for his family to come, prayed for the saviour to save him but no one came. He never had a chance of freedom from this dehumanising servitude. The nauseating smell of urine in the oven baked air, the dank humidity brought him despair. I found him with a fever from the infection and naked but for tattered cotton shorts.

I demanded to know from the authorities the gravity of his crime, the length of his sentence, the weight of evidence. There was none, not a shred of paper where his name was typed, his case number shown, his existence recognised. There was no record of his detention because, according to the police and the warden and the guards, it never happened. There was no conviction, no punishment, and no unlawful arbitrary detention. Jamie never existed on the official records like the disappeared, the abducted, and the victims of rendition. He was a non-person to them. His imprisonment was just a mistake they told me. No one was to blame, so take him away and cause us no trouble, they said. The gate clanged open, Jamie was pushed out petrified and shocked. He was in a daze and could not understand that the misery was over, the torture had ended, and he was a slave no more. He boarded the van and he was dressed in a clean t-shirt and shorts and we brought him for a meal. Soon he was on the way to the PREDA Children's Home where hundreds of rescued kids have been welcomed, recovered, and reunited with their families. Jamie recovered despite the abuse and traumatic experience but he would never be the same, his childhood was stolen forever. Eventually, we found his parents. They came and hugged him and they held each other and cried together.

By the year 2000, we had set up the PREDA jail rescue team that was visiting the jails several times a week, researching the cases of the kids found behind bars and bringing their cases to the attention of the court asking for custody. However, we had not succeeded in releasing anyone. There was no rule of court that would allow the Judge to release children like Jamie to a private home. The law did direct that minors be placed in homes run by the national and local government but there were hardly any. Care for the kids was not a priority for the politicians. Kids don't vote, they are poor and have no influence, powerless and worthless. In fact as we have seen, these are pests to the politicians that spoil the false image of a nice clean and tidy city. There is nothing that tells better the truth about a town or city than the children. Their bodies lying asleep in doorways, curled up in pushcarts, languishing behind prison bars, cry out louder than any speech or newspaper article. Their presence is an indictment of misrule corruption and wilful neglect of the poor and the powerless.

We planned to open a home for those we rescued if ever we could raise the money. Most of the children and youths detained were boys. There was outrage a few years previously when it was revealed the girls were being raped in the police stations when arrested for vagrancy. The girls were now sent to the government-run girls home in Marilacc Hills, or the Haven in Pampanga. Many of the girls found trafficked and enslaved in brothels were unable to be sheltered and helped by the government agency, DSWD, for lack of facilities and funds. We offered to house them but the cooperation by government officials is slow and reluctant. They send them home to the parents on the next bus out of town. Most return on the next bus back. From time to time, the PREDA rescue team still finds street girls in the detention cells and now gets them out quickly before they get raped or abused and bring them to the existing PREDA home for girls which is almost at full capacity. We are in the process of providing a new home for them.

The children in prison were until recently considered non-persons, worthless and beyond help. That was and is completely wrong. They might be rebellious, angry and prone to criminal acts but we have to see the influence of society on them and what the adult world offered them, practically nothing but condemnation and punishment, in the home, school and then in jails. I had to show the world that these children had rights, value and had a God-given dignity despite their poverty and deprivation of basic rights and education in this wealthy resource-filled country. The widespread poverty and jailing of kids is the crime of the rich, because they run the country from top to bottom. They have the political and financial power and their relatives are the key officials in every government department working for their patrons well being, prosperity and protection. The children are not criminals but the adults would like to brand them and treat them as such and be rid of the responsibility to help them.

PREDA Foundation was a member of a coalition of charities drafting changes in the juvenile justice law that would exempt youths, age fifteen-years-old and below, from criminal liability and those fifteen to eighteen would be exempt from prosecution unless it was proven they acted with discernment. It would allow for rehabilitation and diversion programmes rather than punishment and prison sentences. We also proposed to decriminalise vagrancy and substance abuse by minors. In 2001, there was no hope of getting the pending law passed by the congress despite nine years of lobbying. It was a dream but one that was still worth pursuing. Those convicted of serious crimes were sent to the national penitentiary. At one time, before the death penalty was abolished in 2006, twelve youth offenders were on death row.

According to a report in *Newsweek* in August 2001 by Mahlon Meyer and Marites Vuitug, there was an estimated twenty thousand children in Philippine prisons. The story described how young boys were being prostituted by other boys and adults in the prisons. We went to the jails of Metro Manila and everywhere, it was the same. Other charities were doing great work but getting the kids out and into the custody of a children's home was a rare event. We tried to get international help and make urgent appeals to the Geneva based UN Human Rights Working Committee on arbitrary detention. In Angeles City jail in June 2002, we found a ten and twelve-years-old boys and two other older minors with adult prisoners in overcrowded cells. They suffered as much as Jamie and we couldn't get them out.

A hardworking and dedicated young Irish Lawyer, James Nunan, came to PREDA for more than six months at his own expense to help us on the many child abuse and human rights cases. He researched and worked on an urgent appeal to the Human Rights Committee in Geneva for the boys in the Angeles City jail. It was a test case, a wake up call for the authorities, we hoped. Darach MacNamara, Barry Mansfield and Gina Dowling and many other volunteers came too and worked to save as many children from prison as possible. Getting them released was still next to impossible.

The UN Working Committee on Arbitrary Detention, made an amazingly swift reply to the presentation of the facts prepared by James. It took only two months for them to reply, usually it takes years. This was a challenge to the Philippine authorities having ignored us for years now they had to pay attention. The answer of the Philippine government authorities to the questions of the committee was sent back to us for comment and we produced evidence that showed that their submitted statements and claims were blatantly false. In the end they released the four children to a government youth centre on July 5, 2002. It was a victory of sorts but the process so laborious that it could only help a few. The Government officials responded to the Human Rights Committee with the lame excuses that said they regretted that the source of information (PREDA) distorted facts to blow up the cases! Delays in the transfer of the three minors, either to the custody of parents, home for children, or drug rehabilitation centres, were to a large extent due to uncooperative or unconcerned parents despite the best efforts of jail authorities, they said. The officials covering their neglect blamed the parents for leaving their children in jail with rapists and murders as if they would be believed. The appeal to the UN and the constant efforts lobbying, advocacy and legal action to force change created an awareness among the court personnel. They wanted to change but how? We were able to visit more jails with less restrictions and red tape to see the conditions under which the children were held and to identify those being detained and document their cases for legal action. Many jail wardens and the head of the bureau of jail management demanded our jail rescue team to get written permission from them and the Judges.

We held rallies, with a hundred children attending, to protest the detention of minors. We marched to the office of the ombudsman with children that had been jailed illegally to file a class action charge against President Gloria Macapagal-Arroyo and those officials responsible for jailing children. By September 6, we published a forty-page report on the situation of kids in prison based on our jail visits and other research in the courts and prison records. We sent it to the Chief Justice Hilario J. Davide Jr, now retired, and who is the Assistant Resident Representative with the United Nations Development Programme(UNDP). Soon after, Amnesty International published their own fact finding report on the awful conditions of children in prison and cited the PREDA report thus confirming its findings.

I contacted all our supporters and began an international letter writing appeal to him and the other members of the Supreme Court to encourage them to change the rules of the court so that minors could be released to the custody of non-government children's homes or to their parents. This is how our helpers and defenders of children's rights around the world were able to help them.

The new Chief Justice Artemio V. Panganiban with a strong reputation as a defender of children's human rights was equally supportive of the reforms. The court administrator Zenaida Delapanio, a children rights advocate for many years, had already prepared these new rules and the Supreme Court had already sent out several circulars ordering Judges to visit jails and to be compassionate in dealing with minors. They were limited because of the inaction of the Congress to enact the new law. But they tried to anticipate it by the new rules. The new rules were vital. Supreme Court justice Reynato Puno was also a leading member that worked for prison reform. He even had a converted container van made into a court on wheels, complete with Judge, Prosecutor and public defender going to the jails to speed up the resolution of long delayed cases. When the rules were changed, the letter writing campaign helped greatly to encourage the justices to focus on the issue when they were so overworked already. Their circulars to the Regional Trial Judges final opened the way for the Judges to release children to our custody. Would they run away once they had a taste of freedom? Would they resort to fighting, stealing and abuse in the centre? After all they were branded criminals already and had seen the prison process at work. We were filled with apprehension and worry but I knew Alex and myself could draw on our eighteen years experience in managing the drug rehabilitation centre and street children's home and shelter that operated successfully from 1975 to 1992. We felt confident we could make it work. I was also campaigning in several countries and in Britain with the help of our partner organisation Jubilee Campaign, set up by Danny Smith and Lord David Alton, I had the support of the cross party committee on children in the House of Parliament. To my surprise and delight I was nominated for the Nobel Peace Prize by a dedicated children's rights advocate and Member of Parliament, Nigel Griffiths from Scotland. He is now the Deputy Leader of the House of Commons (Parliamentary Secretary). In the Upper House, Lord Raymond Hylton and Lord David Alton never lost an opportunity to promote children's rights and support our work. This nomination in 2001 was soon followed by an Italian human rights award of the city of Ferrara from the Associazione Gruppo. The nominations and the award helped to increase public awareness of the important issues of the campaign to free children from prison and from the exploitation and enslavement in the sex tourist industry. That is the purpose of awards and nominations in my opinion. There were more to come.

Then to our delight on February 28, 2002, the Chief Justice Davide Jr. signed the new rules and they took effect the following April 15. Now there was a chance to have the Family Courts to implement the diversion provisions and send the children to non-government children homes. This was not as easy at it seemed, some Judges were mindful of the harsh demands of the complainants to have the children jailed. They had to be approached by PREDA social workers to be made to drop their opposition to the transfer of the accused children to PREDA Home for Boys. We renovated an existing building on the PREDA property and turned it into a centre for boys with the help of generous supporters. We were ready.

Then in May 2003 the Anti-trafficking of Persons Act known as Republic Act 9208 was passed and signed by the President after years of lobbying too. This would give us a bigger chance to oppose the abduction of women and children, however, like most women and child protection laws they are not enforced and the exploitation went on. Our task was just as daunting. But we had help from our German supporters. Kindernothilfe was still backing up and supporting the children we were rescuing, and others having recovered were restored and reintegrated with their families when it was safe and secure to do so. Otherwise we found a distant relative to care for the child and we continued to support the schooling and make follow up visits. Cordaid of the Netherlands, Caritas and Heks of Switzerland were equally supportive in all this work and individual people who made it their mission to see the children were saved and the abusers jailed and made accountable for their crimes against the children.

In June 2003, I discovered filthy cells in the childcare centre run by Olongapo city government. I thought the centre was helping the children like Rosie and no kids would be jailed. How wrong I was. We rescued children from the main police jails and stations on a regular basis and we were getting kids out of jail in Metro Manila and now had a new home for them, but what I discovered right in our own backyard was equally shocking as anything I had seen in Metro Manila jails. I sent my undercover staff go into the OCARE children's and women's care centre and quietly visit the back rooms. The staff were distracted by the donations we brought. They carried them off to the office and locked the doors to get what they could, just as we had expected they would, and we presented our seminar for the children. Two of the PREDA team were able to visit the children and women locked up in the back rooms. They found them to their dismay, shock and revulsion locked behind bars in tiny padlocked detention cells. There behind a sealed door, the secrets were revealed. Young boys were lying in a stench filled prison cell. No bed, no chair, nothing but a filthy hole in the floor filled with human waste and smelling to high heaven.

Later, when they were released, PREDA organised a seminar at a beach resort in Iba, Zambales for the street kids who had all suffered in the secret cells. Representatives from the Human rights commission were invited to hear the testimony and it was duly given and recorded. They told how men were brought in to impose discipline and control the youths. They were beaten with sticks, deprived them of food and water. The guards knocked their heads against the bars. They had to sleep on the concrete floor and buckets of cold water were thrown on them at night. Faeces spread from the blocked toilet hole around the cell and they could not lie down for over twenty-four hours. There was no place to wash and clean themselves. The food was rice and scraps of boiled vegetable, and a piece of fat leftover from the staff dinner, the kids said. The plastic plate was left on the floor outside the bars and they had to reach out full stretch to get it. This was the joke the guards loved to play and enjoy, to see the child prisoners crying with hunger and to place the food just out of reach. It was a kind of torture. Then with their foot they would push it closer and closer to the outstretched arm and then pull it back amid roars of laughter. It was inhuman; dogs would have had it better.

In the cell beside them, two middle-aged women were together in the cramped cell under similar conditions as the boys. They were claimed to be mentally disturbed and were left sitting in their own urine and excrement as the hole in the floor was also blocked and overflowing. The stench was overpowering. The PREDA staff described it as nauseating. There was no screen on the barred windows and flies and mosquitoes, even cockroaches swarmed all over the cells. Malaria and dengue were just a bite away. Hunger was streaked across their faces. In the end cell, a mother sat lonely and forgotten, her little boy was outside the bars crying uncontrollably. All of this was caught for evidence of abuse and inhumane treatment. If this happened in a prisoner of war camp it would be condemned as a violation of a human right and violation of international agreement. The rights for the children and women were systematically violated. They had done no crime, had not been charged with any violation and yet they were imprisoned by a cruel family dynasty, a regime that ruled the city without care or compassion. Yet they gathered and posted on billboards UNESCO awards, "Most Child Friendly City" and other face-saving public lies. These conditions were captured on camera testified to by witnesses and victims and then all the evidence was sent to the authorities. We protested, we published and it was all to no avail. Nothing changed. We wanted to call on the Red Cross to come and see but the former Mayor Richard Gordon, now a Senator, was then the powerful Secretary of Tourism and he was the long time distinguished Governor of the Philippine Red Cross and his wife was the Mayor who was accountable for the jailing of the women and children. There is no way the Red Cross in the Philippines will ever investigate such conditions in Olongapo city, although the Swedish Red cross was unofficially made aware of these systematic acts of torture and abuse they continued.

Eventually, after years of protest, the more reasonable, respectful and cooperative brother, Bong Gordon, took over Olongapo City Hall from Mayor Katherine Gordon. There was a change. The secret women and child cells of Olongapo City were closed in 2004. The political interests of the Governor of the Red Cross and those of his wife converged. The organisation was effectively paralysed.

The Mission team from Germany and the actors and members of Tatort team who made a TV drama in Germany about the work of PREDA came out to visit us in September 2003 and unveiled a huge portrait of Pia. She is a famous young girl who was first trafficked for sexual exploitation when she was eleven-years-old. Then sold to a German sex tourist at fourteen and brought to Boracay Island Resort where she was rescued. PREDA helped her recover and finish school and college as a nursing aide. She became an outspoken advocate of children's rights. To celebrate International Children's Day on September 19 that year I went to Germany with Pia. She was well known there because she had testified against her abuser in a German court in 1996. The abuser was convicted; one of the first ever sentenced under the extra judicial legislation designed to catch these abusers when they abuse children abroad and then escape back to their home country. They don't leave their activity at the airport either. They are paedophiles without borders. Pia is busy studying and advising children about the dangers of internet chat rooms, blind dating, abduction, child abuse and inspiring victims of sexual abuse to speak out and get help and justice. Missio, one of our partners in Germany organised a speaking tour, TV performances and opportunities in promoting PREDA Fair Trade as an answer to poverty and migration. The Television talk show of Johannes B. Kerner drew 2.8 million viewers.

The six children that were rescued from the sex bars of Angeles City the previous year were doing well at the PREDA home for girls. They had a difficulty adjusting for the first three months. They had been trafficked as sex slaves to the Angeles city sex clubs with names like G-string, Fantastic, and Lollypop Cambodia. *Slavery* is an appropriate description of this kind of exploitation. They are trained to be docile, submissive with threats of worse to come if they don't behave. Many people think all such girls are coerced and held against their wills. In some cases that is true. Those working as dancers and escorts for sale in the sex club it is not so. They are illiterate girls from rural villages that had been taken out of elementary school to work on the farm. Many had been sexually abused in the home or neighbourhood and running away to the bright lights was common. They had heard of the success of other girls and they dreamed of the bright lights and wanted to join them. In comparison to tending pigs and chickens and gathering bananas for the rest of their lives, the sex club is paradise to them. They are told that the Mamasan, the old prostitute past her prime, is her mother image. The owner operator, usually a foreigner (Irish, English, American, Australian, German) is the "Big Daddy". The next prostituted women is the eldest sister and so on. Big Daddy is to be always pleased, pampered and petted, they are taught. He is a *god* for the sex workers, providing their daily allowances. In this corruption of the family bonding, so important to the Filipino soul, the heart of Filipino culture is pressed into the service of sex industry for controlling and domesticating the sex workers at a young age. It should be a cause of outrage instead it is encouraged.

A man named Agnew featured as a leading club operator in Angeles city in the BBC Spotlight investigative programme some years ago. He was never charged in court. But the young underage girls, one only thirteen, rescued from the bars claimed he was their Big Daddy. He said he was only a decorator. One of the girls left PREDA in a fit and went back to the clubs in Angeles City. She had been contacted by her mother, who was on drugs, and told her that her brothers and sisters were starving. She had to send money and, instead of asking us to help, she ran away to the clubs to earn again. She enticed two young girls to go with her who had never been to a club but were abused in the home. Immediately we ran off missing child notices with the photos of the children and rushed over to Angeles City and distributed them to all the tricycle drivers. The news spread and the marketability of the children fell to zero. All the pimps would be scared now that they were publicized as minors and people were looking for them. To be caught with them would bring on kidnapping charges and worse. It worked, within twenty-four hours we had the children back at the PREDA centre. The experienced girl stayed out for ten days and then volunteered to return. Today, she has completely reformed, is a great student and an active advocate of children rights like Pia.

When we did eventually open a home for children in conflict with the law in 2003, we soon showed the authorities that they are not criminals. Of the several hundreds of children that got help at the centre, only a few ever left the PREDA Home for Boys without permission and they went home and later returned. Fewer still returned to jail. It is a thriving open home with no need for shackles, guards, gates, fences, violent restraint, punishment or even harsh verbal reprimand. There is nothing to escape from, only much to stay for. This is how we helped change the awful situation for the better.

In February 2004, another landmark law was passed. This is the Philippine Republic Act 9262, signed by the President on International Women's Day, the Anti-violence Against Women and their Children Act. This was greatly welcomed in our work. We discovered that many of the mothers of the abused children are themselves abused, beaten and threatened by the husband or the live-in partner. This allows him to get away with the child abuse because the mother is scared to report it less she be beaten black and blue. Now that was declared a crime and her chances of getting justice is much higher. The new law gave women the chance to bring charges against the abuser and any domestic violence is now a crime. In the past the law enforcers considered that a domestic affair is not a crime. Now we had another tool to use in our work to reduce the abuse of women and children. Our daily seminars and workshops were going daily all over the province spreading the good news of the dignity of each man, woman and child and showing them how to protect themselves from abuse and violence. This was peace making at its best.

That October of 2003, I was invited to Geneva to make a presentation to the members of the UN Human Rights Committee on child prisoners. PREDA was invited by the World Organisation Against Torture and Amnesty International Filipinos to be one of three NGOs to state the situation on human rights in the Philippines. In our area of expertise so far, the government was in non-compliance with the International Convention on Civil and Political Rights. We were to give an alternative report, knowing that the government report is hazy, blurred and economical with the truth. It was thirteen years since the Philippine Government had complied with its reporting obligations. This was an important opportunity for us to set the record straight and bring the truth to the attention of the world, those who were interested of course. We had no formal opportunity to make a presentation, as it was the Philippine Government that was being challenged. We (representative of the NGOs) met the members during the lunch hour. To be sure, I got their attention by a picture presentation. I had a strong, powerful collection of photographs of children behind bars like those in the secret cells of the Olongapo (OCARE Centre). Some were shocking and depicted the real plight of children in a graphic way. They all gathered around the laptop computer to watch and I had the chance to give them an eyeful of reality. The human rights agencies were terrific in convincing the committee members that the violation of human rights in the Philippines was widespread and serious. The government had tried to make it rosy and greatly improved.

After that, the questioning to the Philippine government representatives was sharp, to the point and tinged with anger. The barrage of questions they couldn't answer devastated the delegates and I felt sorry for them, they had been ill prepared and briefed. They had to ask for a recess to call Manila to get data to answer the Committee. Some government delegates did not even understand the power and purpose of the Committee.

By the end of 2003, we had enough funds to complete the renovation of the old home for street children and we formally opened the new home for boys-in-conflict-with-the-law on the upper hillside overlooking the Subic Bay. It was a big step forward for us to translate the lobbying and the campaigning for these kids with actually getting them out of prisons and into a proper home. Here, there would be no guards, no gates, no walls nor fences. It was not to be an alternative jail or prison or guarded facility, it is more like a summer camp style home where there is order, planned schedules, educational activities, group dynamics, formal education, skilled education, occupational therapy, counselling and emotional release therapy. Together with these there are sports, outings, picnics, indoor games and spiritual and values formation seminars. I believe in a totally open home in a wooded environment where trust, affirmation, encouragement and respect are the main healing tools for the young people scarred from prison abuse and injustice. It had to be a place where the likes of Jamie could easily heal and find his real self and ability to make a useful and meaningful life. Myself, Alex and the staff were soon interviewing candidates for the new staff and then we were busy training them in the principle of health and human development through affirming respect and non-confrontations. I couldn't find any manual or handbook on how to operate such an open centre for kids from prison based on developing trust, respect and a belief in themselves. So we had to write our own. We banned all forms of violence, physical, verbal, psychological and emotional. We trained the staff to cope tactfully and professionally with emotional unruly boys. It was a dream and a vision that we hardly expected to succeed but we just had to try it, disappointed as we feared we might be. The Judges that came to visit asked to see the detention centre, the fences and walls. They were perplexed and worried when we told them there were none. We persuaded them that prison does not work for young people, it is a college for criminals. Walls and gates are not necessary if the young people are treated and respected and given trust and training for a better future. Some were sceptical; others said they would try it and now are glad they did because it works. We promised that we would bring the boys to the court hearings and complete their legal process.

Eventfully, we were able to have up to seventy percent of the cases against the boys dismissed. Many had already been in jail for up to six months in horrific conditions yet no charge was proven against them. Most of the children came from the notorious jails of Metro Manila. We had to travel three hours several times a week to attend the hearings. Many times they were postponed when we arrived. The expenses piled up but we kept rescuing more and more after the breakthrough with the change in the rules of court. The success was gratifying, hardly any one of the boys assigned by the courts to the PREDA left without permission. All this important work is still going on day by day as I write. The dedicated Filipino staff at the PREDA Children's Centre are working in twelve different projects. These socio-pastoral services to the poor and the abandoned are expanding as more and more children are brought for healing and protection. Finally, we got the TV cameras inside the prisons and the cells to show the world the secret that the officials tried to hide; thousands of child prisoners abused, raped and malnourished. With the help of Danny Smith of Jubilee campaign and Chris Rogers of the British Independent Television

(ITV) we documented the terrible conditions and suffering of the children behind bars. This was broadcast in August 2005 and it caused outrage and a flurry of government denials and cover up. The Philippine Senate was moved to pass the Juvenile Justice Bill but the Lower House showed no shame and ignored the terrible conditions even when we showed them the ITV/CNN. I talked to the congressional wives group at a special meeting in the Manila Polo Club to persuade them to pressure their husbands. To little avail. In September I was invited to the speak at the US Congressional Committee for International Relations, sub-committee for African children. The members led by Chris Smith were very moved when I showed them the ITV/CNN report and they wrote a letter to President Arroyo to help end the violations of children rights in prisons. In their letter they asked the Philippine authorities to give PREDA the use of an abandoned Government building and some land for a children's home and vocational training area. Although the provincial Governor and Municipal Mayor of Castellijos approved the use of two hectares of waste land, the derelict buildings were not approved and the Pinatubo Foundation, which was supposed to develop the area for the victims of the eruption fourteen years ago and failed to do so, is blocking the desperately needed children's home. The hardened heart of Pharaoh couldn't have been as obstructionist as that. Then in November I was invited back to Washington DC to address another committee interested in Filipino children's rights and they too were shocked at the revelations of children behind bars. They asked that the Philippine Government to help us too. It was all to no avail.

Even the US congress had little influence when it came to getting the Filipino politicians to help little children. No wonder that some congressional wives told me with some bitterness not to bother talking to them but instead to the congressmen's young mistresses. In January I got Chris Rogers to return to the Philippines for a follow up story to see if anything had changed for the children in prison. We went into the prisons again with hidden cameras at some risk since the officials had not forgotten the expose of the previous August. This was broadcasted on the first week of February 2006 and was seen in Ireland and all over the world. It was even stronger and more hard-hitting than the first. It showed kids squeezed into small cells like chicken cages where they squatted on shelves one on top of the others looking out behind bars in subhuman conditions. There was international shame and revulsion and President Macapagal-Arroyo certified the Juvenile Justice Bill as urgent that same week and after a few weeks more it was passed by Congress. The President ordered all children released from the municipal jails and confined in Camp Diwa, Bicutan, outside the city. It was a more spacious prison for kiddies nevertheless. One day four young teenagers tried to escape over the high razor-wire topped wall. They were blasted with shotguns and two suffered severe hits and were wounded on the legs and had to be operated on. Two others with less serious wounds were released to the custody of PREDA. They are happily going to school everyday as respected students, well dressed and with immense personal self-respect. They want to stay as long as possible at the PREDA Home. The two others are still on crutches in Camp Diwa and can't be transferred to PREDA yet. After nine years of lobbying, campaigning and praying we finally saw the new law through. Now we are doing all we can to see it implemented and that no children are ever placed behind bars again or blasted with shotguns.

Chapter Thirty-Four

When people ask me if I ever felt like giving up, I answer, "Yes, many times." It was in 2001 when I felt most like quitting yet the team work led by Alex and Merly, the prayers and support of many that kept me going despite the growing pressure and harassment from the sex Mafia and death threats which are always unnerving.

All of us want to see the end of abuse, exploitation and injustice and everybody can do something meaningful to make this a better world for children before our time is up and we have to leave. People ask me from time to time what they can do. What good can we do in this world during our short stay to make people less hungry and happier? What can we leave behind that will endure to mark our existence besides a headstone in a lonely cemetery? That's what I ask myself too and the answer for me is to live a purposeful and meaningful life that does good for those with less than I have. People can work for justice and end the slavery of children from their own homes and communities. They can pick up their pen, lift the phone, write an e-mail and lobby politicians, journalists, church people and campaigners, urging them to get involved and make a difference. Others who heard the call and answered are out on the streets campaigning and fundraising in their community – changing the lives of the poor for the better.

People who want to change the unfair way things are in the

world can do much good and inspire others by living honest lives, share what they can afford, give their names and reputations to support petitions and protests. Bad situations can be changed by lobbying politicians to change policies and redirect funds and resources to suffering children instead of helping business cronies or some corrupt government in a developing country.

It is working for goals like these that keeps me going and the whole PREDA team which has grown to sixty-seven qualified committed Filipinos rescuing children, giving them therapy, education, a new start and bringing the criminal abusers to justice despite harassment, opposition threats and dangers of all kinds.

I started PREDA with Merly and Alex on a shoestring budget, a frayed one at that. "Well God had a plan for you," Fr Tom told me many years ago. It unfolded with the years. The hard times came with the good, and the good were spent overcoming the hard. Nor could I, or the PREDA team, expect a smooth trouble free run if we set out to imitate Christ in some small way like we were taught from childhood. In the seminary, the first spiritual book I was given was the *Imitation of Christ*. According to that we could expect to be threatened, harassed, falsely accused, put on trial and even jailed like Fathers Brian Gore and Niall O'Brian and their team of human rights workers.

In human rights work there is always rejection and opposition, but there is resilience and empowerment too. Thousands of missionaries and dedicated church workers and human right advocates give their lives for others, many are harassed, jailed and even killed. They are the unseen selfless friends of the enslaved, where they are, God is too. That's why they spend their lives, despite hardship, at peace, courageously enduring discomfort and hardship in the fields and forests, shantytowns and slums, garbage pits and prisons. Thousands of brave social workers and people's organisers have been tortured and assassinated by death squads on the orders of land grabbers, corrupt politicians and despots. Some bishops and clergy are happier cloistered in churches and rectories than out supporting the Christens risking their lives for the dignity of the human person that Christ died for. They want others to wash their feet and have forgotten that it was Jesus who washed the feet of his apostles. "I came to serve and not be served," he said. Those brave bishops and courageous Christians who have spoken out and have taken a stand for justice and human rights are the hope and inspiration of the church and the people. The poor need to know that God is with them and in them. For us to meet God, we must meet the captives, the oppressed, the hungry, the blind and the wretched of the earth. We are called to be in solidarity with them and work for justice in anyway we can. Everyone can do something to make this a better world and to end the crimes against children. We need to make God, infinite goodness, alive and active in the world, to prolong and extend His presence. How else can anyone believe there is a caring and loving God at all?

There is no other way to be a Christian but to remain authentic to the words and deeds of Jesus of Nazareth. Real Christianity may be difficult to find in the crypts and cathedrals, yet it is far from dead in the Philippines or in the hearts and minds of the millions of Filipinos who work abroad. They carry their faith within and most share all they can earn with their impoverished families in the Philippines. The churches are filled with vibrant communities that believe in taking a stand for justice and truth. Faith and love of neighbour is alive in all those people living with the poor and even dying with them and for them. I have met so many and they make me ashamed that I have not nearly as much enough faith as they have. "No greater love can anyone have than to give their life for their friend," Jesus said. That kind of love is what we see practiced by missionaries in the deserts of Darfur, the jungles of Africa, the workers in the refugee camps. The socially committed journalists and people of all faiths that stand with the poor and risk their lives for justice all over the world are the living saints of today. That selfless sacrifice is not news and does not sell magazines and newspapers, so few know about them and their lives of passion and power that is changing the world for good. These superheroes of faith and fortitude give all and ask nothing in return, yet they get the world. They find the meaning of life in the wretched and the poor by lifting them up, restoring life, healing the wounded and the sick, releasing the captives, giving life to the hungry, light to the blind, empowering the downtrodden and above all restoring truth and justice in word and deed. That's what I want to do, where I want to be, now and forever.

THE END

Also published by Killynon House Books

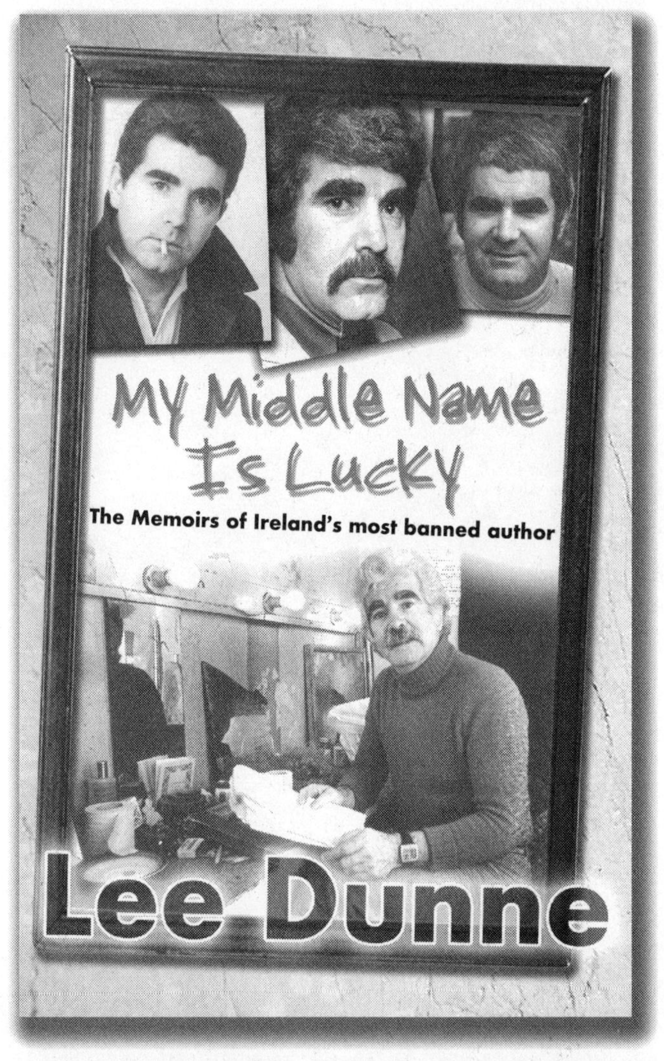

The autobiography of one of Ireland's most controversial writers, Lee Dunne, who had eight books and two movies banned.

ISBN: 1-905706-04-9

Also published by Killynon House Books

PRAISE FOR LEE DUNNE'S PADDY MAGUIRE IS DEAD

The most detailed and horrifying expose of alcoholism written in this country. Amazingly, Dunne now holds the honour of being the most banned author in Europe.

Sunday Independent

In any other country, it would be regarded as didactic. Here it is branded as "indecent and/or obscene" because it reveals exactly and honestly what it is really like to be an alcoholic

John Broderick, Hibernia

ISBN: 1905706022

Also published by Killynon House Books

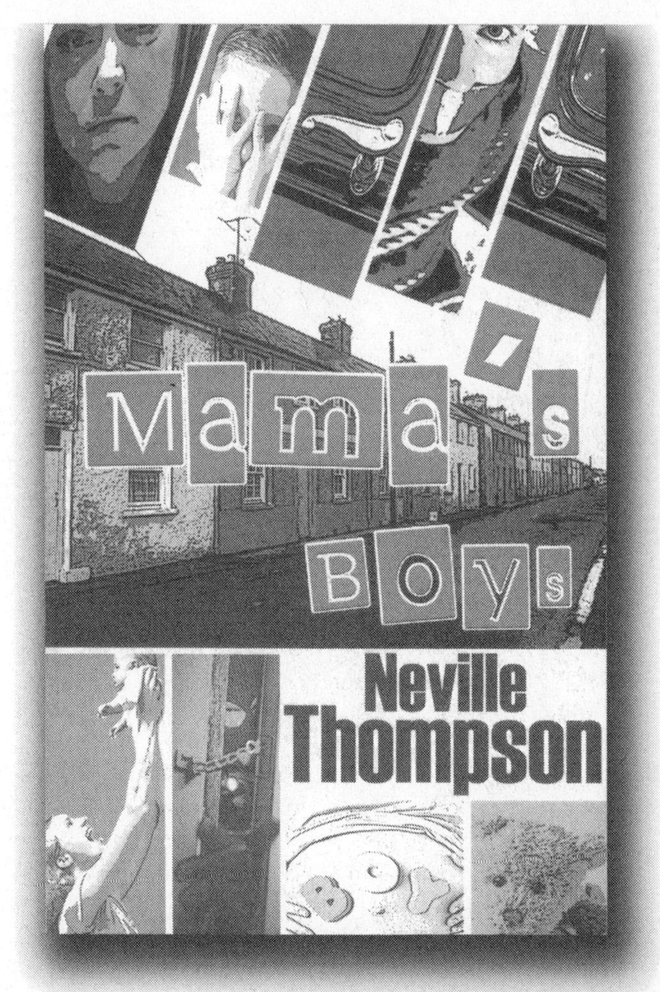

PRAISE FOR NEVILLE THOMPSON

The dialogue snaps and crackles with black humour
Evening Herald

Realism so gritty it's like the concrete of Ballyfermot between your teeth.
RTE Guide

Strong cinematic characteristics with definite shades of Tarantino.
U Magazine

ISBN: 1905706030